GRANVILLE'S
New Strategy of
Daily Stock Market Timing
for Maximum Profit

GRANVILLE'S
New Strategy of
Daily Stock Market Timing
for Maximum Profit

JOSEPH E. GRANVILLE

Prentice-Hall, Inc.　　　　　*Englewood Cliffs, N.J.*

Prentice-Hall International, Inc., *London*
Prentice-Hall of Australia, Pty. Ltd., *Sydney*
Prentice-Hall of Canada, Ltd., *Toronto*
Prentice-Hall of India Private Ltd., *New Delhi*
Prentice-Hall of Japan, Inc., *Tokyo*

Tenth Printing . . . . . December, 1981

Library of Congress Cataloging in Publication Data

Granville, Joseph Ensign
  Granville's New Strategy of daily stock market timing
for maximum profit.

  Includes index.
  1. Stocks. 2. Speculation. I. Title. II. Title:
New strategy of daily stock market timing for maximum
profit.
HG6041.G69 1976   332.6'45   76-5900
ISBN 0-13-363432-9

Printed in the United States of America

A Word from the Author

This new work essentially springs from my first stock market book, *A Strategy of Daily Stock Market Timing For Maximum Profit,* which was published in 1960. That book stood the test of time largely because there have been no deviations in human nature. People still respond to the stimuli of fear and greed in the same predictable fashion as they did then or any time before. Market analysis depends heavily on the assumption that the public will continue to respond to such stimuli in the future in an identical manner. While truth is never out of date, the passage of time does make some increasing demands on an author, when dealing with such a dynamic subject as the stock market, to update the material. New ideas emerged, and old ideas required a thorough review in the light of modern day markets which can easily generate 30 million share days. This new book is an attempt to bring it all together and provide the reader with an entirely new concept of the market "game."

While I had stressed the great importance of technical market indicators 16 years ago, their number has grown to such an extent that attempts to follow them all may now produce confusion rather than clarity. For this reason, some of the lesser indicators covered in the first book are deleted, not because they weren't valid, but because they were redundant. The same results are capable of being achieved by following a lesser number of more important indicators. But the core of the first *Strategy* book is retained and expanded here into a more complete theory of the game.

Much space was devoted in the first book to the day-to-day indicators. Some of that material is retained here, but the stress now is definitely put on the big picture, underscoring where the market stands in the overall bull-bear cycle, in other words, determining what the time is on the market clock. The major factor of time is brought into the picture to serve in the role of the kingpin indicator. By placing the market in a tight cyclic mould, the eternal struggle between the bulls and the bears presents more easily defined patterns, and one can better understand the modus operandi of the market game.

I have sought to explain as clearly as possible the very nub of the game itself, the anachronism between technical data and fundamental data. That factor, which is the very heart of the market, has never, to my knowledge, been clearly spelled out. Technical data stems from the market itself, being the language of the market. If investors understood it and analyzed it correctly, they would all either want to buy at the same time or sell at the same time. An impossible situation would be created since every game requires an opponent, and in this game nobody can buy anything unless someone else sells, and nobody can sell anything unless someone else buys. The clear majority of people involved in the market in any way do not follow the market itself. If they did, they would all be technicians, and the game could not exist. That clear majority consists of fundamentalists, people who largely follow fundamental data—earnings, management changes, new products, the economy, etc. That large, majority group makes its decisions based on such fundamental data.

One might inject a question at this point and ask why both groups couldn't be right at the same time, in other words could bullish technical data occur simultaneously with fundamental data which is also bullish? Such a phenomenon might exist for very brief periods of time, but it is a situation that cannot last. Let me put it this way—the market is a game of futures, the market itself always talking about tomorrow. Fundamental data largely deals with today, statements of fact reflecting something that has already happened. Fundamental data cannot be successfully superimposed over technical data. It lags behind the technical data by about nine months, on the average. This is the antagonism between the two sets of data that makes a market and the "game" possible. It explains why a technician (one who follows the language of the market) acts on the buy signal given by a stock, a stock that a fundamentalist wouldn't touch at that point in time. The market says buy but fundamentals say sell. The fundamentalist might cite the stock's earnings deficit or some negative news concerning the company as his reason for not buying it. Several months pass and the technician gets a sell signal. Usually by then the fundamentals have improved to such a point that the fundamentalist would now be interested in buying the stock from the technician. Now, if you took the fundamental data and shifted it back nine months on the time scale, then both technician and fundamentalist would have seen eye to eye and bought the stock, but then who would be the seller? So you see, this anachronism between technical and fundamental data has to exist or there would be no market, no game.

How can a stock give a buy signal when perhaps the news is bad, its earnings are down and it is otherwise unattractive? The answer is simple. Somebody wants it because he is looking ahead and thus he begins to accumulate it while the fundamentally oriented public is willing to sell it to him. Remember, technicians look ahead while fundamentalists look backward. That smart money accumulation cannot be hidden. It shows up in terms of volume, specifically measured by on-balance volume. Thus the market renders such buy signals right in full view of the fundamentalists who sell rather than buy because the data they follow won't render a buy signal until about nine months later when the technician is then ready to sell the stock back to them at a much higher price.

That anachronistic feature is so important that it explains why this book stresses that news is of generally little value (contrary to public opinion), that fundamental analysis creates a major trap (contrary to public opinion), that stock earnings is the big sucker play (contrary to public opinion). It also explains why much more space is devoted to my latest researches in volume study, making the detection of stock accumulation and distribution almost a science. My on-balance volume concept was first introduced in the *Key* book back in 1963. Being brand new at the time, the concept had not been polished to a finished state. It has been developed since then by trial and error, and it has been determined that some of the principal errors involved the correct interpretation of the important Climax Indicator. Most of the latest research on the Climax Indicator and Field Trends was done after the 1973-74 bear market. It is felt that these new studies were warranted including a ten-year past performance of the Climax Indicator.

The Barron's Confidence Index, which was dealt with extensively in the original book, is deleted. It is an indicator based on bond yields, and it has fallen into disrepute, not because of any change in the validity of the theory, but because the Confidence Index itself is no longer considered reliable. It fell out of bed in the late months of 1970, when a clear majority of the technical market indicators were clearly bullish. Again in the spring of 1975 the Index made a similar decline. At this writing it is uncertain as to whether the Index is making a valid projection of the future direction of the Dow-Jones Industrial Average or not. This time the Index might be working, but its reliability has been impaired since it became overpublicized in the original book.

For the past 12 years I have written and published a weekly market letter, a natural outgrowth of my six years with E.F. Hutton & Company. Many of the ideas in this book were first tossed about in the letters. From this collection of ideas developed since 1963, I have culled out the ones strong enough to walk out of the laboratory on their own two feet and have sought to incorporate them in an overall theory of the repeating market game, a game set in a cyclic mould covering a period of 4 to 4½ years. Some of these ideas introduce new perspectives in technical analysis (and reaffirm old ones), draw a new psychological profile of the market, involve new experimental techniques, and deal with the role the market will play in the years ahead in an intriguing drama studded by the devastating problems of inflation, gold, and even the survival of capitalism as we know it today.

A great deal of this book was written against one of the most disturbing backgrounds the market has ever had. In the 1973-74 bear market, Wall Street was so buffeted by crises that it was thought by a growing number of people to be dangerously incapable of defending itself from total collapse and possible extinction. The brokerage industry was hobbling along as best it could, seeking to serve a totally disillusioned public, a people caught up in the daily struggle to stay ahead of a mounting inflation that threatened to tear away at the basic fabric of our democratic society.

A growing doubt as to the future of the economy was whipped up to a national frenzy of fear and was reflected by a major slide in stock prices. That fear syndrome had done its work again, effectively, ironically blinding the public at the point of maximum investment and speculative opportunity. By late 1974 the down cycle correlating with maximum fear had reached its extreme. Inasmuch as the stock market game is played on a field bounded on each end by these goalposts of fear and greed, once an extreme has been reached, the action reverses itself and heads back in the opposite direction toward the other extreme. The market is constantly in the process of working toward one of those extremes and is seldom static.

Unable to maintain a continued uptrend or downtrend at the point of these greed and fear extremes, the market makes a long-term reversal at the most illogical of times, completing one cycle and embarking on another of generally similar length. But, now stressing the anachronism between the market and fundamental data, what would appear to be illogical market action to the uninformed becomes very logical to the informed. Months after one of those seemingly illogical market moves, fundamental data confirms the market logic. At that point, however, the market may be marching to a different drummer, a new tune to be replayed by the fundamental band perhaps nine months later.

Writing against the storm of controversy in late 1974 that perhaps the market had gone too far, perhaps beyond the point of return, some very astute thinkers contended that there was no way out of the 1974 inflationary dilemma except via a depression. They maintained that the stock market was doomed to play out its role in a tragedy climaxed in a crash severe as that of 1929. They maintained that the market had not seen its bearish extreme.

Increasingly conscious of the time limit imposed on each cycle in the market game, this writer could not buy that fatalistic thesis, certainly not the argument that a total market crash and depression was inevitable and in immediate prospect. Perhaps a few years from now, yes, from a much higher jumping off point, but not in 1974 when technical analysis underscored such a radically oversold position, an extreme to be reckoned with. Once again technical analysis identified the true nature of the extremes then in question and forecasted the important reversal.

As Bernard Baruch kept repeating to himself that two and two still makes four, inevitably one must keep returning to technical analysis for the ultimate answers the market will render. Technical analysis is the language of the market. It is the only way the market can convey what it is doing and what it intends to do. It comes ahead of all collateral studies such as economics, history, psychology, etc. in terms of pure market intelligence.

The market reflects the way people act at a given moment in time. Since we are dealing with an auction market made up of buyers and sellers, technical analysis assigns each of them into categories of smart money and the not-so-smart money. The movements of each category reflected in the daily market action, and the most revealing statistics (which we call market indicators) tell us what the smart money is doing. Smart money is simply money that purchases stocks before prices rise and moves out of stocks before prices fall. The smart money can hide its intentions in many ways, but it cannot hide all of its intentions from the market. The market indicators reflect all these things in terms of price changes, volume changes, fluctuating short interest statistics, the changing number of stocks making new highs and lows, the number of stocks advancing as opposed to the number declining, which stocks make the most active list, and many other changes all comprising technical data which must constantly be consulted.

Technical analysis can never become a science anymore than reading human nature can. If it was a science like physics, chemistry, or mathematics, then everybody would be capable of reading the market alike, all drawing similar conclusions. Obviously, if all people read the market the same way, there would be no auction and no market. It is the injection of the anachronistic fundamental crowd that makes the market possible.

Technical analysts do not always reach the same conclusions, however. Such analysis is an art similar to playing the piano. Most people can't play the piano at all; a large number of people do play adequately; a very small number of people are virtuosos. Technical analysis, being the language of the market, is subject to interpretation. Since the skills of interpreters of the stock market vary, they differ over the meaning of every piece of data. Part of the answer, of course, is that they are not all looking at the same thing, or if they are, they are looking with varying degrees of understanding.

The nub of the problem, as it applies to indicators, is that while they may be crystal clear in definition and theory, they often break down in practice and render false signals, almost as if the market at those infrequent times goes out of its way to lay a false trail to mislead the general public. Because of this, we of course would not place total reliance on any particular market indicator. Each one of them has at some particular time been ineffective, outweighed by a number of other indicators. The way to avoid that danger as much as possible is to follow enough indicators to counteract any possibility that they could all be wrong simultaneously. The indicators covered in this book should more than suffice.

Technical analysis has come a long way since the initial *Strategy* book in 1960, as predicted then by this writer that it would. Probably the most lasting impression the book made here in the United States was the adoption of the 200-day moving average trendline, a device so built into the current literature of chart analysis that it is now taken for granted. It was certain that technical analysis would move into a new golden age as the world grew smaller and information and its effects on stock prices was more quickly disseminated. But, instant intelligence notwithstanding, all markets everywhere duplicate the identifiable footprints of human nature and can be "read." The market "game" is played in Australia, England, Japan or anywhere there are free decisions to buy or sell.

Perhaps one of the silliest notions to come along in recent years is the oft flaunted Random Walk Theory, which presents the thesis that stock prices move at random. If true, then stock technicians have been wasting their time for half a century, seeking to find patterns where there were none. It is with pleasure that such notions are put permanently to rest, notions perhaps mathematically amusing to their perpetrators but having no basis in fact. Ironically, it is the very science of mathematics itself which disproves the random walk theorem as applied to securities markets.* Since the stock market is the collective opinion of human beings, and since human beings cannot perform in a random manner, it follows (in the form of an Aristotelian syllogism) that the stock market cannot perform in a random manner. Of course stock technicians always knew this but from time to time had to stop what they were doing to defend themselves from these unfounded attacks from the random walkers.

In the stock market game portrayed throughout this book, you will constantly be encountering the words accumulation and distribution. There is nothing random about stock accumulation or distribution. It is a planned

---

*Dan Pedoe in *The Gentle Art of Mathematics,* first published in 1958, as much as exploded the Random Walk thesis when stating with perfect authority that *human beings cannot perform in a random manner.*

activity having definite construction and purpose. There could be slight distortions which might be assigned to random buying or selling pressures, but such randomness has never made a case for itself concerning its ability to upset and make unrecognizable the premeditated plans of stock accumulation or distribution. Technical analysis will never be superseded by more effective methods of reading the market because all such effective methods now and in the future will simply join the growing family of current effective methods all under the common roof of technical analysis. It has to be that way because the market can only impart its intelligence in its own language, the language which comprises technical analysis. Even with the more perfect tools described in this book, no market success can be attained or promised without application. Staying on top of the "game" requires the input of new sets of data on a daily basis. That's the key to getting the most out of the introduced on-balance volume (OBV) technical method. The payoff to those who persist in the daily work will be greater market success and maximum profits.

Everybody is interested in the future, and therefore the book concludes with a look at it—the market future, the future of gold and a practical plan to effectively control inflation without a rise in taxes.

Joseph E. Granville

PERSISTENCE

Nothing in the world can take the place of persistence. Talent will not; nothing is more common than unsuccessful men with talent. Genius will not; unrewarded genius is almost a proverb. Education will not; the world is full of educated derelicts. Persistence and determination alone are omnipotent. The slogan "Press On" has solved and always will solve the problems of the human race.

—Calvin Coolidge

To my wife, Polly, and our eight children
who waited patiently for the game to end
and a return to normality.

Contents

Chapter 3

The Volume Complex

Chapter 4

How You Can Win the Game (The Grand Strategy of Stock Trading)

Chapter 5

A Look at the Future

1

The Game

The stock market is a game. All references to the business situation, corporate profits, liquidity, interest rates, employment, etc. are market strategies to ensnare the game players into looking at factors which are often extraneous to what the market is about to do. The late Gerald Loeb described playing the market as a "battle." A battle implies an opponent. In this book the market battle is specifically set down in terms of a game; one seeks to beat the market by reading the correct signals, and the market seeks to outwit you in a series of false signals. Perhaps the market will make much more sense to you when viewed in this light.

This is no easy "how to do it" book which throws out a set of rules and exhorts you to simply follow them toward an assured victory. The market is too clever to allow for a widely circulated blueprint of rules to quickly unlock its secrets, providing too easy a breakthrough. No, the market is a far tougher opponent. The average stock market book invariably talks of "laws," "principles," and "rules." Using every strategy to outwit the game player, the market breaks laws, violates principles, and makes exceptions to the rules. I would like to describe the market in strict terms of blacks and whites, saying that if this happens, then this will happen. Such razor sharp descriptions conflict with reality. The market, being a far more wily opponent, is more adept in the use of greys and the subtle art of camouflage in all its forms anything it can use to lay down a smoke screen to mislead the uninitiated.

In order to dispel the smokescreen and avoid the many booby traps set by the market, we are going to use the only effective counter-strategy, *technical analysis*—the language of the market. Technical analysis is the art of tracking the market, following the footsteps of the "smart money" crowd. The "smart money crowd" is no mysterious "THEY." It is simply a collection of people who are reading the market correctly, seeing through the maze, unconfused by this hall of mirrors. The identification of that smart crowd is constantly changing, but we are not interested in who they are. We are only interested in their footprints. One might ask at this point, why try to follow a set of footprints which can be quickly sanded over by a treacherous opponent, an opponent who always has the chips in his favor, an opponent playing with a stacked deck? You've all heard the expression "All's fair in love and war." While the market can do seemingly outlandish things, it too in all fairness must succumb to a readable *pattern.* In other words, after all the smoke has cleared, it must be said that the market *made sense.* The market has a set path to follow. By the rules of the game, it can set traps, create false paths, lengthen or extend a price swing, *but it is not allowed to destroy the true path.* The smart money, however, will always find its way through the maze correctly and not be fooled by the hall of mirrors. Most important of all, *the game is played by the clock* but not like the game of basketball or football, where there is an exact measurable time cycle. It is more like baseball, where the game can go into extra innings, and the time span on each inning is highly variable, sometimes a short inning there and a long inning following it or vice versa.

So now we have the two KEY WORDS which keep the market within the bounds of fairness: PATTERN and TIMING. The market must give us a logical and predictable pattern to follow, and it is held to a predictable cycle of bull and bear markets, each such market characterized by bull and bear market *phases,* usually three such phases assigned to the bull market and three phases assigned to the bear market. In fairness to the market's opponents, the market is not allowed to strip its gears on the order of these phases. The market does not, for instance, to go from Bull Phase One to Bear Phase Two or from Bear Phase One to Bull Phase One. Once a new bull market starts, the market must follow a pattern which takes it through that bull market and then into and through the bear market that follows it just as certainly as night follows day. The market follows this natural law of progression and has always done so. It, like nature, is held to that law of progression. When you look at your watch and it reads five o'clock in the afternoon, you know that five hours later it is going to be dark. When you determine that the market is traversing the final phase of a bull market, you know that x hours later darkness will descend upon the market. When you determine that the market is traversing the final phase of a bear market, you know that x hours later you will be enjoying the sunrise of a new bull market. So then, the market is ordered to always move *forward* in its predictable pattern.

Knowing this, it comes down to *knowing what time it is on the market clock.* Those who can read the market clock correctly will beat the market, find their way through the maze, outwit the hall of mirrors, and achieve the high monetary return guaranteed to all such winners. In order to know what time the market clock reads, it is necessary to correctly label the *phase* the market is going through. This is done by thoroughly understanding the *characteristics* of each phase. As a doctor diagnoses a disease by identifying characteristics or symptoms, so then do we label a market phase by characteristics only seen in that particular market phase. Sometimes there is a confusing *overlapping* of such characteristics, but taken *as a body,* market phases should be identifiable at all times. In fact, if one misreads the market phase *this alone is almost enough to automatically throw him out of the game.* So then, 1 cannot emphasize enough the importance of calling the market phases correctly. In my *Strategy* book I left much of the discussion of market phases until last, putting far too much stress on the day-to-day market action. It is of course important to get the day-to-day feel of the market, but being stretched out on the rack from time to time as a market loser, one at last respects the predominance at all times of the BIG PICTURE, the main thrust of the market, what the Dow Theorists call the *primary trend.* That trend traverses all three phases of a bull market and all three phases of a bear market. It is the tide that sweeps one to fortune or disaster. Unless one swims with that tide, one will drown. The longer the game is played, the more one will come to respect the Dow Theory, the theory that always keeps things in their correct perspective, putting the primary trend first, the intermediate trend second, and the day-to-day trend last. In the *Strategy* book I championed the day-to-day trader, laying down the language of the market in day-to-day terms. While we had some brilliant successes, it was always the intermediate trend which surpassed the daily trend in importance *and the primary trend that held sway over all.* You can't beat City Hall. You must be in harmony with the *primary* trend of the market if you ever hope to crack the market maze and find your way through the hall of mirrors.

In order to understand the primary trend, one must first get a grasp on what the game is all about, the basic *philosophy* of the market from start to finish. The entire market cycle always starts at a point of excessive fear, runs through to a point of excessive greed, and then runs through and returns to a point of excessive fear. Being an *auction* market, where for every buyer there is a seller and for every seller there is a buyer, someone must be right and someone must be wrong. They can't both be right. The investor who did the right thing is automatically part of the smart money crowd, and the one who did the wrong thing is among the market losers. *There is no third category.* In other words, market winners buy and sell from market losers. Technically, it is *easiest* to do the right thing in the market, but psychologically it is the *hardest* thing to do. It is easiest to buy stocks at the market bottom because so many people are willing to sell them to you, but it is the hardest thing to do psychologically because fear is the force that blinds. It is easiest to sell stocks at a market top because so many people are willing to buy them from you, but it is the hardest thing to do psychologically because greed is the force that blinds, the instinct that tells you stocks are going still higher when the technical action of the market says they are going lower. Right here, in order to join the smart money crowd, one must *counteract crowd psychology*. Without a knowledge of market phases it is very difficult to do because there are times when the crowd is right and the minority suffers losses. You will be introduced to the various "psychological" indicators later on and shown how to use them. Since everybody can't buy at the same time and sell at the same time (and wouldn't if they could), we have an "out of gear" situation always occurring between the smart money and less informed money. When the smart money is confident the crowd is fearful. When the crowd is confident the smart money is fearful. Everybody can't be fearful or confident at the same time, otherwise no stock would change hands. Therefore market sentiment on the whole must always be *out of gear*.

Some years ago Richard Russell, the greatest living Dow Theorist, stated an important principle. He demonstrated that during the first *two thirds* of a bull market, the public is fearful and during the *final third* becomes confident. That confidence lasts through the *first two phases* of the ensuing bear market, turning to fear again during the *final phase* of the bear market. Since there are always two sides to the market coin, what is the smart money doing during that entire market cycle? Obviously the smart money is confident during the first two phases of the bull market, turning fearful during the bull market third phase. Their fear of the market lasts through the first two phases of the ensuing bear market and then turns again to confidence during the third and final phase of the bear market. Now we have a *market*. While the smart money is buying stocks during the first two phases of the bull market, the public is selling them. The big shift takes place during the third phase of the bull market. Now the smart money distributes the stock previously bought, and the public joyfully takes it off their hands. The smart money continues to unload stocks during the first two thirds of the bear market as the public is still buying with misplaced confidence. Most of the smart money selling is done by the time the bear market third phase rolls around, and now the public starts dumping stocks, right into the hands of a newly confident smart money crowd. This point is the most easily forgotten when stock prices are collapsing during the third phase of a bear market. Market analysts tend to forget at such times that the market is an *auction* market, that somebody is *buying* those stocks as the public sells them. The buying and selling of stocks by the smart money crowd is called *accumulation* and *distribution*. If you are to beat the market you must accumulate stocks while the public is fearful and distribute them while the public is confident. That is the *name of the game*.

	Bull I	Bull II	Bull III	Bear I	Bear II	Bear III
The Public	Fearful	Fearful	Confident	Confident	Confident	Fearful
The Smart Money	Confident	Confident	Fearful	Fearful	Fearful	Confident

The smart money starts to seriously accumulate stocks during the third phase of a bear market and begins to distribute them during the third phase of a bull market, taking full advantage of the public's renewed confidence in the market. This sounds like a rather simple process. It is simple if one can correctly label what phase the market is passing through, and therein lies the rub, the lengths the market will often go to to disguise the primary trend, often making Bull Phase III look like Bull Phase II or even Bear Phase II look like Bull Phase I. Looking at the economic cycle is seldom much help inasmuch as that cycle merely produces the obvious psychological impact on the public, the cycle bottoming during the first or second phase of a bull market when the public is fearful and peaking in the first or second phase of a bear market, long after the market has topped out, leaving a confident public to hold the bag.

THE INDICATORS

Now, we want to determine the market phase by the position of the many indicators available to us. In reviewing these indicators we will ask some searching questions about each one of them, questions such as the following:

1. What does the indicator reflect?
2. What does it tell you about the smart money?
3. What does it tell you about the public?
4. Does it suggest what stage or phase the market is going through?
5. Why is it happening?
6. What would an *opposite* reading mean?
7. Could you get these figures in a bull market?
8. Could you get these figures in a bear market?
9. Where has it been, and where is it going?
10. Is it high or low by previous standards?

11. Is it susceptible to false signals?
12. Can it be proved invalid by other indicators?

Those are but a few of the kinds of questions that must be asked of the indicators. Nothing can ever be taken for granted where the market game is concerned, it being an endless battle. The indicators can be classified as *major, minor,* and *miscellaneous.*

THE MAJOR INDICATORS

The Advance-Decline Line

Of all the indicators discussed in this book, *I consider the advance-decline line to be the single most important technical tool.* It is a pure technical indicator based entirely on daily market statistics. It is simply the extension of the daily plurality of issues traded on a cumulative basis expressed in either a continuing column of figures or charted on a graph.

Each day the newspapers publish the number of issues traded and then break that figure down into the number of advancing and declining issues and the number of stocks unchanged. The difference between the number of advancing issues and the number of declining issues is the daily plurality. This daily plurality is then added or subtracted each day cumulatively to determine the advance-decline line.

How to Set Up Your Own Advance-Decline Line

An advance-decline line can be set up at any time, and the course of this line will correspond exactly with that of all advance-decline lines constructed prior to your line by other people. The purpose of the advance-decline line is to inform you in the broadest sense whether the market as a whole is actually gaining or losing strength. By setting up this running record of daily plurality, you will find that the cumulative differential between the daily advances and declines reflects an over-all upward force or downward force existing in the market. More often than not, *a major change in the direction of the market should show up here before it will in any of the other indicators.*

Set up a simple 7-column table under the following headings:

1. Date
2. Advances
3. Declines
4. Cumulative Advances
5. Cumulative Declines
6. Cumulative Differential (The Advance-Decline Line)
7. The Dow-Jones Industrial Average

Suppose you started your Table with the March 20, 1974 market, for example. On that day there were 668 stocks having made price advances and 674 having shown a price decline. The differential was a reading of -6, practically a standoff. However, the Dow-Jones Industrial Average had jumped 4.77 points. The next day the advance-decline line dropped again, 579 issues rising and 788 declining. However, the Dow-Jones Industrial Average went up by 3.13 points. The declining plurality of 209 on the second day is added to the plurality of -6 and the cumulative differential for the two days is now -215. On the third day (March 22) the advance-decline line took a further drop, 541 stocks advancing and 836 declining. However, once again the Dow-Jones Industrial Average rose, this time jumping 2.66 points. This phenomena of an advancing Dow and a declining advance-decline line continued for a couple of more sessions, and then the Dow average collapsed, a typical experience when the advance-decline line fails to confirm upside action in the Dow. These examples are put in tabular form below:

TABLE OF ADVANCES AND DECLINES

Date	Advances	Declines	Cumulative Advances	Cumulative Declines	Cumulative Differential	Dow-Jones Industrials
3/20/74	668	674	668	674	- 6	872.34
3/21/74	579	788	1,247	1,462	-215	875.47
3/22/74	541	836	1,788	2,298	-510	878.13
3/25/74	578	803	2,366	3,101	-735	881.02
3/26/74	687	657	3,053	3,758	-705	883.68
3/27/74	341	1,053	3,394	4,811	-1,417	871.17
3/28/74	191	1,299	3,585	6,110	-2,525	854.35
3/29/74	459	917	4,044	7,027	-2,983	846.68
4/ 1/74	483	896	4,527	7,923	-3,396	843.48

The theory behind the advance-decline line is best described in terms of what I chose to call the "bathtub" analogy. Picture the market as a bathtub. Advancing stocks raise the water level and declining stocks lower the water level. True market strength or weakness is determined by that water level. When the Dow-Jones Industrial Average is rallying and the water level of the entire market is not rising with it, we have developing trouble on our hands. Conversely, when the Dow-Jones Industrial Average looks weak but the water level of the market is virtually unchanged or only slightly lower, then we can say that the true picture of the market is relatively stronger than the picture of weakness proclaimed by the most followed of all market averages.

In a conventional bull market, the early months of rise show the advance-decline line and the Dow-Jones Industrial Average to be in gear on the upside in a happy marriage. The market bathtub is filling up. However, this happy combination eventually breaks down, and the honeymoon is over. The Dow-Jones Industrial Average continues upward on its merry way but the advance-decline line is no longer in step, going sideways to lower. We now have a broken marriage on our hands. While the public is mesmerized by the rising Dow, the market water level is going down. What were once two factors climbing hand in hand are now two factors seriously out of gear. The cycle always shows a strict order in this technical phenomenon: (1) in gear, (2) out of gear, and then (3) in gear. When this divergence between the Dow-Jones Industrial Average and the advance-decline line occurs in a bull market, the usual order of events predicts that the Dow-Jones Industrial Average will get back into gear with the advance-decline line on the downside. We then have a bear market on our hands until the advance-decline line stops going down.

At the end of the line on the downside, we again look for important *divergences,* the out-of-gear movements which will predictably be followed by the in-gear movement between the Dow-Jones Industrial Average and the advance-decline line on the upside.

Now let us look at our bathtub again. You've all heard the expressions by losers in the stock market game of "I took a bath," or "the market took a bath." Physically, *you cannot take a bath unless there is enough water in the bathtub to do so.* In other words, if the advance-decline line was theoretically low enough, *you couldn't take a bath in the market.* So then, *the probabilities of taking a bath in the market are the greatest when the water level of the market bathtub is the highest and just starting to go down, and the least when practically all the water has run out of the tub.*

Viewing this analogy again with the Dow-Jones Industrial Average in mind, we can draw some interesting conclusions as to the movements of the "smart money" crowd. Anybody who is among the first to detect a new trend in the market and act upon that discovery is automatically among the "smart money" crowd. If he moves out of the market or goes short when the level of the market bathtub has crested and is just starting to come down he is acting on the advance-decline line information that the bull market for most stocks is over. His short selling is probably premature because the Dow-Jones Industrial Average is still rising and still carrying a few hundred stocks along with it. Now look at the bathtub. The smart money is the *first to the exits* when the water level of the market stops rising and starts to come down while the Dow is still rising. How does water get out of the tub? Through the drain of course. So then, the smart money under these technical conditions is the first to flow through the drain. Their *money outflow* represents the *bottom layer of water* in the market bathtub. Obviously the water closest to the drain in the tub is the *first to hit the drain* when the water level starts to go down. Or, likened to a *market pyramid,* the *foundation* starts to crumble first, and the top of the pyramid is the last to fall.

If the "smart money" is the first to leave the market bathtub in a cresting market, it follows that the "dumb money," the top layer of water in the market bathtub, is the *last* to leave the tub, the last water to drain out. Since the bulk of the stocks are hitting the drain before the Dow-Jones Industrial stocks (the blue chips), it follows that the Dow-Jones Industrial stocks and other blue chip issues late in the bear market will be the *last stocks to flow through the drain.* The next time you take a bath, watch the water go out of the tub. When the last of the water approaches the drain, *watch how the flow is speeded up.* That phenomenon of *acceleration* is a common characteristic of *terminal* moves. You can note the same characteristic with the gas in your automobile. After you have filled up it seems like the gauge is very slow at first to come down from the "FULL" designation. After you see it drop to the quarter tank level and begin to approach the reserve or "EMPTY" marking it seems to *accelerate on the downside.* Pick up an hourglass, and you can watch the same phenomenon. The sand level seems to drop very slowly at first, but when the top layer is almost empty the sand runs out very fast, for it is *the accelerated terminal action.* So then, the "dumb money" is the last to leave the market when a bear market is terminating, *and it leaves very fast at or near the time when the faucets are going to be turned on to fill the bathtub once again for a whole new cycle.* After the market has been declining for many months, the final drop, the accelerated rushing of the last water to the drain, is characterized by the precipitous drop straight down in the Dow-Jones Industrial Average. You now know there is no more water left in the tub to take a bath in because the advance-decline line has been going down *for a much longer period of time* than the Dow. The precipitous drop in the Dow is the last of the surface water hitting the drain.

With all the water out of the market bathtub, no new bath will be taken *until the bathtub is refilled.* This means that the faucets must be turned on again and the drain closed. A new bull market is about to take place. The "smart money" was the first to leave the bathtub when it was cresting, *and it is equally certain that the "smart money" is the first to flow back into the tub when they are convinced that the tub is empty.* The identification of the smart money crowd, however, is constantly changing. An investor can be part of the "dumb money" crowd deep in a bear market and then become one of the first to detect a new long-term uptrend, acting immediately and correctly on this new discovery. He now is part of the new "smart money" crowd. This smart money then becomes the *bottom* layer of water, the "foundational" factor upon which the new bull market will grow, upon which all the other layers of water in the bathtub will lie. Smart money must always be at the *bottom* layer of the market bathtub because it is *first in and first out.* Dumb money sits up on the surface of the tub water because it is *last in and last out.*

Now you see, of course, that the major function of the advance-decline line as a key market indicator is *denoting whether money is flowing into the market bathtub or out of it.* The indicator can now be fitted into the market phase diagram. Obviously the advance-decline line is going to trend upward during the first phase of a bull market, pushed higher by the confident smart money crowd. There is no question about that. In the second phase of a bull market the line will also be trending higher *but it either tops out late in the second bull phase or early in the third bull phase,* reflecting developing fears on the part of the smart money crowd. *The advance-decline line then trends lower all through the first two phases of a bear market and most if not all of the third bear phase.*

For a very long time analysts believed that the advance-decline line acted the same on market bottoms as it did on tops, bottoming well ahead of the Dow-Jones Industrial Average. Two glaring exceptions to that belief have completely revised that earlier notion. In the 1962 market decline, the Dow bottomed in June of that year. Four months later a new decline relating to the Cuban missile crisis drove the advance-decline line to a new low for the year, a decline which was *not* confirmed by a new low in the industrial average. A similar technical event took place following the 1970 market bottom. The industrial average bottomed in late May, and six weeks later the advance-decline line sank to a new low, a move which the industrial average failed to confirm. The conclusion is that the advance-decline line is the most reliable indicator of an approaching market top but is subject to some question on market bottoms, either turning with the Dow or a short time thereafter. It is therefore NOT considered to be an infallible bottom indicator. This is more understandable when one considers what is going on during the transition from the third and final phase of a bear market to the first phase of a new bull market. As the smart money begins to move back into the market on the buying side and the public is still leaving the market, one can see how for awhile more stocks could be declining than advancing, thus accounting for the upturn in the advance-decline line after the Dow-Jones Industrial Average has already recorded the low.

Much has been written in stock market books about the advance-decline line, but very little has been said about the very *long-term* implications of this indicator. How many people, for example, are aware of the fact that the advance-decline topped out in 1956 and thereafter trended lower for 18 years? In this case suppose someone demanded that the A-D line better the 1956 peak before getting back into the market. He would have found himself out of the market for 18 years. Obviously then, the A-D line has to be interpreted within the shorter 4 to 4 1/2 year market cycles rather than in such long periods as 18 years. It is difficult to explain *why* the A-D line trended lower for 18 years but easy to explain *how* it did this. Consider the mechanics of the indicator briefly. If a stock declines by an eighth of a point, it has contributed toward a drop in the A-D line. Now suppose that stock previously rose by a *full point* and then dropped an *eighth of a point* for the next *eight* market sessions. After those eight sessions, the price of the stock is the same as when the move started, and yet the advance-decline line is much lower. What must have happened between 1956 and 1974 was an alternating series of advances and declines whereby *most* of the advances were in terms of *points* and most of the declines were in *fractions* of points.

What happened before 1956? Between 1938 and 1956, the advance-decline line trended higher. In that period the opposite mechanics took place. In that 18-year period there was an alternating series of advances and declines whereby most of the advances were in fractions of points and most of the declines were in points. Prior to 1938 we find that the A-D line had generally trended lower since 1920, and thus the evidence supported the thesis of the *long-term waves* in the movements of the advance-decline line.

Theoretically there is no limit to how high the advance-decline line can go, but there is a *mathematical limit* to how low it can go, and this became an irresistible and overpowering argument by late 1974 that a brighter future lay ahead for the stock market, such evidence coming into view at a time when least likely to be believed. Consider the following figures: Let us say that 2,000 different stocks are listed on the New York Stock Exchange and that the average price is $40 a share. Now we can calculate a *theoretical maximum drop* for the advance-decline line, assuming that each stock drops an eighth of a point at a time:

$$2000 \times 40 \times 8 = 640{,}000$$

The formula shows that the A-D line cannot drop by more than 640,000 because at minus 640,000 all stocks would be priced at zero. Between 1968 and 1974, the A-D line dropped by approximately 113,000, and quite a bit more if one goes back to 1956. At the December, 1974 bottom in the advance-decline line trend, *the line had wiped out everything going all the way back to 1942!* As the following chart shows, there is *long-term support* back at the 1942 A-D line levels. So then, not only was the advance-decline line making an important cyclical bottom in 1974 in accordance with the 4 to 4 1/2 year cycle, but it is seen here to have completed a very important long-term 18-year downswing *implying an equally long-term upswing ahead.*

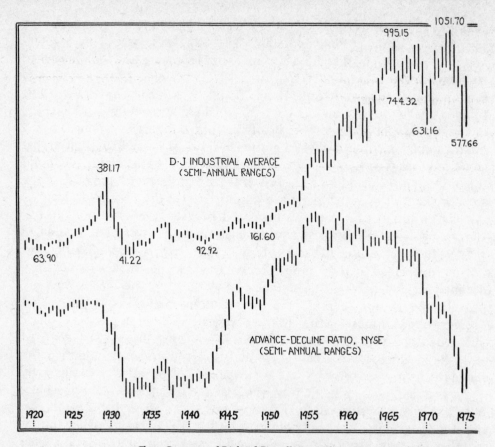

Chart Courtesy of Richard Russell, Dow Theory Letters, LaJolla, California

   The long-term implications here strongly suggest that between 1974 and 1992, each bull market will have an advance-decline line reading above the previous bull market A-D line peak, and that each bear market low will have an A-D line reading above the previous bear market low, just the opposite of what the experience was between 1956 and 1974. So then, the long-term chances of beating the stock market game now are better than they have been in years! I first made this statement at a time when half the country was looking for a depression, when hundreds of brokerage firms were in serious difficulty, and at a time when millions of people had left the stock market.

   While the advance-decline line is a powerful market indicator, one cannot always make a mechanical forecast of where the Dow is headed based on that indicator. Russell stated that past history suggests that in cases of extended price-breadth divergence, the Dow resolves the problem in favor of the A-D line. This is generally true *up to a point*. I already cited the cases where the new A-D line lows in October, 1962, and July, 1970, were NOT followed by new lows in the Dow-Jones Industrial Average. At this writing we have a third instance, the December, 1974 A-D line low not followed by a new low in the Dow-Jones Industrial Average. The time factor here seems to predominate. *When the cyclical influences call for a new bull market upswing, the A-D Line will stop going down regardless of a mechanical prediction based on that line as to where the Dow is headed.*

Throughout the bear market of 1973-74, the extreme pessimists were looking for the Dow to drop to 500 and lower, and, as the long-term chart shows, a prediction for a drop to as low as 92.92 in the Dow could *mechanically* have been made simply because the A-D line descended all the way back to 1942 levels. During the bear market of 1973-74, one famous commentator predicted that the Dow would have to drop to the 450 level because the A-D line had by then dropped to a level 30% under where it was in May, 1970, when the Dow stood at 631. That is one fallacy regarding the advance-decline line that should definitely be avoided; making a Dow forecast based solely on the position of the A-D line usually works out very well the first or second time, but when the time cycle calls for an up market, such mechanical forecasts of a lower Dow go out the window. During the bear market of 1968-70, I fell prey to the same reasoning because it so strongly supported my bearishness all the way down from Dow 986 to Dow 631. To project the Dow based on the A-D line is at best only partially successful. For awhile in a down market the method looks excellent, the Dow breaking down to each level previously predicted by the A-D Line. Then all of a sudden the Dow turns, and the A-D line projections never take place. Here is an actual case: In April, 1969, the A-D Line made the first of three downside projections for the Dow. The first prediction was made on April 22, when the A-D Line broke under the March 25, 1968 low, thus predicting a coming move in the Dow down to 825.15. The Dow stood at 918.59 on the day of the prediction. That first prediction was fulfilled a little over three months later when the Dow moved down to 818.06 on July 25, 1969. Meanwhile on June 6, of that same year, the A-D Line gave out with the second prediction. It broke the October 7, 1966 low, thus projecting a lower Dow reading coming of 744.32. All well and good. Seven months later, on January 30, 1970, the Dow closed at 744.06. That fulfilled the second A-D Line prediction. Meanwhile the A-D Line had given the third projection. On December 17, 1969, it had dropped to the lowest level seen since 1951, when the Dow had had a range of 161 to 276. To have *mechanically* followed the A-D Line at this point, one would have simply predicted a further drop in the Dow to the 161 to 276 area. However, the Dow STOPPED going down at 631 on May 26, 1970. So then, a Dow projection based on the A-D Line level is only *good up to a point*. By late 1974, with the A-D Line having dropped back to levels not seen since 1942, a mechanical projection of a lower Dow to come would be increasingly suspect because an A-D Line having trended lower for 18 years was in itself *radically oversold* and could no longer make a valid prediction of lower Dow levels to come.

While there have been exceptions from time to time in what the advance-decline line is telling us, *it never departs from its basic message*, which is that either water is flowing into the market bathtub or out of it. The rules on the advance-decline line laid down in the original *Stragegy* book have stood the test of time.

Rules On the Advance-Decline Line

1. When the Dow-Jones Industrial Average falls in the face of a rising advance-decline line, the market is going to go up.
2. When the Dow-Jones Industrial Average advances in the face of a declining advance-decline line, the market is going to go down.
3. The severity of the market reaction is signalled by the degree and duration of the disparate movement.
4. The power of the advance is signalled by the degree and duration of the disparate movement.
5. The advance-decline line, taken alone, does not pinpoint the timing for these signalled advances or reactions but merely indicates that they are going to take place at some not-too-distant time.
6. When the Dow-Jones Industrial Average approaches any previous top and the advance-decline line is below the reading which corresponded to that top, then the market situation is bearish.
7. When the Dow-Jones Industrial Average approaches a previous low and the advance-decline line is well above where it was at the time of the previous low, then the market situation is bullish.
8. When the advance-decline line is lower as the market approaches a previous low, then a downside penetration is imminent. (NOTE: THIS IS THE RULE THE MARKET MOST OFTEN MAKES AN EXCEPTION TO WHEN THE BACKGROUND CONDITIONS FOR A MAJOR BOTTOM ARE PREVALENT.)
9. If the advance-decline line is higher as the market approaches a previous high, then a bullish upside penetration can be looked for.

Is there a case on record where the advance-decline line trended lower for many months against a rising Dow-Jones Industrial Average and this disparity was later resolved by the A-D line getting in gear with the rising Dow rather than the other way around? Yes. Back in April, 1963, the A-D line topped out after trending higher since the 1962 market bottom. Thereafter, the line diverged, working lower as the Dow worked higher. Very briefly the Dow got in gear with the lower A-D line at the time of the Kennedy assassination in November of that year, but another technical problem emerged thereafter. As the Dow got stronger in 1964, the A-D Line persisted in failing to confirm the rise, remaining for many months under the April, 1963 peak. But in this case the Dow prevailed rather than the A-D Line, and by October of 1964, the A-D Line confirmed the Dow strength by bettering the April, 1963 peak, a technical event with few, if any, precedents. Well, we don't play the game following just one indicator no matter how important that indicator is. If you play the game that way, the market can fool you every time that particular indicator makes the kind of exceptional move that most indicators do on relatively rare occasions. That is why we are always looking at a *collection* of indicators. In the famous 1963-64 A-D Line exceptional performance, the *time factor* was the predominating influence, the market having come off of a major bottom in 1962. Keeping in mind the 4 to 4 1/2 year market cycle, it wasn't likely that the April, 1963 peak in the A-D Line was a major one inasmuch as the market bathtub had not filled up enough yet. So then, no flat statement can ever be made regarding where the market is going based on a single indicator. It is well, however, to put the greatest reliance on a group of indicators affecting *the greatest part of the market.* Such indicators cannot be rigged and distortions are less likely to occur. The Advance-Decline Line, then, is an ideal indicator to always follow carefully for these reasons inasmuch as it is based on the daily action of *all* stocks.

Daily Highs and Lows

Every day the market statistics reveal the number of stocks recording new highs and lows for the year. It is very important always to be aware of those figures which, like the advance-decline line, *indicate whether the market bathtub is filling up or is being emptied.* It is not important to know whether there are more new highs than lows or visa versa. Such a one-shot revelation would tell you nothing. What is important here is the *trend.* Is the number of new highs expanding or contracting? Is the number of new lows expanding or contracting?

Obviously, a major uptrend in the market must be accompanied by an *expanding* number of stocks making new highs. You will note the emphasis here on the word *expanding.* If I had stated that a major uptrend in the market must be accompanied by a greater number of stocks making new highs than lows, I would be wrong. Major uptrends *start* with more new lows than highs, and major downtrends start with more new highs than lows. So we have to know where we have been before we know where we are going with this indicator. Let us start at the beginning, the start of a major market up-trend, a new bull market. A new bull market starts when an old bear market ends, right at the bottom. The bottom will reveal hundreds of stocks at new lows with virtually none at new highs. Here then is the case of a bearish extreme being bullish, more new lows than highs having expanded to a point where a further expansion of new lows is unlikely to occur. One could actually buy and sell stocks over the long pull based on these high/low extremes, but as you will see later on, this would be futile unless one could be pretty sure what time it was on the market clock.

Like all indicators, the high/low indicator must be interpreted in terms of how it relates to other major indicators. In that respect it called the 1974 bottom better than any other indicator. On September 13, 1974, the high/low indicator showed zero stocks at new highs and 661 at new lows with the Dow-Jones Industrial Average closing sharply down at 627.19. Based on the high/low indicator alone, there was absolutely no doubt that the market was vastly oversold. Every major market bottom had always shown a number of new lows ranging from 500 to well over 800. This was probably the true bottom. Now it only remained to pinpoint the bottom in the major averages. On October 4, the Dow-Jones Industrial Average sank to an intra-day low of 573.22, closing at a new low of 584.56. A look at the high/low indicator on that day was highly revealing. While the popularly followed Dow indicator proclaimed a new closing low at 584.56, the high/low indicator showed two stocks at new highs and 235 at new lows, *a vast improvement since September 13*. There was no guesswork here. Here is cold technical fact. The Dow-Jones Industrial Average stands at a new low and the high/low indicator tells us that *426 stocks have come off their lows*. The Dow low was subsequently tested successfully on December 6, the industrials sinking to an intra-day low of 572.12 but lacking a confirming move by the Transportation Average. On that day the number of new lows expanded from 156 to 297 but was still such a far cry from the climactic number of 661 recorded on September 13 that the evidence by then was more than overwhelming that the market had scored a major cyclical change for the better. This was clearly seen when *relating* the movements of the high/low indicator with the movements of the Dow averages. The high/low indicator revealed a major *non-confirmation* of the October 4 weakness in the industrial average, and it did this *following* an historical oversold condition reflected by 661 new lows.

Subsequent Dow lows on a contracting number of new lows is not of itself enough evidence upon which to proclaim a new bull market. If this phenomenon occurs at the wrong time on the market clock, it only implies a rally ahead rather than a new bull market. The market threw such a technical curve in 1973, and if one overrelied then on the high/low indicator, one would have had to say that a major bottom had been recorded on May 21, 1973, in terms of *internal* market action, and on December 5, 1973, in the Dow. Here is what happened: On May 21, 1973, the number of new lows expanded dramatically to 858, the largest number since the 1970 market bottom, the Dow-Jones Industrial Average sinking that day to 886.51. On December 5 of that year the Dow broke to a new low of 788.31, but the number of new lows had contracted to 559. A strong rally did ensue, but it turned out to be another rally in a bear market. At that time I placed too much reliance on the high/low indicator. I even went so far as to underscore the presence of a "reverse head-and-shoulders" pattern in the number of new lows, pointing out that there were 571 new lows on March 23, 1973, 858 on May 21, 1973, and 559 on December 5, 1973. It all looked good in theory, *but it was ten months too soon on the market clock.* Overstating the importance of a single indicator too often results in great disappointment.

Can the opposite happen? Can the number of new highs rise sharply to several hundred, only to break down thereafter and not be a bear market? Yes. A classic case occured in 1963. April 15, 1963 showed 184 stocks at new highs, a figure that was to break down to only nine new highs by July of that year. As market history subsequently showed, 1963 turned out to be *too early in the market cycle* to have placed undue reliance on the high/low indicator as a forerunner of serious trouble. I stated previously that the advance-decline line had also topped out in April, 1963, only to come back and better the level in October, 1964. There was a case of *two* major indicators presenting a *premature* bearish configuration, not likely to be genuine so soon after a major market bottom such as the one recorded in 1962. Conversely, it was too soon for the bullish high/low figures to be genuine in 1973 after a major cyclical top.

One must put great emphasis on the cyclicality of the market when interpreting the high/low indicator. Coming off of a major bottom, the number of new lows is seen to contract rapidly, and a few months later there may be virtually no new lows and a couple of hundred new highs. Correcting that first upwave, the large number of new highs is going to contract. If the Dow advances while that happens, then the correction in the averages is going to be more severe and protracted. If the Dow declines with the contraction in new highs, the reaction is likely to be less severe and in all probability a normal correction in a continuing bull market. When this phenomenon occurs within a year after a major market bottom, it is historically not the start of a new bear market (1963 example). At this point it is important to keep in mind the posture of most stocks at a major market bottom. Since most major market bottoms occur in the *latter* half of the calendar year, a rapid expansion of new highs will be seen in the early months of the new calendar year simply because the calendar is changed and by March the number of new highs is based on the new calendar year. The *prices* of those stocks may still be well *below* the previous bull market highs; this explains why the number of new highs can contract rapidly on the first correction and not be the forerunner of a new bear market. It is too soon. Later in the cycle, however, 2 to 2 1/2 years after the bottom, a contracting number of new highs (especially with a continued rise in the Dow) is a serious thing indeed. The ultimate downturn in the averages may be several months off, but the peaking out in the number of new individual stock price highs always occurs first. The countdown toward a new bear market has then started.

Late in a bull market the number of individual new highs will reach several hundred, and that figure will become very difficult to sustain. The indicator will have come full cycle from the bottom when several hundred stocks were making new lows and virtually none were making new highs. Inasmuch as the bull market peak in this indicator will include the topping out of many so-called low priced stocks, and inasmuch as we know that low-priced stocks top out before the blue chips, this also explains why the number of new highs tops out before the Dow-Jones Industrial Average. That also correlates with the experience of the advance-decline line which also has a pretty consistent record of topping out before the Dow.

As with all major indicators, maximum market intelligence is derived from watching for *non-confirmations* with the Dow. If the Dow advances against the background of a downtrend in the number of new highs, there is trouble ahead and, conversely, if the Dow declines against the background of a marked reduction in the number of new lows, a very definite upturn ahead is signalled. Whether those signalled turns are merely transitory rallies or declines will depend on where the market is in the 4 to 4 1/2 year market cycle. We are not going to get very excited about a decline coming within a year after a major market bottom, nor are we going to get excited about an advance occuring within a year from a major market top. Those changes may be good money-making advances or declines, but they are not likely to be major changes in the prevailing trend.

Summing up this indicator, here is what it tells us: Like the advance-decline line, it tells us whether the water is flowing into the market bathtub or out of it. It tells us when the bathtub is full and when it is empty. It does this by a series of *non-confirmations* with the Dow at the top and a series of *non-confirmations* with the Dow at the bottom. When there are several hundred new lows *late in the market downcycle,* and the number of new lows is reduced on a new Dow low, we then know that the *smart money* has re-entered the market on the long side. The bulk of the investing public would never be attracted to the market in the face of several hundred new lows, *and that is what keeps the game going.* Obviously everybody can't get in at the bottom and out at the top because *there is no second public.* Smart money must buy from "dumb" money and smart money must sell to "dumb" money. The only way to make money in the market is to buy low and sell high, and thus the greatest buying opportunities in the market must occur when there are several hundred new lows. The greatest selling opportunities must be when there are several hundred new highs. Yet the general public, always fulfilling its role as the "fall guy," won't touch the market when there are several hundred new lows and won't leave the market when there are several hundred new highs. So then, this important indicator tells you that the public is out of the market when there are several hundred new lows and definitely in the market when there are several hundred new highs.

As for the stage of the "game," this indicator is the most reliable at the "extremes," the times it most pays to be right on the market. The indicator, like the market, always look ahead. When the indicator shows several hundred new highs, why is this happening? It is happening because good news is *anticipated.* When the good news arrives the indicator shows a reduction in the number of new highs because *the market does not discount good news twice.* When hundreds of new lows are recorded the market *anticipates* bad news ahead. When the bad news arrives there is a reduction in the number of new lows for the same reason. This is something which the public as a whole will never grasp. If they did, the game would be over. I will go into this in greater detail when discussing the important subject of *news.*

Time

How could *time* itself be a market indicator? Not only is this fourth dimensional factor an indicator, but it could very well be THE indicator. When one is caught up in the day-to-day excitement of playing the market game it is very easy to forget about the market clock. But every game has its limit, and when that limit is reached the game is over *regardless of everything.* Football coaches constantly are aware of the game clock. Basketball players always know what time it is on the game clock. But in the stock market the tendency is to watch everything *but the clock.* Something happens (and there is always something happening), and the impact of that happening sends out a series of waves producing emotional responses. If it is the outbreak of war we normally respond with fear. If the President is assassinated we are numbed with immediate shock. If an enemy nation with which we are not at war attacks or confiscates U.S. property, or otherwise provokes a serious incident, we are normally gripped with anger. All these events would normally prod us into selling stocks. On the other hand, we normally respond with relief after a long strike is settled. We rejoice after a long war ends. We bask in a sense of new security when there is assured prosperity about us and we know the economy is strong. In these cases we normally respond by buying stocks.

When all those conditions are not related to what time it is on the market clock, they have all probably produced the wrong reactions on our part, and then it is like being called out of the game by the coach, forced to sit on the bench and ponder what went wrong. If we sold stocks when war broke out in Korea back in 1950, we did the wrong thing because the market clock said the bulls had plenty of time left in the game. If we sold stocks when President Eisenhower had a heart attack in 1955, we did the wrong thing because the market clock also said the bulls had plenty of time left on the upside. If we sold stocks when Treasury Secretary George Humphrey warned of a "depression that would curl your hair" back in 1957, we did the wrong thing since the market clock at that time showed the bearish game practically over. If we bought stocks on the news that the long national steel strike of late 1959 had ended in early January, 1960, we did the wrong thing because the market clock showed the bears in possession of the ball with time to go. If we sold stocks on the news that President Kennedy had been assassinated, we did the wrong thing because the market clock showed the bulls getting possession of the ball in 1962 with plenty of time left in the game to go. If we sold stocks when war broke out in the Middle East in June, 1967, we did the wrong thing because the market clock showed the bulls getting possession of the ball in 1966 with plenty of time left in the game. If we bought stocks in 1972 when the economy was strong and it looked like the U.S. was finally getting out of Viet Nam with a negotiated cease fire agreement, we did the wrong thing because the market clock showed that it was too late in the bull game, the bulls having had possession of the ball since 1970. If we smartened up and bought stocks on the next Middle East war in late 1973, we did the wrong thing because it was too early in the bear game, the bears getting possession of the ball in January, 1973.

So then, *we learn that events are always secondary to the time in which they occur.* We cannot learn from the events themselves because *they produce different responses at different times on the market clock.* War is bullish early in a bull cycle. War is bearish early in a bear cycle. Peace is bullish early in a bull cycle. Peace is bearish early in a bear cycle. Prosperity is bullish early in a bull cycle (an unlikely occurence). Prosperity is bearish early in a bear cycle. Recession is bullish late in a bear cycle or early in a bull cycle. I can go on and on. Examples are endless.

We had one of the greatest bull markets of all time from 1942 to 1946 when the U.S. was at war with Germany, Italy, and Japan. The Viet Nam war involved the U.S. from 1961 to 1973, yet in that period the market carved out three bull markets and three bear markets, the market making the final peak at the end of the war. Similar comparisons can be made involving the long dollar crisis, inflation, and many other major problems stretching back an entire generation. Throughout it all the market game was played in isolation from all those outside events, *subservient only to the time factor.*

Like the ancient mariner, we have to chart our position by following the fixed stars and constellations of technical market phenomena and set our watches thereby. We have to start somewhere, and so *we must look at the market clock in terms of the last well defined major bottom.* That is a *fixed* star. We will base all our bull market timing strategies from that date forward. *Such major bottoms have generally occurred every 4 to 4 1/2 years, and the record on this is indeed impressive.* The bull and bear cycles have to be sandwiched between that time span. In other words, if we get a typical three phase bull cycle stretching the overall rise to 32 months since the previous major bottom, then we can look for a bear market generally lasting from 16 to 22 months inasmuch as the entire bull and bear cycle will probably terminate 48 to 54 months from the previous major bottom. If the bull cycle is more extended and lasts 44 months as it did between 1962 and 1966, then the next bear cycle has to be short, ten months or less, as it was between February and October, 1966.

Further mapping out our fixed stars, we apply our knowledge of other technical phenomena which provide *timing landmarks* along the way. For instance, the bull market is strongly confirmed by an upside penetration of the 200-day moving average trendline by the Dow, something that generally takes place *during the first four months* after a major bottom. If that occurs we have full proof that the market is in the *first phase* of a new bull cycle, and we can have confidence that the ultimate bull market peak is many months away. Generally *half* of the losses in the industrial average in the preceding bear market are recovered by the Dow no later than the *sixth month* after the major bottom, so when that occurs we have further solid technical proof where we stand in the full cycle, a very bullish posture indeed. As previously shown, the 50% Principle works best in bull markets. The first six months in a new bull market are generally the easiest to read when we have those fixed stars of technical knowledge to go by.

After the first six months off the bottom have passed, the going gets a little more difficult. By this time we probably experience *a temporary topping out by the number of individual new highs as well as the important advance-decline line.* The overall advance after the six month period is well publicized, and the next important development in the market is a *normal* technical reaction. That reaction occurs *six months* after the importance of the major bottom was *widely recognized.* Major bottoms are usually widely recognized for what they are within three months after they occur. This means that the *smart money early buyers* will be cashing in for six-month capital gain profits *increasingly* in the *seventh, eighth,* and *ninth* month following the major bottom. Those three months are therefore subject to a *normal* technical reaction. The general public, still having fresh memories of the previous bear market, doesn't recognize the importance of the bottom until six months after it has been passed. Therefore, *12* months after the major bottom, a portion of the public helps to create selling pressure by taking a six-month capital gain.

Meanwhile, the smart money, coming back in on the completion of the first normal reaction, is eligible for capital gains profits in the *fifteenth* month after the major bottom. A large portion of the public also bought in on the first reaction completed in the ninth month, and they too are eligible for capital gain profits in the *fifteenth* month. This implies that the reaction slated for the fifteenth month will be more severe. It would be expected that the Dow-Jones Industrial Average would trace out a full scale secondary reaction, one even turning the 200-day moving average trendline down. Such a reaction would typify the type of decline ordinarily expected in the *second* phase of the bull market. The first phase ended with the topping out of the new highs and the advance-decline line. At this point it can be surmised that half of the bull market is over. Add *15 months* to that date and make a mental note to be completely out of the market *30* months after the major bottom.

Following the completion of the mid-cycle secondary reaction, the Dow is expected to turn very strong, making an upside penetration of the 200-day line again. It goes on to breaking out to a new bull market high. In doing this it causes the 200-day line to come up and surpass the previous high, thus tracing out an upward zigzag. At this point of upward zigzag in the 200-day line, the *third* phase of the bull market starts. This important move generally occurs around the *twenty-fourth* month after the major bottom. From there on in for the *next six months,* steadily mounting technical deterioration is expected to occur. Every distributive device described in this book comes into full play: stock splits, mounting secondary offerings, increasingly good news and often very heavy volume. Late in that final six-month period there is recorded one technical *non-confirmation* after another on the upside, the Dow making the last fling to another new high long after the smart money has made its exit. The bull market is over.

The timing landmarks are different in the bear cycle. *The length of the bear market will have a definite relationship to the length of the previous bull market.* If the 30-month model worked out, then a bear cycle lasting 18 to 24 months must be allowed for. In the middle of that cycle the rally that fools the majority must be expected to occur. It occurred on schedule in the short 1966 bear market. It was exactly on schedule in the 1968-70 bear market and was equally on schedule in the 1973-74 bear market. If the bull cycle turns out to be an unusually long one, say 40 months, for example, then the bear cycle will be a short eight to 14 months. *Very seldom do the combined bull and bear cycles stretch beyond 54 months.*

This then is the *time model* of the market game. *It even goes beyond the importance of the technical market indicators* because even a bullish message being shouted out by a key technical indicator can be cancelled out if the *time limit* for the bulls is up. No matter how bearish the technical indicators are they are utterly meaningless if the market clock (reading 48 to 54 months after the previous major bottom) says the game for the bears is over.

Oftentimes one may be waiting for a typical third phase upward movement in a long bull market. There is a perfect example of following the market clock first and the phases second. If the normal time limit has been met or exceeded for a bull market, one should sell anyway without waiting for a third phase movement which may not come.

The Dow-Jones Industrial Average

The Dow-Jones Industrial Average is the most widely watched of all market indicators. Because of this, it is notorious for playing tricks on those who fail to peer beneath this outer layer of the market. Being but one part of the entire market, the Dow industrial average moves most reliably when it moves in step with the entire market. It is when the Dow industrial average *walks alone* that an important reversal is in the making. Its movements must be confirmed constantly by the Dow-Jones Transportation Average, the advance-decline line, the high/low indicator and several other key indicators in order to maintain the trend then in progress.

Being so widely followed, it is natural to expect that in terms of the game tactics this is the indicator most responsible for keeping the majority in the market at the top and out of the market at the bottom. It does this by moving out into new high ground without confirmation and into new low ground without confirmation. While the smart money is selling out in other market areas, the unsuspecting public largely senses no immediate market danger as the Dow industrials are working into new high ground. Conversely, as the Dow breaks to a new bear market low, the public is not likely to suspect that the smart money has been accumulating stocks elsewhere in the list for several months. Such was the case on the 1973 top and 1974 bottom, and the scenario has been replayed over and over with variations, important technical non-confirmations occurring involving, in varying combinations, the

Dow-Transports, advance-decline line, high/low indicator, and the Standard & Poor 500 Stock Index.

The market seems to sense when an indicator becomes too popular and shifts its stance elsewhere to keep the public mystified as long as possible. For example, for many months prior to the January, 1973 top, the advance-decline line had been trending lower and the divergence from the rising Dow led into a steep and protracted market decline. By vowing to watch the advance-decline line more carefully in the future, one would have missed the earliest months of the 1974 bottom because then one would have followed the Dow-Jones Industrial Average into new low ground in early December of that year, waiting for the advance-decline line to bottom out which finally did so on December 23, almost three months after the last confirmed bottom of October 4, 1974. The Dow industrials, in breaking to a new low on December 6 of that year, did so on its own, a move that was not confirmed by the Dow-Jones Transportation Average or by the high/low indicator. So then, when the Dow walks alone, watch out! It usually signals an important top or bottom.

When the Dow embarks on one of these solitary walks, either marching into new high ground or breaking into new low ground, it usually does so by concentrated buying or selling in two or three of the 30 stocks, thus creating a suspicious looking type of run-up or decline. This concentration in two or three of the Dow stocks heavily weights the move in the average itself, but the distortion is immediately spotted by comparing the swing in the industrials to the daily change in either the Standard & Poor 500 Stock Index or the New York Stock Exchange Index. The thumb rule for such comparisons is to multiply the Standard & Poor reading by ten, the differential serving to record the disparity between the two averages. An increasingly positive disparity is obviously bearish for the industrial average and an increasingly negative disparity is equally bullish.

The Dow-Jones
Transportation Average

Like the Dow-Jones Industrial Average, the Dow-Jones Transportation Average is a vital segment of long, intermediate, and day-to-day market forecasting. Its major purpose as an indicator is to provide bullish and bearish signals based on confirmations or non-confirmations of strength or weakness in the Dow-Jones Industrial Average. No major forecast of stock market trends is complete without some reference made to what this indicator is saying. The long record of the stock market is replete with instances of such important confirmations or non-confirmations occuring at the most critical times.

The 50% Principle

A great deal has been written about the 50% Principle but nowhere has anyone taken the time to put it to the test and see how often it serves as a beautiful trap. The theory is very logical, best explained in terms of the physical movement of the seesaw. A seesaw is in equilibrium at the 50% level, perfectly horizontal. Once that equilibrium is disturbed and one half of the seesaw goes above the 50% level, it will then keep going all the way as far as it can. The other half of the seesaw will make a compensating movement in the opposite direction, going as far as it can. The market application of the Principle states that if a market decline retraces more than 50% of the advance, then the entire advance is likely to be wiped out. Conversely, if the market retraces more than 50% of a decline, the theory holds that the entire decline will be retraced. Retracements of less than 50% would indicate that the original movement is still in force. Below is a study of every market swing since the 1970 bottom, scoring the theory on each swing.

Dates of Swing	Dow Swing	50% Level	Retraced To	Follow-through	Theory Score
5/26 to 6/3 (70)	631.16 to 713.86	672.51	684.21	Rallied to 720.57	Perfect
6/3 to 6/12 (70)	713.86 to 684.21	699.03	700.00	Rallied to 720.57	Perfect
6/12 to 6/19 (70)	684.21 to 720.57	702.39	701.00	Declined to 669.36	Perfect
6/19 to 7/7 (70)	720.57 to 669.36	694.96	696.00	Rallied to 735.08	Perfect
7/7 to 7/17 (70)	669.36 to 735.08	702.22	707.35	Rallied to 773.14	Perfect
7/17 to 8/13 (70)	735.08 to 707.35	721.21	722.00	Rallied to 773.14	Perfect
8/13 to 9/8 (70)	707.35 to 773.14	740.24	747.47	Rallied to 783.68	Perfect
9/8 to 9/22 (70)	773.14 to 747.47	760.30	761.00	Rallied to 783.68	Perfect
9/22 to 10/7 (70)	747.47 to 783.68	765.57	764.00	Declined to 753.56	Imperfect
10/7 to 10/29 (70)	783.68 to 753.56	768.62	769.00	Rallied to 779.50	Imperfect
10/29 to 11/11 (70)	753.56 to 779.50	766.53	765.00	Declined to 754.24	Imperfect
11/11 to 11/18 (70)	779.50 to 754.24	766.87	767.00	Rallied to 890.06	Perfect
11/18 to 2/16 (71)	754.24 to 890.06	822.15	868.98	Rallied to 916.83	Perfect
2/16 to 2/22 (71)	890.06 to 868.98	879.52	880.00	Rallied to 916.83	Perfect
2/22 to 3/18 (71)	868.98 to 916.83	892.90	899.37	Rallied to 950.81	Perfect
3/18 to 3/24 (71)	916.83 to 899.37	908.10	909.00	Rallied to 950.81	Perfect
3/24 to 4/28 (71)	899.37 to 950.81	925.09	924.00	Declined to 905.78	Imperfect
4/28 to 5/27 (71)	950.81 to 905.78	928.29	923.06	Declined to 873.10	Perfect
5/27 to 6/7 (71)	905.78 to 923.06	914.42	913.00	Declined to 873.10	Perfect
6/7 to 6/28 (71)	923.06 to 873.10	898.08	899.00	Rallied to 903.40	Imperfect
6/28 to 7/12 (71)	873.10 to 903.40	888.25	887.00	Declined to 839.59	Perfect
7/12 to 8/10 (71)	903.40 to 839.59	871.49	872.00	Rallied to 920.93	Perfect
8/10 to 9/8 (71)	839.59 to 920.93	880.26	883.47	Rallied to 901.80	Imperfect
9/8 to 9/27 (71)	920.93 to 883.47	902.20	901.80	Declined to 825.26	Perfect
9/27 to 10/7 (71)	883.47 to 901.80	892.63	891.00	Declined to 825.26	Perfect
10/7 to 11/1 (71)	901.80 to 825.26	863.53	843.17	Declined to 810.53	Perfect
11/1 to 11/4 (71)	825.26 to 843.17	834.21	833.00	Declined to 810.53	Perfect
11/4 to 11/15 (71)	843.17 to 810.53	826.85	822.14	Declined to 797.97	Perfect
11/15 to 11/17 (71)	810.53 to 822.14	816.33	815.35	Declined to 797.97	Perfect

Dates of Swing	Dow Swing	50% Level	Retraced To	Follow-through		Theory Score
11/17 to 11/23 (71)	822.14 to 797.97	810.05	811.00	Rallied to	917.22	Perfect
11/23 to 1/18 (72)	797.97 to 917.22	857.59	889.15	Rallied to	950.18	Perfect
1/18 to 1/26 (72)	917.22 to 889.15	903.18	904.00	Rallied to	950.18	Perfect
1/26 to 3/6 (72)	889.15 to 950.18	919.66	928.66	Rallied to	968.92	Perfect
3/6 to 3/13 (72)	950.18 to 928.66	939.39	940.00	Rallied to	968.92	Perfect
3/13 to 4/18 (72)	928.66 to 968.92	948.79	947.00	Declined to	925.12	Perfect
4/18 to 5/9 (72)	968.92 to 925.12	947.02	948.00	Rallied to	971.25	Perfect
5/9 to 5/26 (72)	925.12 to 971.25	948.18	947.00	Declined to	934.53	Imperfect
5/26 to 6/9 (72)	971.25 to 934.53	952.89	951.61	Declined to	926.25	Perfect
6/9 to 6/21 (72)	934.53 to 951.61	943.07	942.00	Declined to	926.25	Perfect
6/21 to 6/29 (72)	951.61 to 926.25	938.93	939.00	Rallied to	942.13	Imperfect
6/29 to 7/6 (72)	926.25 to 942.13	934.19	933.00	Declined to	910.45	Perfect
7/6 to 7/20 (72)	942.13 to 910.45	926.27	927.00	Rallied to	973.51	Perfect
7/20 to 8/14 (72)	910.45 to 973.51	941.98	935.66	Declined to	935.66	Imperfect
8/14 to 9/25 (72)	873.51 to 835.66	854.58	955.00	Rallied to	955.15	Imperfect
9/25 to 9/28 (72)	935.66 to 955.15	945.40	945.00	Declined to	921.66	Perfect
9/28 to 10/16 (72)	955.15 to 921.66	938.40	939.00	Rallied to	1036.27	Perfect
10/16 to 12/11	921.66 to 1036.27	978.96	1000.00	Rallied to	1051.70	Perfect
12/11 to 12/21	1036.27 to 1000.00	1018.13	1019.00	Rallied to	1051.70	Perfect
12/21 to 1/11 (73)	1000.00 to 1051.70	1025.85	1025.00	Declined to	947.92	Perfect
1/11 to 2/27 (73)	1051.70 to 947.92	999.81	979.98	Declined to	922.71	Perfect
2/27 to 3/7 (73)	947.92 to 979.98	963.95	963.00	Declined to	922.71	Perfect
3/7 to 3/23 (73)	979.98 to 922.71	951.34	952.00	Rallied to	959.14	Imperfect
3/23 to 3/29	922.71 to 959.14	940.92	940.00	Declined to	923.46	Imperfect
3/29 to 4/5 (73)	959.14 to 923.46	941.30	942.00	Rallied to	921.21	Perfect
4/5 to 4/11 (73)	923.46 to 967.41	945.43	945.00	Declined to	921.21	Perfect
4/11 to 5/1 (73)	967.41 to 921.21	944.31	945.00	Rallied to	956.58	Imperfect
5/1 to 5/8 (73)	921.21 to 956.58	938.89	938.00	Declined to	886.51	Perfect
5/8 to 5/21 (73)	956.58 to 886.51	921.54	922.00	Rallied to	930.84	Imperfect
5/21 to 5/25 (73)	886.51 to 930.84	908.67	908.00	Declined to	885.91	Perfect
5/25 to 6/4 (73)	930.84 to 885.91	908.37	909.00	Rallied to	926.78	Imperfect
6/4 to 6/12 (73)	885.91 to 926.78	906.34	906.00	Declined to	869.13	Perfect
6/12 to 6/25 (73)	926.78 to 869.13	894.95	894.64	Declined to	870.11	Perfect
6/25 to 6/28 (73)	869.13 to 894.64	881.88	881.00	Declined to	870.11	Perfect
6/28 to 7/6 (73)	894.64 to 870.11	882.37	883.00	Rallied to	936.71	Perfect
7/6 to 7/27 (73)	870.11 to 936.71	903.41	903.00	Declined to	851.90	Perfect
7/27 to 8/22 (73)	936.71 to 851.90	894.30	895.00	Rallied to	901.04	Imperfect
8/22 to 9/6 (73)	851.90 to 901.04	876.47	880.57	Rallied to	987.05	Perfect
9/6 to 9/13 (73)	901.04 to 880.57	890.80	891.00	Rallied to	987.05	Perfect
9/13 to 10/26 (73)	880.57 to 987.05	933.81	933.00	Declined to	869.88	Perfect
10/26 to 11/14 (73)	987.05 to 869.88	928.46	891.33	Declined to	788.31	Perfect
11/14 to 11/16 (73)	869.88 to 891.33	880.60	880.00	Declined to	788.31	Perfect
11/16 to 12/5 (73)	891.33 to 788.31	839.82	840.00	Rallied to	851.14	Imperfect
12/5 to 12/10 (73)	788.31 to 851.14	819.72	819.00	Declined to	800.43	Imperfect
12/10 to 12/13 (73)	851.14 to 800.43	825.78	826.00	Rallied to	880.69	Perfect
12/13 to 1/3 (74)	800.43 to 880.69	840.56	840.00	Declined to	823.11	Imperfect
1/3 to 1/10 (74)	880.69 to 823.11	851.90	853.00	Rallied to	872.16	Imperfect
1/10 to 1/17 (74)	823.11 to 872.16	847.63	847.00	Declined to	803.90	Perfect
1/17 to 2/11 (74)	872.16 to 803.90	838.03	839.00	Rallied to	891.66	Perfect
2/11 to 3/13 (74)	803.90 to 891.66	852.78	852.00	Declined to	839.96	Imperfect
3/13 to 4/8 (74)	891.66 to 839.96	865.81	866.00	Rallied to	869.92	Imperfect

Dates of Swing	Dow Swing	50% Level	Retraced To	Follow-through		Theory Score
4/8 to 4/18 (74)	839.96 to 869.92	854.94	854.00	Declined to	827.67	Perfect
4/18 to 4/25 (74)	869.92 to 827.67	848.79	849.00	Rallied to	865.77	Imperfect
4/25 to 5/9 (74)	827.67 to 865.77	846.72	846.00	Declined to	795.37	Perfect
5/9 to 5/29 (74)	865.77 to 795.37	830.57	831.00	Rallied to	859.67	Imperfect
5/29 to 6/10 (74)	795.37 to 859.67	827.52	827.00	Declined to	759.62	Perfect
6/10 to 7/11 (74)	859.67 to 759.62	809.64	805.77	Declined to	751.10	Perfect
7/11 to 7/24 (74)	759.62 to 805.77	782.69	805.00	Declined to	751.10	Perfect
7/24 to 8/1 (74)	805.77 to 751.10	780.43	781.00	Rallied to	797.56	Imperfect
8/1 to 8/7 (74)	751.10 to 797.56	774.33	774.00	Declined to	647.92	Perfect
8/7 to 9/4 (74)	797.56 to 647.92	722.74	677.88	Declined to	627.19	Perfect
9/4 to 9/6 (74)	647.92 to 677.88	662.90	662.00	Declined to	627.19	Perfect
9/6 to 9/13 (74)	677.88 to 627.19	652.53	653.00	Rallied to	674.05	Imperfect
9/13 to 10/4 (74)	627.19 to 674.05	650.62	650.00	Declined to	584.56	Perfect
9/19 to 10/4 (74)	674.05 to 584.56	629.30	630.00	Rallied to	673.50	Imperfect
10/4 to 10/14 (74)	584.56 to 673.50	629.03	633.84	Rallied to	674.75	Perfect
10/14 to 10/28 (74)	673.50 to 633.84	653.67	654.00	Rallied to	674.75	Perfect
10/28 to 11/5 (74)	633.84 to 674.75	654.29	654.00	Declined to	577.60	Perfect
11/5 to 12/6 (74)	674.75 to 577.60	626.17	627.00	Rallied to	786.53	Perfect
12/6 to 3/17 (75)	577.60 to 786.53	682.06	743.43	Rallied to	770.26	Imperfect
3/17 to 3/24 (75)	786.53 to 743.43	764.98	765.00	Rallied to	770.26	Imperfect
3/24 to 3/27 (75)	743.43 to 770.26	756.84	756.00	Declined to	742.88	Perfect
3/27 to 4/7 (75)	770.26 to 742.88	756.57	757.00	Rallied to	858.73	Perfect

The 50% Principle is most important *when applied to entire bull and bear markets,* measuring the closing Dow-Jones Industrial Average from the bear market low to the bull market high, dividing by two and applying that halfway level to the ensuing bear market. The Principle states that when the decline in the Dow carries below the halfway mark of the previous bull market, a full retracement will follow. When the advance in the Dow carries above the halfway mark of the previous bear market, a full retracement will follow.

When reviewing the three bull and bear markets between 1962 and 1974, one finds that the figures are of great interest, not only because they reveal the great importance of this Principle *but because we can begin to formulate some rules based on it.* On June 26, 1962, the Dow recorded a major bottom at 535.76. Almost four years later the Dow peaked on February 9, 1966, at 995.15. The halfway level of that entire advance was 765.45. A closing below that level of 765.45 on the 1966 market decline would have predicted a further drop by the market below the 535.76 level. On August 29, 1966, the Dow closed down at 767.03, stopping just short of the 50% level. It rallied sharply into September and then plunged below the halfway mark of 765.45, stopping at 744.32 on October 7, 1966. That proved to be the bottom, *one of the major foolers by the 50% Principle.*

We now have a measurable decline from the 1966 high of 995.15 to the 1966 low at 744.32. The 50% level stood at 869.73. If the Dow could rally above that point in that new bull market, the Principle would predict a full recovery to the 995.15 level. On March 17, 1967, the Dow closed up at a new bull market high of 869.77. Right at that point the Principle was stating that the market was headed higher with certainty. Bearing out the Principle, the Dow trended all the way up to a closing high of 985.21 on December 3, 1968. If one had insisted on a classic 100% full recovery of the previous bear market, looking for another 10-point advance in the Dow, one would have tripped up at a very critical point because that turned out to be the bull market high, just 10 points short of the 100% retracement level.

The bear market of 1968-70 had started, and as it gained downside momentum the 50% level of the previous advance became increasingly important to watch. The 50% level of the 1966-68 advance stood at 864.76. That level was broken on the downside in July 1969, and, despite many technical rallies in between, the relentless bear trend carried the Dow down to the May 26, 1970 bottom at 631.16. Here the 50% Principle was perfect, the July, 1969 decline predicting a new low below the 744.32 low of 1966.

Now the new bull market of 1970-73 was underway, and we had a measurable bear market decline from 985.21 to 631.16 on which to compute the new 50% target level. The new 50% level stood at 808.18. On December 3, 1970, the Dow closed up at 808.53, and the Principle was now projecting a bull market termination point above the 985.21 bull market peak of 1968. True to form, the ultimate peak was reached by the Dow on January 11, 1973, at 1051.70, a remarkable victory for the 50% Principle.

Now a new bear market got started, and the previous measurable advance from 631.16 to 1051.70 assigned the new 50% level at 841.43. Throwing in a "rally that fools the majority" fooler, the Dow dropped to 851.90 on August 22, 1973, holding just above the 50% level, and then rallied all the way back up to 987.05 by October 26, 1973. Embarking on a new plunge, the Dow broke under the 50% level on November 26, 1973, and at that point the Principle was predicting a bear market low below the 631.16 bear market low of 1970. True to form, the Dow hit the low point of 577.60 on December 6, 1974, another victory for the Principle.

The new bull market was underway, and we had the measurable 1973-74 decline from 1051.70 to 577.60 upon which to compute a new 50% level. This time the 50% level stood at 814.65. Climbing on a "wall of worry," the Dow rocketed ahead to surpass the 50% level on April 15, 1975. According to the Principle, *here was a prediction that the Dow would make a full recovery in the months ahead to the 1051.70 peak of early 1973.* In terms of past performance the move might be aborted 21 points past the halfway level as happened on the 1966 decline, or it might stop 10 points short of the old high as happened on the upside in 1968 but, in the main, those exceptions are not too bothersome. The record shows that in the *bull market swings* retracing more than 50% of the previous bear market decline proved to be very bullish in every case. Inasmuch as the 1973-74 drop was so severe, it pointed to a much wider and more extended bull market swing from the 1974 low, the Dow theoretically having another 237 points to rise above the April 15, 1975 closing level of 815.08.

An observation can be made here regarding the *timing* of the 50% penetrations. You will note in the earlier descriptions that the 50% level was penetrated *earlier* in bull markets and *later* in bear markets. Since the bull cycles are generally always longer than the bear cycles, the upside penetrations of the 50% level are far more important in bull markets than they are in bear markets, allowing for the better part of two years until the bull peak. In the bear markets the downside penetrations of the 50% level only allowed several months more for the downtrend. The timing record is shown below:

Market Cycle	50% Penetration	End of Cycle
1966 Bear Market	8 months later	1 month later (fooler)
1966-68 Bull Market	5 months later	21 months later
1968-70 Bear Market	7 months later	10 months later
1970-73 Bull Market	6 months later	24 months later
1973-74 Bear Market	11 months later	11 months later
1974-? Bull Market	6 months later	? months later

The extreme importance of upside penetrations of the 50% level in bull markets is now fully apparent, and it can now be assigned a key place in the timing structure of the entire market cycle. Obviously such penetrations do not occur in the third phase of a bull market and they do not occur in the second phase. Such a penetration must be assigned to the *first* phase of a new bull market, enabling one to home in on where the market stands in the entire cycle. It becomes one of the most reliable of tools, almost totally reliable in bull markets but open to slight question during bear markets. Inasmuch as the market game is played with a *cyclical time limit*, the 50% Principle is an invaluable aid in helping to reveal what time it is on the market clock.

So then, April 15, 1975 made technical history, over half of the entire 1973-74 drop in the Dow recovered. In the light of previous experience with the 50% Principle during bull markets, we can look for a termination of the bull market which started in October, 1974, some 21 to 24 months after the April 15, 1975 date. Adding that time span would bring us up to the January to April, 1977 time segment. This was in harmony with my earlier projections of a final top in late 1976 or early 1977.

While the Principle is a definite help in defining the parameters of bull market peaks or bear market bottoms many months in advance, it is never a reason for complacency. No matter how accurate the longer range market forecast is, based on the Principle, it affords no protection against the sharp intermediate or secondary downswings which occur during all bull markets or against the equally sharp secondary rallies which take place during bear markets. A suitable example of this is seen in the 1970-73 bull market. The penetration of the halfway level of the previous cycle occurred on December 3, 1970, an historical technical occurrence. Though it predicted a new Dow high to occur almost two years later, the overall time span included the sharp secondary downtrend which occured in 1971, a drop which carried the Dow all the way down from 950.81 to 797.97.

Market students interested in researching the action of the Principle prior to 1962 will discover, as this writer did, that the Principle bears out the earlier conclusions, that it is *most reliable in bull markets* and less than reliable in bear markets. To fortify this conclusion, let us look at the bull market of 1957-61. That total swing took the Dow from 419.79 to 734.91. The 50% level stood at 577.35. That was the critical level to watch in the 1961-62 downswing. It was penetrated on the downside by 0.42 on May 28, 1962, five months after the 1961 top. Like the 1966 drop, Dow Theorists were fooled. Instead of the Dow continuing to drop all the way back down to the 1957 low of 419.79, *it completed the down cycle one month after the penetration of the 50% level,* bottoming on June 26, 1962, at 535.76. Now having a measurable decline from the 1961 high at 734.91 to the 1962 low at 535.76, the new 50% level became 635.33, the level to watch in the new bull market which started in June, 1962. That level was penetrated on the upside in November, 1962, five months after the June bottom. That bull market peaked in January, 1966, a full 38 months after the upside penetration of the 50% level, *further positive proof of the astounding validity of such upside penetrations in a bull market.*

Some analysts have attempted to apply the 50% Principle to the super cycles, bridging the four-year cycle. Such analyses have led to *super traps.* For instance, some analysts stayed bearish in 1962 after the bottom because, as we have already seen, the Dow retraced more than 50% of the 1957-61 rise in 1962. To further implement their bearishness, they applied the 50% Principle to the entire 1949-61 advance measured from Dow 161.60 to 734.91, coming up with a 50% level of 488. They projected a drop to that level and lower, but the 1962 market fooled them and bottomed at 535.76, a level still not broken half a generation later. Trying to apply the Principle to the super cycle, let us now stretch it from 1949 to the 1966 Dow top at 995.15. On that time spread the 50% level is computed at 578.37, a level not broken on the 1966 downturn. Next we come to the still wider time spread of 1949 to the 1968 top at 985.21. The 50% level on that wider time spread stood at 573.40, a level not broken on the 1968-70 bear market. Stretching the time span to the 1973 Dow high of 1051.70, we come up with a 50% level of 606.65, *a level which was penetrated on the 1973-74 bear market.* However, what happened? Instead of a cataclysmic market crash so widely predicted, the Dow bottomed slightly below the critical long-range 50% level, the closing low seen at 577.60.

In conclusion, we can summarize the value of this important indicator as follows:

(1) The maximum importance and reliability centers on the better than 50% retracements of previous entire bear market declines, pinpointing the breakthrough as occurring in the *first phase* of a new bull market with almost two years to go until the final bull market peak.
(2) It has little reliability in bear markets retracing more than 50% of the previous entire bull market, just as often setting up a bear trap as forecasing further decline.
(3) It has very little value when applied to super time cycles, again more often than not setting up a bear trap.
(4) It has better than average accuracy when applied to short-term market swings.

In concluding this discussion of the 50% Principle, we must look back to the 1929 crash and the aftermath action. In the *first* phase of the 1962-66 bull market, the 1966-68 bull market, the 1970-73 bull market, and the rise commencing in 1974 more than 50% of the preceding bear market decline was retraced, a strongly valid longer range bullish forecast of much higher markets to come in each case. Yet in each case, soon after the 50% level was penetrated, those who remained bearish on the market would haul out the 1929 case to rationalize their faulty conclusion that those first phase bull advances were merely rallies in continuing bear markets. The 1929 crash, occurring between September and November of that year, was more than 50% retraced by the spring of 1930, but the move was followed by new collapses to new lows as we all know. The bears wished to show that the more than 50% retracement of the 1929 crash was a major trap. The Principle was not really at fault, however. I stated here that *valid* applications of the principle entail measurements based on *completed* bull or bear markets. The market crash between September and November, 1929 was obviously not a complete bear market and thus the 1930 fooler. This should put that matter to rest so that we don't have to hear anymore about how the 50% Principle let everyone down in 1930. The example was a poor one in attempts to defend a bearish attitude in the market years of 1963, 1967,

1970, and 1975. Application of the Principle in those bullish years was all based on previously *completed* bear markets.

Disparity Index

Almost invariably, market tops and bottoms are accompanied by a disparate movement, a separating of the ways between the general market and the Dow-Jones Industrial Average. At bottoms the Dow outpaces the general market on the downside, and at market tops the Dow usually outpaces the market on the upside. Expressed another way, the market acts better than the Dow at bottoms and worse than the Dow at tops. Such disparities stem from imbalances that occur within the Dow average itself as stocks that are capable of making wide price swings create such upside and downside distortions, DuPont being famous in that respect. In my *Strategy* book I had introduced the disparity concept and had used the Standard & Poor 500 Stock Average as the measurement of the general market, multiplying that average by ten so as to equate with the Dow-Jones Industrial Average. A rise in the Standard & Poor 500 of 0.25 on a given day, for instance, accompanied by a 7-point gain in the Dow would immediately indicate a disparate upside movement of 4 1/2 Dow points (S & P change times ten subtracted from the Dow). Such day-to-day disparate movements can be corrected before they build up to significant proportions, but if they are not quickly corrected and are allowed to build up to a significant spread, then it becomes increasingly easy to predict a general market reaction to the disparity as well as the probable degree of the predicted Dow swing. For instance, suppose positive disparity between the general market and the Dow had built up over a period of months to 60 points. That would be considered a very dangerous spread, the Dow being 60 points higher than where the general market says it should be. It would imply a coming reaction of 60 points. However, since the general market would also be declining on a 60-point drop in the Dow, the dangerous positive disparity would point to a drop *greater* than 60 points in order to correct the disparity.

All disparities are subject to total correction. They never exist indefinitely. In the transition from bull market to bear market, we would look for the highest positive disparity around the peak of the bull market and zero or even negative disparity at a bear market bottom. *Negative disparity is always bullish.* It is usually seen when there is maximum disbelief that the market can rise.

Since the New York Stock Exchange developed its index *of all stock prices* on the Big Board back in 1966, we can make an exact distinction now between the Dow-Jones Industrial Average and the general market. The New York Stock Exchange Index is therefore preferable to the Standard & Poor

500 Stock Index in measuring disparity. Many newspapers do not include the Standard & Poor figures, but all financial sections report the daily changes in the New York Stock Exchange Index. The Disparity Index is not always conveying a message, but when it does have something to say it speaks out clearly and leaves little room for doubt.

Inasmuch as the blue chip issues\constitute the last group to hit bottom in a bear market, one would start looking for the very bullish *negative disparity* late in a bear market. The final 50-point drop in the Dow-Jones Industrial Average in the 1973-74 bear market was a total deception but was very easy to read from many technical standpoints. However, it must have fooled a great many people because heavy buying didn't begin to come into the market until early 1975 when the upturn was far more obvious. But, one of the rules the market itself is held to in the game is that it is not allowed to completely cover up what it is doing. It played fair in 1974, giving many key signals to the approaching major bottom. One of them was negative disparity, another was a major non-confirmation between the Industrials and Transports, and still another was a climax in the number of individual new lows a full three weeks before the Dow bottom. A much more subtle fooler was seen in the Dow-Jones Industrial Average *divisor*. While half the country was looking for a crash and a depression, thinking that the 1974 bottom in the Dow was below that of 1970, the research in this book shows that both the 1968-70 and 1973-74 bear markets showed *identical drops* in terms of the declines in the total number of points for all the Dow industrial stocks, *but because the 1973-74 period had a lower Dow divisor, the Dow average went under the 1970 low.* Were it not for that lower divisor, the Dow would have bottomed out at 697.70 instead of 577.60, a matching loss of 354 points in the Dow average, *artificially ballooned* to a loss of 471 points on the 1973-74 downturn. While one might say that the market was cheating, it actually held to the rules of the game. The divisor is constantly being printed in the *Wall Street Journal,* and the market considers ignorance of these facts no excuse for the uninformed players.

One should be equally alert to constantly tracking disparity. While many people were fooled by the Dow-Jones Industrial Average breaking the October 4, 1974 low of 584.56 and dropping to 577.60 on December 6, 1974, the broadly based Standard & Poor 500 Stock Index *advanced* in the same period from 60.96 to 64.13. Multiplying the 3.17 differential by ten according to the thumb rule, we come up with a *rise* of 31.70 points. Comparing that with the *loss* of 6.96 points in the Dow-Jones Industrial Average, we show *negative disparity* of 38.66 points on the final Dow low of December 6, 1974, a very bullish reading.

In the same period we find that the still more broadly based New York Stock Exchange Index (composite) rose from 33 to 34. Multiplying the differential by 30 according to the thumb rule, we come up with a rise of 30.00 points. Comparing that with the loss 6.96 points in the Dow-Jones Industrial Average, we come up with *negative* disparity of 36.96 points, very close to the Standard & Poor showing.

Now, between December 6, 1974, and May 14, 1975, the Dow-Jones Industrial Average rose from 577.60 to 858.73, an advance of 281.13 points. Checking out the Standard & Poor 500 Index first, we find that it rose from 64.13 to 90.53 in the same period. Multiplying the differential by 10, we come up with a total gain of 264.00 points. With a Dow gain, however, of 281.13 points, what was once *negative* disparity at the bottom had now been translated to *positive* disparity of 17.13 points by May 14, 1975. In the same period the New York Stock Exchange Index rose from 34.00 to 48.01. Multiplying the differential by 30, we come up with a total gain of 420.30 points. That shows a continued *negative* disparity of 139.17 points which would normally be extremely bullish for the Dow. However, there is obviously a discrepancy here. It is highly unlikely that the Standard & Poor 500 would show positive disparity while the New York Stock Exchange Index (covering all big boards stocks) would show negative disparity.

Reworking the figures in terms of *percentage gains* should eliminate the discrepancy. The Dow gain from 577.60 to 858.73 was a gain of 48.6%. The Standard & Poor 500 Stock Index gain from 64.13 to 90.53 was a gain of 41.1%. The New York Stock Exchange Index gain from 34.00 to 48.01 was a gain of 41.2%. The discrepancy is eliminated, the gains in the two broader indices *practically identical*. What was sought to be demonstrated is seen here: the *negative* disparity (bullish) at market bottoms and the transition to *positive* disparity (bearish when looking extreme) on the approach to a top. By May, 1975, the percentage gains showed the Dow *outpacing* the market.

The reader is carried through this little exercise so as to illustrate the possible fallacies in assigning multiples to the broader indices when comparing their movements to the Dow-Jones Industrial Average. While assigning a multiple of 30 to the New York Stock Exchange Index has worked for some periods of time, it certainly didn't apply in the example given here. A multiple of approximately 18.8 saw the New York Stock Exchange Index perfectly in line with the Standard & Poor 500 Index. In order to be perfectly correct in all computations of disparity, I would recommend only using *percentage change* comparisons. That revises the multiple method used in the first *Strategy* book.

The 200-Day Moving Average of the Dow

This is a powerful analytical tool heavily relied on by technicians as an effective guide to the major market movement. Being a 200-day moving average of the Dow-Jones Industrial Average, the indicator is not prone to making many false signals. The changes are very small and slow to come by. It takes a powerful and sustained downtrend in the Dow industrial average to turn the 200-day line down and keep it going down, and it takes an equally strong uptrend in the Dow to turn the 200-day line around and point it upward again. The 200-day line effectively differentiates between primary market declines and declines in a bull market as well as primary advances and rallies in a bear market. A rally in a bear market seldom has the staying power to turn a declining 200-day line around. In a bear market such rallies usually produce a sequence of confrontations whereby the Dow-Jones Industrial Average comes up and hits the declining trendline and then retreats to new lows. On the other hand, it is a mathematical requirement that to turn the 200-day line up after a long decline, the Dow-Jones Industrial Average must obviously rise above the line, and therefore we must put great stress on the importance of such line crossings. After the 200-day line has been falling for many months and the Dow manages to come up and cross the line, such upside penetrations have served among the more reliable confirmations of a new bull market.

The normal market behavior after such an important upside breakthrough by the Dow through the 200-day line is for the Dow to continue advancing for several months accompanied by a smooth and uninterrupted rise in the 200-day line. The Dow eventually gets to a point where it can no longer advance, having reached the rallying peak of the initial bull market advance. The Dow average then starts a series of declines back toward the 200-day line. It either holds at the line and turns up again or it drops beneath the line. Market history tells us that in neither case does the bull market end on that rally termination and initial decline. Even if that first corrective phase turns the 200-day line down, market history has shown the staying power of the bull movement to be strong enough to turn the 200-day line up again to a new high, thereby producing an upward zigzag movement in this important indicator. Market history also tells us that it is after the upward zigzag movement in the 200-day line is effected that it is time to look for Pandora's box of technical troubles to pop open. The last two times that the 200-day line bettered the initial bull market peak, thus producing such an upward zigzag, was in October, 1968 and May, 1972, both periods closely preceding major Dow peaks.

I did not refer to this *zigzag movement* by the 200-day line in the *Strategy* book. It is stressed now because it may turn out be our most reliable indication of bull market peak periods. Obviously the Dow-Jones Industrial Average has to move out to new highs in order to push the slower-moving 200-day line above the earlier bull market peak, and it is on those new highs that we would expect the technical deterioration of a failing advance-decline line and other signs of important technical market deterioration to show up.

While the longer term zigzag movement in the 200-day line now will always be taken as an alert of an impending major top in the Dow, the initial upside penetration of the trendline after many months of decline will always be treated as a very important confirmation of a new bull market. *All penetrations of the trendline must always be weighed as to where in the typical market cycle they are occurring.* Upside penetrations in January, 1967, August, 1970 and January, 1975, all had one thing in common. They all occurred shortly after major cyclical bottoms in the Dow had been recorded, *and thus they all confirmed new bull markets.* Three months after the October 7, 1966 bottom the Dow went through the 200-day line, making the upside penetration on January 11, 1967. History proved the move to be a valid bull market confirmation. Following the same timing, one could have made a similar projection following the May 26, 1970 Dow bottom, predicting a very bullish upside penetration of the trendline by late August of that year. The actual penetration occurred on August 21,1970, a technical bullseye, and confirmed the new bull market. One could have made a similar projection following the 1974 Dow bottom, dating the bottom as October 4, 1974, because that was the last date of confirmed new lows (rails did not confirm the lower December, 1974 industrial low), looking for a very bullish upside penetration of the trendline to occur in January, 1975. It occurred on January 27, 1975, and the rise thereafter was every bit as sensational as that following the 1967 and 1970 penetrations. In every case the upside penetration of the trendline occurred within four months or less after the major market bottom.

Other upside penetrations of the trendline occurred too late in the typical market cycle to have the same degree of bullish indication. The famous upside penetration of December, 1971, was necessary *in order to effect the later upside zigzag movement in the trendline itself,* but it was signalling the terminal upswing in the trendline rather than the very bullish and more sustained initial upleg. The upside penetration of the line in September, 1973, was too soon after the cyclical January, 1973, top to be a valid indication of a new bull market. So then, check out all line penetrations with the *market time factor,* keeping in mind how many months old the bull or bear market is.

The Important Subject of Non-Confirmations

Why are confirmations and non-confirmations so all-important in the study of indicators and where the market is headed? When all the major indicators are moving in one direction we can say that one confirms the other, and the likelihood is very strong that the market will continue in that direction. When the indicators are clearly out of gear, not in harmony with the prevailing direction of the Dow-Jones Industrial Average, an important reversal is close at hand. Now I want to make a very important distinction. *A confirmed move in any direction is just as prone to reversal, but in the clear majority of cases such reversals are very temporary.* Experience has shown that *it is the non-confirmations that produce the important changes of market direction.*

In terms of the game, let us picture the market as a football game between supply and demand. In a bear market, supply has the ball and is running hard to score a first down. The first down is made (market makes a new low). Now supply tries for the second down and is thrown for a five-yard loss (the Dow rallies 5 points). However, supply still has the ball (the trend is down) and then succeeds in advancing 15 yards to make a new first down (another confirmed market low). On the next play the supply team is thrown for a ten-yard loss (the Dow rallies 10 points) but once again successfully overcomes the deficit with a brilliant 25-yard end run to score another first down (another confirmed market low). In this example the supply team always had possession of the ball (the trend), and every advance by the team across the field was confirmed by new first downs (every market low was confirmed). Nevertheless, the team had temporary setbacks (market advances), but these were temporary because the supply team made the necessary first down (confirmed new lows) in each case and never lost possession of the ball (market trend remained down).

Now picture the demand team making a strong comeback leading toward victory over the supply team (a bull market). In order to change the trend of the game the demand team must get possession of the ball. It can do this by either interception or by the repeated failure of the supply team to make a first down. Failure to make a first down on the part of the supply team would be likened to the failure to a score a new confirmed market low, and at that point the demand team gets possession of the ball and the market trend is reversed to the upside, such reversals following major downside non-confirmations. The demand team remains in possession of the ball for the remainder of that period (bull market), all setbacks on the field from then on proving temporary (unconfirmed market declines within a bull market).

Summing up, we can now formulate some buying and selling rules.

Buying Rules

1. Buy on any decline that follows a confirmed advance.
2. Buy into any unconfirmed decline.

Selling Rules

3. Sell on any advance that follows a confirmed decline.
4. Sell into any unconfirmed advance.

The Four Warning Rules

5. Never buy into a decline that follows an unconfirmed advance.
6. Never buy into a confirmed decline.
7. Never sell into an advance that follows an unconfirmed decline.
8. Never sell into a confirmed advance.

General Motors

Much has been written over the years about General Motors as a market forecaster. Being in the forefront of the bellwether stocks, it always pays to track the stock and be aware of any signals it might be flashing. The common thumb rule states that *if GM fails to make a new low for four months then a strong market has been confirmed, and failure to record a new high for four months confirms a weak market.* The stock has shown better *leading* characteristics on market tops rather than on bottoms. On market bottoms the stock was making new lows *after* the Dow bottoms of 1966, 1970, and 1974. Reliance at those times on the General Motors Four-Month Rule would have kept one bearish several months past the actual market lows. However, the keyword here is *confirmation.* No market downturn is going to be serious unless General Motors *confirms* the downturn. No market rise is going to be important unless General Motors *confirms* the upturn. When used this way, the indicator will never get you into trouble.

The Six Months Indicator

The Six Months Indicator is applied to important market lows in order to know when to expect the influence of selling generated by those who bought at the bottom and are now eligible to take a six-months capital gain. By applying this yardstick to the low points in previous starting bull markets, we can draw some interesting conclusions. For instance, is the indicator most effective measured from actual Dow bottoms or from more widely recognized bottoms? Going back to 1962 we measure off six months from the June low and we come up with December, 1962. No reaction took place at that time. Measuring six months from the Cuban Missile Crisis bottom of October, 1962, we come up with April, 1963. Interestingly enough, the number of new highs peaked on April 15 that year, but the Dow continued to work higher until May 31, running into a *normal* June-July decline. Assuming the June-July decline to reflect six-month capital gain selling, we can work it back and say that the 1962 bottom was importantly *recognized* in December, 1962, enough stock having been bought at that time to turn the market down six months later on capital gain selling pressures. That bull market had a long way to go and the first effects of capital gain selling was to produce only a normal reaction in a continuing bull market. In other words, we are not concerned about those initial pullbacks early in the bull cycle. We should be concerned when applying the six-month yardstick *late in the cycle.* For instance, the market made an important low in June, 1965. It was not *recognized* as an important low until August, 1965. Adding six months to August, 1965, we come up with the important bull market top of February, 1966.

Next we come to the 1966 bottom which took place on October 7, 1966. Adding six months to that date we have April, 1967. The Dow had temporarily peaked at 876.67 on March 23, dropping in a normal reaction to a low of 842.43 on April 10. A new high on May 8 at 909.63 was followed by a wider reaction to 847.77 on June 5. Working it back, we can say that the 1966 market bottom was recognized widely enough in November, 1966, to produce the 62-point reaction six months later. A much wider reaction occurred after the September 25, 1967 top at 943.08, reflecting capital gain selling by those who bought in March, 1967, where the 1966 bottom was still more widely recognized. Applying the yardstick *late in the bull cycle,* we add six months to the important intermediate bottom of March, 1968, and we come up with September, 1968. However, the importance of the March, 1968 bottom was not recognized widely until April and May, and adding six months brings us up virtually to the peak of that bull market.

As for the 1970 bottom, adding six months to May of that year brought us up to November where no reaction was encountered. The importance of the 1970 bottom was not *recognized* until after the 200-day line penetration late in August. That brings us up to almost March, 1971. Since an important decline got started following the April 28 high at 950.81, we would have to work it back and say that the importance of the 1970 bottom was most widely recognized in October, 1970. Up until that month the Dow Transports had not confirmed the bull market advance but made a very bullish move through the 200-day moving average trendline.

In the next bull cycle we add six months to the October 4, 1974 date of the confirmed lows and come up with April, 1975. No reaction occurred simply because October, 1974, was not where the bottom was widely *recognized.* The next bottom occurred on December 6, 1974, the famous and extremely bullish unconfirmed industrial low. Adding six months to that date, we could expect the pressures of six-month capital gain selling to show up in June, 1975, and more so by July, 1975, the Dow temporarily topping out sometime in May, 1975. According to this study, it would be a normal corrective downswing in a continuing bull market. Another downswing would be expected to occur later in 1975, leading into an intermediate bottom probably occuring around the middle of 1976. Once that bottom is recognized as such (one or two months later), we add six months to that date of recognition and come up with a possible bull market peak in February, 1977.

The Short Interest Ratio

The ratio of the monthly short interest to the average daily volume for that month constitutes the short interest ratio. The theory of the short interest ratio contends that when the ratio is above 1.50, the market is bullish, and when it is near or below 1.00, the market is bearish. Experience has shown that when the ratio approaches 2.00, it is extremely bullish, and on such readings stocks can be bought with maximum confidence. A ratio of 2.00 would mean that the monthly short interest stood at twice the average daily volume for that month. The last time the ratio was at such a level was in July, 1970, which was certainly a time to buy stocks. *On all other readings the indicator is of very questionable value.* It is best used in conjunction with other indicators. All bearish forecasts based on this indicator have failed the test of time. The year 1932 presented the greatest historical buying opportunity in the stock market, and the short interest ratio stood at 0.75. However, it was also under the 1.00 level in 1933, 1934, 1935, 1936, and 1937, as well as 1938, 1939, 1940, 1941, 1942, and 1943. It managed to stay above 1.00 in 1944 but went under again late in 1945 and all of 1946. Only under briefly in 1947, the indicator didn't go under again until mid-1948. It was again under in 1950, early 1953, early 1955, one brief reading in 1956, and again late in 1959. The Dow, meanwhile, between 1932 and 1959, went from approximately 41 to over 680, thus burying the effectiveness of the short interest ratio as an indicator on moves under 1.00. Readings after 1959 were equally worthless. They sometimes coincided with good market swings but primarily because of the movements of other more reliable indicators, not because of the effectiveness of the short interest ratio.

The Head and Shoulders

There are many time tested chart formations which always alert the technician to a definite impending price development. One of the major formations is the "head and shoulders," so named because three peaks in the Dow average show the middle one standing out as the "head" with the lesser first and third peaks representing the "shoulders." The theory behind this formation states that the peak of technical power is reached on the "head." Thereafter, the right shoulder advance indicates the loss of technical power, the inability to return to the "head" peak. The stage is then set for a testing of the "neckline," the major chart support level which is in line with the reaction level following each of the three price peaks. The theory then states that a move through that neckline is very bearish. Such a statement is made with good authority inasmuch as the neckline would consist of four reaction lows (three pyramids would have four equivalent low points). One would certainly have to respect a move breaking under four reaction lows. The ensuing move is usually sharply perpendicular.

Conversely, if you turn the "head and shoulders" upside down you are confronted with the very bullish "reverse head and shoulders." In this formation the extreme of the bearish price movement is shown by the central decline, or "head" and the failure of the bears to extend their case is then shown by the right shoulder decline which terminates well above the "head" low. The next test is shown on the ensuing rise toward the "neckline," a line of four price levels which have heretofore demonstrated resistance against higher prices. A move about that "neckline" is extremely bullish, usually resulting in a sharply perpendicular advance. Classically, volume tends to peak as the "head" is formed.

A perfect "head and shoulders" formation is very rare. What is usually encountered when one is seen is a drooping right shoulder. Sometimes chartists stretch their analysis quite a bit to show a valid "head and shoulders." However, one should always be on the watch for them because they usually signal major advances or declines, as the case may be.

Through bitter experience I have learned *the extreme importance of placing this particular chart formation in the proper context with the typical market cycle.* In other words, I would place extreme importance on a "head and shoulders" formation in the Dow-Jones Industrial Average *occurring 1 1/2 to 2 years after a major bottom,* that formation probably coinciding with a major market top. I would place equal importance on a "reverse head and shoulders" formation in the Dow occurring one to two years after a major market top, that formation probably coinciding with a major market bottom. In other words, the "head" in each case represents either a bull market peak or a bear market bottom as the case may be. *Anything in between is subject to the gravest errors of interpretation.*

Back in 1970, leaning heavily on cyclical and other market evidence, I predicted a rise in the Dow to over 1000, such a level to be seen in 1972. Coming off a bottom then at 631, such a prediction was met with almost total disbelief. By 1972, however, with the Dow persistently moving up and staying above the 900 level, many more had joined the "Dow 1000" school, including Secretary of the Treasury John B. Connally who made a public prediction in early 1972 that the Dow would top the 1000 level that year. Among my arsenal of bullish arguments was *a rather rare long-term four year reverse head and shoulders chart formation in the Dow.* The important "neckline" connected the important market tops of December, 1968, May 1969 and April, 1971. A move through the December, 1968 Dow closing level of 985.21 would virtually guarantee a sharp perpendicular advance up through the 1000 level as previously predicted. On November 9, 1972, the neckline of that great reverse head and shoulders formation was penetrated, the Dow closing up that day at 988.26. Three market sessions later the Dow crossed the 1000 level for the first time in history on a closing basis. In my November 17, 1972 market letter I stated that I had no qualms about the next 50 points up, mentioning then my concern about expected downside signals to occur around the Dow 1050 level. Up to that point my market record was virtually perfect, the market peaking at 1051.70 on January 11, 1973. Rather than an intermediate correction at that point, however, a major bear market ensued which was not to bottom out until October 1974. I had been correct on just about every facet of the market from the 1970 bottom up to the 1973 top, so much so that I began to put too much importance on some of the indicators that had led to my success on that long advancing period, notably the discovery of that long-term four-year reverse head and shoulders formation in the Dow. Since it was *long-term* in nature, I felt then that it implied *long-term* bullish implications once that neckline was penetrated. Instead, the penetration was followed by a blowoff 50-point advance to a major bull market peak. In other words, the neckline penetration was bullish in the *short term* only, having no long-term bullish implications. The lesson learned here is the importance of where in the typical market cycle the head and shoulders formation occurs. A reverse head and shoulders formation *occurring 30 months after the May 1970 market bottom* could have nothing more than a *short term* bullish implication. If the neckline penetration had occurred in early 1971, it would have had the longer term bullish implications, *but such a penetration occurring almost four years after the previous market peak encountered the devastating terminal effects of the 4 to 4 1/2 year market cycle, an influence that was almost certain to translate an otherwise long-term bullish influence into a short-term one, in this case a two-month blowoff to an aging bull market.*

Such an experience enables one to state some pretty definite *rules* on head and shoulder formations:

(1) Place great bullish importance on any reverse head and shoulders formation that occurs in a reasonably short time following a new bear market Dow low, especially when that low is approximately 4 to 4 1/2 years following the previous bear market low.

(2) Place great bearish importance on any head and shoulders formation that occurs in a reasonably short time following a new bull market

(3) Dow high, especially when that high is approximately 4 to 4 1/2 years following the previous bull market high.

(3) If a reverse head and shoulders formation occurs late in a bull market, the move through the neckline has only very short-term bullish implications, probably leading into the final blowoff.

(4) If a head and shoulders formation occurs late in a bear market, the move below the neckline has only very short-term bearish implications, probably leading into a selling climax and the termination of the bear market.

Probably no better defined "neckline" has occurred than that which was traced out on the 1974 market bottom when a very bullish looking reverse head and shoulders formation appeared which was later aborted, a move which completely baffled the bears. It started when the Dow bounced to 677.88 on September 6, 1974. That was followed by a drop to a new bear market low at 627.19 on September 13, setting up the left shoulder of a reverse head and shoulders formation. The next rise carried the Dow up to 674.05 on September 19, falling just short of the September 6 resistance level of 677.88. The next drop carried the Dow perpendicularly lower in 11 consecutive declines to a new bear market low at 584.56 on October 4, that drop forming the "head" of the reverse head and shoulders formation. That sharp extended drop produced an almost equal and opposite reaction on the upside, the Dow catapulting ahead to a rally high of 673.50 on October 14. The rise was once again checked in the growing area of upside resistance shown by the earlier interim highs of September 6 and 19. Now we had the left shoulder and the head of our bullish formation, and it only remained for the right shoulder to be formed followed by a breakout through the neckline. Obviously, the 627.19 level of September 13 was critical. Following the October 14 top, the Dow once again fell back, checking the decline at 633.84 on October 28, a move which appeared to form the right shoulder of the reverse head and shoulders formation. The Dow bounced sharply back up to 673.03 by October 30, retreated a little and then bounced sharply up to 674.75 by November 5. Once again it fell back a trifle and then made one final upward attempt on November 11, the Dow failing then to get above 672.64. So here we saw no less than six Dow rally tops within nine weeks within a 5-point narrow band, the clearly defined neckline. Then the market pulled one of its famous "foolers," seeking to destroy the opposition in one stroke. From the November 11 Dow level of 672.64, the industrial average zigzagged sharply lower, *aborting* the right shoulder on November 18 at 624.92. That so encouraged the bears that they all fell into a glorious "bear trap," the Dow careening lower to 577.60 by December 6. Of course there were so many downside non-confirmations on that move that it should have been clear to them that they were looking right at a major confirmed bottom, a market that was set to go no lower, the true bottom having already occurred in September and October.

The value of this example was seen in subsequent market action. The well-defined neckline was still intact, showing the valid line of upside resistance. *A move through that line would have the same very bullish implications even though the reverse head and shoulders formation had been aborted in November, 1974.* One of the most bullish days in market history occurred on January 27, 1975. It was on that day that the neckline was brilliantly penetrated, the Dow rocketing ahead from 666.61 to 692.66. That one move coincided with an upside penetration of the Dow 200-day moving average price line, a valid Dow Theory Bull market confirming signal and the highest volume seen in market history up to that time. A short three months later the Dow was up well over 800 and still going strong.

Anytime a "head and shoulders" formation is detected and is followed by an aborting move, a move either aborting just a shoulder or even the head, don't succumb to the obvious and become very bullish when it is an aborted head and shoulders, or very bearish when it is an aborted reverse head and shoulders without checking out the move thoroughly in terms of *all the major indicators.* Such aborted moves have often coincided with famous bull and bear traps. While every major market bottom and top has been accompanied by important downside and upside non-confirmations between the major indicators, the combinations differ just enough on each cyclical terminal point so as to trap all those who put too much reliance on one or two key indicators. Many examples of this abound. One such example is found in *odd lot short sales.* That indicator called the 1962, 1966, and 1970 bottoms perfectly but if one had waited for a similar run-up in odd lot short sales to signal the end of the 1973-74 bear market, one would have missed that great market bottom. Another key example was the precipitous decline in the Barron's Confidence Index between June and August, 1970, dropping sharply from 97.0 to 88.0, misleading many people who placed too much confidence in that indicator to believe that a further sharp drop in the Dow lay ahead when that average had already scored a major bottom in May of that year.

Speculation Index

American Stock Exchange volume as a percentage of New York Stock Exchange volume constitutes the Speculation Index. The purpose of this indicator is to alert us to the times when the degree of speculation is dangerously high, notably in the third phase of a bull market. *In other phases the indicator is almost useless.* The last time it was flashing a timely warning was back in 1968, a year of the rampaging bull, a year when it was standing room only in boardrooms across the country. In that year American Stock Exchange volume was running about 60% of the big board volume, well above the redline warning level which is around 45%. Those high readings are relatively rare but when they occur (anything over 45%) *make a total exit from the market.* You may be a bit premature in relation to the final Dow top but the risks are too great to wait around. The stock market was so popular in 1968 that the Exchanges shortened the trading hours, closing early at 2:00 P.M. in order that the backrooms could catch up on the excessive paperwork. The crowded boardrooms, the excessive popularity as shown by the very high Speculation Index, and the early Exchange closing all spelled out upside excesses and the Dow made the final peak on December 3, 1968. Of course that was quite a few months after the Speculation Index began to flash the warnings, but I am sure that anyone would have counted himself very fortunate to have sold stocks at anytime during 1968 when one considered the sharp drops that lay ahead in the 1969-70 bear market.

Stressing the vital importance of always looking at all the major indicators, the Speculation Index proved its *uselessness* at a major market top in late 1972. As the Dow was going through the 1000 level in November 1972 the Speculation Index stood at a very low reading of 21.54%, indicating that there were no signs of speculation at that time. If one had been putting equal stress on low Speculation Index readings as on high readings, then that indicator proved expensively useless at the 1972 market top because there are no reliable guidelines as to what low level the Index has to reach to be reliably bullish. As a matter of fact, the Index was under 20% throughout most of 1973 and all of 1974, and those otherwise bullish low readings never were effective. Not until early October, 1974, did the Index bottom out and then at a ridiculously low level of 9%. Who was to know that this Index would drop that low before the market bottomed out?

There was an indication, however, that would have led one to believe that October, 1974, was the exact opposite of December, 1968, or January, 1973. If shortening the trading hours in 1968 was a bearish omen for the market, *it stood to reason that lengthening the hours would be a bullish omen.* On October 1, 1974, the New York Stock Exchange started the lengthened sessions, closing at the unprecedented late hour of 4:00 P.M. Is it any surprise then that the market bottomed out on October 4, 1974, ending the worst bear market since the 1930's?

We are therefore only concerned here with the very high Speculation Index readings, 45% and higher. Those high readings are reliably bearish but the low readings give little or no indication of when a bear market is going to bottom out.

The Low-Priced Stocks

The analysis of low-price stock movements can often be more confusing than revealing when used to pinpoint what phase the market is going through. The most popular notion regarding their movement is that their blow-off move is reserved for the third and most speculative phase of a bull market. However, if one is depending on such a third phase speculative movement, the end of a bull market could catch one offguard. There is nothing certain about a sharp upswing in low-priced stocks during a bull market third phase. It is equally probable, and even a bit more common, that low-priced stocks generally do well during the first two phases of a bull market and that the action becomes choppy and less predictable during the third phase. While it has been pointed out that there was an equal lack of reliability in putting too much stress on the Speculation Index (that Index extremely toppy in 1968 but relatively depressed on the 1972 market top), low-priced stock movements are equally uncertain. The two major choices for a topping out in the group involve phase two terminal points or phase three terminal points. As the advance-decline line seldom rises through all three bull market phases, usually topping out during the second phase, a peaking in the low-priced stocks during the second phase would go hand in hand with the topping out of the advance-decline line. On the other hand, there could be a sharp upswing in the third phase corresponding to a 1968-type performance in the Speculation Index. I therefore could not class the movement of low-priced stocks among the major market indicators although one should always be aware of what the group is doing. The best Index to follow is Barron's Low-Priced Stock Index.

THE DAY-TO-DAY INDICATORS

In some respects the stock market trend is easier to recognize in the broader sweep of its primary and intermediate term swings than in its day-to-day movement, but the market usually has something to say every day and it is important to listen. If we don't, we increase the chances of perhaps missing something important. Every longer-term trend, whether it be a short one of three weeks, an intermediate one of three months, or a longer one of nine months, consists of a series of daily trading sessions all put together. If you are determined to lick the enemy of loss and stay on top of this game, *the market demands that you adopt a routine of daily surveillance.* First of all, *it is a case of knowing what to look for* and secondly, *the quick and accurate interpretation of your findings.* The stock market is its own best indicator and *tips its hand as to what it is going to do the next day 95% of the time.*

In order to make a daily forecast, the first requirement is a copy of the morning edition newspaper containing a complete financial section. In that section will be found the key daily market indicators. Of course they are not so labeled and therefore must be identified as such. The majority of the day-to-day indicators are derived from six segments of the daily financial section:

1. Dow-Jones Averages
2. 15 Most Active Stocks
3. Standard & Poor Indices
4. New York Stock Exchange Index
5. What Stocks Did
6. Odd-Lot Figures

1. Dow-Jones Averages

While newspapers may differ a bit in the way they present the market statistics, *they all show the Dow-Jones Averages,* which consist of four averages. Those consist of an average for the Industrial stocks, an average for the Transportation stocks, an average for the Utility stocks, and a combined average of those three segments, the 65 stock average (30 industrials, 20 transports, and 15 utilities). In this table is also shown the high and low reading for each average as well as the closing level together with the increment of daily change in terms of so many points.

From this simple set of daily statistics we can derive the following Key Market Daily Indicators:

    5 - 6 Disparity
   15 - 16 Weighting
   23 - 24 Overdueness
   33 - 34 Reversals
   37 - 38 The 3-Day Rule
   45 - 46 General Motors Indicator
   47 - 48 The Closing
   51 - 52 Rebounds and Declines

That is a total of sixteen different indicators (considering both directions). Included here are Indicators #11 and #12 as well as #43 and #44 derived from the Dow-Jones Industrial Stocks. A preliminary simple task is to *memorize the names of the 30 Dow-Jones Industrial Stocks:*

Allied Chemical	Esmark	Owens Illinois
Alcoa	Exxon	Procter & Gamble
American Brands	General Electric	Sears Roebuck
American Can	General Foods	S.O. of California

American Telephone   General Motors   Texaco
Anaconda   Goodyear   Union Carbide
Bethlehem Steel   International Harvester   U.S. Steel
Chrysler   International Nickel   United Technologies
DuPont   International Paper   Westinghouse Electric
Eastman Kodak   Johns Manville   Woolworth

2. 15 Most Active Stocks

The table of the most active stocks traded contains 15 issues. From these published statistics we can derive the following additional indicators:

     7 - 10 Leadership
     11 - 14 Features

Here are eight more daily market indicators, bringing our workable total up to 24.

3. Standard & Poor Indices

The Standard & Poor market averages are usually contained with the Dow-Jones averages, providing a means of comparison. The S & P averages consist of 425 industrials, 15 railroads, 60 utilities, and an average of those 500 stocks. From these averages we derive four more indicators:

     17 - 20 Genuity

We now have a workable total of twenty-eight daily market indicators.

4. The New York Stock Exchange Index

This index involving all stocks traded on the New York Stock Exchange was put into use in 1966, several years after the first edition of the *Strategy* book. Involving all the big board stocks, it is far more representative of what the market did than the Dow-Jones or Standard & Poor averages. It provides an additional test for checking out daily genuity. Rather than complicating the picture and showing this another set of daily indicators, it is lumped in with the Standard & Poor, both those averages used to test the genuineness of a move in the Dow-Jones Industrial Average. As long as one or the other average shows the in and out-of-gear movements with the Dow we have a clear expression of daily genuity.

5. What Stocks Did

In this section we find the number of stocks traded, the number which advanced and the number declining. Here we also find how many stocks made new highs for the year and how many made new lows for the year. Completing this section, we find the volume figures for the day. This section produces the following additional daily market indicators:

  1 - 4 Plurality
21 - 22 Dullness
25 - 28 Light Volume
29 - 32 Heavy Volume
39 - 40 Churning
53 - 56 Highs and Lows

This raises our workable total to 48 daily indicators.

6. Odd-Lot Figures

These are sometimes seen in a different part of the financial section. From these figures we pick up two additional indicators:

49 - 50 Odd Lots

Now we're up to fifty daily market indicators.

In addition to the six most vital segments of the daily financial section which must be faithfully examined each day, the following six miscellaneous indicators can be added to the previous list:

35 - 36 Gold Indicator
41 - 42 News Reflections
43 - 44 Erratic Price Movement

From here on, all indicators referred to in this section on day-to-day forecasting will be called *points. All the favorable points have even numbers and all the unfavorable points have odd numbers.* Testing out an actual day in the market, we will base our calculations on the published figures for January 27, 1975. Using a daily formula technique, a forecast of the January 28 market will now be determined.

We will now pull out each indicator in the order that it occurs. The first thing to check on is *plurality,* an examination of the Dow-Jones Industrial Average in relation to the advances and declines. The statistics for the January 27 session show that the Dow-Jones Industrial Average rose by 26.05 points. Further down, under *What Stocks Did* we see that 1,476 issues advanced and 189 declined. Point 4 now comes into play:

Point 4. When the number of advances outnumbers declines together with a rise in the Dow-Jones Industrial Average, then the market advance is likely to continue.

The figure 4 then becomes the first number in the composition of the *daily market forecasting formula.*

There was no disparity between the Dow-Jones Industrial Average and the Dow-Jones Transportation Average, both of them rising in gear. The disparity indicator therefore was not activated on January 27.

We now check the *quality of leadership,* and this is done by examining the type of stocks seen in the list of the 15 most active stocks. Here we see such well known names as Kresge, Southern Company, McDonalds, Merrill Lynch, Borden, Union Carbide, Minnesota Mining and General Motors. It is obvious that the market advance had good quality leadership. That brings Point 10 into play:

Point 10. If the quality of market leadership improves on an upswing in the Dow-Jones Industrial Average, then it indicates that the market advance is likely to continue.

The figure 10 is added to the figure 4 as the second number in the daily forecasting formula. Our formula now looks like this:

4 - 10

Continuing, we now check the *features* which is nothing more than an examination of the gains and losses among the 15 most active stocks so as to determine whether the *net drive of the market* was on the upside or downside. Here we find that 13 out of the 15 stocks posted gains, one being unchanged, and one declining, a very strong showing. This brought Point 14 into play:

Point 14. When a majority of the 15 most active stocks are up on the day along with an advancing Dow-Jones Industrial Average, then the advance is likely to continue.

Our daily forecasting formula now looks like this:

4 - 10 - 14

It was seen that there were no upside distortions, none of the Dow-Jones Industrial stocks contributing undue weight to the reading of the average. The weighting indicator was therefore not brought into play.

Now we check to see if the other main averages were in gear with the Dow-Jones Industrial Average, showing commensurate gains. We see that the

New York Stock Exchange was fully in line with the Dow industrial advance, and so we know that the advance by the Dow-Jones Industrial Average was a *genuine* one. We call this factor *genuity*. This check brings Point 20 into play:

Point 20. If the advance in the Dow-Jones Industrial Average is genuine (matched by an equal or greater gain in the Standard & Poor 500 Stock Index or the New York Stock Exchange Index) then the market advance is likely to continue.

Our daily market forecasting formula now looks like this:

$$4 - 10 - 14 - 20$$

Volume figures showed a very significant change, jumping sharply from 20, 667, 850 to 32,130,000 shares, a record. This brought Point 30 into play.

Point 30. A rise on heavy volume with a good quality of market leadership means the advance can continue.

Our daily forecasting formula now looks like this:

$$4 - 10 - 14 - 20 - 30$$

Among the miscellaneous indicators is the *Gold Indicator*. Regarded as a contra-cyclical group, an advance in the golds is considered bearish and a decline in the golds is considered bullish. On January 27, the gold stocks declined. This activated Point 36.

Point 36. A decline in the gold stocks implies that the general market will advance.

Our daily forecasting formula has now been expanded to look like this:

$$4 - 10 - 14 - 20 - 30 - 36$$

We now look to see what *General Motors* did, this being the key bellwether stock. We find that General Motors advanced 7/8ths of a point on January 27, and thus Point 46 came into play:

Point 46. General Motors has a distinct tendency to top out ahead of the general market and therefore, as long as this stock is advancing, the general current trend of the market is healthy and is expected to continue rising.

The daily forecasting formula is lengthened again to read like this:

$$4 - 10 - 14 - 20 - 30 - 36 - 46$$

Next we examine the *closing,* ascertaining whether the Dow-Jones Industrial Average had a strong closing. This is done by comparing the intra-day high and low figures for the Dow against the closing level. We see in this particular instance that the intra-day high for the Dow stood at 698.69 and the intra-day low at 678.43. In view of the fact that the Dow closed at 692.66, we can consider that a strong close. This then brings Point 48 into play.

Point 48. In the absence of overnight news, a strong closing in the market usually spills over with further strength seen the next day.

Now the daily formula reads like this:

$$4 - 10 - 14 - 20 - 30 - 36 - 46 - 48$$

Next we check the odd-lot figures, finding that 187,500 shares were purchased and 313,500 shares were sold. This activated Point 50.

Point 50. A trend toward decreased odd lot buying on balance is a bullish indication for the market.

Now the formula is lengthened again to read as follows:

$$4 - 10 - 14 - 20 - 30 - 36 - 46 - 48 - 50$$

To complete the daily forecast, we look at the state of the *highs and lows.* Here we see a good increase in the number of individual new highs, jumping from 20 to 40. This activates Point 54.

Point 54. A trend of expanding new daily highs is bullish.

This completes our daily forecasting formula for January 27, 1975, the formula reading as follows:

$$4 - 10 - 14 - 20 - 30 - 36 - 46 - 48 - 50 - 54$$

The above one-day formula contains *ten* bullish points (even numbers) and not a single bearish point. Being extremely bullish, the formula *calls for an up day to follow.*

On January 28, 1975, the Dow-Jones Industrial Average rose 2.11 points.

At first glance, the successful prediction of a market advance on a one-day basis may not appear to be too significant. However, a clear indication of what the Dow-Jones Industrial Average is expected to do each day represents *a giant step toward assured stock trading profits.* Just to be able to make a pure daily market forecast will be regarded as a real victory for those people who previously were news headline readers. Here is a forecast *made purely by the market itself,* as all market forecasts should be made. With repeated practice one will soon be able to explore the very guts of market intelligence in a matter of minutes when picking up the morning paper, one's eye then naturally attracted to the vital market information. One will soon gain a feel for the day-to-day timing which is so important in constructing a winning market strategy.

Successful day-to-day timing embraces the collective application of many indicators in order to assure a technically reliable forecast. Many people have their various favorite indicators which are closely followed. Some follow three, four, or five things they feel are significant. Others may follow five or ten market indicators. More astute market students may follow 15, 20, or even 30 indicators embracing not only technical factors, but also fundamental and psychological factors. When it is realized that there are actually *hundreds* of indicators constantly in play, a new market concept is necessary, the requirement to weight the market impact of the technical indicators *on balance.* Keeping the market forecasts *technically pure,* only *market* indicators are employed in the daily forecast. If ten indicators point to a market advance and five suggest a market decline, the *balance* is bullish (favorable) and the market is expected to rise the next day. If seven indicators are bearish (unfavorable) and three are bullish, then the unfavorable balance calls for a market decline the next day. Some indicators alone are almost powerful enough to turn the market up or down, and it then requires many additional offsetting influences to overcome those solitary power signals. One may make a market forecast based on five indicators all pointing in the same direction, and yet those five may be in the *minority* portion of the total number of indicators used here, thus causing a market forecast based on that minority portion to go awry. The theory is reduced to a daily formula derived from the indicators which apply that day. The reader easily learns to recognize with a little practice which combinations are most favorable or unfavorable.

In order to get a true feel of the daily market and be able to make daily forecasts based solely on what the market is saying, a familiarization with the 56 basic day-to-day indicators is necessary. You can then check your daily newspaper financial section to see which of these points apply.

THE 56 BASIC DAY-TO-DAY INDICATORS

1. When the number of declines outnumbers advances together with a rise in the Dow-Jones

Industrial Average, then the market is on the verge of a decline.

2. When the number of advances outnumbers declines together with a fall in the Dow-Jones Industrial Average, then the market is on the verge of an advance.

Plurality

3. When the number of declines outnumbers advances together with a fall in the Dow-Jones Industrial Average, then the decline is likely to continue.

4. When the number of advances outnumbers declines together with a rise in the Dow-Jones Industrial Average, then the market advance is likely to continue.

5. When the Dow-Jones Transportation Average moves more negatively than the Dow-Jones Industrial Average, then this is considered to be a signal for a near-term decline in the Dow-Jones Industrial Average.

Disparity

6. When the Dow-Jones Transportation Average moves more positively than the Dow-Jones Industrial Average, then this is considered to be a signal for a near-term advance in the Dow-Jones Industrial Average.

7. If the quality of market leadership deteriorates on an upswing in the Dow-Jones Industrial Average, then it is pretty reliable evidence that a near-term decline is in the making.

8. If the quality of market leadership deteriorates on a downswing in the Dow-Jones Industrial Average, then it is pretty reliable evidence that a near-term advance is in the making.

Leadership

9. If the quality of market leadership improves on a downswing in the Dow-Jones Industrial Average, then it indicates that the market decline is likely to continue.

10. If the quality of market leadership improves on an upswing in the Dow-Jones Industrial Average, then it indicates that the market advance is likely to continue.

11. If losses predominate among the 15 most active stocks and the Dow-Jones Industrial Average is down, the market is expected to fall the following day.

12. If gains predominate among the 15 most active stocks while the Dow-Jones Industrial Average shows a decline, it is likely that the next day in the market should be an up day.

Features

13. If losses predominate among the 15 most active stocks and the Dow-Jones Industrial Average is up, the market is expected to go down the next day.

14. If gains predominate among the 15 most active stocks and the Dow-Jones Industrial Average advances, then the market is expected to rise the next day.

15. A noticeable advance in one or more Dow-Jones Industrial stocks such as DuPont, resulting in a gain for the industrial average, is an indication that an intermediate high is at hand and that a subsequent decline lies ahead.

Weighting

16. A noticeable decline in one or more Dow-Jones stocks such as DuPont, resulting in a loss for the industrial average, is an indication that an intermediate low is at hand and that a subsequent advance lies ahead.

17. If the advance in the Dow-Jones Industrial Average is not genuine (a less than commensurate gain made by the Standard & Poor 500 Stock Index or New York Stock Exchange Index) then the rise is suspect.

18. If the decline in the Dow-Jones Industrial Average is not genuine (a less than commensurate dip

made by the Standard & Poor 500 or New York Stock Exchange Index) then the decline is suspect and the next move may be an upward one in the Dow-Jones Industrial Average.

Genuity*

19. If the Dow-Jones Industrial Average declines and is matched by an equal or greater decline in the Standard & Poor 500 or New York Stock Exchange Index then the decline is likely to continue.

20. If the advance in the Dow-Jones Industrial Average is genuine (matched by an equal or greater gain in the Standard & Poor 500 or New York Stock Exchange Index) then the advance is likely to continue.

21. When dullness prevails following a previous advance, that is bearish.

Dullness

22. When dullness prevails following a previous decline, that is bullish.

23. Five or six or more consecutive daily advances in the Dow-Jones Industrial Average heighten the probability of a quick downside reversal.

Overdueness

24. Five or six consecutive declines or more in the Dow-Jones Industrial Average heighten the probability of a quick upside reversal.

25. A rise on light volume lacks conviction, especially if the quality of the market leadership is poor.

26. A rise on light volume is not necessarily bearish if the quality of market leadership is good on the upswing.

Light Volume

27. A decline on light volume is not necessarily bullish if the quality of market leadership is high on the decline.

---

*The thumb rule used in testing for genuity is to multiply the net change in the Standard & Poor 500 Stock Index by ten and compare that result with the net change in the Dow-Jones Industrial Average. When using the New York Stock Exchange Index, experience shows that 30 is the best multiple to use. Now, however, this technique has been substituted by comparing the percentage gains rather than using multiples. (See page 50.)

28. A decline on light volume is especially bullish if the quality of market leadership deteriorates on the decline.

29. A rise on heavy volume with a deteriorating quality of market leadership indicates that a reaction is near.

30. A rise on heavy volume with a good quality of market leadership means the advance can continue.

Heavy Volume

31. A decline on heavy volume with the quality of market leadership good on the dip indicates a further decline.

32. A decline on heavy volume with the market leadership of poor quality suggest a bullish near-term reversal of direction.

33. When the Dow-Jones Industrial Average runs up to a new rally top followed by a failure to hold the gains of the day, the market direction is about to turn down.

Reversals

34. When the Dow-Jones Industrial Average sinks to a new low on an intermediate decline and closes well above the lows of the day, the market direction is near-term bullish.

35. When the gold group picks up strength across the board, then the market usually follows soon afterwards with a reaction.

Gold Indicator

36. When the gold group turns weak across the board, then the market usually follows soon afterwards with an advance.

37. There are seldom ever more than three consecutive sharp daily advances. The fourth day sees either a reduced rate of climb or a sharp decline.

The 3-Day Rule

38. There are seldom ever more than three consecutive sharp daily declines. The fourth day sees either a reduced rate of decline or a sharp rebound.

39. After the market has been rising for a few days and follows this with a small net change in the Dow-Jones Industrial Average on heavy volume, this churning action is the normal prelude to an important bearish reversal.

Churning

40. After the market declines sharply for a few days and follows this with a small net change in the Dow-Jones Industrial Average on heavy volume, this churning action is the normal prelude to an important bullish reversal.

41. When the market turns a deaf ear on bullish news, that is a bearish indication.

News

42. When the market disregards bearish news, that is a bullish market indication.

43. After the market has been advancing for some time and there occurs very erratic action in a stock on the upside, this is typical of pre-top action.

Erratic Price Movement

44. After the market has been declining for some time and there occurs very erratic action in a stock on the downside, this is typical of pre-bottom action.

45. A declining trend for General Motors is a distinct signal for caution as far as the market, as measured by the Dow-Jones Industrial Average, is concerned.

The General Motors Indicator

46. General Motors has a distinct tendency to top out ahead of the general market and therefore, as long as this stock is advancing the general current trend of the market is healthy and is expected to continue rising.

47. In the absence of overnight news, a weak closing in the market usually spills over with further weakness seen the next day.

The Closing

48. In the absence of overnight news, a strong closing in the market usually spills over with further strength seen the next day.

49. A trend toward increased odd lot buying on balance is a bearish indication for the market.

Odd Lots

50. A trend toward decreased odd lot buying on balance is a bullish indication for the market.

51. Technical declines are much more likely to follow sharp advances rather than periods of slow and gradual rise.

Rebounds and Declines

52. Technical rebounds are more likely just to follow sharp declines rather than periods of simple erosion.

53. A trend of expanding new daily lows is bearish.

54. A trend of expanding new daily highs is bullish.

Highs and Lows

55. A reduction in the number of new highs is bearish.

56. A reduction in the number of new lows is bullish.

2

You Can't Win the Game
Without Knowing
These Things

NEWS IS OF GENERALLY LITTLE VALUE

Traders and investors get into more trouble and make more expensively wrong decisions by following news than for any other reason. So heavily influenced by the news, the majority get lost in the maze, unable to see what the smart money is doing. News is also important to the smart money because they understand the role news plays in the market game, and they can usually act most effectively under the protective cover of news. They know that the news misleads the opposing game players into selling them stocks when the smart money wishes to buy and into buying their stocks when the smart money decides that the time has arrived for distribution. As a market aid, *news is of little or no value in playing the market game successfully. News is generally for suckers.* It misleads more often than it guides. It creates mistimed fears which provoke selling at the wrong time and raises hopes which encourage the buying of stocks at the wrong time. The reason why news has very little relationship to what the market is going to do is simply because *the market is moving on tomorrow's news,* and thus the current news is a stale factor to the market.

I might add a distinction here. News is not important. It is the way the market *reacts* to the news that is important. If the news is bad and the market acts well in the face of it, that is a *bullish reaction,* a positive sign that the market is marching to the tune of a different drummer. Reading the bad news proves to be no aid in making the correct market decisions. Most people would be better off not having read any news, because more often than not bad news causes bad selling, mistimed selling. If the market is undergoing smart money accumulation, it is generally able to withstand the onslaught of a barrage of bad news because the market had already anticipated the news weeks or months before. The news is *current* but the market is moving on the *future*.

If it were possible to report tomorrow's news today and devote the entire newspaper to futuristic but realistic reporting, there would be a closer correlation between news and the market. Then the market game would take on an entirely different contour. The price swings would be wider than they currently are. When news was bad there would be far more sellers and still fewer buyers, and thus prices would have to drop much more before trades could be executed. Conversely, when news was good there would be far more buyers than sellers, and prices would have to climb to greater heights before trades could be executed. It is the *out-of-step timing* between news reporting and market action that enables the market game to be played so successfully by the smart money, preying on the public's overreliance on current news as a guide to what the market is going to do.

Strange as it may seem to the uninitiated, if one is looking for market guidance one would actually be better off never reading a newspaper or news magazine. As stated earlier, if one wants market guidance one can only get it from the *market itself*, guidance dictated by the *technical* action of the market. The technical action conveys the message whether stocks are being accumulated or distributed in significant amounts. That is all one needs to know, and such information will never be found on the front page of your newspaper or in your favorite news magazine.

The public at large must be kept pessimistic on stocks long after a bear market has ended, enabling the smart money to buy stocks from them under the cover of the then prevailing bad news. That is the name of the game. It takes place during every major market bottoming period, just as the public is kept optimistic on stocks long after a bull market has peaked, enabling the smart money to distribute stocks to them at the top dollar.

October 4, 1974 marked a major bottom in the stock market, terminating the bear market which had previously prevailed. Five days after that bottom I wrote an article summing up the technical action of the turn, proclaiming the start of a new bull market. The article was met with total disbelief and was rejected by a number of top publications. However, *Financial World* decided to run it in their November 20 issue, placing it next to another article having a diametrically opposite market opinion. A week later I placed an ad in the same magazine entitled MARKET CALLS FOR MASSIVE ACCUMULATION. It was a large ad, taking up almost half a page. Casting no reflection on the pulling power of *Financial World* but merely to point up *the prevailing psychology* of the time, I received virtually no response, perhaps three or four subscription orders for my market letter. Yet answering that ad could have produced fortunes for many people in the weeks and months thereafter. The market had made a major turn from the bottom, a move greeted by mass disbelief.

Six weeks after the October, 1974 bottom a particularly bad day was reported on November 18, when the Dow-Jones Industrial Average knocked down 22.69 points. The decline did not produce a new low inasmuch as the technical or internal action of the market had already forecasted a successful testing of the lows ahead. The market was offering one of the greatest arrays of super bargains since the depression days of 1932, but here is what the Associated Press dished out the next morning to the American public:

WORRIES FUEL SELLOFF

The stock market gave way under the pressure of recession worries Monday and fell into its sharpest drop in nearly a year. The Dow Jones average of 30 industrials slid 22.69 to 624.92 for its biggest drop since it lost 26.99 January 9th. Nearly 10 times as many issues declined as advanced on the New York Stock Exchange, with the final margin reading 1,382 to 140 among the 1,824 issues traded.

For several weeks it has appeared the market has been balanced between those who feared a severe economic slump and those who hoped for a milder period of softness that would help cool inflation down without doing much lasting damage. With Thursday's report by the government that wholesale prices continued to soar in October, and subsequent talk of new layoffs and business cutbacks, however, it appeared that by Monday morning the optimists had at least temporarily lost their nerve.

The Dow sank some 15 points in the first hour under active selling. The pace of activity quieted after that—Big Board volume finished at a moderate total of 15.23 million shares-but prices found little support. The Dow's close was at its lowest since October 8, when it finished at 602.63 in the midst of a recovery from the 12-year closing low it had hit a few days before.

One source of the decline at the outset was the expectation that Chrysler Corp. might have to order a broad-scale shutdown of its facilities next month because of lagging new car sales. Chrysler Chairman Lynn Townsend told a mid-afternoon press conference there would be a 50,000-unit production schedule cutback, but denied that any general shutdown was planned. Chrysler shares slid 5/8 to 8 1/2 in active trading. General Motors fell 1 1/2 to 31 3/4 and made a new 20-year low of 31 1/2 during the session, while Ford lost a point to 30 3/8.

Anxiety over possible delays in ending the nationwide coal strike, another evident factor in the market's general weakness, touched off declines in such coal issues as Pittston, down 1 3/4 to 32, and North American Coal, off 1 3/4 at 24 1/2. Occidental Petroleum, the Big Board volume leader, lost 1 1/4 to 12 7/8. The company, which has a large coal subsidiary, said it would take legal steps to block any takeover bid by Standard Oil of Indiana. Indiana Standard was off 2 3/4 at 85.

Coca Cola, which reported flat third quarter earnings and said it was studying a switch to last in-first out inventory accounting, tumbled 6 1/8 to 48 7/8. The Big Board's composite stock index lost 1.38 to 36.76. The American Stock Exchange market value index was down 1.73 to 67.03. Houston Oil & Minerals, the Amex's most-active issue, fell 3 5/8 to 23 3/8. In the over-the-counter market, the NASDAQ composite index closed at 62.09, down 2.32.

Meanwhile, a war scare in the Middle East drove the dollar to a precipitous plunge on Europe's main money markets, and the price of gold reached record highs. Dealers said the flight from the American currency was spurred by fears that an Arab-Israeli conflict could prompt the Arabs to impose another oil embargo against the United States. Later reports of reduced Middle East tension failed to calm foreign exchange markets.

Gold is a traditional hedge during times of monetary uncertainty. There was a rush to buy it because of the rumors of war and reports that South Africa might hold back gold production to force prices higher.

The British pound rose by almost two cents against the dollar from $2.315 to $2.3345, but sterling did badly against European currencies. Its performance added up to 20.7 per cent depreciation in the pound's value since it was floated 18 months ago.

Analysts said the main cause of the pound's trouble was the prospect of industrial unrest after British coal miners rejected a bonus plan aimed at increasing coal production.

The Coca Cola Company announced plans to sell its soda in recyclable plastic bottles. The company displayed samples of the bottles, called "the easy goer," behind plexiglass in an exhibit at the National Soft Drink Association Convention in Atlantic City, New Jersey. In a statement issued by the company's Atlanta, Georgia headquarters, Board Chairman J. Paul Austin said, "The major consumer benefits of the plastic bottle includes its light weight, durability, ease of handling and recyclability."

The giant Ingalls Shipyards in Pascagoula, Mississippi, were shut down Monday after most workers of the firm's first production shift honored picket lines and did not report for work. The pickets were set up after the company's contract with various unions expired Sunday morning.

Negotiations to avert a permanent shutdown of United Parcel Service operations in the metropolitan New York area will be resumed in Washington at 10 A.M. today.

Gulf Power Company, which serves 172,000 customers in 10 Florida counties, asked the Public Service Commission for an emergency rate increase of $19 million a year. A spokesman said the request would raise the price of electricity for residential customers by $5.28 a month for each 1,000 kilowatt hours. The company said the emergency increase, if granted, would be in effect only until the Public Service Commission made a ruling, expected in December, on a request for a permanent increase.

The Federal Energy Administration is studying a tax credit to purchasers of good-mileage cars, free home insulation for the poor, and the already rejected 30-cent gasoline tax as possible fuel-saving measures.

The Federal Reserve Board confirmed that it began easing its restraints on the nation's money supply in August. The Fed released, with a 90-day lag to discourage speculation, the minutes of its Open Market Committee, which regulates the ebb and flow of the money supply through purchases and sales of government securities.

Analysts had widely noted in August an apparent easing of the Fed's tight money policies. The easing was reflected in declining interest rates. The release of the August committee minutes showed that the Fed had targeted growth for the money supply at from 4.75 per cent to 6.75 per cent.

(End of daily A.P. report)

Most of the report made *pretty dismal reading.* Now hear this: Less than 90 days later Chrysler stock was over 11, General Motors hit 40, and Ford bettered 37. Pittston was at 45, North American Coal at 27 1/4, and Occidental Petroleum was pushing 16. *Coca Cola was up close to 80.* Wholesale prices were declining, the coal strike had long since been settled, and the rumored Middle East war remained in the rumor stage. While the price of gold had closed on November 18 in London at $190.50 an ounce, it was sharply lower by mid-February at $178.60 an ounce. The only item related to the true course of the market was the Federal Reserve shift in the monetary policy, action already taken into account by the market in its bottoming of October 4, 1974. So there you have it, *a clear cut demonstration of what little value news is in relation to the true course of the market.* Yet that is what the public is being subjected to every day. They read their newspapers and their weekly news magazines and feel that they are up on the market when in actuality *they are following something that has little or nothing to do with the current market action.* News is the diabolical mechanism which triggers most of the action in keeping the market game going, constantly misleading the uninformed and providing the smart money crowd with the necessary "cover" to disguise their market tactics from the casual market observer.

*   *   *   *

As further proof of the service the media provides in making the accumulation of unwanted stocks easier for the informed buyers, let us examine the on-balance volume figures for the three major automobile stocks at the time of their *maximum unpopularity* in late 1974 and early 1975, attempting to correlate the market action with the news.

Date	Chrysler		Ford		General Motors	
12/ 5/74	-71,100	7.25	0	30.50	-127,000	29.13
12/ 6/74	-139,000	7.13	-46,500	30.13	29,300	29.38
12/ 9/74	-224,300	7.00	8,500	30.36	29,300	29.38
12/10/74	-138,200	7.63	89,200	32.00	214,400	30.50
12/11/74	-54,000	8.13	152,300	32.63	377,400	31.25

Associated Press December 12, 1974

"Auto stocks picked up ground after President Ford met with company officials and labor leaders to discuss the industry's problems. . . . . Chrysler additionally reported that four of the five plants it shut down for December would be reopened in January."

Date	Chrysler		Ford		General Motors	
12/12/74	49,000	8.50	219,200	33.25	565,400	32.00
12/13/74	-1,000	8.38	188,600	33.00	468,700	31.88

Associated Press December 14, 1974

"Chrysler Corp. extended the shutdown of one of its plants into February and Ford Motor Co. announced new layoffs. That means 106,000 auto workers have been indefinitely laid off."

Date	Chrysler		Ford			General Motors	
12/16/74	-65,200	8.00	236,100	UP	33.50	308,700	31.75
12/17/74	-65,200	8.00	263,400	UP	33,75	446,500	33.38
12/18/74	-135,500	7.63	312,700	UP	34.13	446,500	33.38
12/19/74	-208,300	7.50	312,700	UP	34.13	244,900	DOWN 32.25

Associated Press December 20, 1974

"In addition, there was General Motors' announcement Wednesday of additional production cutback and layoff plans for the first quarter of next year. The shares of GM, the world's largest industrial corporation, slipped 1 1/8 to 32 1/4 in active trading Thursday."

Date	Chrysler			Ford		General Motors		
12/20/74	-273,700	DOWN	7.25	262,900	33.63	105,000	DOWN	31.25

Associated Press December 21, 1974

"Auto stocks lost ground in the wake of a series of layoff and production cutback announcements recently for next year's first quarter. General Motors was down 1 at 31 1/4; Ford Motor lost 1/2 to 33 5/8, and Chrysler slipped 1/4 to 7 1/4."

Date	Chrysler			Ford		General Motors		
12/23/74	-370,200	DOWN	7.13	221,100	33.25	-47,900	DOWN	30.00

Associated Press December 24,1974

"General Motors, bracing for another disastrous year, says the auto industry can hope for only modest improvements in 1975 even if the government acts quickly to end the recession.

In a year-end statement, GM Chairman Thomas A. Murphy predicted industry car sales in 1975 would be up slightly from the depressed 1974 levels.

But he cautioned that his expectations depend on 'prompt government actions to restore consumer confidence and to stimulate the economy.'

Calling 1974 the 'most turbulent in postwar automotive history,' Murphy intimated that the ailing industry could be in even worse shape next year without new energy, fiscal and monetary policies.

'The outlook for the American automobile industry hinges directly and importantly on how soon and how effectively the nation's economy can recover from the present recession,' he said."

Date	Chrysler			Ford			General Motors		
12/24/74	-326,400		7.63	256,300		33.63	30,400		30.50
12/26/74	-388,700	DOWN	7.50	323,600	UP	34.25	136,800		31.50
12/27/74	-485,900	DOWN	7.38	280,800		33.50	37,300		30.75
12/30/74	-622,900	DOWN	7.13	230,100		33.25	-107,100	DOWN	30.25
12/31/74	-469,900		7.25	268,000		33.38	66,500		30.75
1/ 2/74	-398,900		8.00	286,900		33.88	162,300	UP	31.88

Associated Press January 3, 1975

"Chrysler Corp. announced further production cutbacks that will result in layoffs of 10,800 workers in the Detroit and St. Louis areas beginning Jan. 6. With the new cutbacks, the firm said, 39,400 of its 117,000 employees will be on indefinite layoff, and 10,050 on temporary layoff.

Nearly 200,00 of the auto industry's 688,000 hourly workers will be laid off next week. Many of the workers are eligible for payment of up to 95 per cent of their regular salary for up to a year during the layoffs, but some auto union officials have said the funds used to pay this compensation will run short before the year is up."

Date	Chrysler			Ford			General Motors		
1/ 3/75	-398,900		8.00	330,700	UP	34.38	257,800	UP	33.63
1/ 6/75	-323,100	UP	8.50	367,200	UP	35.25	389,000	UP	35.13
1/ 7/75	-226,800	UP	9.25	333,800		34.88	511,400	UP	35.38
1/ 8/75	-107,200	UP	9.38	277,600		34.75	666,200	UP	35.50
1/ 9/75	-182,700		9.25	317,600		36.50	780,500	UP	37.13
1/10/75	-182,700		9.25	354,000		36.75	653,000		36.63
1/13/75	-72,800	UP	9.38	297,800		36.50	810,900	UP	37.00

Associated Press January 14, 1975

"Lynn Townsend, chairman of Chrysler Corp., said Monday that the company had embarked on a long range restructuring that would leave it considerably smaller and leaner but able to operate profitably in a smaller market. In one of the most pessimistic assessments of the auto industry's future ever to come from a top auto executive, Townsend said in an interview in his office: 'We are making no assumptions here, in controlling and operating our company, that the market ever is going to get better than 6 million cars.'

Last year the total car market in the U.S. was 8.8 million cars. In 1973 the auto industry sold a record 11.4 million cars, including both domestic and imported cars. Domestic car sales in 1973 totaled about 10 million.

In the long range planning for Chrysler, the most hard pressed of this nation's big three auto makers, Townsend indicated he was assuming that the auto industry could remain at its current depressed levels for a long time."

Date	Chrysler		Ford			General Motors	
1/14/75	-130,900	9.25	240,100	DOWN	36.25	658,600	36.63

Associated Press January 15, 1975

"Meanwhile, U.S. auto sales during the first 10 days of 1975 could be headed for their lowest level in the post-World War II period. Figures released Tuesday showed sales industrywide were down an estimated 33 per cent. With three of the four major auto companies reporting Tuesday, sales declines from 1974 levels arranged from 27 per cent at General Motors to 52 per cent at American Motors. Chrysler deliveries were off 47 per cent. Ford Motor Co. was expected to report similar results today.

Based on the estimate, industry sales for the period would be about 93,000 units—a daily rate of 11,600. A GM company analyst said that would be substantially worse than in 1958, the previously recorded low for the period."

Date	Chrysler			Ford		General Motors	
1/15/75	-207,800	DOWN	8.88	275,700	36.50	796,400	37.38

Associated Press January 16, 1975

"Auto assemblies were cut nearly one-quarter to an annual rate of 5.4 million units. That means cars were coming off the assembly line at a rate 35 percent below a year earlier, when the market had already been hit with the oil embargo. Since manufacturer and dealer inventories of new cars are still at near-record levels, the outlook is for further cutbacks, the Fed said."

Date	Chrysler			Ford		General Motors		
1/16/75	-207,800	DOWN	8.88	275,700	36.50	918,800	UP	37.63
1/17/75	-251,800	DOWN	8.75	242,100	35.88	835,800		37.25
1/20/75	-251,800	DOWN	8.75	216,100	DOWN	35.75	755,200	37.13

Associated Press January 21, 1975

"The Department of Transportation said it has asked a federal court to order General Motors to notify the owners of an estimated 816,000 older model cars that the cars contain what the department alleges are safety-related defects. The department said one suit asks that GM be ordered to notify the owners of 1965 and 1966 Chevrolets and 1966 Buicks built before March 28, 1966, that a fire hazard exists from allegedly faulty carburetor plugs in the Rochester Quadrajet carburetors. It is estimated 375,000 vehicles were involved.

The second suit asks that GM be ordered to notify the owners of 1965 through 1968 model Buick Electra 225s and Buick Wildcats and early production 1970 model Cadillacs (except El Doradoes) that are equipped with cruise control that an alleged defect exists in the engine mounts. The department estimated 441,000 vehicles were involved in that suit."

Date	Chrysler			Ford			General Motors		
1/21/75	-208,700		9.13	185,400	DOWN	35.63	679,200		36.50
1/22/75	-208,700		9.13	210,800		36.00	774,300		37.38
1/23/75	-152,100		9.50	141,200	DOWN	35.75	699,000		37.00
1/24/75	99,800	UP	10.00	221,900	UP	36.00	799,000	UP	38.50
1/27/75	326,500	UP	11.50	288,900	UP	37.25	991,800	UP	39.38
1/28/75	326,500	UP	11.50	249,900		37.00	1,197,400	UP	39.50
1/29/75	441,000	UP	11.63	295,000	UP	37.38	1,334,100	UP	39.88
1/30/75	312,100		11.25	241,300	DOWN	36,88	1,224,400		38.50
1/31/75	397,300		11.50	197,800	DOWN	36.75	1,224,400		38.50

Associated Press February 1, 1975

"About 37, per cent of the auto industry workforce will be on temporary or indefinite layoff next week as most major automakers expand production cutbacks. According to industry figures released this week, 254,000 hourly workers out of a total workforce of 684,000 will be on temporary or indefinite layoff next week. That is an increase of about 6,000 over this week."

Date	Chrysler		Ford		General Motors	
2/3/75	317,700	11.25	230,600	37.25	1,124,500	38.38

Associated Press February 4, 1975

"Autos were mixed, as January car sales came in. General Motors, posting a 10 per cent decline in sales over January a year ago, fell 1/8 to 38 3/8. Chrysler, whose sales plummeted 60 percent, slipped 1/4 to 11 1/4."

Date	Chrysler			Ford			General Motors		
2/4/75	86,300	DOWN	10.00	3,900	DOWN	34.25	516,700	DOWN	35.63

Associated Press February 5, 1975

"More than half the Dow's decline stemmed from large drops in the two auto issues in the average-General Motors, which fell 2 3/4 to 35 5/8 and Chrysler, off 1 1/4 at 10. Elsewhere in the auto group, Ford Motor was down 3 at 34 1/4 and American Motors slipped 3/8 to 4 3/8.

All four auto stocks were among the 15 most active issues on the Big Board, with GM topping the list on turnover of 607,800 shares. Analysts traced the pressure on the stocks to GM's lowering of its dividend late Monday to 60 cents a share from the 85 cents paid in each quarter last year.

One analyst said the company's cash position was sufficient to allow it to maintain the dividend at last year's rates. For that reason, he said, investors were evidently reading the directors' decision to reduce the payment as an expression of concern on their part over the industry's longer term prospects. GM also reported a 2 per cent drop in fourth quarter profits, while American Motors was posting a $5.6 million loss for its fiscal first quarter ended Dec. 31.

With the GM news confronting it, as well as the gloomy forecasts on inflation and unemployment in President Ford's budget message to Congress Monday, it appeared the market was going to be in for a rough day. But traders were apparently heartened by the fact that the selling didn't spread far beyond the auto group."

Date	Chrysler			Ford			General Motors		
2/ 5/75	244,700		10.25	126,800		35.13	741,800		37.25
2/ 6/75	159,000		10.00	55,400		34.25	546,000		35.38
2/ 7/75	97,500		9.75	55,400		34.25	708,600		35.75
2/10/75	33,300	DOWN	9.50	55,400		34.25	583,300		35.50
2/11/75	119,700		10.25	129,400	UP	34.50	736,900	UP	35.88
2/12/75	231,900		10.75	207,600	UP	36.00	833,100	UP	36.88

Associated Press February 13, 1975

"Since mid-January GM, Ford, Chrysler and American Motors have offered cash rebates of from $200 to $600 on selected new models in an effort to boost sales. All four programs are scheduled to end Feb. 28.

The companies say the sales pace in late January was double the rate in the early part of the month because of the rebates. However, deliveries for the entire month were off 16 per cent from the depressed levels of January 1974 and gave the industry its worst performance for that month in 14 years.

The firms paid out an estimated $30 million in rebates to customers in the last 10 days of January.

Wall Street analysts say the companies cannot afford to expand or continue the rebates because they are operating on thin profits. Ford, Chrysler and American Motors will lose money in the current quarter, while GM is expected to break even or report a small profit, the analysts say.

Industrywide, 208,000 of the 684,000 hourly auto workers are on indefinite layoff this week, the most since the industry's severe sales slump began 16 months ago. In addition, some 45,000 workers are on temporary layoff at 14 car and truck plants shut down this week."

Date	Chrysler			Ford		General Motors		
2/13/75	74,300		10.63	106,100	35.50	1,026,100	UP	37.63
2/14/75	-13,300	DOWN	10.25	161,300	35.75	1,139,900	UP	38.00
2/18/75	-246,600	DOWN	9.75	115,900	35.13	1,037,100		37.75

Associated Press February 19, 1975

"A dividend cut by DuPont Co., the chemical giant, and a steep fourth-quarter loss reported by Chrysler Corp. helped set the Dow-Jones average of 30 industrials back about six points in the morning........Chrysler Corp., another active NYSE stock, fell 50 cents to $9.75. The company announced over the weekend it lost $73.5 million in the fourth quarter of 1974."

Date		Chrysler			Ford		General Motors		
2/19/75	-430,100	DOWN	9.38	81,300	DOWN	35.00	968,900		37.38
2/20/75	-430,100	DOWN	9.38	30,600	DOWN	34.13	968,900		37.38
2/21/75	-298,300		9.75	149,200		34.88	1,180,100	UP	39.00
2/24/75	-298,300		9.75	56,700		34.13	1,069,800		38.13
2/25/75	-351,100		9.63	-13,100	DOWN	32.88	982,300		37.25

Associated Press February 26, 1975

"The rebates, and now the price-cutting tactic, were launched to stimulate a car market in its worst slump since World War II.

The companies say the rebates have helped perk up sales but are too expensive to continue indefinitely. The firms also have been making drastic reductions in output to reduce burdensome supplies of unsold models.

Some 207,000 of 683,000 hourly workers are on indefinite layoff due to the production cutbacks."

Date		Chrysler			Ford		General Motors		
2/26/75	-283,200	UP	9.88	69,600		33.38	1,074,100		37.75
2/27/75	-191,600	UP	10.13	-100,400	DOWN	32.50	1,144,200		38.25
2/28/75	-152,800	UP	10.25	-41,000		33.00	1,209,500	UP	39.00
3/ 3/75	- 83,300	UP	10.63	65,900		33.38	1,407,600	UP	39.88
3/ 4/75	- 83,300	UP	10.63	286,500	UP	34.38	1,254,100		39.63

Associated Press March 5, 1975

"A last minute sales surge under expiring rebate plans apparently failed to materialize in February as purchases of U.S.-made cars headed for an eight-year low. General Motors, Chrysler and American Motors reported Tuesday that sales in the final eight days of February were even lower than the depressed levels of a year ago, when fuel shortages sent the industry into an unprecedented sales slump. Ford Motor Co. will release its figures today. Analysts said it is unlikely that Ford sales would surpass those of a year ago. The analysts predicted that sales of all domestic makes for February and the final period would be the lowest for a February since 1967."

Date		Chrysler			Ford		General Motors	
3/5/75	-83,300	UP	10.63	286,500	UP	34.38	1,380,800	40.00

Associated Press March 6, 1975

"The automakers have been among those hardest hit by declining sales. Ford Motor Co. said that its car sales at the end of February were 6 per cent higher than the levels of a year ago when the oil embargo and energy crisis prompted people to buy fewer autos. But sales for the entire month of February were down 6.4 per cent from the same period of 1974. Ford, the nation's second largest automaker, was the last of the major U.S. car manufacturers to release sales figures for last month. It was the only company to show a sales gain in the final eight days of the month. Ford sales and a strong showing by imports boosted total car sales in February above year earlier levels for the first time in 17 months."

Date		Chrysler			Ford		General Motors		
3/6/75	-41,400	UP	10.88	368,900	UP	35.13	1,471,100	UP	40.63

Associated Press March 7, 1975

"General Motors said it will have more workers furloughed next week than at any time in the auto industry's 18-month sales slump. It will operate all 23 of its U.S. assembly plants but at reduced schedules."

Date		Chrysler			Ford		General Motors		
3/ 7/75	69,000	UP	11.13	454,300	UP	36.00	1,597,200	UP	41.25
3/10/75	162,100	UP	11.38	521,100	UP	37,25	1,720,000	UP	41.88
3/11/75	55,900		11.13	623,200	UP	37.50	1,904,700	UP	42.25
3/12/75	156,900		11.50	552,500		37.25	2,060,200	UP	42.38
3/13/75	111,900		11.38	506,500		37.00	2,060,200	UP	42.38

Associated Press March 14, 1975

"In early March auto sales reports, a sharp decline at Ford Motor and a drop at American Motors balanced out gains by General Motors and Chrysler. GM shares were unchanged at 42 3/8; Ford slipped 1/4 to 37; Chrysler was down 1/8 at 11 3/8; and AMC rose 1/8 to 6 5/8."

Date		Chrysler		Ford			General Motors		
3/14/75	111,900		11.38	388,100	36.75	2,220,700	UP	44.13
3/17/75	30,300	DOWN	11.00	473,000	37.38	2,384,600	UP	45.88
3/18/75	- 33,300	DOWN	10.88	473,000	37.38	2,204,900		44.00
3/19/75	- 71,200	DOWN	10.75	444,700	36.88	2,056,700		42.63

Associated Press March 20, 1975

"Special unemployment benefit funds at Chrysler and General Motors are expected to run dry this spring, leaving more than 130,000 laid off auto workers in bleak financial straits. Chrysler's fund could be exhausted by the first week of April and GM's could run out by mid-May due to massive, unprecedented industry layoffs, according to United Auto Workers union projections. The Supplemental Unemployment Benefit (SUB) funds, a unique cushion designed to see auto workers through temporary layoff periods, were not designed to cope with recession-level furloughs. Laid off assemblers who now collect an average $170 a week in SUB pay and unemployment compensation, will lose an average $90 a week when the funds run out, leaving them and their families with $89 a week income."

Here is a record of the Associated Press market headlines covering the market action in late 1974 and early 1975. In the light of what happened, judge for yourself the power of the press and the important role it plays in the market game, scaring people when stocks should be bought and causing them to look elsewhere when stocks should be sold. The headline occurs the morning after each market closing.

Date		Dow–Jones Industrial Average	Associated Press Headline
September	30, 1974	607.87	STOCK MARKET SLUMPS TO NEW LOW
October	1, 1974	604.82	MARKET RECOVERS EARLY 14-POINT LOSS
October	2, 1974	601.53	DOW CLOSES AT 601.53
October	3, 1974	587.61	DOW CLOSES AT 587.61, RECORD LOW
October	4, 1974	584.56	
October	7, 1974	607.56	DOW CLOSES AT 607.56
October	8, 1974	602.63	DOW CLOSES AT 602.63, OFF 4.93 POINTS
October	9, 1974	631.02	MARKET SHOWS SHARPEST GAIN OF THE YEAR
October	10, 1974	648.08	DOW SURGE CONTINUES, CLOSES AT 648.08
October	11, 1974	658.24	MARKET POSTS BROAD GAINS
October	14, 1974	673.50	STOCK MARKET SHOWING STRONG GAINS
October	15, 1974	658.40	MARKET DIPS AGAIN
October	16, 1974	642.29	MARKET DIPS TO 642.29
October	17, 1974	651.44	DOW CLIMBS 9.15 TO 651.44
October	18, 1974	654.88	PROFIT TAKING PUSHES BACK EARLY RALLY
October	21, 1974	669.82	DOW CLOSES AT 669.82, UP 14.94
October	22, 1974	662.86	INFLATION NEWS PUSHES MARKET INTO DOWNTURN
October	23, 1974	645.03	AUTO NEWS PUSHES DOW INTO SLIDE
October	24, 1974	636.26	DOW DIPS TO 636.26 AT CLOSING
October	25, 1974	636,19	RECESSION TALK STALLS TRADING
October	28, 1974	633.84	SUGAR, GOLD STAR IN OTHERWISE LACKLUSTER MARKET
October	29, 1974	659.34	SHARP RALLY ERUPTS IN STOCK MARKET
October	30, 1974	673.03	STOCK MARKET BUILDS SECOND SHARP GAIN
October	31, 1974	665.52	OCTOBER: BEST GAIN IN YEAR
November	1, 1974	665.28	NO FIREWORKS; MARKET QUIETLY GOES NOWHERE
November	4, 1974	657.23	COAL TALK SNAG BRINGS BROAD MARKET PULLBACK
November	5, 1974	674.75	STOCKS JUMP HIGH
November	6, 1974	669.12	PROFIT TAKING ERASES EARLY MARKET GAINS
November	7, 1974	671.93	MARKET STOPS AND GOES, END UP
November	8, 1974	667.16	COAL STRIKE FEARS, ECONOMY DOUBTS STALL MARKET
November	11, 1974	672.64	MARKET DRIFTS UP, AGAINST FLOW OF BAD NEWS
November	12, 1974	659.18	COAL STRIKE CONCERN SHOWS
November	13, 1974	659.18	UPS, DOWNS COME OUT EVEN

Date	Dow–Jones Industrial Average	Associated Press Headline
November 14, 1974	658.40	PRICES YIELD TO INERTIA FINISH UNCHANGED IN DULL TRADING
November 15, 1974	647.61	INFLATION, RECESSION, WOBBLY $ WORRIES PULL MARKET LOWER
November 18, 1974	624.92	WORRIES FUEL SELLOFF
November 19, 1974	614.05	RECESSION FEARS HIT AGAIN
November 20, 1974	609.59	STOCK PRICES BACK DOWN AGAIN
November 21, 1974	608.57	MARKET NOT SHAKEN BY ACTION AGAINST AT & T
November 22, 1974	615.30	EIGHT DAY LOSING STREAK ENDS WITH A WHIMPER
November 25, 1974	611.94	WORRIES HOBBLE MARKET: IT LIMPS TO MILD DECLINE
November 26, 1974	617.26	RALLY GIVES MARKET MODERATE GAIN
November 27, 1974	619.29	EARLY ADVANCE SLIPS TO SLIM GAIN
November 29, 1974	618.66	MARKET SUFFERS POST HOLIDAY DOLDRUMS
December 2, 1974	603.02	STOCKS TAKE A POUNDING
December 3, 1974	596.61	DOW NEARS 12 YEAR LOW
December 4, 1974	598.64	DOW ENDS BELOW 600 AGAIN
December 5, 1974	587.06	WORRIES PUSH STOCKS LOWER
December 6, 1974	577.60	DJ AVERAGE HITS NEW 12 YEAR LOW
December 9, 1974	579.94	MARKET FINDS LITTLE INSPIRATION
December 10, 1974	593.87	(No market coverage)
December 11, 1974	595.35	(No headline)
December 12, 1974	596.37	INVESTORS WAITING
December 13, 1974	592.77	MARKET SLIDES LETHARGICALLY
December 16, 1974	586.83	MARKET DRIFTS AIMLESSLY, FALLS
December 17, 1974	597.54	RALLY BRINGS SOME SCATTERED GAINS
December 18, 1974	603.49	MARKET RALLIES BRIEFLY IN SECOND DAY ADVANCE
December 19, 1974	604.43	RECESSION WORRIES STALL SHORT MARKET RALLY
December 20, 1974	598.48	INFLATION, SPREADING SLUMP BRING DECLINE
December 23, 1974	589.64	STOCK PRICES SHARPLY LOWER; TRADING ACTIVE
December 24, 1974	598.40	
December 26, 1974	604.74	MARKET REGISTERS MILD GAIN
December 27, 1974	602.16	GLOOMY REPORTS KILL RALLY, PUSH PRICES DOWN
December 30, 1974	603.25	TAX SWITCHING BRINGS BUSY DAY, LOWER PRICES
December 31, 1974	616.24	RALLY CLOSES OUT POOR YEAR
January 2, 1975	632.04	LUKEWARM DEMAND FOR GOLD SENDS STOCK PRICES HIGHER
January 3, 1975	634.54	STOCKS RISE AS BUYERS FORESEE RECESSION FIGHTING MEASURES
January 6, 1975	637.20	MARKET GAINS AGAIN
January 7, 1975	641.19	MARKET GAINS AT A SLOWER PACE

Date		Dow–Jones Industrial Average	Associated Press Headline
January	8, 1975	635.40	MARKET WEAKENS, DECLINES
January	9, 1975	645.26	STOCKS GAIN IN LATE SURGE
January	10, 1975	658.79	MARKET RALLY VIGOROUS, TRADE HEAVY
January	13, 1975	654.18	PROFIT TAKING ERASES EARLY GAINS
January	14, 1975	648.70	INDIFFERENT REACTION TO FORD'S PROPOSALS
January	15, 1975	653.39	COAL MINING, INSULATION ISSUES-MENTIONED BY FORD–LEAD RISE
January	16, 1975	655.74	STOCK PRICES SHOW LITTLE CHANGE
January	17, 1975	644.63	UNEASINESS ABOUT RECESSION'S LENGTH, DEPTH CAUSES SETBACK
January	20, 1975	647.45	DULL MARKET WAITS FOR ECONOMIC DEVELOPMENTS
January	21, 1975	641.90	STOCK MARKET RALLY FALLS SHORT
January	22, 1975	652.61	LATE TRADING BRINGS GOOD GAIN
January	23, 1975	656.76	MARKET ZIGZAGS UPWARD WITH HOPES, DOUBTS
January	24, 1975	666.61	DOW CLIMBS TO HIGHEST CLOSING LEVEL SINCE EARLY NOVEMBER
January	27, 1975	692.66	BIG DAY ON THE MARKET
January	28, 1975	694.77	STOCKS CONTINUE RISE IN FAST PACED MARKET
January	29, 1974	705.96	
January	30, 1975	696.42	FRENZIED WINNING STREAK SNAPPED
January	31, 1975	703.69	CLOSING RALLY SETS RECORDS
February	3, 1975	711.44	MARKET PAUSES, PULLS STEADILY AHEAD
February	4, 1975	708.07	MARKET REBOUNDS
February	5, 1975	717.85	
February	6, 1975	714.17	PROFITEERS, BUYERS IN MARKET SLUG-FEST
February	7, 1975	711.91	STOCK MARKET STAGGERS, RECORDS MODERATE LOSS
February	10, 1975	708.39	TRENDLESS MARKET FALLS AFTER INTEREST SCARE
February	11, 1975	707.60	MARKET CHANGES LITTLE ON QUIET DAY
February	12, 1975	715.03	GOOD GAIN IN SHORT SESSION
February	13, 1975	726.92	STOCK MARKET SOARS TO SIX MONTH HIGH
February	14, 1975	734.20	MARKET CLIMBS AGAIN
February	18, 1975	731.30	PRICES DIP AT BAD NEWS
February	19, 1975	736.39	MARKET CLOSES MIXED
February	20, 1975	745.38	MARKET IGNORES BAD NEWS, MAKES SOLID ADVANCE
February	21, 1975	749.77	
February	24, 1975	736.94	STOCK PRICES RETREAT; DROP BROAD BUT ORDERLY: ANALYSTS
February	25, 1975	719.18	MARKET SUFFERS SHARPEST DROP IN THREE MONTHS
February	26, 1975	728.10	MARKET RECOVERS SOME OF GROUND LOST LATELY
February	27, 1975	731.15	GLOOMY NEWS RESTRAINS STOCKS TO SLIGHT GAIN

Date		Dow–Jones Industrial Average	Associated Press Headline
February	28, 1975	739.05	PRIME RATE CUTS KEEP MARKET AHEAD
March	3, 1975	753.13	HOPES OF OIL PRICE BREAK SPARK STOCK SURGE
March	4, 1975	757.74	OIL PRICE BREAK INSPIRES SECOND HEAVIEST DAY; PRICES GAIN A BIT
March	5, 1975	752.82	MARKET DRIFTS DOWNWARD; INVENTORIES MOVING?
March	6, 1975	761.81	WHOLESALE PRICE DROP, HOPE FOR EASING OF OIL PRICE SEND STOCKS UP
March	7, 1975	770.10	RATES FALL, MARKET UP
March	10, 1975	776.13	EIGHTH GAIN IN LAST NINE SESSIONS
March	11, 1975	770.89	PROFIT TAKING PULLS PRICES DOWN
March	12, 1975	763.69	PROFIT TAKING, SAD OUTLOOK BLAMED AS MARKET TAKES FALL
March	13, 1975	762.98	SHOWING INDECISIVE
March	14, 1975	773.47	INVENTORY STATISTICS ENCOURAGE MARKET
March	17, 1975	786.53	OPTIMISM BRINGS RISE
March	18, 1975	779.41	PROFIT TAKING PUSHES PRICES DOWN IN ACTIVE, TURBULENT SESSION
March	19, 1975	769.48	DOWNTURN MOVES INTO SECOND DAY
March	20, 1975	764.00	THIRD STRAIGHT LOSS
March	21, 1975	763.06	SLUGGISH MARKET DRIFTS LOWER
March	24, 1975	743.43	LOSS SHARPEST OF '75
March	25, 1975	747.89	NARROW GAIN POSTED
March	26, 1975	766.19	HOPES FOR TAX CUT BOOST STOCK PRICES
March	27, 1975	770.26	WINNING STREAK CONTINUES
March	31, 1975	768.15	STOCK MARKET STRAGGLES LOWER BUT FINISHES QUARTER WITH GAINS
April	1, 1975	761.58	STOCKS IN BROAD DECLINE
April	2, 1975	760.56	TROUBLED MARKET DROPS AFTER BRIEF RALLY TRY
April	3, 1975	752.19	STOCKS REFLECT UNEASINESS
April	4, 1975	747.26	WORST WEEK OF YEAR
April	7, 1975	742.88	WARY MARKET DECLINES AGAIN
April	8, 1975	749.22	TECHNICAL RALLY BREAKS STRING OF SIX DECLINES
April	9, 1975	767.99	STOCKS MAKE GOOD GAIN
April	10, 1975	781.29	MARKET RUNS UP ANOTHER STRONG GAIN
April	11, 1975	789.50	MARKET HITS EIGHT MONTH HIGH
April	14, 1975	806.95	MARKET SOARS ABOVE 800
April	15, 1975	815.08	INDUSTRIAL OUTPUT DROPS SLIGHTLY
April	16, 1975	815.71	LATE RALLY WIPES OUT EARLY LOSS
April	17, 1975	819.46	STOCKS RISE, VOLUME BIG
April	18, 1975	808.43	MARKET LOSS 1ST IN 8 DAYS
April	21, 1975	815.86	HOPES OF VIET SETTLEMENT BOOST MARKET
April	22, 1975	814.14	TIRED MARKET FEARS INTEREST HIKES, FALLS
April	23, 1975	802.49	INTEREST HIKE WORRIES PUSH PRICES DOWN

Date		Dow—Jones Industrial Average	Associated Press Headline
April	24, 1975	803.66	(No Headline)
April	25, 1975	811.80	PROFITS LOWEST SINCE WORLD WAR TWO
April	28, 1975	810.00	STAGNANT STOCK MARKET SLIPS SLIGHTLY
April	29, 1975	803.04	PROFIT TAKERS PUSH PRICES LOWER
April	30, 1975	821.34	BLUE CHIP RALLY BOOSTS DOW TO 10 MONTH HIGH
May	1, 1975	830.96	MARKET ADVANCES SHARPLY AGAIN
May	2, 1975	848.48	MARKET PUTS ON ANOTHER BURST OF POWER
May	5, 1975	855.60	IMPORTS HOG CAR MARKET; DETROIT LOSING
May	6, 1975	834.72	BLUE CHIPS SAG STOCKS BY 20.88
May	7, 1975	836.44	ERRATIC MARKET SHIFTS BETWEEN PROFIT TAKING AND OPTIMISM OVER ECONOMY'S PROSPECTS
May	8, 1975	840.50	STOCKS WITH SMALL PRICE TAGS OFFSET BAD NEWS
May	9, 1975	850.13	INVENTORY CUT NEWS SPURS MARKET RALLY
May	12, 1975	847.47	MARKET SHOWS LITTLE SHOCK AT SHIP SEIZURE
May	13, 1975	850.13	SHIP SEIZURE SQUELCHES MARKET RALLY
May	14, 1975	858.73	STOCK MARKET CLIMBS TO 11 MONTH HIGH
May	15, 1975	848.80	SLUGGISH RETAIL SALES PUSH PRICES DOWN
May	16, 1975	837.61	PROFIT GRAB CUTS STOCKS
May	19, 1975	837.69	MARKET CLOSES AHEAD
May	20, 1975	830.49	ECONOMY'S SLUMP, INFLATION WORSE THAN PREVIOUSLY ESTIMATED
May	21, 1975	818.68	INFLATION QUICKENS AS HIGHER MEAT PRICES BOOSTS GROCERY COSTS
May	22, 1975	818.91	(No headline)
May	23, 1975	831.90	DROP IN PRIME RATE SPURS BIG MARKET RALLY
May	27, 1975	826.11	PROFIT TAKING SIDETRACKS MARKET'S EARLY RALLY TRY
May	28, 1975	817.04	CONCERN OVER FORD'S ENERGY PLAN FORCE MARKET DOWN
May	29, 1975	815.00	QUIET MARKET WANDERS; FINISHES SESSION DOWN
May	30, 1975	832.29	MARKET REACTS TO GOVERNMENT'S REVISED ECONOMIC PREDICTIONS

No News Is Good News

It holds that if news in itself is so often associated with market traps, then all market movements *in the absence of news* may very well be more significant than if accompanied by news. Widely predicted advances for the market are not as bullish as are the *unadvertised* advances. Put another way—an advance on news is not as bullish as an advance on no news. For a decade market letter writers always left themselves an escape hatch by stating that if peace came in Viet Nam, all bets were off, and the market could be expected to go through the roof. When a real breakthrough was made in late 1972, the market took off from already high levels, *but it was a widely advertised advance by then.* The bear market of 1973-74 started in January, 1973, and was well underway by the time the formal cease fire agreement was signed in Paris. In reverse—widely predicted declines for the market are not as bearish as are generally unadvertised declines. A decline on news is not as bearish as a decline on no news. The January, 1973 decline started amidst a general absence of specific bearish news. This news phenomenon always seems to take on maximum significance *at all the major turning points.* So typically during the start of a bull market, the market rises in the absence of news or, to put it another way, it rises in the absence of the kind of news which would be expected to put the market up. In other words, the news remains generally bearish but the market rises in the face of it. Think back to 1970 and how bad the news was and how the market rose off that May bottom and kept going in the face of it. Think back to the 1974 bottom and how bad the news was and how the market kept going up in the face of it. In both cases it was a generally *unadvertised* advance, the best kind to have.

It ties in with Humphrey Neill's Theory of Contrary Opinion which, if taken by itself, can lead one into all kinds of difficulties because it is most valid *at the turning points.* Such turning points are associated with *excesses.* Popularity is not bad. Overpopularity is. The more prevalent an idea is the more likely the market is to reverse during its widest acceptance.

As stated in the first *Strategy* book, these observations caution against following the crowd on a sharp advance promulgated by supporting newspaper headlines and lead to the general advice to sell on the good news. When the market is going up and majority opinion wonders why, then that is a reliable signal to buy. Stocks are often best bought while there is a general selling stampede promulgated by bearish newspaper headlines. When the market is going down and nobody in general seems to know why, sell. The public is more often led by their emotions, *but the technical indicators are unemotional.* Trust the indicators and distrust the emotional appeals which sway the public.

A market going up on good news cannot sustain itself as long as a market going up on bad news. Conversely, a market going down on bad news cannot sustain the decline as long as a market going down on good news. It is all connected with belief or disbelief as the case may be. The 1970-71 market offered a striking example. Coming off the Dow 631 bottom in May, 1970, the averages marched higher on the typical wall of worry which accompanies all important bull moves. The economy was still in the throes of recession and the public was waiting for an official pronouncement from Washington that it was turning around. The Dow climbed all the way from 631 to 940 between May 26, 1970 and April 16, 1971, a thrilling ascent of 309 points in the face of public disbelief. Then on that day of April 16, 1971, the Commerce Department *made it official,* announcing that the economy in January, February, and March 1971, *recorded the steepest one quarter rise since 1958.* The *disbelief* which had accompanied the 309-point rise *was transformed into belief.* The market had largely advanced on *no news,* an extremely bullish move. Now the advance *had taken on news* AND THAT WAS A WARNING. *The technical market indicators moved in the opposite direction of the public thinking.* While bullish when the public disbelieved, they registered trouble shortly after the psychological shift of April 16, signalling a peak on April 28 at 950.81. So the industrial average rose 309 points on disbelief and a mere 10 points more on belief. Look how well the market had sustained itself on bad news and public disbelief and how shortlived the further advance became once the news turned good and disbelief gave way to belief.

For many months during the 1973-74 decline, the government persisted in saying that the country was not in a recession. President Nixon stated many times that there would be no recession. Later in the downturn, President Ford was equally reluctant to label the downturn a recession until it became all too obvious. By that time the market had reached bottom, and by the time President Ford announced to the American people in his January, 1975 State of the Union address that he had *bad* news to report, the Dow already had a firm grip on the wall of worry, clearly in the early stages of a new bull market.

As this is being written, the Dow-Jones Industrial Average has climbed 281 points up that worry wall, rising from 577 to 858 between December 6, 1974, and May 14, 1975. The rise was accomplished against the background of a bad economic recession. The technical indicators throughout the rise were seldom stronger until, as in the spring of 1971, serious upside resistance began to come into evidence. It only remained for an official announcement from Washington that the recession was over or some other widely circulated story that the recession was ending in order to complete the almost identical 1970-71 pattern.

Almost exactly coinciding with the peak of the great 281-point initial rallying phase of the bull market, the May 19, 1975 issue of *U.S. News and World Report* came out with the cover story entitled "First signs of recession's end." Here is one of the most vivid examples I could give you of the existence of the anachronistic posture of news in relation to the stock market. Subtract *nine months* from May, 1975, and you get August, 1974. In August, 1974, the market was in the very terminal slide leading toward the October 4, 1974 bottom. The true internal bottom for the market occurred on September 13, 1974. So then, what the market saw as a major buy signal in the fall of 1974 *is matched fundamentally nine months later* (official government announcement of ending recession probably occurring in summer of 1975).

In other words, if you could take the May-June-July 1975 news and move it back nine months to the fall of 1974, *then technicians and fundamentalists alike would all want to buy stocks simultaneously, and the market game would end for lack of sellers.* Dwell carefully on this for a moment, it being of such paramount importance. *It is the very nub of the market game.* The market moved on futures and the fundamentalists moved on news. I think all fundamentalists are from Missouri because they have to be shown. A fundamentalist cannot buy a stock when all fundamentalists *disbelieve* that stocks can go up. They must be SHOWN. They have to BELIEVE that stocks will go up. They have to have a major news magazine tell them that the recession is over. So what happens? They have their fundamental evidence many months after the major bottom, and they come into the market with confidence. They buy. Who is selling? Why, of course, the technicians who bought in the fall of 1974 on *market evidence* which is perpetually proven to be superior to fundamental evidence.

Now, for a still deeper insight into this tremendously important anachronistic spread between technical data and fundamental data, here are the opening lines of the May 19, 1975 *U.S. News and World Report* story about the ending recession: "The slump that started late in 1973 will touch bottom in the next few weeks." That single sentence again confirms the anachronism between the market and the news. Subtract nine months from the fall of 1973 and you get the January, 1973 market top! The market started to discount the future recession nine months before it began! Now if we could take the news as it existed in the fall of 1973 and go back with it nine months, we would have had a situation in January, 1973, where technicians and fundamentalists alike would all want to sell. That was impossible. The game would end. In reality, the fundamentalists bought from the technicians all the way down, and by the time there was evidence that a slump was starting, the market made an intermediate bottom in December, 1974, and rallied strongly for four months.

I can't help but dwell on this a bit, it being so basic to the market game. Think for a minute about the hundreds of millions of dollars involved in the total media effort of publishing magazines, publishing newspapers, putting on TV broadcasts, the cost of radio time, etc. in order to inform the people about business and the economy, AND IT ISN'T WORTH FIVE CENTS as far as telling the public when to buy stocks. Not only is that heavily bankrolled media effort *totally irrelevant* to what the stock market is saying, *but it results in keeping the public constantly on the wrong side of the market.* It is the biggest single enemy the public will ever have in their generally losing efforts in the market game. An equally appalling amount of money is wasted each year by Wall Street brokerage houses on their research departments, most of which are devoted to *fundamental* research. It can be proven over and over that such fundamental data *comes down the tube too late to do most investors any good.* Most corporate good news has long since been discounted by the stocks, and the same anachronistic feature exists: technical data and those who follow it exploiting fundamental data and its followers every time.

If you doubt this in any way, I would suggest that you go to your local library and take the time to match up the market and the news *by going back nine months with the news and matching it with the Dow Jones Industrial Average.* By doing that you will then generally find that the market and the news agree! It otherwise can't happen. Can you imagine a big national magazine exhorting the public to rush in and buy stocks in October, 1974? Equally impossible, can you imagine listening to TV in January, 1973, and being told that all the top economists agree that the market is at a major top? On the contrary, IN ORDER TO KEEP THE MARKET GAME GOING, top economists were very bullish in January, 1973, and extremely pessimistic in October, 1974. So much for economics. It is the handmaiden of the fundamental crowd. Once you become completely oriented to the technical market approach you will view all major economic developments as TRAPS. When weighing such developments, give them the NINE MONTH TEST. Go back nine months and see if technicians and fundamentalists would then have agreed on the probable course of the stock market, checking out what the market had done in that nine-month period. If the economic development was bullish and the market had generally gone up for the previous nine months, the development had already been discounted and technicians would sell on the news as the fundamentalists bought. If the development was bearish and the market had generally gone down for the previous nine months, then it had been discounted and the technicians would be buying stock from the fundamentalists impressed into selling on the development.

The Major Trap of Fundamental Analysis

An ideal equilibrium will never exist in the market. It has no part in the market game and never will. Such a theoretical balance would mean that a slide rule computation showing U.S. Steel to be worth $60 a share would also be accompanied by U.S. Steel going across the tape at 60. If the stock rose to 65, just enough selling pressure would develop to bring it back to 60, and if it dropped under 60, just enough buying would come in to put it back up to 60. It would stay at 60 until the next earnings report and then out would come the slide rules and a new equilibrium figure would be computed to which the market price would adhere. Such an exact cause and effect relationship between fundamental changes and the price of a stock is ridiculous and is almost totally irrelevant to the game the market plays, a game between accumulators and distributors, measured not in values but in terms of *force regardless of values,* a game almost totally dependent on *timing.* Giving this a little thought, *the fundamental analysis of stocks has little or no part to be played in the successful winning of the market game.* Anyone who has bought a stock based purely on fundamental considerations can attest to their shock when the market game then in progress completely ignored those considerations, tossing their stock on the vicious waves of the high seas of supply and demand. Such fundamentalists, not accustomed to the perpetual market game, were either pushed into becoming investors, holding declining stocks in a bear market, or pressured to sell them too early in a bull market. Such investors became the "required fall guys" in the market game because somebody has to hold stocks in a bear market, and somebody must be ready to supply stocks to the smart money buyers in a bull market. Not being attuned to the faster movements of the speculator, the stock *investor* largely plays the sucker role, not being able to divorce himself from the market game whether he likes it or not.

The most compelling demonstration of wholesale market stupidity continues to be shown by the allegiance to the precepts of the fundamentalist school, so many of them laid down by the "father of fundamental security analysis," Benjamin Graham. Graham actually frowned on stock speculation, feeling that there were no sound principles to guide the speculator in the market. Yet Graham or his many followers could never buy or sell a stock without becoming involved in the "game," a game almost totally foreign to fundamental stock analysis. Closer to the real truth of the matter, it is the speculator who does have the sound principles to guide him in the market *while there are no sound principles to guide the investor in the market.* As we go along you will see the total truth of that statement. After all, the market is an entity far more subject to *supply and demand pressures* rather than to values. As I have said so often, any young person who is seriously out to learn all he can about the market will do well to study all he can about *psychology* and he might minor in economics *or even skip the subject completely,* it having so little to do with the market. Economics scarcely takes into consideration *how people feel,* and it is those mass feelings

translated into supply and demand pressures which more often than not
trample down all the careful but irrelevant work done by the fundamentalist
in their misdirected efforts to determine such things as appraised values,
estimated earning power, multipliers, and asset values.

Here are Benjamin Graham's rules for the appraisal of common stocks
used as a guide for the timing of purchases or sales. I leave it up to the reader
to decide which methods are relevant to the market game, and, for that
matter, which methods are simpler and more accurate, the Graham method
or the method of reading the language of the market itself, the technical
methods described throughout this book:

(1) The appraised value is determined by (a) estimating the earning
power, (b) applying thereto a suitable multiplier, and (c) adjusting, if
necessary, for asset value.

(2) The earning power should ordinarily represent an estimate of average
earnings for the next five years.

(3) The above estimate should be developed preferably from a projection
of the dollar volume and the profit margin. The starting point is the
actual exhibit over some period in the past. Under conditions existing
in early 1949 there is no "normal period" of past years which can be
accepted as a direct measure of future earning power. However, an
averaging of the results of an unusually good period and a subnormal
period might be acceptable, i.e., giving 50 per cent weight to the
1936-40 average after taxes and 50 per cent weight to 1947-48 or
1946-48.

(4) When figures of earlier years enter into the calculation, proper
adjustment should be made for subsequent changes in capitalization.

(5) The multiplier should reflect prospective longer term changes in
earnings. A multiplier of 12 is suitable for stocks with neutral
prospects. Increases or decreases from this figure must depend on the
judgment and preferences of the appraiser. In all but the most
exceptional cases, however, the maximum multiplier should be 20
and the minimum should be eight.

(6) If the tangible-asset value is less than the earning-power value
(earning power times multiplier), the latter may be reduced by some
arbitrary factor to reflect this deficiency. Our suggested factor is as
follows: Deduct one-quarter of the amount by which the earning-
power value exceeds twice the asset value. (This permits a 100 per
cent premium over tangible assets without penalty.)

(7) If the net-current-asset value exceeds the earning-power value, the
latter may be increased by 50 per cent of the excess to give the final
appraised value.

(8) Where extraordinary conditions prevail—such as war profits or war restrictions, or a temporary royalty or rental situation—the amount of the total probable gain or loss per share due to such conditions should be estimated and added to, or subtracted from, the appraised value as determined without considering the abnormal conditions.

(9) Where the capitalization structure is highly speculative—that is, where the total of senior securities is disproportionately large—then the value of the entire enterprise should first be determined as if it had common stock only. This value should be apportioned between the senior securities and the common stock on a basis which recognizes the going-concern value of the senior claims. (Note difference between this treatment and a valuation based on dissolution rights of the senior securities.) If an adjustment is needed for extraordinary conditions, as referred to in (8), this should be made in the total enterprise value, not on a per-share-of common basis.

(10) The more speculative the position of the common stock—for whatever reason—the less practical dependence can be accorded to the appraised value found.

(11) Appraised values should be taken as a definite guide to current purchase or sale only if they exceed or fall below the market price by at least one-third. In other cases they may be useful as a supplemental fact in analysis and investment decisions. (Benjamin Graham's rules are quoted from *A Treasury of Wall Street Wisdom,* the 1966 classic edited by Dr. Harry D. Shultz and Samson Coslow.)

If that is what is required to appraise a stock then let the fundamentalists have it all. The technician wants no part of it. Everything there involves *estimates* which are nothing more than *guesses:* the application of multipliers where the figure is *arbitrarily* chosen, again just a *guess; projections* which assume that the future will follow along the lines of the past; *guesses* as to prospective longer term changes in earnings; individual judgments and preferences which may differ widely from appraiser to appraiser; the introduction of more *arbitrary* factors as needed; and finally, a sliding scale of dependence according to how speculative the stock may be. Even if all those were valid methods to beat the game, such lengthy calculations would not find the market standing still so as to allow the appraised value to be relevant to the price of the stock in question. Whatever the *market* does is a *technical* situation, and you cannot successfully apply *fundamental* methods to a *technical* situation. That is like trying to mix oil and water. It is only logical that *technical* methods correctly analyze *technical* situations.

Earnings—The Big Sucker Play

Probably no greater deception faces the average market follower than the general overemphasis on corporate earnings as a reliable guide to where the price of a stock is headed. Yet 99% of all market followers are grounded in the belief that what a company earns is the very guts of what the stock market is all about. *They couldn't be more wrong.* When a company reports that it earned $4 a share in a given year, it is an incontestable fact, no argument about that. That fact, however, may be completely irrelevant to what the price of the stock is now going to do. The reason is very simple and yet most people give it very little consideration. The fact that the company earned $4 a share is a statement of knowledge *up to that moment.* It provides no hint whatsoever what the company is going to earn *in the future.* Inasmuch as stock prices are made on *future* expectations, what the price of the stock now does *has little or no relationship whatsoever to the fact that the company just reported annual earnings of $4 a share.* There lies the nub of the great deception, entrapping the majority to buy at the wrong time and sell at the wrong time, caught up in the cruelest hoax the market game can play on the innocent, those brought up upon the importance of corporate earnings. Bunk, pure bunk! What usually happens is that the smart money sees the $4 earnings as a probable peak, and they start selling to the suckers who think they have caught hold of a growth stock. The price of the stock starts falling in the face of the high earnings but the faithful majority hang on. Probably a year later the company reports reduced earnings of $1.20 a share, and the faith of the majority is shaken. They then sell in the face of the bad news near the lows as the smart money scoops up the shares to start the game all over again.

Do you think the writer is too cynical? I'll tell you a true story. Back in the early 1960's, when I was writing the market letter for E.F. Hutton & Co. in New York, I recommended a well-known stock as a short sale in the 80's. A few days later the comptroller of the company called me and invited me to have lunch with him. He said that he wanted the opportunity to present his bullish case, believing that I was making a serious mistake in recommending the stock as a short sale. We then met and I patiently listened to him discuss such things as cash flow, mounting orders, a record backlog of orders, their outlook for the industry, rising prices for their basic product, and just about every other bullish fundamental statistic he could throw at me. At the conclusion of the luncheon he asked me if I was going to continue to recommend the stock as a short sale. I told him that I recognized him as an authority in his business and that I didn't question anything he told me. However, I also told him that the price of his company's stock *had absolutely nothing to do with anything he had said.* I simply told him that the price of his stock was subject to the simple laws of supply and demand and that, currently, *supply was outstripping demand.* He asked why. I said that I didn't know why, only that it was happening and that was the all-important fact. I then shocked him by stating that my charts suggested a very sharp price drop coming into the low 40's. He laughed and said that such a move was out of the question inasmuch as he was the chief financial officer of the company and that such a projection completely conflicted with their fundamental projections.

We met again when the price of the stock was down in the low 60's, and again he held to his earlier beliefs that the stock was fluctuating in a normal range, although reluctantly conceding that the short sale in the 80's was working out. To make a long story short, we met once again several months later when the stock was down in the low 40's. This time his attitude was completely different. The basic price of his product had been sharply cut, they were contemplating the closing of two West Coast plants, and there was a reported layoff of personnel. He told me that they had become quite pessimistic about the immediate future of the industry and were doing some selling. He then asked me if I was going to continue recommending the stock as a short sale and that he too believed the stock was headed lower. I simply told him that we had covered our short sales a week before and were now recommending the stock as a purchase, a stock now technically oversold. Again he was distressed because he had sold a block of stock a few days previously, thinking that the poor fundamentals might drive the price down into the 20's. As the news got worse the stock recovered from the 40's back to the mid-60's in several weeks.

That is a typical gambit of the market game. Here was the comptroller of the company, a man trained to know every financial transaction his company was involved in, a man who understood his product, his key personnel, his sales, where the economy was headed. He probably had excellent training in economics and was probably Phi Beta Kappa. He undoubtedly knew his business from top to bottom, *but the business of the stock market is something almost totally removed from ordinary business, almost completely divorced from orthodox economics.* It was no wonder that the comptroller of this well-known company knew everything about the company *but had no idea where the stock was headed.*

Yet those who get their first training in Wall Street are assigned to read and study Graham & Dodd, and the complete fundamental approach is so hammered into their subconscious minds that they can never completely rid themselves of the hinderance and become pure market technicians. They are taught immediately to put too much stress on the importance of dividends, yields, and price/earnings ratios. These are all the dodges of the game, devices to entrap the majority into holding stocks when they should no longer be held, BECAUSE THE CONTINUATION OF THE GAME DEPENDS ON SOMEBODY TO ALWAYS BE HOLDING STOCKS.

I recall that back in 1967 I encountered a woman who had inherited 4,000 shares of American Telephone common stock, then yielding 4.3%. I told her that the stock, then selling for around $52 a share, appeared to be headed lower, and I suggested that she sell it. She was horrified by the suggestion. First of all, she said that she depended on the income. I told her that she could do a lot better than 4.3% and suggested that she switch into Ligget & Myers, then yielding 6.84%. I pointed out that such a switch would increase her dividend income by about 60%. She was not impressed. She made it clear that Telephone stock had been held by her family for years, and she was not going to be the first to break the tradition by moving out of it. Furthermore, Telephone stock had maximum safety. Her clinching reason for not wanting to switch was that she would not feel right being in a tobacco stock since she and her family had never approved of smoking.

It was not an extreme case. As a matter of fact, it was rather typical of the flimsy reasoning behind the holding of some stocks which should have been jettisoned a long time ago and the refusal to buy other stocks which would have produced immediately improved benefits. She had said that she held the stock for income yet she refused to increase that income. Her argument regarding safety didn't hold water because Liggett & Myers had paid a $5 dividend every year since 1948 with the exception of 1955 when it paid $4 and 1959 when it paid $5.75. Her remarks regarding her aversion to buying the stock of a company in the tobacco business were completely irrelevant. The simple question here was did she or did she not want to increase her dividend income. Apparently she didn't. She was not going to better her lot and break a family tradition. If I had stacked up over $5,000 in cash on the table before her and lit a match to it she would have deemed me crazy. Yet her determination to accept $8,944 in dividend income every year rather than $14,227 produced the same results than if she had made the switch and then went ahead and literally burned up, 5,283 crisp new $1 bills.

People are going to do what they do in the main regardless of any educating influence. The continuation of the market game depends to some degree (a considerable one) on maintained ignorance because somebody always must hold stocks which should otherwise have been sold when the trend is down. It is a pretty safe bet that that woman still held her 4,000 shares of Telephone stock right up through the high interest period of 1974 when U.S. Treasury bills were yielding over 9%. I used to think many years ago that if I wrote a stock market book revealing all the secrets of the game that the book would kill the game. Everybody would then know the right time to buy and the right time to sell. Then there would be nobody around to sell to the buyers and nobody around to buy from the sellers. No one has to worry about such a book ending the market game, not when it can be endlessly demonstrated that there is more maintained stupidity in this business than in probably any other business in the world. The best intelligence available will never reach more than a fraction of the population at any time, and even the majority of those who avail themselves of it will in time forget what they learned. Margaret Mitchell's *Gone With the Wind* was one of the greatest of all bestsellers, yet read by a small fraction of the population. The true language of the market, technical, all of it, will never be heard by more than a small fraction of all market followers because the majority of those involved in the market are bombarded with mistimed fundamental data which nine times out of ten hasn't a blessed thing to do with where the price of a stock or the market itself is headed. The media is the biggest enemy of the small investor, mostly headlining the wrong news at the wrong times, playing on his misguided reliance on fundamentals and his normal fears and greeds. One of the biggest culprits appears to be corporate earnings for the simple reason that it is so logical that a stock should rise on improved earnings and fall on reduced earnings. Actually, it is never quite that simple although the simple will always believe it to be so.

The fallacy of corporate earnings as a guide to what the price of the stock is going to do is best illustrated in terms of the price/earnings ratio. If the price of a stock exactly correlated with the earnings, then the price/earnings ratio would be a constant. A stock having a price/earnings ratio of 10 would be expected to rise from 30 to 50 as the per share earnings rose from \$3 to \$5 and would be expected to plummet to 12 if the per share earnings dropped sharply from \$5 to \$1.20. But this simple formula based on a non-existent correlation breaks down in actual practice. We know this to be true *because all price/earnings ratios widely fluctuate.* The very fact that p/e ratios fluctuate *points up the poor correlation between earnings and stock prices.* A good correlation would be reflected by a near constant p/e ratio. In actual practice, however, we have seen the Dow sell at an overvalued 20 times earnings in the early 1960's which was far short of the Dow peak in early 1973 at 16.5 times earnings, and we have seen the sharply undervalued p/e reading for the Dow in the fall of 1974 at under 6. The actual figures force us to conclude that the market either overvalues stocks or undervalues stocks. That is no brilliant discovery, but it does underscore the fallacy of earnings. If a stock earns \$3 a share and the earnings are increased to \$4 a share, *the increased earnings provide no clue whatsoever as to whether the market will overvalue or undervalue the improved earnings figure.*

Yet the expensively maintained research departments of the large brokerage houses, mutual funds, banks, insurance companies etc. continue to pore over corporate earnings reports, still thinking that to be the key to successful stock selection when the fluctuating p/e ratios say the answer lies in forecasting coming overvaluation and undervaluation. Fundamental analysis is poorly equipped to predict periods of overvaluation and undervaluation.

That is a function of *technical* analysis since overvaluation and undervaluation is reflected by stock prices and stock *prices* belong to the technician, not the market fundamentalist. If a stock is to become overvalued or undervalued it won't be a function of the earnings, but rather of the net result of supply and demand, two major factors totally divorced from corporate earnings. Yet such stress is placed on price/earnings ratios that the daily stock tables now include the figures, just one more solid piece of evidence that *the newspapers are major tools in the game,* increasingly making the public conscious *of something that is totally irrelevant to what a stock is likely to do.*

Probably the finest work I have ever seen which completely repudiated the importance of corporate earnings in timing stock purchase or sale was published by Arthur Merrill in late 1973. He presented a chart of the Dow-Jones Industrial Average against the background of the constantly changing price/earnings ratios and that chart clearly revealed the *rhythmical lag* in corporate earnings behind the movement of the stock average. It showed the rise in earnings as the market fell out of bed in 1966, the drop in earnings as the market underwent a strong 1967 recovery, the rise in earnings as the market carved out the plateau 1968 top, the still rising earnings curve as the market plunged in 1969, the great market turn to the upside in 1970 as earnings continued to turn down, the upturn in earnings as the market went into a sharp 1971 correction, the sharper upturn in earnings as the market made the great plateau 1972 top, the still sharper rise in earnings as the market plunged in 1973 and 1974, and the great 1974 upturn in the market as earnings leveled off and started to decline. The chart is shown on page 105.

Interest Rates—An Effective Game Camouflage

Interest rates play an effective role in keeping the general public out of the stock market at the time when the smart money is moving in. A high level of interest rates is thought to be bearish for the market and low rates bullish. Actually this is not so. It is the *direction* interest rates are moving in that is important. In late 1974, the prime rate peaked at 12%, the Federal Reserve Board deciding in August to adopt a new policy of monetary ease. That action set the stage for the stock market bottom which soon followed. Now it was time for the smart money to make their move, having become confident as opposed to the still highly pessimistic public. Historically high interest rates at this point were no longer a bearish influence on the market because the *direction* those rates were about to move in was bullish. The smart money is always the *first* group to take advantage of a new trend and the general public is the *last* group. The influx and efflux of money in the market is largely geared to interest rates and psychology. Once it is

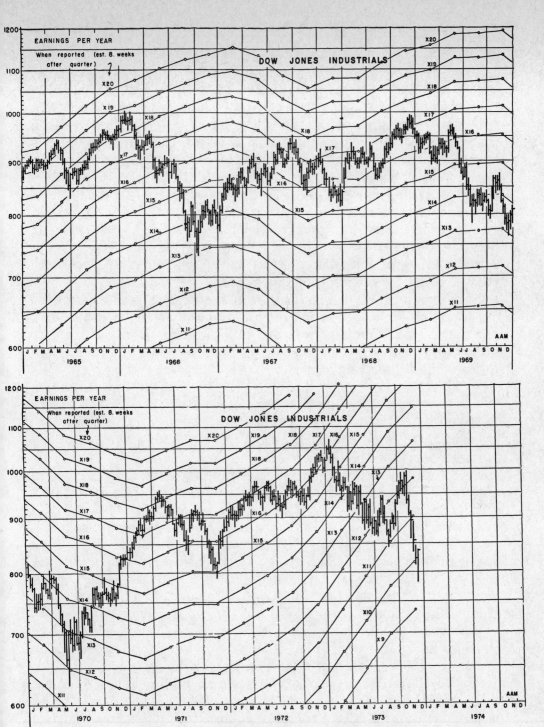

Chart Courtesy of Arthur A. Merrill, Technical Trends, Chappaqua, New York

determined that rates have peaked, the market is ripe for upturn, and once it is determined that rates have bottomed, the market is ripe for downturn. When rates peaked in September, 1974, it was apparent then that the way was at last cleared for a new bull market in stocks. This largely explains why bank trust officers are generally slow to get with the new trend because as rates start to work lower they are still comparatively high, and portfolio managers and their clients would rather cling to those comparatively high rates of return as long as possible rather than risk the money in the market. But the market looks ahead, sensitive to the first evidence that there is a change in the interest rate cycle. So if you have a trust fund don't ever expect any miracles. The bank will keep you mostly liquid for many months after the stock market has bottomed, simply because high interest rates (still high but coming down) is the most effective way the smart money has of keeping the public out of the market and pessimistic while their initial program of stock accumulation begins.

When rates continue to drop (many months after the market bottom), the public will at last jettison their fixed income portfolios and commit funds, previously locked up to take advantage of high interest rates, to the equity market. By this time the smart money *at last has a market which can absorb their starting distribution programs.*

The Stock Split—Major Game Strategy

Thumb rule: If a stock has been in a strong advance and then a split is announced, *the stock is normally seen to be on the verge of a decline and can either be sold and bought back cheaper or sold short.*

Time has not eroded the effectiveness of this rule. The stock split is used as both a single stock indicator and collectively as a market indicator. Most stock splits usually occur after long price advances and their occurrence is taken to mean *distribution.* The stock is being passed from strong hands into weak hands. Upon such split news the early buyers become early sellers, leaving the late buyers holding the bag. Stock splits are generally regarded as *good news.* Good news always provides a cover for those who wish to distribute stock and thus one who buys split stock is playing into the hands of those distributors.

The buying public, always more attracted to good news than bad news, somehow interpret stock splits as offering them a bargain, a stock previously selling at $150 a share now offered at $50 a share on a 3-1 split. They temporarily forget that the stock capitalization is tripled on the split, and as time goes by they tend to *completely forget.* Stock splits occur so as to increase the marketability of the shares, it obviously being easier to induce a buyer to buy a stock at 50 rather than 150.

Stocks which have had long price run-ups become stock split *candidates* long before any announcement is made. When announcements come in those cases, one should take *immediate* action, and there are three options open:

(1) Sell, (2) Go short with a protective stop, (3) Go short against the box if it is important for tax purposes to protect a long term capital gain. If a stock has had a *moderate* advance and a surprise split announcement is made, *then immediate action is not required* and would probably be wrong if taken. The market quickly adjusts to surprises, and in such a case the stock would have some further run-up in price. However, the general theory of stock going from strong hands into weak hands still holds and a more extended decline could be anticipated following such a stock split run-up.

Collectively, the number of companies splitting their stock provides us with an extremely reliable *general market indicator.* In the first phase of a bull market *there is no need to increase the marketability of shares.* They are already at their lows and in a most marketable condition. Not enough time has elapsed to produce the kind of price run-ups which normally precede announced stock splits. Stock splits become more frequent during the second stage of a bull market and *reach their maximum number during the third stage.* During the third stage of a bull market the smart money, no longer confident about the primary trend, *seek to unload their high priced wares on a now confident public* and find a most suitable cover for their distributive tactics by taking advantage of every stock split announcement to give the public all the stock they have.

As a very general rule, one can be increasingly confident in the working of the stock split thumb rule after a bull market has been in force for *1 1/2 years.* Once that amount of time has elasped, the bull market can be considered *mature,* the collective number of stock splits will be quite high, and one can safely assume that the smart money will be looking for every convenient market exit to duck out under the guise of strength.

In a bear market, stock splits are relatively rare. There is no need to increase the marketability of shares inasmuch as the primary downtrend is already doing it in the most painful way.

What about *reverse* splits? A reverse split is much rarer than the ordinary split. Instead of lowering the price of the stock and increasing the stock capitalization, the stock is *raised* in price and the capitalization *reduced.* Why should that be done? Since it is the *opposite* of a stock split, it holds that it should reflect *the opposite of distribution.* So then, assume that a reverse stock split reflects *accumulation* and is therefore *bullish.* But, one may ask, isn't it easier to accumulate a low-priced stock rather than making the shares more expensive? Actually, no. Suppose a stock is very depressed, selling at $2 a share with a capitalization of 10,000,000 shares. If you owned a block of that stock and had held it for a long time, there would be little compulsion for you to want to sell it at the low price of $2 a share. Suppose now that a group of insiders wished to strengthen their control of the company. Instead of making the public want to buy the stock, in this case they would want to create an inducement to make the public want to *sell* the stock. The price has to be put up. Along comes the announcement of a 1-5 reverse split. The stock, previously seeming nonrespectable at $2 a share, now is put up to $10 a share. The public, holding the stock for a long time at $2 a share, is much more likely to want to do a little selling. The insiders pick up the stock at $10 a share because now they find it easier to pick up a *larger* percentage of 2,000,000 shares when the public is in a selling mood rather than a smaller percentage of 10,000,000 shares when the public wouldn't sell. So the general rule on reverse stock splits is the reverse of the stock split thumb rule. A reverse stock split is bullish, suggests accumulation, and the stock should be bought on such announcements. Actually a reverse stock split is a cheaper method for a company to buy in its own stock rather than a tender offer. A tender offer is always made *above the market* so as to speed up the process of accumulation. A reverse stock split may achieve the same purpose *but always holding to market prices.*

One has to be particularly careful in a situation where a stock has had a string of stock splits over the years since such splits tend to hide the tremendous increase in the share capitalization. Suppose a stock is split 3-1 every time it reaches 100 and the initial move started when the stock was selling at 33 with a capitalization of 300,000 shares. After the third split the stock is still priced at 33 but the capitalization has grown from 300,000 shares to 8,100,000 shares. The price of 33 tends to hide the fact that the stock had risen in price from 33 to approximately 900. A late buyer at 33 doesn't realize that is paying 900 based on the old capitalization. The potential supply of the stock now is outstripping the new demand for the stock. So then, each stock split weakens long-term demand and increases the likelihood of an extended price decline.

Another general rule regards the *degree* of the split. The harder the stock is to sell—the greater the split. Low splits of 3-2 or 2-1 are common for stocks selling under $100 a share, but when it comes to distributing a very high-priced stock, it may require a split of 5-1 or even 10-1 to do the job. The general rule is to increase the bearishness on the higher splits.

When a *Dow-Jones industrial stock* splits, it introduces an important change in *volatility* which may have fascinating consequences on the long-term outlook. The Dow-Jones Industrial Average is computed each day by adding the closing prices of the thirty stocks and dividing that total by a *divisor.* Every time a Dow-Jones industrial stock splits *the divisor is lowered.* All the 30 industrial stocks are weighted evenly in the average, and thus a stock split on one of them *will increase the volatility of all of them*. Back in the late 1950's and early 1960's, the divisor on the Dow average stood at over 4. In other words, it required more than a 4-point advance in DuPont, for example, to raise the average a full point. Over the years as a Dow stock would occasionally split, the divisor got lower and lower until by May 1975 the divisor had dropped to 1.598. This means that it now only requires a change of roughly 1 5/8 in any Dow stock to change the average by a full point. It is then obvious that the *volatility* of the Dow Average has been steadily increasing over the years. Like a knife, volatility cuts two ways. The Dow is capable of rising more points than it was 15-20 years ago but, as demonstrated in the 1973-74 bear market, it was also capable of making a sharper drop in terms of points lost.

This subject of Dow *volatility* is one I seldom see discussed anywhere. The public views the Dow-Jones Industrial Average strictly empirically, thinking that a Dow level at 850 is the same as 850 was ten years ago. The two levels could not be identical since each period had a *different* Dow divisor. This raises some interesting questions. The 1973-74 drop in the Dow from 1051.70 to 577.60 totalled 471 points with a divisor at 1.598. Multiplying the point drop in the average by the divisor, it required a total point drop among the 30 industrial stocks amounting to 752 points to produce the drop of 471 points in the average. The 1968-70 drop in the Dow from 985 to 631 totalled 354 points with an average Dow divisor during the period of 2.12. Multiplying the point drop in the average by the divisor, it required a total point drop among the 30 industrial stocks amounting to 752 points to produce the drop of 354 points in the average. *Point for point the drop in the Dow stocks in the 1968-70 period was identical with the drop in the 1973-74 period.* Amazing. Now let us go back to the 1966 drop. In that decline the Dow dropped from 995 to 744 with an average divisor of 2.40. Multiplying the decline of 251 points by the divisor, we see that it required a drop of 582 points in the Dow stocks to produce the drop of 251 points in the Dow average. How about the 1962 drop? Between December, 1961, and June, 1962, the Dow dropped from 734.91 to 535.76, a total drop of 199 points with an average Dow divisor of 3.30. In that drop it required a total point drop among the Dow industrial stocks of 657 points to produce the 199 point drop in the Dow average.

Now one can begin to see some interesting distortions. *The drop in Dow points in the 1961-62 decline was much greater than in 1966, yet the record books say that the Dow dropped 199 points in 1962 and 251 points in 1966.* That hidden divisor is the culprit. In the table below are shown these distortions in all the major bull and bear swings since 1957:

Market Cycle	Swing in Dow Average	Average Divisor	Swing in Dow Points
1957-61	+315	4.40	+1,386 points
1961-62	-199	3.30	- 657
1962-66	+459	2,65	+1,216
1966	-251	2.40	- 582
1966-68	+241	2.20	+ 530
1968-70	-354	2.12	- 752
1970-73	+420	1.70	+ 714
1973-74	-471	1.59	- 752

Studying the above table, one can now spot an important flaw in the Dow-Jones Industrial Average. While it had registered an all-time high in January, 1973, at 1051.70, that high was only made possible by the *increasing volatility* of the average as shown by the *steadily reducing* divisor. If one computes the actual point swings among the Dow industrial stocks and adds them in a cumulative fashion the table now looks like this:

Market Cycle	Swing In Dow Points	Cumulative Swing in Dow Points
1957-61 Bull	+1,386	+1,386
1961-62 Bear	- 657	+ 729
1962-66 Bull	+1,216	+1,945
1966 Bear	- 582	+1,363
1966-68 Bull	+ 530	+1,893
1968-70 Bear	- 752	+1,141
1970-73 Bull	+ 714	+1,855
1973-74 Bear	- 752	+1,103

This revealing table shows the true top in terms of the Dow stocks themselves as 1966 and not 1973. The dropping divisor created a 50-point distortion on the upside in making the 1973 top. The continued drop in the divisor created a 50-point distortion on the downside on the 1974 bottom inasmuch as the Cumulative Point Swing column shows the true level of the Dow, in terms of the stocks themselves, as just very slightly under the 1970 low.

Now we can surmise some interesting things regarding the future. Averaging all the bull swings in the Dow points (not the average, the points) we find that the average upswing in Dow stock points is 961 points (each of the 30 Dow stocks averaging a 32-point gain). At the rate the divisor is dropping, suppose the average divisor stood at 1.25 throughout the bull market which started in 1974. On that basis an average bull swing in the bull market starting in 1974 would take the Dow Average up 768 points. Adding that figure to the 1974 low of 577.60, we come up with a Dow level of 1345.60. If the greatest swing of 1957-61 was repeated with a low divisor of 1.25, the Dow Average increase would be an astounding 1,108 points.

Adding that to the 1974 bottom would project a Dow Average bull market peak of 1,685. If the smaller bull market rise of 1966-68 is repeated off the 1974 bottom, then the lower projected Dow Average level of 1001.60 comes into view. These projections by themselves mean nothing, of course, other than to show *the power of Dow volatility,* all other things remaining equal.

There is no question about future distortions lying ahead. While DuPont or any other Dow stock back in 1957 was required to rise by almost 4 1/2 points to contribute a rise of a full point in the Dow Industrial Average, the requirement was sharply reduced to about 1 5/8 points by 1975. Back in 1964, DuPont stock topped out at about $300 a share, dropping to under $100 a share in both the 1970 and 1974 bottoms. Suppose, for example, that one stock in a new bull market made a full recovery to the old high of $300. *That one swing would add approximately 103 points to the Dow-Jones Industrial Average!* The real fun will begin when someday the divisor drops to under 1.00. When that happens we'll see some 50-point swings in the Dow in one day. However, the volatility knife cuts both ways, but it certainly is a factor to take into consideration when projecting the extent of major bull and bear market swings.

Presidential Election Year Markets

With great accuracy, the market projections described in the original *Strategy* book based on the table of Presidential Election year Markets generally came to pass. Favorable market years were assigned 1964-65 and 1968 as far as the table extended. No revision of the original text is necessary, only the adding of future election years to the table which is done here, extending the series to the year 2000.

With few major exceptions the stock market has shown a tendency to work higher during Presidential Election years. The exceptions, however, are as interesting and illuminating as are the adherents to the higher trend. In order to ascertain which election years are most likely to come under the exceptional heading, it is necessary to do some grouping based on past performance under the headings of most favorable, favorable, neutral, slightly unfavorable, and unfavorable, To begin with, a guiding observation is made which favors election years ending in the number 4. This is based on the observation that years ending in 5 have been almost invariably good years in the stock market, and these advances have been particularly good following the election years of 1904, 1924, 1944, and 1964. The assumption here is that the stock market will be rising in 1984 and 1985. Expectations of an outstanding stock market year for the year 1975 were based on the "5" observation.

Election years (Presidential) ending in zero have more often constituted the exceptions to the generalization that the market has a tendency to work higher in such years. Such was the case in 1920 and 1940, and 1960 pretty much turned out to be a "zero" year as then expected. The year 1980 is the next probably "exceptional" year.

Election years ending in the figure 8 have shown a tendency toward higher stock prices but with less vigor than the years ending in the number 4. Years ending in the number 2 have been neutral on balance. Years ending in the number 6 have been slightly favorable. These years are now placed in their appropriate columns:

Neutral	Favorable	Unfavorable	Most Favorable	Favorable
1892	1896	1900	1904	1908
1912	1916	1920	1924	1928
1932	1936	1940	1944	1948
1952	1956	1960	1964	1968
1972	1976	1980	1984	1988
1992	1996	2000		

Getting back to the mid-decade, favorable stock market years (years ending in 5), it is seen that the stock market was rising in 1885, 1895, 1905, 1915, 1925, 1935, 1945, 1955, 1965, and was outstandingly strong in the early months of 1975. In addition to this, all these rises spilled over into the 6th year of the decade, and thus the stock market was seen to still be rising in 1886, 1896, 1906, 1916, 1926, 1936, 1946, 1956, and for a short while in 1966. However, it is seen that the rises in those years were closer to their terminal points than they were in the year before. Therefore, Presidential Election years ending in the number 6 were followed by sharp reactions the following year. This was seen in the 1917, 1937, and 1957 declines *and serves as a warning for the year 1977.* The over-all record shows a greater inclination for stock prices to fall the year after a Presidental Election, but in the "zero" years such an assumption could be expensively deceptive. Here is an impressive record of consistency in that respect with a few exceptions: The economic upset years of 1837, 1857, 1869, 1873, 1893, 1921, 1929, 1937, 1949, 1957, 1969 and 1973 all had one thing in common, the post-Presidential Election occurrence, again a warning for the year 1977.

A brief reference is made here regarding the Presidential death cycle, a cycle having had no more than passing repercussions on the stock market or none at all. The cycle apparently started in 1840 and the President elected then and every twenty years thereafter has died in office: Harrison, Lincoln, Garfield, McKinley, Harding, Roosevelt, and Kennedy. The cycle has never been explained. One story has it that Indian Chief Tecumseh put a curse on Harrison after the Battle of Tippecanoe and that this curse has continued to modern times. It of course adds interest to who the occupant in the White House will be in 1980. But as for providing market impact, the death of a President would only have such maximum impact according to where in the market cycle it occurred. Harding died in August, 1923, when the market was in the throes of a new bull market. There was scarcely a ripple. Roosevelt died in April, 1945, with the market booming along in another bull market, again no market impact. Kennedy, shot in November, 1963, created a two-hour debacle in the market which immediately ushered in the Johnson bull market.

3

The Volume Complex

THE NEW VOLUME TECHNIQUES

In the ensuing pages I will reintroduce the original concept of on-balance volume, the use of field trends, and the important Climax Indicator. In the review table below, the total daily volume is added to a cumulative total whenever the price of the stock closes higher than the day before, and it is subtracted whenever the price of the stock closes lower than the day before. On the days when the stock closes unchanged in price, the running cumulative volume total remains unchanged. That cumulative volume figure is what I have called on-balance volume, or OBV. Now we watch carefully for upside and downside *breakouts* in the OBV figures, marking upside breakouts with an UP designation and downside breakouts with a DOWN designation. As long as these UP and DOWN designations are *zigzagging* higher, it is said that the field trend is a *rising* one. If the UP and DOWN designations are not in gear (neither zigzagging higher or lower), it is said that the field trend is *doubtful.* When the clusters of UP and DOWN designations are *zigzagging lower,* then it is said that the field trend is a *falling* one. The best way to learn is by doing, and so we will apply the OBV analytical technique to one of the Dow-Jones industrial stocks during the first phase of the bull market which started in October, 1974.

U.S. STEEL

Date	Price	Volume	On–Balance Volume	Designation	Field Trend
10/4 /74	37.25	40,000	40,000		
10/7 /74	38.75	27,900	67,900		
10/8 /74	38.50	28,900	39,000		
10/9 /74	40.50	32,700	71,700	UP	
10/10/74	41.13	57,700	129,400	UP	
10/11/74	41.25	56,300	185,700	UP	

Date	Price	Volume	On–Balance Volume	Designation	Field Trend
10/14/74	41.63	49,300	235,000	UP	
10/15/74	40.13	87,200	147,800		
10/16/74	40.00	30,400	117,400		
10/17/74	41.50	22,900	140,300		
10/18/74	42.00	92,800	233,100		
10/21/74	42.25	34,100	267,200	UP	
10/22/74	40.50	47,400	219,800		
10/23/74	39.00	59,100	160,700		
10/24/74	38.75	37,600	123,100		
10/25/74	38.88	33,400	156,500		
10/28/74	39.00	17,700	174,200		
10/29/74	41.63	35,400	209,600		
10/30/74	42.25	64,900	274,500	UP	
10/31/74	42.25	34,700	274,500	UP	
11/1 /74	41.25	43,600	230,900		
11/4 /74	39.88	76,000	154,900		
11/5 /74	40.00	32,000	186,000		
11/6 /74	40.00	57,300	186,000		
11/7 /74	38.75	71,200	114,800	DOWN	
11/8 /74	38.00	119,800	- 5,000	DOWN	
11/11/74	38.13	42,700	37,700		
11/12/74	37.00	47,600	- 9,900	DOWN	
11/13/74	38.25	56,700	46,800	UP	
11/14/74	38.50	56,200	103,000	UP	
11/15/74	38.00	23,600	79,400		
11/18/74	36.88	35,700	43,700		
11/19/74	36.25	66,400	- 22,700	DOWN	FALLING
11/20/74	37.13	34,800	12,100		FALLING
11/21/74	37.75	27,000	39,100		FALLING
11/22/74	38.00	15,600	54,700		FALLING
11/25/74	37.75	15,300	39,400		FALLING
11/26/74	38.75	17,100	56,500	UP	FALLING
11/27/74	39.13	26,400	82,900	UP	FALLING
11/29/74	38.75	10,400	72,500		FALLING
12/2 /74	38.00	31,300	41,200		FALLING
12/3 /74	37.25	43,600	- 2,400	DOWN	FALLING
12/4 /74	37.63	47,900	45,500		FALLING
12/5 /74	36.50	25,900	19,600		FALLING
12/6 /74	36.25	40,100	- 20,500	DOWN	FALLING
12/9 /74	35.75	27,500	- 48,000	DOWN	FALLING
12/10/74	36.50	30,800	- 17,200		FALLING
12/11/74	36.63	26,000	8,800		FALLING
12/12/74	37.13	26,500	35,300		FALLING
12/13/74	36.75	31,000	4,300		FALLING
12/16/74	36.63	23,400	- 19,100		FALLING
12/17/74	37.25	24,300	5,200		FALLING
12/18/74	37.63	19,400	24,600		FALLING
12/19/74	37.75	13,700	38,300	UP	FALLING
12/20/74	37.50	22,100	16,200		FALLING
12/23/74	37.13	17,700	- 1,500		FALLING

Date	Price	Volume	On–Balance Volume	Designation	Field Trend
12/24/74	37.00	13,500	- 15,000		FALLING
12/26/74	37.63	5,100	- 9,900		FALLING
12/27/74	37.75	14,100	4,200		FALLING
12/30/74	37.63	14,200	- 10,000		FALLING
12/31/74	38.00	40,200	30,200	UP	FALLING
1 /2 /75	38.50	10,300	40,500	UP	FALLING
1 /3 /75	39.63	18,000	58,500	UP	FALLING
1 /6 /75	39.50	16,200	42,300		FALLING
1 /7 /75	39.50	19,400	42,300		FALLING
1 /8 /75	39.38	13,800	28,500		FALLING
1 /9 /75	39.88	24,700	53,200		FALLING
1 /10/75	41.00	48,900	102,100	UP	DOUBTFUL
1 /13/75	40.38	21,600	80,500		DOUBTFUL
1 /14/75	40.00	18,900	61,600		DOUBTFUL
1 /15/75	40.88	18,900	80,500		DOUBTFUL
1 /16/75	40.75	26,300	54,200	DOWN	DOUBTFUL
1 /17/75	41.00	14,000	68,200		DOUBTFUL
1 /20/75	40.88	16,100	52,100	DOWN	DOUBTFUL
1 /21/75	40.88	18,300	52,100	DOWN	DOUBTFUL
1 /22/75	40.75	35,000	17,100	DOWN	DOUBTFUL
1 /23/75	42.00	55,700	72,800	UP	DOUBTFUL
1 /24/75	43.63	58,500	131,300	UP	RISING
1 /27/75	44.75	77,000	208,300	UP	RISING
1 /28/75	45.00	82,800	291,100	UP	RISING
1 /29/75	45.88	77,200	368,300	UP	RISING
1 /30/75	46.38	78,800	447,100	UP	RISING
1 /31/75	47.25	38,900	486,000	UP	RISING
2 /3 /75	48.13	91,900	577,900	UP	RISING
2 /4 /75	47.63	126,600	451,300		RISING
2 /5 /75	48.63	91,300	542,600		RISING
2 /6 /75	49.25	142,300	684,900	UP	RISING
2 /7 /75	50.00	121,800	806,700	UP	RISING
2 /10/75	49.00	104,300	702,400		RISING
2 /11/75	47.63	106,800	595,600		RISING
2 /12/75	47.38	56,700	538,900		RISING
2 /13/75	47.25	103,300	435,600	DOWN	RISING
2 /14/75	48.00	48,900	484,500		RISING
2 /18/75	47.88	47,300	437,200		RISING
2 /19/75	48.25	59,000	496,200	UP	RISING
2 /20/75	49.75	95,500	591,700	UP	RISING
2 /21/75	50.00	105,300	697,000	UP	RISING
2 /24/75	49.25	59,400	637,600		RISING
2 /25/75	48.88	43,500	594,100		RISING
2 /26/75	49.75	59,800	653,900		RISING
2 /27/75	47.88	78,100	575,800	DOWN	RISING
2 /28/75	49.13	48,300	624,100		RISING
3 /3 /75	50.25	190,900	815,000	UP	RISING
3 /4 /75	51.50	183,900	998,900	UP	RISING
3 /5 /75	52.00	137,900	1,136,800	UP	RISING
3 /6 /75	52.50	107,700	1,244,500	UP	RISING
3 /7 /75	53.00	92,000	1,336,500	UP	RISING

Date	Price	Volume	On–Balance Volume	Designation	Field Trend
3 /10/75	52.88	96,900	1,239,600		RISING
3 /11/75	53.63	156,000	1,395,600	UP	RISING
3 /12/75	53.25	81,400	1,314,200		RISING
3 /13/75	52.88	118,800	1,195,400	DOWN	RISING
3 /14/75	55.00	160,400	1,355,800		RISING
3 /17/75	56.00	131,000	1,486,800	UP	RISING
3 /18/75	57.13	244,000	1,730,800	UP	RISING
3 /19/75	56.38	154,700	1,576,100		RISING
3 /20/75	56.50	108,100	1,684,200		RISING
3 /21/75	57.38	89,400	1,773,600	UP	RISING
3 /24/75	55.88	81,900	1,691,700		RISING
3 /25/75	56.00	95,200	1,786,900	UP	RISING
3 /26/75	57.50	98,900	1,885,800	UP	RISING
3 /27/75	58.50	75,700	1,961,500	UP	RISING
3 /31/75	58.75	102,200	2,063,700	UP	RISING
4 /1 /75	57.75	62,100	2,001,600		RISING
4 /2 /75	57.63	70,300	1,931,300		RISING
4 /3 /75	55.88	72,500	1,858,800		RISING
4 /4 /75	55.75	62,600	1,796,200		RISING
4 /7 /75	55.38	66,600	1,729,600		RISING
4 /8 /75	55.50	33,500	1,763,100		RISING
4 /9 /75	57.38	41,500	1,804,600		RISING
4 /10/75	58.88	116,100	1,920,700		RISING
4 /11/75	60.00	114,400	2,035,100		RISING
4 /14/75	60.63	95,800	2,130,900	UP	RISING
4 /15/75	61.63	132,500	2,263,400	UP	RISING
4 /16/75	61.88	99,700	2,363,100	UP	RISING
4 /17/75	62.88	142,900	2,506,000	UP	RISING
4 /18/75	61.88	79,300	2,426,700		RISING
4 /21/75	63.00	70,300	2,497,000		RISING
4 /22/75	62.50	58,900	2,438,100		RISING
4 /23/75	62.25	54,800	2,383,300	DOWN	RISING
4 /24/75	63.25	83.700	2,467,000		RISING
4 /25/75	64.50	105,100	2,572,100	UP	RISING

What you see here in the table of daily on-balance volume readings for U.S. Steel constitutes the daily recording exercise required in order to stay completely abreast of the technical condition of a stock. In order that the exercise is thoroughly understood, each of the OBV breakouts will be pointed out. The first breakout was an upside one occurring on October 9, 1974. The OBV figure of 71,700 was higher *than the last previous* high which was 67,900 on October 7. The breakout therefore got an UP designation. After reaching 235,000 in a series of UPS, OBV fell back rather sharply to 117,400 on October 16. In view of the fact that the last previous low was 39,000, the drop to 117,400 received no down designation. OBV turned at that point and went straight up to a new high at 267,200, bettering the previous high of 235,000. Another UP designation was recorded. Still another OBV high was recorded on October 31, thereby completing the first *cluster* of UP designations. One or more UP or DOWN designations in a group constitutes a cluster. These clusters help denote the true volume trend of the stock. We look for such clusters in either an upward zigzag formation or a downward zigzag formation. When either a previous high or low in the OBV figures is broken without forming a zigzag formation in the clusters, the field trend is termed doubtful. A downward zigzag in the clusters constitutes a falling field trend, and a rising zigzag in the clusters constitutes a rising field trend. The usual transition of growing strength shows a stock going from a falling trend to a doubtful field trend to a rising trend.

On November 7, 1974, the U.S. Steel OBV dropped to 114,800. The last previous low was 154,900 recorded on November 4. Going under a previous low constituted a downside OBV breakout, and thus we see the first DOWN designation in the review. We still don't know anything yet about the field trend because we only have two clusters to work with. OBV then dropped further, stopping at -9,900 on November 12 and completing the cluster of DOWN designations. A new UP was recorded on November 13 as OBV bettered the immediate previous high of 37,700. Another rise occurred on November 14, and that completed the second cluster of UP designations. On November 19 the OBV fell to a new low at -22,700 thereby getting a new DOWN designation. That DOWN designation was under the previous DOWN of November 12 and for the first time here we can identify the field trend for U.S. Steel. It is a falling field trend *as shown by the downward zigzag in* OBV clusters. It takes *four* clusters to identify a field trend. The significant OBV level is always *the last one to occur in a cluster*. So in this case we see an UP at 274,500 on October 31, a DOWN at -9,900 on November 12, an UP at 103,000 on November 14, and a DOWN at -22,700 on November 19, a clearly identified downward zigzag in the OBV clusters. *Once a field trend has been identified it remains in force until proved otherwise.*

The next cluster of UP designations was completed on November 27 at 82,900. Since that figure was well below the previous UP at 103,000, the field trend remained the same, a pattern of descending UPS and DOWNS. The falling field trend was reinforced on December 9, when a new cluster of DOWNS saw OBV at a new low of -48,000. Thereafter, a feeble series of UP designations was telling us nothing as late as January 3, 1975, the UP designation at 58,500 still under the previous 82,900 level of November 27. However, on January 10 the entire technical posture of the stock changed for the better. On that day OBV moved up to 102,100, thereby bettering the 82,900 reading of November 27. This meant that the latest cluster of UP designations had broken the pattern of the downward zigzag cluster pattern. Not yet in a rising zigzag, however, the field trend status shifted on that day from falling to doubtful.

The next test was to see that the new DOWN designations held above the previous DOWN designations, a required condition setting the stage for a rising zigzag in the OBV clusters. All the OBV had to do was hold above the -48,000 level of December 9 on the next series of DOWN designations. The test was beautifully passed when the next series of DOWN designations was completed at 17,100 on January 22. All that remained now was for OBV to move up and pass the 102,100 level of January 10 to put the stock in a strong rising field trend status. Two days later this was accomplished, OBV breaking out to 131,300 on January 24. The field trend status changed from doubtful to rising.

From there on out for the remainder of the period reviewed it was all technical peaches and cream, OBV constantly zigzagging higher. Reporting just the last OBV figure in each cluster it went this way from mid-January, 1975 on: 17,100, 806,700, 435,600, 697,000, 575,800, 1,395,600, 1,195,400, 2,506,000, 2,383,300, and 2,572,100.

THE CLIMAX INDICATOR

In order to compute the daily Climax Indicator, all the on-balance volume breakouts for the 30 Dow-Jones industrial stocks are counted each day, and the net figure constitutes the Climax Indicator or CLX. For instance, if eight stocks had upside breakouts and three had downside breakouts then the CLX reading for that day would stand at +5. A single reading is meaningless. Where the CLX takes on significance is when it is placed alongside the Dow-Jones Industrial Average each day. We can see if advances or declines in the Dow are technically justified by the CLX. For instance, if the Dow average jumps 10 points on a given day and the CLX falls from +8 to +4, there is a definite loss of technical strength on the rise in the average and a decline would be expected. How much of a decline would depend on where the market stood in the normal cycle. The CLX is especially useful when the Dow is making either new highs or new lows because those could be critical market turning points, and the critical nature would be denoted on whether the CLX confirmed the new high or low. Since I created the indicator with that test in mind, originally applying it to the testing of selling climax bottoms, I gave it the name *Climax* Indicator, and the name has been used ever since. However, over the years it has become not only important at major market bottoms and tops but also a very valuable tool in daily application, constantly testing the Dow movements each day for their validity.

It is a dynamic volume indicator, and, by my definitions of volume always taking precedence over price in terms of importance, this indicator will always tell you more about the true technical state of the 30 Dow industrial stocks than will the Dow-Jones Industrial Average itself. Since everybody looks at the *price* average, you have to look at the *volume* movements within the Dow which *precede* the price movements. Since you are concerned here with only on-balance volume *breakouts,* you are dealing with the most *dynamic* type of indicator.

The indicator was created in August, 1961. Having had no past performance to go on at that time, my original concept of the CLX was simply that of an indicator which measured the oversold or overbought status of the market. With only 30 stocks in the Dow-Jones Industrial Average, it is obvious that the maximum readings possible for the indicator would be a -30 on the downside and a +30 on the upside. But, since all stocks never move totally in concert, the actual experience has shown downside moves terminating under -20 and upside moves terminating long after readings of +20 or higher are seen. I had not realized back in 1961 that the greatest importance of the Climax Indicator lay not in a given reading such as -20 or +22 but in the confirmations and non-confirmations of the Dow industrial average, *especially the latter.*

It was learned early in the experience with the CLX that there are definite top and bottom formations, an identifiable *pattern* in the numerical series of CLX readings. Very broadly speaking, here is a typical bottom series: -22, -11, -4, +3, +1, -5, -16*, +2, +10. The CLX drops sharply to an oversold status of -22 as the Dow average registers a very sharp drop. Immediately there is a sharp rebound but the CLX is unable to better the +3 level. A renewed decline sets in, the CLX falling back to +1, then to -5, and sharply lower to -16. On the -16 CLX reading *the Dow drops to a new low.* That is *bullish* because the CLX *did not confirm the new Dow low.* It shows that there was less technical sting on the new Dow low than on the day the -22 reading was recorded. It denotes a downside *exhaustion* and the next important move should be up. The CLX then rebounds from -16 and betters the previous high reading of +3, reading +10 in this case. What we have here is the *rising zigzag* CLX formation: -22, +3, -16, +10 where the Dow makes a new low on the *third* CLX reading in the series of zigzags. This type of CLX zigzag is very important to watch for.

Conversely, the pattern on market tops show the same technical characteristic. Here is a typical series of CLX figures denoting a Dow top: +20, +10, +14, +18*, +13, +8, +11*, +4, +1, -2, +1, +5*, 0, -3, -10. First we see the full extent of technical power on the upside with the very strong CLX reading of +20. The Dow stays near the top and then breaks out on the +18 CLX reading, showing a very slight loss of technical power. It backs off a bit from the high and then the average scores another high, this time on the reduced technical power of a +11 CLX reading. A little wider reaction follows but the average manages to eke out still another high, this time the CLX only managing to climb to a weak +5 reading. Thereafter, the CLX comes down and breaks the previous low of -2, making the bearish downward zigzag formation: +20, -2, +5, -10, the Dow making a new high on the *third* figure in the zigzag series. Again it is a case of *exhaustion*, this time on the upside. Look at it this way: It takes a certain amount of CLX strength to support the weight of the Dow average. In the example just given of a typical top series, suppose the Dow made a series of highs at 950, 960, 980, and 985, and these were dead weights to be lifted by the number of men represented by the CLX figure. In the first case we had 20 men lifting 950 pounds which was no problem. On the second high we had 18 men lifting 960 pounds, a little more work but still no problem. On the third high we had 11 men lifting 980 pounds, much more of an exertion but still no major problem. On the fourth high, however, we had five men struggling to lift 985 pounds, a real backbreaker. They collapsed under the strain and the Dow came tumbling down.

Here is how the CLX worked on some of the major tops and bottoms:

The 1962 Bottom

Date	Dow Average		Climax Indicator	Comment
June 14	563.00	LOW	-28	Vastly oversold
June 15	578.18		+ 2	Too sharp a rise to be maintained
June 18	574.21		- 1	Heads lower for major test
June 19	571.61		- 6	Heads lower for major test
June 20	563.08		-12	Heads lower for major test
June 21	550.49	NEW LOW	-18	Downside Non-confirmation
June 22	539.19	NEW LOW	-24	Downside Non-confirmation
June 25	536.27	NEW LOW	-20	Downside Non-confirmation
June 26	535.76	NEW LOW	-13	Downside Non-confirmation Bottom
June 27	536.98		- 8	Readying for the upside
June 28	557.35		+ 8	Required upward zig zag

The 1966 Top

Date	Dow Average		Climax Indicator	Comment
Jan. 5	981.62	HIGH	+13	Maximum upside strength recorded
Jan. 6	985.46	HIGH	+12	Upside Non-confirmation
Jan. 7	986.13	HIGH	+ 5	Upside Non-confirmation
Jan. 10	985.41		+ 4	Normal pullback
Jan. 11	986.85	HIGH	+ 7	Losing strenght on the highs
Jan. 12	983.96		+ 2	Normal Pullback
Jan. 13	985.69		+ 5	Losing Strength
Jan. 14	987.30	HIGH	+ 3	Further Loss of Strength and another non-confirmation
Jan. 17	989.75	HIGH	+ 8	Inadequate Strength
Jan. 18	994.20	HIGH	+ 8	Inadequate Strength
Jan. 19	991.14		0	Readying for further pullback
Jan. 20	987.80		0	Normal pullback
Jan. 21	988.14		+ 2	Insignificant Rise

Date	Dow Average	Climax Indicator	Comment
Jan. 24	991.42	+ 1	Losing strength again
Jan. 25	991.64	- 4	Necessary downleg forming and another non-confirmation
Jan. 26	990.92	- 5	Growing technical weakness
Jan. 27	990.36	- 3	Remaining technically weak
Jan. 28	985.35	- 7	Downleg extended
Jan. 31	983.51	- 9	Further extension of necessary downleg
Feb. 1	975.89	-14	Necessary downleg completed
Feb. 2	982.29	+ 1	Inadequate strength
Feb. 3	981.23	0	Normal pullback
Feb. 4	986.35	+ 9	Inadequate rise
Feb. 7	989.69	+ 9	Technically weak rise
Feb. 8	991.03	+ 6	Still another non-confirmation
Feb. 9	995.15 HIGH	+10	Final non-confirmation
Feb. 10	990.81	+ 4	Starting crucial confirming downleg
Feb. 11	989.03	- 1	Confirming downleg underway
Feb. 14	987.69	- 3	Further technical weakness
Feb. 15	981.57	- 7	Down movement accelerating
Feb. 16	982.40	- 7	Meaningless rise
Feb. 17	975.27	-13	Further downside acceleration
Feb. 18	975.22	-11	No strength here
Feb. 21	966.48	-14	Very weak formation
Feb. 23	960.13	-16	Very bearish downward zig zag

The 1966 Bottom

Date	Dow Average	Climax Indicator	Comment
Aug. 29	767.03 LOW	-21	Maximum internal weakness
Aug. 30	775.72	- 2	Necessary upleg underway
Aug. 31	788.41	+ 5	Gaining very short term strength
Sept. 1	792.09	+ 8	Short term up pattern extended
Sept. 2	787.69	+ 5	Normal pullback
Sept. 6	782.34	- 3	Normal pullback
Sept. 7	777.39	-10	Normal pullback
Sept. 8	774.88	- 9	Downside non-confirmation
Sept. 9	775.55	- 6	Picking up short term strength
Sept. 12	790.59	+ 8	Short term strength extended
Sept. 13	795.48	+12	Necessary upleg extended
Sept. 14	806.23	+12	Necessary upleg almost complete
Sept. 15	814.30	+16	Necessary upleg complete
Sept. 16	814.30	+ 9	Signal for final decline
Sept. 19	810.85	+ 1	Final decline underway
Sept. 20	806.01	- 5	Final decline underway
Sept. 21	793.59	-12	Broke under Sept. 7 level
Sept. 22	797.77	- 2	Very weak rise
Sept. 23	790.97	- 9	Decline accelerating
Sept. 26	792.70	- 5	Meaningless rise
Sept. 27	794.09	- 3	Meaningless rise
Sept. 28	780.95	-13	Rapid downside acceleration

Date	Dow Average		Climax Indicator	Comment
Sept. 29	772.66		-21	Important test dead ahead
Sept. 30	774.22		-13	Meaningless rise
Oct. 3	757.96	LOW	-21	CLX triple bottom and important downside non-confirmation
Oct. 4	763.19		- 8	A one–day bounce
Oct. 5	755.45	LOW	-11	Another downside non-confirmation
Oct. 6	749.61	LOW	-13	Another downside non-confirmation
Oct. 7	744.32	LOW	-15	Final downside non-confirmation
Oct. 10	754.51		- 1	Coming rapidly off the bottom
Oct. 11	758.63		+ 2	Looking more bullish
Oct. 12	778.17		+11	Strong rise and Dow breakout
Oct. 13	772.93		+ 8	Normal pullback
Oct. 14	771.71		+ 4	Normal pullback
Oct. 17	778.89		+ 5	New strength maintained
Oct. 18	791.87		+12	Zig zagging higher
Oct. 19	785.35		- 1	Normal pullback
Oct. 20	783.68		0	Normal pullback
Oct. 21	787.30		+ 2	Neutral day
Oct. 24	787.85		- 3	Neutral day
Oct. 25	793.09		+ 3	Needs more CLX strength
Oct. 26	801.11		+11	Good pickup in strength
Oct. 27	809.57		+16	Got the required strength

The 1968 Top

Date	Dow Average		Climax Indicator	Comment
Oct. 4	952.95	HIGH	+14	Maximum internal strength
Oct. 7	956.68	HIGH	+11	Loss of internal strength
Oct. 8	956.24		+ 7	Normal setback
Oct. 10	949.78		- 4	Normal setback
Oct. 14	949.06		+ 2	Renewed rise ahead
Oct. 15	955.31		+ 6	Further rise ahead
Oct. 17	958.91	HIGH	+ 2	CLX non-confirmation
Oct. 18	967.49	HIGH	+ 7	CLX non-confirmation
Oct. 21	967.49	HIGH	+ 6	CLX non-confirmation
Oct. 22	963.14		+ 2	Normal pullback
Oct. 24	956.68		0	Normal pullback
Oct. 25	961.28		0	CLX non-confirmation
Oct. 28	957.99		- 4	Wider pullback ahead
Oct. 29	951.08		- 5	Still pulling back
Oct. 31	952.39		+ 2	Meaningless rise
Nov. 1	948.41		- 6	Still on required downleg
Nov. 4	946.23		- 3	CLX says downleg completed
Nov. 6	949.52		+ 1	Final upswing underway
Nov. 7	950.65		+ 1	Final upswing underway
Nov. 8	958.98		+12	Final upswing underway
Nov. 12	964.20		+12	CLX non-confirmation
Nov. 13	967.43		+ 7	CLX non-confirmation
Nov. 14	963.89		+ 4	Normal pullback
Nov. 15	965.88		+ 5	Inadequate strength
Nov. 18	963.76		- 1	Normal pullback
Nov. 19	966.75		0	Inadequate strength
Nov. 21	964.69		- 3	Normal pullback

Date	Dow Average		Climax Indicator	Comment
Nov. 22	967.06		+ 4	Final upswing still in progress
Nov. 25	971.35	HIGH	+ 9	Still inadequate strength
Nov. 26	979.49	HIGH	+11	Still inadequate strength
Nov. 27	976.32		+ 2	Normal pullback
Nov. 29	985.05	HIGH	+ 8	CLX non-confirmation
Dec. 2	983.34		+ 6	Normal pullback
Dec. 3	985.21	HIGH	+ 1	Flagrant non-confirmation. The top
Dec. 5	977.69		- 4	More apparent technical weakness
Dec. 6	978.24		- 3	Meaningless rise
Dec. 7	979.36		- 4	CLX non-confirmation
Dec. 10	977.67		- 1	Upside hesitation
Dec. 12	977.13		- 3	Normal pullback
Dec. 13	981.98		+ 2	Inadequate strength
Dec. 16	976.32		- 2	Confirming downleg underway
Dec. 17	970.91		- 9	Bearish downward zig zag

The 1970 Bottom

Date	Dow Average		Climax Indicator	Comment
April 28	724.33	LOW	-24	Maximum CLX weakness
April 29	737.39		- 3	Sharp but meaningless bounce
April 30	736.07		- 3	Further slide ahead
May 1	733.63		- 3	Unable to stabilize
May 4	714.56	LOW	-15	Some hope for a rebound. Non-confirmation
May 5	709.81	LOW	-12	Some hope for a rebound. Non-confirmation
May 6	718.40		1	Just a bounce
May 7	723.07		+ 1	Just a bounce
May 8	717.73		- 1	Recent gains not holding
May 11	710.07		- 7	Set to make new lows
May 12	704.59	LOW	-12	Another non-confirmation
May 13	693.84	LOW	-17	New weakness confirmed
May 14	684.79	LOW	-22	Must have necessary upleg
May 15	702.22		- 1	Necessary upleg
May 18	702.81		+ 2	Upleg completed
May 19	691.40		-10	Going into the final slide
May 20	676.62	LOW	-20	Building for climax bottom
May 21	665.25	LOW	-20	CLX measures some developing down-side resistance
May 22	662.17	LOW	-14	CLX non-confirmation
May 25	641.36	LOW	-21	CLX stays above the April 28 level
May 26	631.16	LOW	-21	CLX non-confirmation, downside exhaustion, final bottom
May 27	663.20		+ 4	Bullish upward zig zag as required

The 1973 Top

Date	Dow Average		Climax Indicator	Comment
Dec. 11 (72)	1036.27	HIGH	+12	Maximum internal strength
Dec. 12 (72)	1033.19		0	Signalling necessary downleg
Dec. 13 (72)	1030.48		- 5	Necessary downleg fully underway
Dec. 14 (72)	1025.06		- 7	Still dropping
Dec. 15 (72)	1027.24		- 6	Meaningless rise
Dec. 18 (72)	1013.25		-14	Pulling back sharply

Date	Dow Average	Climax Indicator		Comment
Dec. 19 (72)	1009.19		-17	Still signalling retreat
Dec. 20 (72)	1004.82		-13	CLX signalling another advance ahead
Dec. 21 (72)	1000.00		-12	Reaffirms new rally ahead
Dec. 22 (72)	1004.21		- 5	New rally underway
Dec. 26 (72)	1006.70		- 1	Normal rise
Dec. 27 (72)	1007.68		- 1	Final rally underway
Dec. 29 (72)	1020.02		+11	Accelerated runup
Jan. 2	1031.68		+16	Final countdown
Jan. 3	1043.80	HIGH	+14	Some loss of strength
Jan. 4	1039.81		+ 5	Normal pullback
Jan. 5	1047.49	HIGH	+ 9	CLX non-confirmation
Jan. 8	1047.86	HIGH	+ 8	CLX non-confirmation
Jan. 9	1047.11		+ 2	Sets stage for final failure
Jan. 10	1046.06		0	Makes final nonconfirmation certain
Jan. 11	1051.70		+ 9	CLX non-confirmation, upside exhaustion, final top
Jan. 12	1039.36		- 1	Rapid breakdown begins
Jan. 15	1025.59		-10	Downward zig zag already completed
Jan. 16	1024.31		- 9	Brief bounce signalled
Jan. 17	1029.12		- 4	Just a bounce
Jan. 18	1029.12		- 5	Renewed CLX weakness
Jan. 19	1026.19		-10	Renewed CLX weakness
Jan. 22	1018.81		-12	Breaks double bottom at -10
Jan. 23	1018.66		- 6	No strength here. Damage already done
Jan. 24	1004.59		-19	Major confirmation of weakness. CLX breaks under December low.

The 1974 Bottom

Date	Dow Average	Climax Indicator		Comment
Sept. 13	627.19	LOW	-24	Maximum internal weakness
Sept. 16	639.78		- 4	Starting necessary upleg
Sept. 17	648.78		+ 5	Necessary upleg extended
Sept. 18	651.91		+ 5	Upleg not completed
Sept. 19	674.05		+15	Necessary upleg completed
Sept. 20	670.76		+ 7	Starting final plunge
Sept. 23	663.72		- 4	Picking up speed on the downside
Sept. 24	654.10		- 8	Dropping rapidly
Sept. 25	649.95		- 7	Insignificant non-confirmation
Sept. 26	637.98		-10	Renewed weakness
Sept. 27	621.95	LOW	-13	CLX non-confirmation
Sept. 30	607.87	LOW	-20	CLX non-confirmation
Oct. 1	604.82	LOW	- 9	Setting stage for final nonconfirmation Non-confirmation
Oct. 2	601.53	LOW	- 8	Non-confirmation
Oct. 3	587.61	LOW	-16	Non-confirmation
Oct. 4	584.56	LOW	-11	CLX non-confirmation, downside exhaustion, final bottom
Oct. 7	607.56		+ 7	Starting initial recovery move
Oct. 8	602.63		0	Normal pullback
Oct. 9	631.02		+18	Bullish upward zig zag as required

REVIEWING THE CLX TOP AND BOTTOM PATTERNS

I have described here the *final zig-zag movement* that accompanies all major tops and bottoms wherein the Climax Indicator forms the zigzag at Points A, B, C, and D with the Dow-Jones Industrial Average recording the maximum high or low at Point C which is marked in each instance as a major CLX non-confirmation. Putting the CLX readings in their ABCD order clinches the CLX zigzag theory and bottom and top non-confirmations.

Market Bottoms

	Point A	Point B	Point C	Point D
The 1962 Bottom	-28	+ 2	-13	+ 8
The 1966 Bottom	-21	+16	-15	+16
The 1970 Bottom	-24	+ 2	-21	+ 4
The 1974 Bottom	-24	+15	-11	+18

Market Tops

	Point A	Point B	Point C	Point D
The 1966 Top	+13	-14	+10	-16
The 1968 Top	+14	- 6	+ 1	- 9
The 1973 Top	+12	-17	+ 9	-19

MORE ON THE FIELD TRENDS

A question certain to be asked at this point concerns the zigzagging movements of the Climax Indicator: Obviously there must be many other times when the CLX zigzags in the A-B-C-D manner described above. How can we differentiate between those zigzags and the major ones described above? The answer pretty much depends on the status of the field trends on the Dow industrial stocks as well as the all-important *time* factor. You saw in the on-balance volume study of U.S. Steel the regularly recurring UP and DOWN designations. Everytime such a designation is made it means that there is an OBV breakout, either on the upside or the downside. Each such breakout contributes toward the Climax Indicator reading for that day. As the major technical status of a stock is shifting it becomes clear that the *quality* of the OBV breakouts also is shifting. You noted in the Steel example that the field trend for the stock bullishly shifted from falling, to doubtful, to rising. It then becomes obvious that a DOWN designation has one kind of technical impact in a falling field trend, another kind of impact in a doubtful field trend, and a much smaller or even insignificant impact in a rising field trend. But in making up the daily Climax Indicator all the UP and DOWN designations are given equal weight regardless of their quality. That does require that one must take into account the field trend mix among the 30 Dow-Jones industrial stocks. For instance, if a clear majority of the Dow stocks were in rising field trends, a low CLX reading of -19 would more likely constitute a buying level, whereas if the majority of Dow stocks were in falling fields trends, the -19 reading would have serious bearish impact implying a further sharp drop in the market. The rule to be kept in mind is as follows: If the field trend mix among the 30 Dow industrial stocks is improving, then high CLX readings take on more importance and low CLX readings take on less importance. If the field trend mix is deteriorating, then the high CLX readings take on less importance while the low CLX readings take on more importance.

In order to demonstrate the changing impact of high and low Climax Indicator readings correlating with the field trend mix of the 30 Dow-Jones industrial stocks, the following data covers the period from January, 1970 to April, 1975:

Dow Field Trends and The Climax Indicator

Week Ending	Field Trend Mix	Net Field Trend	Highest CLX	Lowest CLX
1/ 7/70	7-15- 8	- 1	+13	- 4
1/14/70	8-14- 8	0	- 2	-15
1/21/70	7-14- 9	- 2	0	-10
1/28/70	4-12-14	-10	+ 1	-17
2/ 4/70	1-15-14	-13	+ 6	-23
2/11/70	1-14-15	-14	+10	- 8
2/18/70	3-14-13	-10	+13	- 4
2/25/70	7-13-10	- 3	+15	+ 2
3/ 4/70	13-10- 7	+ 6	+16	+ 1
3/11/70	14-10- 6	+ 8	+ 6	-10
3/18/70	13-11- 6	+ 7	- 4	-16
3/25/70	14-10- 6	+ 8	+22	- 8
4/ 1/70	13-11- 6	+ 7	+16	- 1
4/ 8/70	13-12- 5	+ 8	+ 6	- 3
4/15/70	9-12- 9	0	+ 5	-11
4/22/70	6-14-10	- 4	- 8	-17
4/29/70	2-14-14	-12	- 3	-24
5/ 6/70	2-15-13	-11	- 1	-15
5/13/70	2-14-14	-12	+ 1	-17
5/20/70	4-10-16	-12	+ 2	-22
5/27/70	1-11-18	-17	+ 4	-21

Week Ending	Field Trend Mix	Net Field Trend	Highest CLX	Lowest CLX
6/ 3/70	1-16-13	-12	+15	+ 9
6/10/70	1-15-14	-13	0	-11
6/17/70	2-13-15	-13	+13	-17
6/24/70	3-12-15	-12	+15	-11
7/ 1/70	3-13-14	-11	- 5	-15
7/15/70	3-13-14	-11	+11	-17
7/24/70	9-14- 7	+ 2	+22	- 5
7/31/70	12-12- 6	+ 6	+ 9	- 4
8/ 7/70	11-13- 6	+ 5	+ 4	- 8
8/14/70	10-13- 7	+ 3	- 1	-12
8/21/70	13-11- 6	+ 7	+22	- 9
8/28/70	16-11- 3	+13	+22	+ 8
9/ 4/70	16-10- 4	+12	+11	- 4
9/18/70	16-10- 4	+12	+ 8	-13
9/25/70	16- 8- 6	+10	+10	-13
10/ 2/70	16- 7- 7	+ 9	+ 5	+ 1
10/ 9/70	17-11- 2	+15	+16	- 3
10/16/70	16-12- 2	+14	+ 4	- 8
10/23/70	14-13- 3	+11	- 1	- 9
10/30/70	11-13- 6	+ 5	+ 3	- 9
11/ 6/70	11-13- 6	+ 5	+12	- 1
11/13/70	12-13- 5	+ 7	+13	-14
11/23/70	10-12- 8	+ 2	+ 7	-11
12/ 2/70	14-12- 4	+10	+25	+ 8
12/ 9/70	15-12- 3	+12	+18	+ 2
12/16/70	14-14- 2	+12	+10	- 1
1/ 6/71	14-12- 4	+10	+18	- 1
1/13/71	14- 9- 7	+ 7	+ 9	+ 1
1/20/71	13-11- 6	+ 7	+10	+ 3
1/27/71	13-13- 4	+ 9	+ 9	- 2
2/ 3/71	11-16- 3	+ 8	+12	+ 2
2/10/71	10-18- 2	+ 8	+ 8	+ 2
2/17/71	11-19- 0	+11	+12	+ 5
2/24/71	12-17- 1	+11	+ 1	-17
3/ 3/71	12-16- 2	+10	+ 4	- 2
3/10/71	12-13- 5	+ 7	+12	0
3/17/71	12-13- 5	+ 7	+17	0
3/24/71	10-15- 5	+ 5	+ 5	-13
3/31/71	11-12- 7	+ 4	0	- 7
4/ 7/71	12-12- 6	+ 6	+ 7	- 3
4/14/71	11-14- 5	+ 6	+10	+ 7
4/21/71	12-13- 5	+ 7	+15	- 2
4/28/71	13-11- 6	+ 7	+ 2	- 1
5/ 5/71	14-10- 6	+ 8	+ 1	-10
5/12/71	14-10- 6	+ 8	+ 5	- 4
5/19/71	10- 8-12	- 2	+ 4	-10
5/26/71	10- 8-12	- 2	- 3	-17
6/ 2/71	10-10-10	0	+ 7	- 4
6/ 9/71	8-11-11	- 3	+ 5	-12
6/16/71	8-11-11	- 3	± 1	- 5
6/23/71	6-11-13	- 7	- 3	-22
6/30/71	7-10-13	- 6	+12	- 1

Week Ending	Field Trend Mix	Net Field Trend	Highest CLX	Lowest CLX
7/ 7/71	8-12-10	- 2	+12	+ 4
7/14/71	8-11-11	- 3	+ 8	-10
7/21/71	8-15- 7	+ 1	+ 3	-12
7/28/71	6-13-11	- 5	+ 2	-14
8/ 4/71	3-15-12	- 9	- 2	-20
8/11/71	2-16-12	-10	+ 3	-11
8/18/71	4-13-13	- 9	+20	- 6
9/ 1/71	5-12-13	- 8	+ 5	- 3
9/ 8/71	10-10-10	0	+13	- 3
9/15/71	11- 9-10	+ 1	+ 4	-10
9/22/71	9- 9-12	- 3	+ 6	-20
9/29/71	7-10-13	- 6	- 4	-14
10/ 6/71	6-12-12	- 6	+10	0
10/13/71	7-14- 9	- 2	+ 8	- 5
10/27/71	3-15-12	- 9	- 9	-14
11/ 3/71	2-15-13	-11	+11	-12
11/10/71	2-15-13	-11	+ 5	- 8
11/17/71	1-16-13	-12	+ 7	-15
12/ 1/71	4-16-10	- 6	+15	- 7
12/ 8/71	7-14- 9	- 2	+14	0
12/15/71	9-13- 8	+ 1	+ 8	- 3
12/22/71	12-11- 7	+ 5	+18	+ 4
1/ 5/72	20- 7- 3	+17	+15	- 7
1/12/72	18-10- 2	+16	+13	+ 1
1/19/72	14-13- 3	+11	+ 4	- 6
1/26/72	8-16- 6	+ 2	- 2	-14
2/ 2/72	11-13- 6	+ 5	+ 5	- 1
2/ 9/72	10-14- 6	+ 4	+ 8	- 3
2/16/72	9-13- 8	+ 1	+ 8	- 3
2/23/72	7-14- 9	- 2	+ 8	-10
3/ 1/72	9-12- 9	0	+ 9	+ 1
3/ 8/72	9-12- 9	0	+13	+ 1
3/15/72	8-13- 9	- 1	+ 1	- 9
3/22/72	8-12-10	- 2	+ 5	-10
3/28/72	10- 9-11	- 1	+ 6	- 5
4/ 5/72	11- 9-10	+ 1	+13	- 5
4/12/72	10-12- 8	+ 2	+11	- 2
4/19/72	10-13- 7	+ 3	+ 6	- 1
4/26/72	9-13- 8	+ 1	+ 2	-18
5/ 3/72	9-11-10	- 1	+ 1	-10
5/10/72	7-12-11	- 4	+ 3	-20
5/17/72	8-11-11	- 3	+11	- 3
5/24/72	9-16- 5	+ 4	+13	+ 5
6/ 7/72	8-17- 5	+ 3	- 5	-12
6/14/72	8-15- 7	+ 1	- 1	-15
6/21/72	6-16- 8	- 2	+ 8	- 1
6/28/72	7-10-13	- 6	- 1	-14
7/ 5/72	7- 9-14	- 7	0	-11
7/12/72	6- 9-15	- 9	+ 8	- 7
7/19/72	5- 9-16	-11	+ 2	-11
7/26/72	6-10-14	- 8	+18	- 5
8/ 2/72	7-10-13	- 6	+11	- 4
8/ 9/72	8-12-10	- 2	+12	+ 1

Week Ending	Field Trend Mix	Net Field Trend	Highest CLX	Lowest CLX
8/16/72	8-14- 8	0	+15	+ 3
8/23/72	10-14- 6	+ 4	+13	+ 2
8/30/72	12-11- 7	+ 5	- 1	- 9
9/13/72	15- 7- 8	+ 7	+14	-13
9/20/72	12- 6-12	0	+ 1	-12
9/27/72	9- 8-13	- 4	+14	-11
10/ 4/72	10- 7-13	- 3	+15	- 3
10/11/72	7-10-13	- 6	+ 2	-11
10/18/72	8- 8-14	- 6	+ 4	-18
10/25/72	10- 9-11	- 1	+20	+ 4
11/ 1/72	12- 6-12	0	+ 9	- 7
11/ 8/72	13-10- 7	+ 6	+16	+ 7
11/15/72	14-10- 6	+ 8	+13	0
11/21/72	16- 9- 5	+11	+12	0
11/29/72	16-12- 2	+14	+ 9	- 4
12/ 6/72	18-11- 1	+17	+ 8	+ 2
12/13/72	19- 8- 3	+16	+12	- 5
12/26/72	16- 8- 6	+10	- 1	-17
1/ 2/73	17- 7- 6	+11	+16	- 5
1/17/73	12-11- 7	+ 5	+ 9	-10
1/24/73	11- 9-10	+ 1	- 5	-19
1/31/73	11- 8-11	0	0	-10
2/ 7/73	6- 8-16	-10	- 3	-16
2/14/73	6-12-12	- 6	+11	-16
2/21/73	5-11-14	- 9	- 2	-10
2/28/73	4-10-16	-12	- 3	-15
3/ 7/73	7-11-12	5	+23	- 1
3/14/73	8-11-11	- 3	+ 6	- 2
3/21/73	5-11-14	- 9	- 5	-16
3/28/73	3-14-13	-10	+10	-19
4/ 4/73	5-12-13	- 8	+12	- 7
4/11/73	5-15-10	- 5	+16	- 7
4/18/73	8-13- 9	- 1	+ 3	- 3
4/25/73	7-15- 8	- 1	+ 4	-15
5/ 2/73	5-17- 8	- 3	+ 8	-14
5/ 9/73	5-19- 6	- 1	+11	0
5/16/73	4-13-13	- 9	- 4	-18
5/23/73	4-10-16	-12	- 7	-23
5/30/73	6- 9-15	- 9	+10	- 7
6/ 6/73	6- 8-16	-10	+ 4	-13
6/13/73	8- 7-15	- 7	+16	-2
6/20/73	4- 8-18	-14	- 3	-20
6/27/73	4- 9-17	-13	+ 8	-11
7/ 3/73	3-10-17	-14	+ 8	-11
7/11/73	6- 9-15	- 9	+17	-10
7/18/73	7-11-12	- 5	+11	- 7
7/25/73	7-16- 7	0	+14	+ 4
8/ 1/73	6-17- 7	- 1	+ 6	-15
8/ 8/73	5-18- 7	- 2	- 4	- 9
8/15/73	3-17-10	- 7	- 6	-20

Week Ending	Field Trend Mix	Net Field Trend	Highest CLX	Lowest CLX
8/29/73	4-15-11	- 7	+16	- 4
9/ 5/73	8-11-11	- 3	+16	+ 8
9/12/73	7-10-13	- 6	+ 8	- 7
9/19/73	9-11-10	- 1	+18	- 3
9/26/73	15-12- 3	+12	+20	+13
10/ 3/73	14-14- 2	+12	+10	+ 1
10/10/73	15-14- 1	+14	+ 8	- 9
10/17/73	14-14- 2	+12	+ 6	- 5
10/24/73	16-12- 2	+14	+ 3	- 9
10/31/73	12-13- 5	+ 7	+17	- 9
11/ 7/73	6-15- 9	- 3	- 5	-20
11/14/73	3-16-11	- 8	+ 1	-22
11/20/73	3-15-12	- 9	+ 4	-11
12/ 5/73	1-11-18	-17	- 8	-20
12/12/73	2-14-14	-12	+14	- 7
12/19/73	2-15-13	-11	+15	-10
1/ 2/74	6-14-10	- 4	+13	+ 3
1/ 9/74	10-11- 9	+ 1	+20	-15
1/16/74	8-12-10	- 2	+ 6	-12
1/23/74	9-11-10	- 1	+12	- 6
1/30/74	9-11-10	- 1	+ 4	-11
2/ 6/74	6-11-13	- 7	- 6	-23
2/13/74	6-11-13	- 7	+ 1	-16
2/20/74	7-11-12	- 5	+13	- 1
2/27/74	11-11- 8	+ 3	+21	+ 9
3/ 6/74	10-11- 9	+ 1	+13	- 4
3/13/74	12-14- 4	+ 8	+14	- 3
3/20/74	11-15- 4	+ 7	+ 2	-15
3/27/74	12-11- 7	+ 5	+ 2	- 8
4/ 3/74	9-13- 8	+ 1	+ 2	-19
5/ 1/74	5-10-15	-10	+13	-19
5/ 8/74	4-13-13	- 9	+ 9	- 2
5/15/74	6-11-13	- 7	+17	- 7
5/22/74	2-11-17	-15	-11	-25
6/19/74	2-19- 9	- 7	+20	-18
6/26/74	4-13-13	- 9	- 1	-22
7/10/74	3-11-16	-13	- 7	-23
7/17/74	2-15-13	-11	+ 8	-13
7/24/74	2-14-14	-12	+12	+ 1
7/31/74	2-12-16	-14	- 4	-14
8/ 7/74	3-14-13	-10	+15	-14
8/14/74	3-13-14	-11	+ 1	-15
8/21/74	1-13-16	-15	- 1	-18
8/28/74	1-10-19	-18	-11	-18
9/ 4/74	1- 9-20	-19	+ 4	-21
9/11/74	3- 8-19	-16	+16	- 8
9/25/74	1-13-16	-15	+15	- 8
10/ 9/74	1-14-15	-14	+18	-16
10/23/74	5-12-13	- 8	+10	-13
11/ 6/74	7-11-12	- 5	+14	- 5
11/20/74	2-19- 9	- 7	- 1	-26

Week Ending	Field Trend Mix	Net Field Trend	Highest CLX	Lowest CLX
12/ 4/74	1-15-14	-13	+ 7	-12
12/18/74	5-14-11	- 6	+ 8	- 5
12/31/74	9-12- 9	0	+13	0
1/15/75	12-16- 2	+10	+22	- 2
1/29/75	20-10- 0	+20	+28	+ 5
2/12/75	20-10- 0	+20	+13	- 4
3/26/75	18- 9- 3	+15	+21	-19
4/ 9/75	14-10- 6	+ 8	+ 7	-15
4/23/75	13- 9- 8	+ 5	+18	-11

Earlier errors in interpreting what had appeared to be the critical Climax Indicator levels, the sharp rises to +20 or higher and the equally sharp drops to levels of -20 or lower, will largely be eliminated by a strict following of the *Net Field Trend*. In the table just shown here enough data is given to clearly show how the Net Field Trend ended the 1968-70 bear market, how it began the 1970-73 bull market and ended, how it behaved throughout the 1973-74 bear market, and how it so ably confirmed the new bull market that started in late 1974. Definite repeating characteristics are seen throughout the market cycle.

Entering the final year of the 1968-70 bear market, the table shows that the Net Field Trend figure was zigzagging bearishly lower, dropping to a low -14 reading on the week of February 11, rallying weakly to a +8 reading the week of March 11, and then crashing down to the bear market low figure of -17 the week of May 27. It reflected the *true trend of the market.*

Entering the bull market starting in 1970, the Net Field Trend figure rallied from the -17 bear market low and quickly moved up to a *plus* level. The figure then stayed in plus territory without exception from July, 1970 to May, 1971, *a characteristic only seen in bull markets.* The first high level was reached at +15 the week of October 9, 1970. Thereafter the figure traced out a normal downward zigzag accompanying the late 1971 market decline, dropping to -12 in late November, 1971. Following that drop, the figure moved up strongly to a +17 reading the week of January 5, 1972, bettering the previous high of +15 recorded in October, 1970, showing the major trend to still be up. It pulled back thereafter normally to -11 in July, 1972 (holding above the November, 1971 decline level) and then shot up to the peak +17 reading in early December, 1972. As the Dow industrial average tacked on the final 50 points of the bull market, the *Net Field Trend* figure steadily dropped from the +17 climactic high reflecting the loss of internal strength. The bull market was over and a new pattern was about to unfold.

The bear market of 1973-74 was vicious and unrelenting and the *Net Field Trend* tells the story. It dropped into minus territory by February, 1973, and stayed there without exception from February to late September, 1973, *a characteristic only seen in bear markets.* The lowest level for the *Net Field Trend* figure on that initial declining period was -14 in June and July of 1973. The sharp market rally in September and October of 1973 had *no sustaining power,* the Net Field Trend figure only able to put together five readings in the plus territory. Following the quick rise to +14, the figure crashed to a new bear market low of -17 in the week of December 5, 1973, breaking under the previous low of -14 seen the previous June and July, thus extending the longer term zigzagging downtrend. This was followed by *insufficient strength* in the spring of 1974, the Net Field Trend figure only able to rally to +8 by the middle of March and well short of the +14 rally figure seen in October, 1973. The figure fell back into bearish minus territory, climaxing at a new bear market low of -19 in early September, 1974. The final 60-70 point drop in the Dow industrial average occurred after the Net Field Trend figure had bottomed at -19, proof that the long bear market was virtually over.

Entering the bull market starting in October, 1974, the Net Field Trend figure rallied from the -19 bear market low and completed the very bullish upward zigzag into plus territory by the middle of January, 1975. Extremely bullish readings of +20 were reached early in the new cycle, attesting to a degree of technical strength which was not expected to go away in a hurry.

In these descriptions of the movements of the Net Field Trend figure covering a period of five years *a basic repeating pattern begins to unfold.* Based on that pattern, a hypothetical model can be set up and the action of the *Net Field Trend* figure in the future should always be checked out against that model.

MODEL ACTION OF THE NET FIELD TREND FIGURE
IN BULL AND BEAR MARKETS

Bull Market Action

1. Rallies from the -17 to -19 bear market low and quickly returns to the plus level, where it remains for many months, hitting peak levels of anywhere from +15 to +20.
2. On an intermediate decline the Net Field Trend figure falls back in the minus zone but holds well above the previous bear market bottom, dropping back normally to the -12 to -14 area.
3. Recovering from the intermediate decline, the Net Field Trend figure rapidly returns to previous high levels, usually bettering them, but, if the previous high was a very strong +20 reading, at least equalling it.

4. One more normal pullback occurs, the Net Field Trend figure holding above the previous intermediate decline level, a figure as low as -11 acceptable.

5. A final burst of strength ends the bull market, the *Net Field Trend* figure peaking out anywhere between +17 and +20. *The peak in that figure occurs three to five weeks before the final Dow top.* As the Dow makes the final run-up, the Net Field Trend figure records a steady fall, reflecting the loss of internal strength

Bear Market Action

1. Declines rapidly from the +17 to +20 bull market peak and within a few weeks is in minus territory where it remains for many months, hitting low levels of anywhere from -14 to -16.

2. On an intermediate advance (the rally that fools the majority), the *Net Field Trend* figure shoots back up into plus territory well short of the previous bull market peak level and cannot stay there more than a few weeks.

3. Breaking down from that rally top, the *Net Field Trend* figure quickly crashes below the previous low, making a new low for the bear market (usually in the -15 to -17 area).

4. Some minor attempts to turn the market around only see the Net Field Trend figure rallying back to the +6 to +8 level at the very best, soon giving way to renewed weakness.

5. Final drop characterized by series of very low Net Field Trend readings, climaxing in the -17 to -19 area. Here the final Dow low may or may not be coincident with the Net Field Trend figure low.

The entire model is geared to the typical 4 to 4 1/2 year market cycle. The *Net Field Trend* figure must be added to the family of *major* market indicators. Its importance lies in not only reflecting the *true volume trend* of the 30 Dow industrial stocks, *but in putting all Climax Indicator readings in the proper perspective.* It then becomes obvious that a high plus reading for the Climax Indicator such as a +20 reading *has no bullish inference if the Net Field Trend figure is in an established downtrend. Conversely, low readings of -20 or lower have no bearish inference if the Net Field Trend figure is in an established uptrend.* The truth of this was always there but this is the first time I have put it down as a formal statement. It explains all previous errors in CLX misinterpretation, errors which had put misplaced faith in high CLX readings especially during bear markets. Too much stress had been previously placed on the empirical value of the Climax Indicator alone without regard to the trend of the market. *Now the CLX is irrevocably locked together with the trend,* and this casts new light and importance on the A-B-C-D zigzags of the Climax Indicator. Let me add here, that the only time a high CLX reading is bullish in a bear market *is when it is reflected by a change of trend within three to five weeks after it is recorded.* Also, *the only time a low CLX reading of -20 or lower is bearish in a bull market is when it is reflected by a change of trend within three to five weeks after it is recorded.* Otherwise all high CLX readings are bullish in a bull market and low CLX readings are essentially bearish in a bear market although very short term they often signal overbought and oversold markets. This represents a tremendous development of refined theory since the Climax Indicator was first introduced in my *New Key* book back in 1963. In those earlier presentations of on-balance volume theory, I had simply assigned overbought and oversold implications to high and low CLX readings regardless of the market trend. Now the indicator becomes far more sophisticated and more sensitive to show up *the market traps* which so often occur at the C point in the A-B-C-D Climax Indicator zigzags. The C point, you will remember, is the point at which the Dow-Jones industrial average makes a new high as the CLX zigzags lower, or the point at which the average makes a new low as the CLX zigzags higher. The C point then becomes the principal *spike or barb* upon which the bears are impaled in a developing upswing, and the bulls are fooled in a developing market downswing. Those deceptions at the C point are what the smart money game followers should constantly be on the watch for. Those are the *key non-confirmations* between the Dow and the Climax Indicator at the C point in the A-B-C-D CLX major zigzags. But when now related to the Net Field Trend figures, each turning point is far better explained, even to the point of explaining why *small declines* follow a bearish downward CLX zigzag in a bull market, and only *limited advances* follow a bullish looking upward CLX zigzag during a bear market.

Upside and Downside Exhaustion Better Explained

In the keeping of daily on-balance volume records for the Dow-Jones industrial stocks, it is found to be additionally important to note the day upon which each Dow stock records its on-balance volume peak. Since each peak can be superseded by new peaks, we are only interested in the last peak recorded. Its importance will grow as time passes, and it is seen that it is not superseded by a new peak. In other words, *we are interested in the dates upon which each Dow stock tops out OBVwise.* In a rising market an increasing number of such Dow OBV peaks would enable one to pinpoint the area of maximum upside *exhaustion.* Picture thirty men carrying an immense weight collectively. The higher the Dow average goes the heavier it gets because there are fewer of these men to carry the increased weight. By the time over half the men quit, the burden on the remaining half is becoming intolerable, and by the time over twenty of them have quit, the Dow average is about to fall of its own weight. It is an ideal technique to follow in order to identify major or intermediate term tops after the Dow has risen several hundred points in an extended rise. Here is an example of the technique in action:

Between December 6, 1974, and May 14, 1975, the Dow-Jones Industrial Average rose 281 points, making a remarkable advance from 577.60 to 858.73 in that short period of time. Without following any technique other than simply recording the daily on-balance volume figures for each of the Dow-Jones Industrial stocks and noting their dates of peaking out, here is how effectively the study of upside exhaustion can pinpoint the area of maximum vulnerability following an extensive Dow rise:

The first stock to top out OBV wise was *International Nickel* on January 29, 1975, *leaving 29 stocks left to support the average.* Then on February 6, *Johns Manville* peaked, *leaving 28 stocks to support the average.* On February 20, *Esmark* topped out, still no problems, *27 stocks still left to support the average.* On February 27, *Owens-Illinois* peaked, *still a comfortable number of 26 stocks remaining to support the average.* On March 4, *Allied Chemical* left the arena of strength, *leaving 25 stocks left to support the average.* On March 5, *Texaco* left the circle of strength, *leaving 24 stocks to support the average.* Then on March 10, *General Electric* reached its OBV peak, *leaving 23 stocks to support the average.* On March 17, *American Can* made its exit, *leaving 22 stocks to support the average.* On March 20, *General Foods* peaked, *leaving* 21 stocks to support the average. Deterioration accelerated a bit in April. On April 14, *American Brands* topped out, *leaving 20 stocks left to support the average.* The next day, April 15, *two* Dow stocks went through the exits, *DuPont* and *Goodyear, leaving 18 stocks to support the average.* On April 16th two more Dow stocks saw their OBV peaks, *Anaconda* and *Procter & Gamble, leaving 16 stocks remaining to support the average.* Now the technical situation was getting critical. On April 25, *Woolworth* saw its peak, leaving 15 stocks remaining to support the average.

The analysis is interrupted briefly here to interject the following point: Experience has shown that once *more than half* of the 30 Dow stocks record OBV peaks, the end of the Dow rise is in sight and deterioration thereafter is rapid. At this point it only required one more Dow stock to reach an OBV peak to enter the closing period of the Dow rise. Here is what happened:

On April 28, *U.S. Steel* peaked, setting the stage for the anticipated May Dow top. *Now there were only 14 Dow stocks remaining to support the average,* and the technical STRAIN soon proved too much. Now note the *speeding up* of the new technical weakness. On May 2, *Bethlehem Steel* peaked, *leaving 13 stocks remaining to support the average.* On May 5, *Exxon* saw its OBV peak, *leaving 12 stocks to support the average.* On May

6, *Alcoa* peaked, *leaving only 11 stocks left to support the average.* Then on
May 9, *two* more Dow stocks peaked, *International Paper* and *Westinghouse
Electric, and the support faction was reduced to only 9 stocks.* On May 13,
American Telephone and *Chrysler* peaked, *leaving but 7 stocks remaining to
support the average.* The next day, May 14, saw *three* Dow stocks reach their
OBV peaks-*Eastman Kodak, General Motors,* and *Sears Roebuck. Now there
were only four stocks remaining called upon to support the average.*
Obviously the average was at the point of quitting the rise. Four stocks
couldn't be expected to carry the other 26. The technical strain by May 14
was intolerable. The Dow had reached the point of upside EXHAUSTION .
The Dow-Jones Industrial Average topped out at 858.73 on May 14!

Now let us put the above valuable information in tabular form, noting the
levels of the Dow-Jones Industrial Average on all the dates of the stock OBV
topouts:

Date	Cumulative Number of Dow Stocks No Longer Supporting the Average	Number of Remaining Stocks Supporting the Average	DJIA
Jan. 29	1	29	705.96
Feb. 6	2	28	714.17
Feb. 20	3	27	745.38
Feb. 27	4	26	731.15
Mar. 4	5	25	757.74
Mar. 5	6	24	752.82
Mar. 10	7	23	776.13
Mar. 17	8	22	786.53
Mar. 20	9	21	764.00
Apr. 14	10	20	806.95
Apr. 15	12	18	815.08
Apr. 16	14	16	815.71
Apr. 25	15	15	811.80
Apr. 28	16 (Majority peaks out!)	14	810.00
May 2	17	13	848.48
May 5	18	12	855.60
May 6	19	11	834.72
May 9	21	9	850.13
May 13	23	7	850.13
May 14	26 MAXIMUM STRAIN	+ THE TOP!	858.73

While the technical warnings were plain in terms of this study, the Climax
Indicator has no peer in pinpointing the exact day of the high, and it did so
on this top in the classic manner. As previously stated, the important tops
are those where the Dow goes to a new high on a progressive drop in the
CLX to a reading UNDER +5, the CLX zigzagging LOWER as the Dow
moves out into new high ground. Reviewing the pertinent figures leading
toward the May 14 peak, note that the Advance-Decline Line broke out

above the March 17 top on May 9 but that the Climax Indicator was the dominant indicator here:

Date	Industrials	Climax Indicator	Highs and Lows		Advance-Declines
3/17/75	786.53	+12 Inadequate Strength	393 –	3	-98,205*
......	......	....	....		......
5/ 2/75	848.48	+18 Great Strength	204 –	9	-99,236
5/ 5/75	855.60	+16 Maintained Strength	194 –	10	-98,942
5/ 6/75	834.72	+ 1 Very Bullish Looking	166 –	7	-99,316
5/ 7/75	836.44	- 1 New Dow High Ahead	81 –	7	-99,187
5/ 8/75	840.50	+ 4 Must See Dow High	155 –	11	-98,717
5/ 9/75	850.13	+12 Working Toward Top	244 –	3	-98,062*
5/12/75	847.47	+ 5 Almost There	186 –	6	-97,963*
5/13/75	850.13	+ 4 Losing Strength Fast	143 –	7	-97,783*
5/14/75	858.73	+ 4 THE TOP	179 –	3	-97,421*

*–New Advance-Decline Line highs.

The March 17 figures are included in the above table so as to show the peak in the number of new individual highs as well as the first peak in the advance-decline line. While the A-D Line did go above the March 17 high, peak strength had obviously already been seen as shown by the reduction in individual new highs. The loss of strength by the Climax Indicator also perfectly reflected the exhaustion at the top.

In relating this last table with the previous one showing the number of Dow stocks having topped out, we have an interesting method of filtering out the portion of the Climax Indicator reading which is technically meaningless. In other words, on May 2 we saw what appeared to be a strong reading of +18. However, the table of OBV peaks showed that on May 2, 17 Dow stocks had peaked out OBVwise, leaving 13 stocks to support the average. The Climax Indicator recorded 18 net upside OBV breakouts and, matching that figure with the 13 Dow stocks still showing strength, we can only conclude that five of the upside breakouts were of a *secondary* nature, not the bullish prime breakouts which signal higher markets. We might say then that the true value of the CLX on May 2 was +13 and NOT +18. Checking out May 5, we had a CLX reading of +16 but on the same day there were only 12 Dow stocks left supporting the average. By the same token, we might say that the true CLX reading was +12 with four Dow stocks making secondary OBV upside breakouts. Then on May 9 the CLX stood at +12, but we know that there were only nine Dow stocks that hadn't yet topped out. So then, the true CLX was really +9 with three Dow stocks making secondary upside breakouts.

These are the correct technical methods to use in positively identifying market upside exhaustion. How about downside exhaustion? The same method works admirably. Without going into a specific stock by stock countdown, suffice to say that seven market sessions prior to the very important intermediate bottom of November 23, 1971, it could be shown that 25 out of the 30 Dow industrial stocks had already shown their OBV lows for the year, leaving but five Dow stocks to fuel any additional market declines. It was perfect example of *downside* exhaustion.

There is a great market truth in all this, at the very heart of the success of technical analysis. Markets never show maximum strength at the Dow top and never show maximum weakness at the Dow bottom. Maximum strength occurs before the Dow top and maximum weakness occurs before the Dow bottom. Picture a mountain climber. When he gets to the mountain peak he is *exhausted,* certainly not the point of his maximum strength. The lesson here is to constantly seek to identify maximum *internal* strengths and weaknesses in the market. Never rely on the Dow-Jones Industrial Average as a guide to such maxima. Its function, aside from camouflaging the true internal condition of the market in order to mislead the uninformed, is to provide a measure of recognizable distortion which is such useful technical information to the informed.

THE TRUE SIGNIFICANCE OF VOLUME

Of all that has been written on the subject of technical stock market analysis, the least explored area appears to be that of *volume.* There have been some significant pioneering efforts, notably those of Harold M. Gartley, but even those great early contributions to volume theory were only *approaches* toward the great kernel of truth and never quite on target. A rather concise statement of Gartley's great work is compacted into a tightly written gem of a chapter in *A Treasury of Wall Street Wisdom* by Harry D. Schultz and Samson Coslow. I will discuss briefly a few of the highlights of Gartley's conclusions, adding new insights derived from my on-balance volume studies.

Perhaps the most obvious reason why the subject of volume is so generally overlooked is because people don't buy at a given volume figure or sell at a given volume figure. They buy at a *price* and sell at a *price.* Human nature being what it is, people therefore are most interested in stock market *prices.* They listen every day for the latest reading of the Dow-Jones Industrial Average, an average of 30 stock *prices.* They turn eagerly to the daily newspaper to see how their favorite stock closed, a closing measured in terms of *price.* They would be bewildered if they were told that the market closed down 18,000,000 or that Ajax Industries closed up 43,800. They are completely oriented to *price.* Because of that *misdirected attention,* they are constantly on the receiving end of *a series of effects,* never probing for the *causes* that produce those effects. I have consistently contended that *volume precedes price* and therefore *volume is a cause and price is an effect.*

Gartley stated that the reason we study volume is because it is believed that it is a measure of *supply of and demand for shares.* If stock X is up 1/4 point on volume of 11,000 shares we must generally assume that the demand for stock X exceeded the supply, even though we know that 11,000 shares were bought and 11,000 shares were sold. In this case the *demand came first,* since it required a 1/4 point increase in price to produce the 11,000 shares of matching supply. Conversely, if a stock declines in price we must assume that *supply came first,* since it required that drop in price before enough demand could be created to produce the auction market balance. Since supply and demand is measured by volume, and since it is demonstrated here that supply and demand make the price trends, then it follows that *volume makes the price trends,* or volume *precedes* price.

These are still generalities. What is usually most lacking in all discussions of volume is the presence of THE PLAN. A stock doesn't move willy nilly from 5 to 20 on a series of random advances or decline from 20 to 5 on a random sequence of price drops. To get from 5 to 20 there must be a PLAN of *accumulation,* and to get from 20 to 5 there must be a PLAN of *distribution.* Don't forget for a moment the GAME. This is a war, *a constant battle to inveigle the uninformed to sell their stock to the accumulators at the low price and to buy it back from them at a higher price when the accumulators are ready to become the distributors.* Without such a PLAN the market would be meaningless and with it the market constantly makes sense. So the key words of the game are *accumulation* and *distribution.* In a war the shots aren't scattered all over the place at random, the firepower is always concentrated on the enemy in a PLAN of battle. In the stock market prices will never reliably show you the plan of battle, but volume will if it is related to patterns of *accumulation* and *distribution.*

The basic truth of the theory of the constant GAME PLAN could only logically be expressed in terms of the *on-balance volume* concept. One day in the market means nothing, several days reveal something *but the longer period of time involved reveals an increasing portion of the current overriding PLAN then extant.* Regardless of which came first, the supply of shares or the demand for them, both supply and demand are *equated* each day in this *auction* market. One cannot say that a stock is being accumulated or distributed based on what happens on a given day. Suppose stock X goes up a point on 50,000 shares. We can say that the demand for stock X came first and was met with a supply of shares equal to the demand. Suppose, however, that the next day the stock dropped a full point on 30,000 shares.

On that day the supply came first and enough demand was created at the lower price to satisfy the auction equation. Now what? After two days, the stock is right back where it started, and the generally uninformed public *sees it exactly that way*, a stock going nowhere. Looking at the *volume*, however, you can see that *something has changed*. On the first day the stock went up on 50,000 shares, and on the second day it went down on 30,000 shares. The price is unchanged BUT THERE IS A RESIDUE OF 20,000 SHARES OF NET DEMAND FOR THE STOCK, a residue neatly disguised from the public view because the public is only interested in prices, and in this case, the stock is showing no price change after two days of trading. *It is that residue that I call on-balance volume.*

Two days of trading, however, cannot reveal a plan of accumulation or distribution. We need more. Just because the on-balance volume now stands at +20,000, we cannot say that the stock is under accumulation. Suppose on the third day the stock drops a quarter point on 40,000 shares. That would drop the OBV from +20,000 to -20,000, and we would then be totally in the dark as to what the stock was likely to do next. *What we have to do is record the on-balance volume long enough until the patterns of accumulation or distribution are revealed.* Accumulation is identified by rising zigzag patterns in the OBV figures, and distribution is revealed by OBV downward zigzags.

Getting back to stock X, let us discuss a series of hypothetical OBV readings, always remembering the following recording rules: (1) When the price closes up, we record the total volume for the day on the upside. (2) When the price closes down, we record the total volume for the day on the downside, *subtracting it from the figures of the day before.* (3) When the price closes unchanged, the OBV reading for that day is ZERO regardless of how high or low the trading volume was. (4) When a stock is selling ex-dividend and shows a net price rise, all the volume is assigned to the upside, and when there is a net price decline all the volume is assigned to the downside. (5) When a stock is split, the same daily recording technique is followed without deviation. Below is an on-balance volume table of stock X. In the table we note every OBV upside breakout with an UP designation and every OBV downside breakout with a DOWN designation.

STOCK X

Date	Closing Price	Volume	Demand Volume	Supply Volume	On–Balance Volume	
Feb. 3	10.00				0	
Feb. 4	11.00	50,000	50,000		50,000	
Feb. 5	10.00	30,000		30,000	20,000	
Feb. 6	9.75	40,000		40,000	- 20,000	
Feb. 7	9.88	15,000	15,000		- 5,000	
Feb. 10	9.75	25,000		25,000	- 30,000	DOWN

Date	Closing Price	Volume	Demand Volume	Supply Volume	On–Balance Volume	
Feb. 11	9.63	40,000		40,000	70,000	DOWN
Feb. 12	9.75	35,000	35,000		35,000	
Feb. 13	9.88	20,000	20,000		15,000	
Feb. 14	10.00	35,000	35,000		20,000	
Feb. 17	9.88	12,000		12,000	8,000	
Feb. 18	10.00	17,000	17,000		25,000	UP
Feb. 19	10.38	45,000	45,000		70,000	UP
Feb. 20	10.63	60,000	60,000		130,000	UP
Feb. 21	10.63	80,000			130,000	UP
Feb. 24	10.50	45,000		45,000	85,000	
Feb. 25	10.25	55,000		55,000	30,000	
Feb. 26	10.00	25,000		25,000	5,000	DOWN
Feb. 27	9.88	30,000		30,000	25,000	DOWN
Feb. 28	10.00	50,000	50,000		25,000	
Mar. 3	10.25	75,000	75,000		100,000	
Mar. 4	10.63	100,000	100,000		200,000	UP
Mar. 5	10.88	80,000	80,000		280,000	UP
Mar. 6	11.00	90,000	90,000		370,000	UP
Mar. 7	10.75	65,000		65,000	305,000	
Mar. 10	10.63	30,000		30,000	275,000	
Mar. 11	10.75	25,000	25,000		300,000	
Mar. 12	10.63	35,000		35,000	265,000	DOWN
Mar. 13	10.88	65.000	65,000		330,000	UP
Mar. 14	11.25	150,000	150,000		480,000	UP
Mar. 17	12.00	200,000	200,000		680,000	UP
Mar. 18	12.50	175,000	175,000		855,000	UP
Mar. 19	12.00	90,000		90,000	765,000	
Mar. 20	12.13	45,000	45,000		810,000	
Mar. 21	11.50	65,000		65,000	745,000	DOWN
Mar. 24	11.88	85,000	85,000		830,000	UP
Mar. 25	12.25	100,000	100,000		930,000	UP
Mar. 26	13.13	145,000	145,000		1,075,000	UP
Mar. 27	13.75	165,000	165,000		1,240,000	UP
Mar. 28	15.00	200,000	200,000		1,440,000	UP
Mar. 31	15.00	165,000			1,440,000	UP
Apr. 1	15.50	175,000	175,000		1,615,000	UP
Apr. 2	15.25	115,000		115,000	1,500,000	
Apr. 3	16.00	190,000	190,000		1,690,000	UP

Between February 11 and April 3, the stock jumped from 9 5/8 to 16. It did not get there through any series of *random* moves. No stock goes from 9 5/8 to 16 at random anymore than a stock drops from 50 to 25 at random. There is always a PLAN, and the only way to discover what the plan is all about is by *detecting the patterns of accumulation or distribution.* We are not going to identify those patterns reliably by price, but rather by on-balance volume, the residue of supply and demand pressures. If we went solely by *price* in the example of Stock X, we would have to say that *the stock was going nowhere* between February 3 and March 13, moving in a tight trading range of 9 5/8 on the downside and 11 on the upside. There was no discernable pattern in the price movement during that period of time. On the other hand, however, *the volume movements revealed a plan of accumulation which was totally evident by March 4.*

The only way such a plan could be revealed is by the technique of on-balance volume, the creation of *a volume advance-decline line.* Nothing else in the table shows such a coherent continuity except the OBV column. Without it, it might be said that the prices of Stock X fluctuated slightly at random and that the push and pull of demand volume and supply volume was also a series of random occurrences. But putting the conflicting demand volume and supply volume figures together and recording a daily cumulative record of the volume *differential,* the figures take on direction and start making some sense. One can see that the OBV bottomed on February 11 at -70,000, moved out to a high of 130,000 on February 20, fell back to -25,000 on February 27, and then broke out to a higher high at 200,000 on March 4. Such an upward zigzag in the OBV figures, measured from each cluster of downside and upside breakouts, put the stock in a *rising field trend* by March 4, and it was evident then that here was *a plan of accumulation* pretty effectively disguised from the eyes of the public. From that point on the OBV zigzagged higher, gaining upward acceleration when the price broke out on the upside on March 14. But the accumulation plan was evident prior to the price breakout, predicting in advance that the price would break out. It is a case of demand pressure building up which later must be translated in terms of higher prices.

Another reason why patterns of accumulation and distribution are pretty well disguised from the eyes of the public is because the buying or selling of a stock seldom produces a one-sided series of supply or demand pressures. Like two boxers in the ring, the bulls and bears are battling it out, first demand getting the upper hand and throwing the punches, and then supply getting in its licks, *but the outcome of the fight is predictable.* Either demand develops a winning pattern or supply develops a winning pattern. The two boxers are never perfectly matched. One must overcome the other, just as a stock reveals by the use of on-balance volume which pressure will dominate and, therefore, which way the price trend will be headed.

The early volume studies were never as specific as this. They treated volume in terms of vague generalities, skirting all around the answer, never quite being able to define what was really happening. Accumulation or distribution might have been suspected as taking place due to various volume characteristics, but not until on-balance volume came along was it possible not only to discover existing accumulation or distribution patterns, but to measure their force exactly.

The primary conception of volume used to be reduced to four statements:

1. When volume tends to increase during price declines, it is a bearish indication.
2. When volume tends to increase during advances, it is a bullish indication.
3. When volume tends to decrease during price declines, it is bullish.
4. When volume tends to decrease during price advances, it is bearish.

Those statements remain valid today, but they are typical of how little volume analysis has progressed, all generalities and no specifics. Those statements have more validity when analyzing the market as a whole but are not necessarily true when applied to the movement of specific stocks. One's participation in the market game is only done via specific stocks and thus applying those generalities regarding volume to specific stock action can be very misleading. One will find in the case histories presented in this book instances of volume tending to increase on a price decline only to lead to strong reversals to the upside when it is discovered that the on-balance volume stayed above a previous low on the volume increase. There are also instances of volume increasing on an advance with the on-balance volume either failing to make a new high or making such a towering high that it turned out to be a *terminal* move and therefore bearish. An equal number of exceptions are found when drawing conclusions from volume decreases. While previously it was pretty much guesswork, on-balance volume reveals why these things happened.

The older methods of analyzing volume generally involved four techniques: (1) Moving averages of volume, (2) Volume Ratios, (3) Correlations of Volume and Price, and (4) Special Group Studies. Let us now apply some of those techniques, discussing their inadequacies when compared with the superior OBV technique.

Moving Averages of Volume

This is done in order to smooth out fluctuations in activity so that trends can be more closely observed. The absurdity of those older methods is now evident in the light of the advanced OBV concept. By using a moving average of volume one is MIXING demand volume and supply volume, and *their important technical identities are destroyed.* Going back to Stock X, let me demonstrate the futility of a moving average of volume:

Between February 3 and March 13, the stock had a trading range between 9 5/8 and 11, and by March 13 the 5-day moving volume average had simply moved up from a low of 23,800 to a high of 82,000 and back down again to 44,000. By March 13 there was no hint that the stock was about to break

STOCK X
(Using a 5-Day Moving Average of Volume)

Date	Closing Price	Volume	5-Day Moving Average
Feb. 3	10.00		
Feb. 4	11.00	50,000	
Feb. 5	10.00	30,000	
Feb. 6	9.75	40,000	
Feb. 7	9.88	15,000	
Feb. 10	9.75	25,000	32,000
Feb. 11	9.63	40,000	30,000
Feb. 12	9.75	35,000	31,000
Feb. 13	9.88	20,000	27,000
Feb. 14	10.00	35,000	31,000
Feb. 17	9.88	12,000	28,400
Feb. 18	10.00	17,000	23,800
Feb. 19	10.38	45,000	25,800
Feb. 20	10.63	60,000	33,800
Feb. 21	10.63	80,000	42,800
Feb. 24	10.50	45,000	49,400
Feb. 25	10.25	55,000	57,000
Feb. 26	10.00	25,000	53,000
Feb. 27	9.88	30,000	47,000
Feb. 28	10.00	50,000	41,000
Mar. 3	10.25	75,000	47,000
Mar. 4	10.63	100,000	56,000
Mar. 5	10.88	80,000	67,000
Mar. 6	11.00	90,000	79,000
Mar. 7	10.75	65,000	82,000
Mar. 10	10.63	30,000	73,000
Mar. 11	10.75	25,000	58,000
Mar. 12	10.63	35,000	49,000
Mar. 13	10.88	65,000	44,000
Mar. 14	11.25	150,000	61,000
Mar. 17	12.00	200,000	95,000
Mar. 18	12.50	175,000	125,000
Mar. 19	12.00	90,000	136,000
Mar. 20	12.13	45,000	132,000
Mar. 21	11.50	65,000	115,000
Mar. 24	11.88	85,000	92,000
Mar. 25	12.25	100,000	77,000
Mar. 26	13.13	145,000	88,000
Mar. 27	13.75	165,000	112,000
Mar. 28	15.00	200,000	139,000
Mar. 31	15.00	165,000	155,000
Apr. 1	15.50	175,000	170,000
Apr. 2	15.25	115,000	164,000
Apr. 3	16.00	190,000	169,000

out on the upside and run to 16 using the moving average volume figures.
Now go back to the on-balance volume figures seen in the original Stock X

table. Those figures will now be directly compared to the five-day moving average figures, and what a revelation!

STOCK X

Date	Closing Price	On–Balance Volume		5-day Volume Average
Feb. 10	9.75	- 30,000	DOWN	32,000
Feb. 11	9.63	- 70,000	DOWN	30,000
Feb. 12	9.75	- 35,000		31,000
Feb. 13	9.88	- 15,000		27,000
Feb. 14	10.00	20,000		31,000
Feb. 17	9.88	8,000		28,400
Feb. 18	10.00	25,000	UP	23,800
Feb. 19	10.38	70,000	UP	25,800
Feb. 20	10.63	130,000	UP	33,800
Feb. 21	10.63	130,000	UP	42,800
Feb. 24	10.50	85,000		49,400
Feb. 25	10.25	30,000		57,000
Feb. 26	10.00	5,000	DOWN	53,000
Feb. 27	9.88	- 25,000	DOWN	47,000
Feb. 28	10.00	25,000		41,000
Mar. 3	10.25	100,000		47,000
Mar. 4	10.63	200,000	UP	56,000

By March 4 it was apparent that on-balance volume had revealed a definite *plan of accumulation,* a clear pattern of a rising zigzag in the OBV upside and downside breakouts making a rising field trend. On the other hand, the five-day moving average of daily volume revealed NOTHING, simply moving up from 23,800 to 57,000 and then staying under the 57,000 level for five straight days as the OBV was making the most revealing upside breakout! But don't take my word for it. Let us move on to a *specific* stock, using the actual OBV figures and moving volume averages for a given period:

BRISTOL MYERS

Date	Price	On–Balance Volume		5-day Volume Average
Oct. 1, 1974	31.38	- 16,700		
Oct. 2, 1974	31.88	2,200		
Oct. 3, 1974	31.63	- 3,600		
Oct. 4, 1974	31.63	- 3,600		
Oct. 7, 1974	32.63	12,700	UP	15,920
Oct. 8, 1974	32.38	- 1,700		15,460
Oct. 9, 1974	34.25	19,800	UP	15,980
Oct. 10, 1974	37.25	57,800	UP	22,420
Oct. 11, 1974	38.88	72,800	UP	21,040
Oct. 14, 1974	40.88	97,100	UP	22,640
Oct. 15, 1974	40.00	57,700		27,640

Date	Price	On-Balance Volume		5-day Volume Average
Oct. 16, 1974	38.88	36,500		27,580
Oct. 17, 1974	40.88	46,800		22,040
Oct. 18, 1974	43.25	57,200		21,120
Oct. 21, 1974	43.63	94,400		23,700
Oct. 22, 1974	42.75	54,000		23,900
Oct. 23, 1974	39.88	39,000		22,660
Oct. 24, 1974	39.75	12,000	DOWN	26,000
Oct. 25, 1974	40.63	25,800		26,680
Oct. 28, 1974	42.25	40,600		22,200
Oct. 29, 1974	44.25	55,000		17,000
Oct. 30, 1974	46.13	104,000	UP	23,800
Oct. 31, 1974	46.50	129,000	UP	23,400
Nov. 1, 1974	47.50	142,200	UP	23,280
Nov. 4, 1974	46.63	124,200		23,920
Nov. 5, 1974	47.50	137,900		23,780
Nov. 6, 1974	49.00	179,200	UP	22,240
Nov. 7, 1974	49.13	189,900	UP	19,380
Nov. 8, 1974	49.63	203,200	UP	19,400
Nov. 11, 1974	48.88	192,500	UP	17,940
Nov. 12, 1974	48.38	156.400		22,420
Nov. 13, 1974	48.00	123,800	DOWN	20,680
Nov. 14, 1974	48.63	133,700		20,520
Nov. 15, 1974	48.00	123,200	DOWN	19,960
Nov. 18, 1974	45.38	96,700	DOWN	23,180
Nov. 19, 1974	44.75	65,000	DOWN	22,240
Nov. 20, 1974	45.38	86,100		19,940
Nov. 21, 1974	46.63	98,400		20,420
Nov. 22, 1974	48.00	112,700		21,180
Nov. 25, 1974	48.50	130,900		19,520
Nov. 26, 1974	50.38	154,800	UP	17,960
Nov. 27, 1974	48.88	121,400		20,440
Nov. 29, 1974	49.63	128,000		19,280
Dec. 2, 1974	47.13	106,400	DOWN	20,740
Dec. 3, 1974	44.88	77,000	DOWN	22,980
Dec. 4, 1974	46.13	100,600		22,920
Dec. 5, 1974	46.75	112,900		18,700
Dec. 6, 1974	44.75	74,100	DOWN	25,140
Dec. 9, 1974	45.63	91,400		24,280
Dec. 10, 1974	48.00	100,300		20,180
Dec. 11, 1974	48.63	115,600	UP	18,520
Dec. 12, 1974	49.63	131,100	UP	19,160
Dec. 13, 1974	47.75	111.300		15,360
Dec. 16, 1974	48.13	126,800		15,000
Dec. 17, 1974	47.88	104,700	DOWN	17.640
Dec. 18, 1974	49.38	158,000	UP	25,280
Dec. 19, 1974	48.13	139,200		25,900
Dec. 20, 1974	48.00	125,600		24,660
Dec. 23, 1974	48.75	148,600		26,160
Dec. 24, 1974	49.38	152,100		22,450
Dec. 26, 1974	49.13	141,500		13,900
Dec. 27, 1974	49.13 ex. div.	147,100		11,260

Date	Price	On–Balance Volume		5-day Volume Average
Dec. 30, 1974	49.25	156,400	UP	10,400
Dec. 31, 1974	50.00	165,600	UP	7,640
Jan. 2, 1975	51.00	181,200	UP	10,060
Jan. 3, 1975	52.00	191,900	UP	10,080
Jan. 6, 1975	52.75	213,700	UP	13,320
Jan. 7, 1975	51.50	203,500		13,500
Jan. 8, 1975	49.88	188,400		14,680
Jan. 9, 1975	49.38	138,000	DOWN	21,640
Jan. 10, 1975	50.50	229,800	UP	37,860
Jan. 13, 1975	49.50	212,600		36,940
Jan. 14, 1975	47.75	188,700		39,680
Jan. 15, 1975	47.75	188,700		38,680
Jan. 16, 1975	47.75	188,700		35,460
Jan. 17, 1975	47.38	166,100		21,620
Jan. 20, 1975	47.25	136,800	DOWN	24,040
Jan. 21, 1975	46.88	121,000	DOWN	22,420
Jan. 22, 1975	47.00	148,600		25,920
Jan. 23, 1975	47.75	194,800		28,300
Jan. 24, 1975	48.75	227,000		30,220
Jan. 27, 1975	50.00	250,200	UP	29,000
Jan. 28, 1975	51.75	279,200	UP	31,640
Jan. 29, 1975	54.50	315,100	UP	33,300
Jan. 30, 1975	54.13	271,000		32,880
Jan. 31, 1975	56.13	304,400		33,120
Feb. 3, 1975	57.25	339,000	UP	35,400
Feb. 4, 1975	57.25	339,000	UP	37,400
Feb. 5, 1975	58.00	362,800	UP	34.980
Feb. 6, 1975	58.38	409,600	UP	35,520

Here is a classic case of how effective on-balance volume is when stacked up against such archaic techniques as a moving volume average. Between October, 1974 and February, 1975, Bristol Myers almost doubled. This dynamic upswing was well revealed by on-balance volume which was making a strong series of up designations in early October while average volume was literally standing still! The upward zigzag in the OBV clusters was seen as early as October 30, the confirming OBV breakout occurring on that date above the previous OBV high of October 14. The moving volume average was virtually static, peaking at 27,640 on October 15 and not bettering that peak until January 10 when the price of the stock was already up in the 50's. The volume average finally peaked at 39,680 on January 14 when the price of the stock stood at 47 3/4, and thus there was no hint from that source that the stock was going to continue rising to 58 3/8 less than a month later. OBV, however, moved up to a new high on January 27, bettering the previous OBV high of January 10, and on that renewed bull signal the stock tacked on almost another 9 points in less than two weeks. Meanwhile the average volume remained under the January 14 peak, misleading analysts putting any credence on average volume.

As previously stated, any technique involving *total* volume as a market indicator is not going to reveal very much. Total volume *mixes* both the supply volume and the demand volume, and thus they lose their vital identities. Any intelligent study of volume *must break it down into the supply and demand components* and then identify which of those components predominates. That is exactly what on-balance volume does. It thereby reveals the *plan,* whether it be a plan of accumulation or a plan of distribution.

Volume Ratios

Years ago great stress was put on the study of *volume ratios.* That technique stressed the greater importance of *relative* data as opposed to the raw figures. One simply would take the raw volume figures for a given stock each day and then divide by the total market volume to get the daily volume ratio. It was felt that volume was only significant when it showed a change in relation to the total volume. Students following that technique claimed that there was no significant peak in volume which did not show up in relative volume, but that there were numerous instances where a notable increase or decrease is not discernible in the raw figures but is clearly apparent in the relative figures. Gartley felt that the greatest value in studying volume ratios versus the raw figures was that when they developed a peak comparable to the highest two or three peaks in the previous year or two, an important development in the price trend was almost always underway; whereas in the raw figures, numerous peaks which appeared to the eye as possibly important were of no significance whatsoever.

The study of on-balance volume completely puts the study of volume ratios in an insignificant light inasmuch as one no longer needs the volume ratio data. It was at best a very inexact technique. One did get some blips on the volume radar screen, but it was never clearly ascertained as to whether the stock was under accumulation or not. Once on-balance volume is used and thoroughly understood, the shortcomings of volume ratios become only too apparent. The now obvious deficiency is that one is taking a volume figure which is not identified in terms of supply or demand volume and is then taking that meaningless figure and comparing it to the total volume, which is also not identified in supply and demand terms. The OBV technique proves over and over that a stock can be under very significant accumulation without ever developing any significantly high volume figures. The Bristol Myers example just recently given showed a stock practically doubling *with the average volume never exceeding 38,000 shares. Accumulation or distribu-*

tion is capable of taking place at any time in a stock on any scale of volume regardless of contractions or expansions in total market volume.

In order to satisfy any remaining doubts regarding the importance of volume ratios, a study is given here of the daily action in *Westinghouse Electric,* showing both the on-balance volume figures and the volume ratios. One will be able to quickly decide which analytical technique is of greater use.

WESTINGHOUSE ELECTRIC

Date	Total Market Volume	Stock Volume	Volume Ratio	OBV	Price
10/ 4/74	15,910,000	188,200	1.1	- 188,200	9.00
10/ 7/74	15,000,000	110,500	0.6	- 77,700	10.00
10/ 8/74	15,460,000	206,300	1.3	- 284,000	9.75
10/ 9/74	18,820,000	122,900	0.6	- 161,100	10.00
10/10/74	26,360,000	169,300	0.6	161,100	10.00
10/11/74	20,090,000	243,900	1.2	405,000	9.13
10/14/74	19,770,000	353,500	1.8	51,500	9.75
10/15/74	17,060,000	168,700	1.0	- 51,500	9.75
10/16/74	14,790,000	141,000	0.9	- 192,500	9.38
10/17/74	14,470,000	151,900	1.0	- 192,500	9.38
10/18/74	16,460,000	106,400	0.6	- 86,100	9.88
10/21/74	14,500,000	247,300	1.7	- 333,400	9.75
10/22/74	18,930,000	170,400	0.9	- 503,800	9.25
10/23/74	14,200,000	140,300	1.0	- 644,100	9.00
10/24/74	14,910,000	168,500	1.1	- 475,600	9.25
10/25/74	12,650,000	149,000	1.2	- 624,600	9.00
10/28/74	10,540,000	117,800	1.1	- 742,400	8.88
10/29/74	15,610,000	129,800	0.8	- 742,400	8.88
10/30/74	20,130,000	119,100	0.5	- 623,300	9.13
10/31/74	18,840,000	148,200	0.8	- 475,100	9.50
11/ 1/74	13,470,000	85,100	0.6	- 475,100	9.50
11/ 4/74	12,740,000	75,500	0.6	- 550,600	9.13
11/ 5/74	15,960,000	161,300	1.0	- 389,300	9.88
11/ 6/74	23,930,000	175,000	0.7	- 564,300	9.50
11/ 7/74	17,150,000	69,700	0.4	- 494,600	9.88
11/ 8/74	15,890,000	76,700	0.5	- 571,300	9.75
11/11/74	13,220,000	135,900	1.0	- 435,400	10.00
11/12/74	15,040,000	122,400	0.8	- 557,800	9.50
11/13/74	16,040,000	141,900	0.9	- 415,900	9.88
11/14/74	12,500,000	52,600	0.4	- 468,500	9.75
11/15/74	12,480,000	81,400	0.7	- 549,900	9.50
11/18/74	15,230,000	88,100	0.6	- 638,000	9.00
11/19/74	15,720,000	168,700	1.1	- 806,700	8.75
11/20/74	12,430,000	100,100	0.8	- 706,600	8.88
11/21/74	13,810,000	61,900	0.5	- 644,700	9.25
11/22/74	13,020,000	82,400	0.6	- 727,100	9.00
11/25/74	11,295,000	73,600	0.6	- 653,500	9.13
11/26/74	13,600,000	63,300	0.5	- 716,800	9.00
11/27/74	14,810,000	150,500	1.0	- 716,800	9.00
11/29/74	7,400,000	104,100	1.5	- 820,900	8.88

Date	Total Market Volume	Stock Volume	Volume Ratio	OBV	Price
12/ 2/74	11,140,000	300,700	2.7	-1,121,600	8.63
12/ 3/74	13,620,000	176,500	1.3	- 945,100	8.75
12/ 4/74	12,580,000	225,200	1.8	- 945,100	8.75
12/ 5/74	12,890,000	141,900	1.1	-1,087,000	8.63
12/ 6/74	15,500,000	213,100	1.4	-1,300,100	8.50
12/ 9/74	14,660,000	87,400	0.6	-1,387,500	8.38
12/10/74	15,690,000	120,700	0.8	-1,266,800	8.63
12/11/74	15,700,000	123,900	0.8	-1,266,800	8.63
12/12/74	15,390,000	76,300	0.5	-1,343,100	8.50
12/13/74	14,000,000	80,200	0.6	-1,423,300	8.38
12/16/74	15,370,000	120,700	0.8	-1,302,600	8.50
12/17/74	16,880,000	91,700	0.6	-1,302,600	8.50
12/18/74	18,050,000	94,700	0.5	-1,302,600	8.50
12/19/74	15,900,000	135,400	0.9	-1,438,000	8.25
12/20/74	15,840,000	165,500	1.0	-1,438,000	8.25
12/23/74	18,040,000	112,800	0.6	-1,438,000	8.25
12/24/74	9,538,000	66,600	0.7	-1,371,400	8.38
12/26/74	11,810,000	64,100	0.5	-1,371,400	8.38
12/27/74	13,060,000	111,400	0.8	-1,371,400	8.38
12/30/74	18,520,000	222,900	1.2	-1,148,500	9.50
12/31/74	20,970,000	239,300	1.1	- 909,200	10.00
1/ 2/75	14,800,000	138,500	1.0	- 770,700	10.13
1/ 3/75	15,270,000	144,900	1.0	- 915,600	9.88
1/ 6/75	17,550,000	194,500	1.1	- 721,100	10.25
1/ 7/75	14,330,000	98,600	0.7	- 622,500	10.75
1/ 8/75	15,600,000	143,800	0.9	- 478,700	10.88
1/ 9/75	16,340,000	95,500	0.6	- 383,200	11.25
1/10/75	25,890,000	203,000	0.8	- 180,200	11.50
1/13/75	19,780,000	173,300	0.9	- 6,900	11.63
1/14/75	16,610,000	131,400	0.8	- 6,900	11.63
1/15/75	16,580,000	121,700	0.8	- 114,800	11.75
1/16/75	17,110,000	120,500	0.7	- 5,700	11.50
1/17/75	14,260,000	69,000	0.5	- 74,700	11.25
1/20/75	13,450,000	74,400	0.6	- 149,100	10.88
1/21/75	14,780,000	102,900	0.6	- 149,100	10.88
1/22/75	15,320,000	64,900	0.4	- 84,200	11.13
1/23/75	17,960,000	65,800	0.4	- 150,000	11.00
1/24/75	20,670,000	62,000	0.3	- 88,000	11.13
1/27/75	32,130,000	140,000	0.5	52,000	11.75
1/28/75	31,760,000	180,500	0.6	232,500	11.88
1/29/75	27,406,000	150,000	0.5	232,500	11.88
1/30/75	29,740,000	438,800	1.5	- 206,300	10.88
1/31/75	24,640,000	296,500	1.2	90,200	11.25
2/ 3/75	25,400,000	364,700	1.5	454,900	11.88
2/ 4/75	25,040,000	142,100	0.6	312,800	11.63
2/ 5/75	25,830,000	97,800	0.4	410,600	11.75
2/ 6/75	32,018,000	193,000	0.6	603,600	11.88
2/ 7/75	20,060,000	106,700	0.5	496,900	11.75
2/10/75	16,120,000	58,300	0.4	438,600	11.63
2/11/75	16,470,000	56,400	0.3	495,000	11.75
2/12/75	19,790,000	74,600	0.4	569,600	12.00

Date	Total Market Volume	Stock Volume	Volume Ratio	OBV	Price
2/13/75	35,160,000	156,300	0.5	725,900	12.25
2/14/75	23,290,000	137,000	0.6	862,900	12.50
2/18/75	23,990,000	94,200	0.4	768,700	12.38
2/19/75	22,192,000	90,300	0.4	768,700	12.38
2/20/75	22,260,000	55,200	0.3	823,900	12.50
2/21/75	24,440,000	76,700	0.3	823,900	12.50
2/24/75	19,150,000	95,200	0.5	728,700	12.13
2/25/75	20,910,000	110,500	0.5	618,200	11.50
2/26/75	18,790,000	101,500	0.5	719,700	11.63

Here we find the volume ratio of Westinghouse Electric fluctuating between 0.3 on the low side and 2.7 on the high side. The high ratio reading occurred on December 2, while the price of the stock was still falling, 13 market sessions prior to the December 19 bottom. The low ratio reading took place on four different occasions: January 24, February 11, February 20, and February 21, 1975, all on advances in the price of the stock. *There appears to be no discernible pattern which might lead toward a conclusion that there is a correlation between the volume ratio and where the price of the stock is headed.* On the other hand, on-balance volume was clearly definitive in identifying the December, 1974 bottom and the massive January, 1975 upside breakout. By May, 1975, the stock was selling at 17 7/8.

THE WHOLE MUST EQUAL THE SUM OF THE PARTS

You have been introduced to the forecasting power of on-balance volume when it is tracing out a definite trend for an individual stock. When OBV trends lower, it is indicating lower prices to come, and when it trends higher, one can look for higher prices to come. *When all the individual OBV trends are lumped together, we then have market on-balance volume.* If there is a preponderance of individual stocks having rising OBV trends, then it must follow that the market as a whole will show a rising OBV trend inasmuch as the whole must equal the sum of the parts. How good an indicator is *market* OBV? Well, let us see. In order to compute market on-balance volume we must add or subtract the daily volume based on the rise or fall of the market each day. If the Dow Jones Industrial Average is up, we cannot always say that the market was up since there are some days when the Dow rose and the market in terms of the broader indices was down. To be consistent, we will add the daily volume on the days the advance-decline line rises and subtract the volume on the days the advance-decline line declines. Since the A-D line is based on *price,* it naturally substitutes for the price of an individual stock when computing OBV for an individual stock. It is the only certain measurement to determine whether the market as a whole is up or down on the day. The review figures below commence a few weeks prior to the 1974 market bottom.

Date	Dow–Jones Industrials	Big Board Volume	On–Balance Volume		Advance–Decline Line	
9 /13/74	627.19	16,070,000	- 16,070,000		- 902	
9 /16/74	639.78	18,370,000	2,300,000		- 846	
9 /17/74	648.78	13,730,000	16,030,000		19	
9 /18/74	651.91	11,760,000	4,270,000		- 42	
9 /19/74	674.05	17,000,000	21,270,0000	UP	1,020	UP
9 /20/74	670.76	16,250,000	37,520,000	UP	1,450	UP
9 /23/74	663.72	12,130,000	49,650,000	UP	1,521	UP
9 /24/74	654.10	9,840,000	39,810,000		893	
9 /25/74	649.95	17,620,000	57,430,000	UP	1,262	
9 /26/74	637.98	9,060,000	48,370,000		652	DOWN
9 /27/74	621.95	12,230,000	36,140,000	DOWN	50	DOWN
9 /30/74	607.87	15,000,000	21,140,000	DOWN	- 855	DOWN
10/ 1/74	604.82	16,890,000	4,250,000	DOWN	-1,043	DOWN
10/ 2/74	601.53	12,230,000	16,480,000		- 726	
10/ 3/74	587.61	13,150,000	3,330,000	DOWN	-1,280	DOWN
10/ 4/74	584.56	15,910,000	19,240,000	UP	-1,262	
10/ 7/74	607.56	15,000,000	34,240,000	UP	- 189	UP
10/ 8/74	602.63	15,460,000	49,700,000	UP	139	UP
10/ 9/74	631.02	18,820,000	68,520,000	UP	1,095	UP
10/10/74	648.08	26,360,000	94,880,000	UP	2,172	UP
10/11/74	658.24	20,000,000	114,880,000	UP	2,813	UP
10/14/74	673.50	19,770,000	134,650,000	UP	3,674	UP
10/15/74	658.40	17,060,000	117,590,000		3,066	
10/16/74	642.29	14,790,000	102,800,000		2,574	
10/17/74	651.44	14,470,000	117,270,000		2,749	
10/18/74	654.88	16,460,000	133,730,000		3,228	
10/21/74	669.82	14,500,000	148,230,000	UP	3,548	
10/22/74	662.86	18,930,000	167,160,000	UP	3,595	
10/23/74	645.03	14,200,000	152,960,000		2,736	
10/24/74	636.26	14,910,000	138,050,000		1,879	DOWN
10/25/74	636.19	12,650,000	150,700,000		1,905	
10/28/74	633.84	10,540,000	140,160,000		1,643	DOWN
10/29/74	659.34	15,610,000	155,770,000	UP	2,322	UP
10/30/74	673.03	20,130,000	175,900,000	UP	2,827	UP
10/31/74	665.52	18,840,000	194,740,000	UP	2,841	UP
11/ 1/74	665.28	13,470,000	208,210,000	UP	2,879	UP
11/ 4/74	657.23	12,740,000	195,470,000		2,480	
11/ 5/74	674.75	15,960,000	211,430,000	UP	3,077	UP
11/ 6/74	669.12	23,930,000	235,360,000	UP	3,412	UP
11/ 7/74	671.93	17,150,000	252,510,000	UP	3,719	UP
11/ 8/74	667.16	15,890,000	268,400,000	UP	3,869	UP
11/11/74	672.64	13,220,000	281,620,000	UP	4,139	UP
11/12/74	659.18	15,040,000	266,580,000		3,490	
11/13/74	659.18	16,040,000	250,540,000		3,104	

Date	Dow–Jones Industrials	Big Board Volume	On–Balance Volume		Advance–Decline Line	
11/14/74	658.40	13,540,000	237,000,000		3,073	
11/15/74	647.61	12,480,000	224,520,000		2,650	
11/18/74	624.92	15,230,000	209,290,000		1,408	DOWN
11/19/74	614.05	15,720,000	193,570,000	DOWN	574	DOWN
11/20/74	609.59	12,430,000	181,140,000	DOWN	224	DOWN
11/21/74	608.57	13,810,000	167,330,000	DOWN	179	DOWN
11/22/74	615.20	13,020,000	180,350,000		628	
11/25/74	611.94	11,300,000	169,050,000		394	
11/26/74	617.26	13,600,000	182,650,000	UP	645	UP
11/27/74	619.29	14,810,000	197,460,000	UP	938	UP
11/29/74	618.86	7,400,000	190,060,000		850	
12/ 2/74	603.02	11,140,000	178,920,000		- 77	DOWN
12/ 3/74	596.61	13,420,000	165,500,000	DOWN	- 877	DOWN
12/ 4/74	598.64	12,580,000	152,920,000	DOWN	- 931	DOWN
12/ 5/74	587.06	12,890,000	140,030,000	DOWN	-1,654	DOWN
12/ 6/74	577.60	15,500,000	124,530,000	DOWN	-2,579	DOWN
12/ 9/74	579.94	14,660,000	109,870,000	DOWN	-2,875	DOWN
12/10/74	593.87	15,490,000	125,360,000		-2,333	DOWN
12/11/74	595.35	15,700,000	141,060,000		-2,089	
12/12/74	596.37	15,390,000	125,670,000		-2,450	
12/13/74	592.77	14,000,000	111,670,000		-2,775	
12/16/74	586.83	15,370,000	96,300,000	DOWN	-3,148	DOWN
12/17/74	597.54	16,880,000	113,180,000		-3,108	
12/18/74	603.49	18,050,000	131,230,000		-2,932	
12/19/74	604.43	15,900,000	115,330,000		-3,122	
12/20/74	598.48	15,840,000	99,490,000		-3,668	DOWN
12/23/74	589.64	18.040,000	81,450,000		-4,306	DOWN
12/24/74	598.40	9,540,000	90,990,000		-3,961	
12/26/74	604.74	11,810,000	102,800,000		-3,816	
12/27/74	602.16	13,000,000	89,800,000		-3,935	
12/30/74	603.25	18,520,000	71,280,000	DOWN	-4,206	
12/31/74	616.24	20,970,000	92,250,000		-3,251	UP
1 / 2/75	632.04	14,800,000	107,050,000	UP	-1,960	UP
1 / 3/75	634.54	15,270,000	122,320,000	UP	-1,205	UP
1 / 6/75	637.20	17,590,000	139,910,000	UP	- 277	UP
1 / 7/75	641.19	14,330,000	154,240,000	UP	132	UP
1 / 8/75	635.40	15,600,000	138.640,000		91	
1 / 9/75	645.26	16,340,000	154,980,000	UP	644	UP
1 /10/75	658.79	25,890,000	180,870,000	UP	1,870	UP
1 /13/75	654.18	19,780,000	200,650,000	UP	2,333	UP
1 /14/75	648.70	16,610,000	184,040,000		2,151	
1 /15/75	653.39	16,580,000	200,620,000		2,356	UP
1 /16/75	655.74	17,110,000	217,230,000	UP	2,645	UP
1 /17/75	644.63	14,260,000	203,470,000		2,297	
1 /20/75	647.45	13,450,000	190,020,000		2,210	
1 /21/75	641.90	14,780,000	204,800,000		2,365	
1 /22/75	652.61	15,320,000	220,120,000	UP	2,615	
1 /23/75	656.76	17.960,000	238,080,000	UP	3,059	UP
1 /24/75	666.61	20,670,000	258,750,000	UP	3,762	UP
1 /27/75	692.66	32,130,000	290,880,000	UP	5,049	UP

Date	Dow–Jones Industrials	Big Board Volume	On–Balance Volume		Advance–Decline Line	
1 /28/75	694.77	31,760,000	322,640,000	UP	5,508	UP
1 /29/75	705.96	27,410,000	350,050,000	UP	6,073	UP
1 /30/75	696.42	29,740,000	320,310,000		5,922	
1 /31/75	703.69	24,640,000	344,950,000		6,386	UP
2 / 3/75	711.44	25,400,000	370,350,000	UP	7,172	UP
2 / 4/75	708.07	25,040,000	345,310,000		6,915	
2 / 5/75	717.85	25,830,000	371,140,000	UP	7,480	UP
2 / 6/75	714.17	32,020,000	403,160,000	UP	7,698	UP
2 / 7/75	711.91	20,060,000	383,100,000		7,458	
2 /10/75	708.39	16,120,000	366,980,000		7,387	
2 /11/75	707.60	16,470,000	350,510,000		7,186	
2 /12/75	715.03	19,790,000	370,300,000		7,776	UP
2 /13/75	726.92	35,160,000	405,460,000	UP	8,334	UP
2 /14/75	734.20	23,290,000	428,750,000	UP	8,491	UP
2 /18/75	731.30	23,990,000	404,760,000		8,377	
2 /19/75	736.39	21,930,000	382,830,000		8,353	
2 /20/75	745.38	22,260,000	405,090,000		8,603	UP
2 /21/75	749.77	24,440,000	429,530,000	UP	8,805	UP
2 /24/75	736.94	19,150,000	410,380,000		8,227	
2 /25/75	719.18	20,910,000	389,470,000		7,132	DOWN
2 /26/75	728.10	18,790,000	408,260,000		7,432	
2 /27/75	731.15	16,430,000	424,690,000		7,755	
2 /28/75	739.05	17,560,000	442,250,000	UP	8,083	
3 / 3/75	753.13	24,100,000	466,350,000	UP	8,854	UP
3 / 4/75	757.74	34,140,000	500,490,000	UP	9,313	UP

Here is an authentic endorsement of *market on-balance volume* as a major market indicator, every bit as important as the advance-decline line and perhaps a great deal more effective. The table begins with the important market session of September 13, 1974, the date of the *true* market bottom as measured by the number of stocks making new 1974 lows that day, a maximum number of 661. Interestingly enough, the market on-balance volume was recorded at -16,070,000 on that day, never dropping under it thereafter. The final downside deception by the Dow while it undoubtedly fooled most market observers watching the industrial average and the advance-decline line at that time, could not fool the on-balance volume indicator, an indicator which had to record any predominant demand for stocks, no matter how slight. It is quite revealing to see here that such predominant demand showed up *prior* to the October 4 lows. Between September 13 and September 25, market OBV jumped from -16,070,000 to 57,430,000, enough of a gain to weather the final seven sessions of the 1973-74 bear market and then record a very bullish non-confirmation of that final drop.

One might say at this point, however, that inasmuch as market OBV can only go up when the advance-decline line goes up, why not just watch the

A-D Line and forget about OBV. True only up to a point. Note the divergence after September 23 between market OBV and the A-D Line, the A-D Line working down to a new low by October 3, *but the OBV remaining importantly above the September 13 low.* This emphatically proved that there was a *residue of predominant demand for stocks* which neither the drop in the industrial average or the advance-decline line could wash away. It proved once again that *volume precedes price.* The further proof of this was even more compelling. On December 6, 1974, the Dow-Jones Industrial Average broke to a new 1974 low accompanied by the advance-decline line breaking sharply under the previous low of October 3. Once again most observers were probably impressed by this show of weakness on the part of the industrial average and the advance-decline line, no doubt believing that the 1974 bear market was being importantly resumed. The December 6 industrial low was accompanied by a very bullish *non-confirmation* on the part of the Dow-Jones Transportation Average, BUT EVEN WITHOUT THAT IMPORTANT INDICATION, THE MARKET ON-BALANCE VOLUME BY ITSELF OFFERED SUFFICIENT PROOF THAT THERE HAD BEEN A GROWING PREDOMINANT DEMAND FOR STOCKS SINCE AS EARLY AS SEPTEMBER 13. On December 6, market on-balance volume stood at 124,530,000, sharply above the 19,240,000 figure of October 4, the day of the last confirmed lows in the Dow averages. Even when the advance-decline line kept going down thereafter to post its final bottom on December 24, the market OBV figure held up at 81,450,000, still well above the October figures. That could only have been possible by virtue of the fact that the market advances were on higher volume than the market declines after September 13. Such an observation has always been judged to be bullish for the market but apparently nobody had attempted to formalize it with an exact measuring technique until on-balance volume was used.

Now note the general overall pattern of the market OBV figures as they sprang higher from the 1974 lows, going from -16,070,000 on September 13 to 281,620,000 on November 11. There was no way the market was going to give that back. It was too emphatic, too overpowering. It was the strongest of all technical indications, *taking precedence over all other technical indicators.* It is hard to believe that the advance-decline line and the Dow-Jones Industrial Average made new lows *after* that internal demand buildup, but that is the window dressing put there to deceive the unwary, those who are swayed by the figures that everybody looks at. This is a serious game and if the market is set to beat you, it will throw a series of conflicting figures in your face every time it gets the chance. However, it can never cover all the tracks. The telltale trail of the smart money *must show up in the on-balance volume figures* because only those figures can reveal whether stocks are being accumulated or distributed. As the table shows, market OBV had risen to 500,490,000 by March 4, 1975, *representing a half a billion shares of predominant demand for stocks.* The OBV came first and then the price advance, as emphatically demonstrated in the great turn off of the 1974 lows. By early March, 1975, the Dow was up about 180 points *but OBV saw it coming first!*

MOST ACTIVE STOCK ON-BALANCE VOLUME

The volume factor being so overwhelmingly important, it would follow that another key market indicator can be derived from computing the on-balance volume of *the most active stocks.* The most active list each day accounts for about 15% of the total daily market volume and, this being where the action is, the OBV seen collectively on those stocks should emphatically confirm or refute other key indicators. The same period of time will be covered in this study, September 13, 1974, through March 4, 1975. Since most daily newspapers list the 15 most active stocks, only those 15 each day will be considered. Many studies of the most active stocks rely on measurements of the top 20 issues as shown each week in *Barron's,* but a study of the top 15 is a more convenient measurement, much more widely available.

Date	Dow–Jones Industrials	15 Most Active Stock On–Balance Volume		Advance–Decline Line	
9 /13/74	627.19	- 701,100		- 902	
9 /16/74	639.78	- 258,400		- 846	
9 /17/74	648.78	- 97,100		19	
9 /18/74	651.91	- 92,600		- 42	
9 /19/74	674.05	1,044,300		1,020	UP
9 /20/74	670.76	895,700		1,450	UP
9 /23/74	663.72	118,200		1,521	UP
9 /24/74	654.10	- 1,157,700	DOWN	893	
9 /25/74	649.95	- 1,612,900	DOWN	1,262	
9 /26/74	637.98	- 2,354,400	DOWN	652	DOWN
9 /27/74	621.95	- 4,075,700	DOWN	50	DOWN
9 /30/74	607.87	- 5,828,200	DOWN	- 855	DOWN
10/ 1/74	604.82	- 7,363,300	DOWN	-1,043	DOWN
10/ 2/74	601.53	- 7,860,500	DOWN	- 726	
10/ 3/74	587.61	- 9,600,900	DOWN	-1,280	DOWN
10/ 4/74	584.56	-10,657,200	DOWN	-1,262	
10/ 7/74	607.56	- 9,388,700		- 189	UP
10/ 8/74	602.63	-10,373,800		139	UP
10/ 9/74	631.02	- 8,457,800	UP	1,095	UP
10/10/74	648.08	- 7,446,400	UP	2,172	UP
10/11/74	658.24	- 6,162,600	UP	2,813	UP
10/14/74	673.50	- 4,081,100	UP	3,674	UP
10/15/74	658.40	- 5,074,300		3,066	
10/16/74	642.29	- 7,194,900		2,574	

Date	Dow–Jones Industrials	15 Most Active Stock On–Balance Volume		Advance–Decline Line	
10/17/74	651.44	- 7,532,900		2,749	
10/18/74	654.88	- 7,780,400		3,228	
10/21/74	669.82	- 7,926,400		3,548	
10/22/74	662.86	- 7,890,600		3,595	
10/23/74	645.03	-10,050,400	DOWN	2,736	
10/24/74	636.26	-10,543,700	DOWN	1,879	DOWN
10/25/74	636.19	-10,614,600	DOWN	1,905	
10/28/74	633.84	-10,590,100		1,643	DOWN
10/29/74	659.34	- 9,435,400		2,322	UP
10/30/74	673.03	- 7,772,200	UP	2,827	UP
10/31/74	665.52	- 7,925,700		2,841	UP
11/ 1/74	665.28	- 8,160,800		2,879	UP
11/ 4/74	657.23	- 9,243,700		2,480	
11/ 5/74	674.75	- 7,576,600	UP	3,077	UP
11/ 6/74	669.12	- 7,393,100	UP	3,412	UP
11/ 7/74	671.93	- 5,778,200	UP	3,719	UP
11/ 8/74	667.16	- 6,541,800		3,869	UP
11/11/74	672.64	- 6,162,900		4,139	UP
11/12/74	659.18	- 7,603,500	DOWN	3,490	
11/13/74	659.18	- 7,645,900	DOWN	3,104	
11/14/74	658.40	- 8,451,800	DOWN	3,073	
11/15/74	647.61	- 8,587,600	DOWN	2,650	
11/18/74	624.92	-10,646,500	DOWN	1,408	DOWN
11/19/74	614.05	-12,391,200	DOWN	574	DOWN
11/20/74	609.59	-12,663,900	DOWN	224	DOWN
11/21/74	608.57	-12,936,600	DOWN	179	DOWN
11/22/74	615.20	-12,227,000		628	
11/25/74	611.94	-12,552,900		394	
11/26/74	617.26	-12,558,800		645	UP
11/27/74	619.29	-12,396,800		938	UP
11/29/74	618.86	-12,844,900	DOWN	850	
12/ 2/74	603.02	-14,480,600	DOWN	- 77	DOWN
12/ 3/74	596.61	-15,130,000	DOWN	- 877	DOWN
12/ 4/74	598.64	-15,276,800	DOWN	- 931	DOWN
12/ 5/74	587.06	-16,401,000	DOWN	-1,654	DOWN
12/ 6/74	577.60	-17,633,000	DOWN	-2,579	DOWN
12/ 9/74	579.94	-17,252,700		-2,875	DOWN
12/10/74	593.87	-15,667,700		-2,333	
12/11/74	595.35	-15,610,800		-2,089	
12/12/74	596.37	-16,391,800		-2,450	
12/13/74	592.77	-16,870,500		-2,775	
12/16/74	586.83	-18,517,900	DOWN	-3,148	DOWN
12/17/74	597.54	-17,982,400		-3,108	
12/18/74	603.49	-18,796,900	DOWN	-2,932	
12/19/74	604.43	-19,758,600	DOWN	-3,122	
12/20/74	598.48	-20,510,500	DOWN	-3,668	DOWN
12/23/74	589.64	-21,940,000	DOWN	-4,306	DOWN
12/24/74	598.40	-21,720,000		-3,961	
12/26/74	604.74	-21,612,100		-3,816	
12/27/74	602.16	-21,648,500		-3,935	
12/30/74	603.25	-22,032,500	DOWN	-4,206	

Date	Dow–Jones Industrials	15 Most Active Stock On–Balance Volume		Advance–Decline Line	
12/31/74	616.24	-20,004,900	UP	- -3,251	UP
1/ 2/75	632.04	-18,645,900	UP	-1,960	UP
1/ 3/75	634.54	-18,374,300	UP	-1,205	UP
1/ 6/75	637.20	-16,334,200	UP	- 277	UP
1/ 7/75	641.19	-16,515,000		132	UP
1/ 8/75	635.40	-16,956,700	.	91	
1/ 9/75	645.26	-16,393,900		644	UP
1/10/75	658.79	-13,487,500	UP	1,870	UP
1/13/75	654.18	-13,532,600		2,333	UP
1/14/75	648.70	-15,560,900		2,151	
1/15/75	653.39	-14,725,400		2,356	UP
1/16/75	655.74	-15,345,900		2,645	UP
1/17/75	644.63	-16,658,700	DOWN	2,297	
1/20/75	647.45	-16,736,300	DOWN	2,210	
1/21/75	641.90	-17,097,900	DOWN	2,365	
1/22/75	652.61	-17,033,500		2,615	
1/23/75	656.76	-16,633,400		3,059	UP
1/24/75	666.61	-14,316,600	UP	3,762	UP
1/27/75	692.66	-11,930,400	UP	5,049	UP
1/28/75	694.77	-12,230,800		5,508	UP
1/29/75	705.96	-11,554,800	UP	6,073	UP
1/30/75	696.42	-14,430,900	DOWN	5,922	
1/31/75	703.69	-11,408,400	UP	6,386	UP
2/ 3/75	711.44	- 8,555,600	UP	7,172	UP
2/ 4/75	708.07	-10,678,700		6,915	
2/ 5/75	717.85	- 8,799,800		7,480	UP
2/ 6/75	714.17	- 9,697,900		7,698	UP
2/ 7/75	711.91	- 8,709,400	UP	7,458	
2/10/75	708.39	- 9,328,600		7,387	
2/11/75	707.60	- 8,755,200		7,186	
2/12/75	715.03	- 6,762,800	UP	7,776	UP
2/13/75	726.92	- 4,687,300	UP	8,334	UP
2/14/75	734.20	- 3,722,400	UP	8,491	UP
2/18/75	731.30	- 2,437,300	UP	8,377	
2/19/75	736.39	- 2,543,200		8,353	
2/20/75	745.38	- 2,447,800		8,603	UP
2/21/75	749.77	- 167,700	UP	8,805	UP
2/24/75	736.94	- 64,000	UP	8,227	
2/25/75	719.18	- 2,347,500		7,132	DOWN
2/26/75	728.10	- 1,782,300		7,432	
2/27/75	731.15	- 1,783,600		7,755	
2/28/75	739.05	- 438,700	UP	8,083	
3/ 3/75	753.13	- 2,479,500	UP	8,854	UP
3/ 4/75	757.74	- 1,760,200		9,313	UP

Comparing the Most Active Stock OBV figures with the Market OBV figures, we immediately encounter *a surprising divergence*. While Market OBV bottomed in September, 1974, the Most Active Stock OBV figures trended sharply lower throughout September, October, November, and

December, 1974, finally bottoming on December 30. When one considers the fact that we are working each day here with only 15 different stocks, such a distortion from the total market OBV is understandable. We are dealing here with a collection of *extremes*. When a stock is advancing on extremely high volume, the popular thing is to jump on board and buy it. Conversely, when a stock is under pressure, dropping on very heavy volume, the popular inclination is to sell it. The most active stocks are sort of in a glass fishbowl. Everybody sees them and is usually influenced by their moves. Such intense attention would create price and volume distortions not indicative of the true trend of the market. Since we know that the true market bottom in 1974 occurred in September of that year, the continued sharp decline in the Most Active Stock OBV figures for three months thereafter must be attributed to tax selling and the misguided dumping of stocks which so often occurs around the time of a major market bottom. That must be true because note how the Most Active Stock OBV figures quickly got in line with the general market after December 30, 1974, more than making up the losses of the previous three months during the first two months of 1975.

The year end distortion in the Most Active Stock OBV figures points up an important conclusion that would not be otherwise possible without the use of these valuable figures. Those statistics prove that tax selling, like news and other factors previously covered, *is another device employed by the market to camouflage the true trend,* influencing the uninformed to usually take the wrong action. People are usually more easily influenced by a small group of stocks which are featured each day by virtue of their high volumes rather than by what the market as a whole is doing. However, for any market upturn to be valid, the Most Active Stock OBV figures must soon be aligned with those OBV figures for the market as a whole, showing the bullish pattern of a sustained trend of rising zigzags in the upside and downside breakthroughs. The MAS OBV shows this uptrend as being confirmed on January 27, 1975, making the first upward zigzag in the OBV figures on that day. Evaluating MAS OBV as a prime technical indicator, I would have to conclude on the evidence presented here that it should be used as a *confirming* indicator rather than one capable of rendering a valid early warning signal.

ADDITIONAL VOLUME STUDIES

Volume is so important as an indicator that it cannot be minimized by lumping it in with a group of price indicators and quickly dispensing with the subject by a few generalities. If one is to beat the market, follow the true trail of the smart money, see through the camouflage or window dressing of false market moves, *one must devote most of one's market study time to the study of volume.* After all, money is either flowing into the market or out of it on balance with the exception of those periods when there is a balance between buying and selling pressures creating an overall neutral movement. In those cases it can be said that stocks in general are neither under accumulation or distribution. It is this money flow which is the circulatory system of the market body. One must understand that system if one expects to make a successful diagnosis of the market, proclaiming it healthy or diseased. Long ago it was once asked: "Is it volume which causes price changes, or do price changes cause volume—the hen or the egg, which came first?" I sought to answer that question with sufficient proof back in 1963 by introducing the concept of *on-balance volume,* an analytical technique which proved by contention that *volume tends to precede price.* It is easier for the market to fool you with *price* changes than with *volume* changes because, human nature being what it is, most people are primarily interested in the *price* of their stock rather than the trading volume. A stock trading for months between 6 3/4 and 9 isn't going to excite the general trading public. The price parameter is narrow, and let us say that the stock is very depressed, down considerably from the high. Now allow me to demonstrate quickly the volume changes in that stock, and when it is ended you will know without a doubt what came first, the chicken or the egg, volume or price.

The example chosen is that of Royal Crown Cola between the short period of October 1, 1974, to January 8, 1975. During that period the price of sugar was climbing out of sight, so who in his right mind would want to seriously buy into a soft drink company? We have a situation here where the fundamentals appear to be bad, thus creating a negative psychological atmosphere, keeping the general trading public out of the stock. In the table below the *on-balance volume analytical technique* is going to be used. It is simplicity itself. Everytime the stock closes at a higher price all the trading volume for that day is going to be *added* to a cumulative total, and everytime the stock closes lower, all the trading volume for that day is going to be *subtracted* from that cumulative total. The cumulative net volume is called the on-balance volume. When the price of the stock closes unchanged there is no change in the on-balance volume. The term on-balance volume will be abbreviated to OBV. In the table UP and DOWN designations are used whenever OBV moves above or below previous highs or lows, such designations showing the OBV breakouts.

Royal Crown Cola

Date	Closing Price	Daily Volume	On–Balance Volume (OBV)	
Oct. 1	7.63			
Oct. 2	7.63			
Oct. 3	8.13	2,500	2,500	
Oct. 4	7.75	4,400	- 1,900	
Oct. 7	8.13	1,400	- 500	
Oct. 8	8.25	3,600	3,100	UP
Oct. 9	8.50	2,800	5,900	UP
Oct. 10	8.38	7,100	- 1,200	
Oct. 11	8.00	7,100	- 8,300	DOWN
Oct. 14	9.00	13,200	4,900	
Oct. 15	8.63	3,300	1,600	
Oct. 16	8.38	1,200	400	
Oct. 17	8.50	1,500	1,900	
Oct. 18	8.75	1,300	3,200	
Oct. 21	9.00	2,300	5,500	UP
Oct. 22	9.00	1,200	5,500	UP
Oct. 23	8.63	1,300	4,200	
Oct. 24	8.50	1,700	2,500	
Oct. 25	8.13	4,300	- 1,800	DOWN
Oct. 28	8.00	1,200	- 3,000	DOWN
Oct. 29	8.25	3,400	400	
Oct. 30	7.88	5,300	- 4,900	DOWN
Oct. 31	7.75	3,500	- 8,400	DOWN
Nov. 1	7.75	2,000	- 8,400	DOWN
Nov. 4	7.63	3,000	-11,400	DOWN
Nov. 5	7.75	3,500	- 7,900	
Nov. 6	7.63	4,400	-12,300	DOWN
Nov. 7	7.38	5,700	-18,000	DOWN
Nov. 8	7.75	4,300	-13,700	
Nov. 11	7.75	4,600	-13,700	
Nov. 12	7.50	3,800	-17,500	
Nov. 13	7.25	7,600	-25,100	DOWN
Nov. 14	7.50	6,100	-19,000	
Nov. 15	7.75	4,500	-14,500	
Nov. 18	7.38	5,600	-20,100	
Nov. 19	7.25	4,300	-24,400	
Nov. 20	7.25	6,300	-24,400	
Nov. 21	7.13	4,000	-28,400	DOWN
Nov. 22	7.00	5,400	-33,800	DOWN
Nov. 25	7.13	2,200	-31,600	
Nov. 26	7.13	3,200	-31,600	
Nov. 27	7.25	2,100	-29,500	
Nov. 29	7.25	4,200	-29,500	
Dec. 2	7.13	4,700	-34,200	DOWN
Dec. 3	7.13	2,200	-34,200	DOWN
Dec. 4	7.38	9,900	-24,300	UP
Dec. 5	7.13	1,700	-26,000	

Date	Closing Price	Daily Volume	On–Balance Volume (OBV)	
Dec. 6	7.00	14,500	-40,500	DOWN
Dec. 9	6.75 (ex-dividend)	2,500	-40,500	DOWN
Dec. 10	6.75	7,200	-40,500	DOWN
Dec. 11	6.88	3,100	-37,400	
Dec. 12	6.75	3,800	-41,200	DOWN
Dec. 13	6.88	4,400	-36,800	UP
Dec. 16	6.75	3,500	-40,300	
Dec. 17	6.75	6,700	-40,300	

Note here that as the price of the stock fell back to 6 3/4 on December 16 and 17, the OBV failed to move under the December 12 OBV low. We could then say (until proved otherwise) that the stock was technically stronger on December 16 and 17 than it was at the same price on December 12. Now note what took place next:

Date	Closing Price	Daily Volume	On–Balance Volume (OBV)	
Dec. 18	6.88	57,100	16,800	UP
Dec. 19	7.13	6,800	23,600	UP
Dec. 20	7.38	15,100	38,700	UP
Dec. 23	7.38	8,900	38,700	UP
Dec. 24	7.63	1,700	40,400	UP
Dec. 26	7.75	6,000	46,400	UP
Dec. 27	8.50	14,500	60,900	UP
Dec. 30	8.88	20,000	80,900	UP
Dec. 31	9.00	11,100	92,000	UP
Jan. 2	9.63	5,100	97,100	UP
Jan. 3	9.75	5,500	102,600	UP
Jan. 6	10.13	5,800	108,400	UP
Jan. 7	10.38	2,500	110,800	UP
Jan. 8	10.50	6,100	117,000	UP
Jan. 9	10.50	5,100	117,000	UP
Jan. 10	10.75	5,900	122,900	UP
Jan. 13	10.75	3,200	122,900	UP
Jan. 14	10.63	3,600	119,300	
Jan. 15	10.50	1,300	118,000	
Jan. 16	10.50	5,800	118,000	
Jan. 17	9.38	7,900	110,100	
Jan. 20	9.88	1,700	111,800	
Jan. 21	9.88	1,200	111,800	
Jan. 22	9.50	2,800	109,000	DOWN
Jan. 23	10.00	3,400	112,400	UP
Jan. 24	10.00	7,000	112,400	UP

The stock continued to trend strongly higher, the price at 16 1/2 by mid-May.

On December 18 the stock advanced in price by the miniscule fraction of 1/8. It had been higher than that for months, so what was all the fuss about?

The *dramatic* change was in the *volume of trading*. The stock did something that it had been unable to do for a long time. *It moved up on very heavy volume*. The heavy volume of 57,100 shares was enough to push the OBV up from a near low of -40,300 to +16,800 in one day, and that new OBV figure dramatically moved out above anything recorded on the upside for the past 2 1/2 months. Being a very depressed stock, the sudden demand for the stock had to be traced to *smart money buying*. The general public is only interested in prices and NOT volume and therefore would not have been suddenly attracted to the stock by the small 1/8 rise from 6 3/4 to 6 7/8. Now that we can see the BUY SIGNAL of December 18 based on *volume*, let us see what the price of Royal Crown Cola did thereafter. As the table shows, the price wasted no time in *following* the dramatic OBV signal, climbing rapidly from 6 7/8 to 10 1/2 over the next 13 market sessions, a percentage gain of over 52%. *Volume precedes price*. One must respect an OBV upside breakout on high volume when the stock has been very depressed. It has to be smart money buying *simply because it couldn't be smart money selling*. The smart money would not have previously owned the stock at those depressed levels.

Was Royal Crown Cola a lucky accident? By the time you finish with this book I am sure that you will agree that it was not. While specifically on this subject of volume preceding price and at the same time showing you how OBV works, here is another example culled from the period of time giving a little more price and volume background:

Kane Miller

Date	Closing Price	Daily Volume	On–Balance Volume	
July 29, 1974	9.63	800	+ 800	
July 30	9.75	200	+ 1,000	
July 31	9.63	1,200	- 200	DOWN
Aug. 1	9.50	1,400	- 1,600	DOWN
Aug. 2	9.50	3,400	- 1,600	DOWN
Aug. 5	9.38	1,600	- 3,200	DOWN
Aug. 6	9.63	1,200	- 2,000	
Aug. 7	10.13	1,500	- 500	
Aug. 8	10.25 (ex-dividend)	3,900	3,400	UP
Aug. 9	10.13	300	3,100	
Aug. 12	10.13	1,000	3,100	
Aug. 13	10.00	2,500	600	
Aug. 14	9.75	1,800	- 1,200	
Aug. 15	9.63	1,000	- 2,200	
Aug. 16	9.63	1,800	- 2,200	
Aug. 19	9.38	3,800	- 6,000	DOWN
Aug. 20	8.88	1,100	- 7,100	DOWN
Aug. 21	9.00	700	- 6,400	

Date	Closing Price	Daily Volume	On–Balance Volume (OBV)	
Aug. 22	8.88	3,300	- 9,700	DOWN
Aug. 23	8.63	1,600	-11,300	DOWN
Aug. 26	8.63	2,800	-11,300	DOWN
Aug. 27	8.50	2,100	-13,400	DOWN
Aug. 28	8.88	5,500	- 7,900	
Aug. 29	8.63	3,500	-11,400	
Aug. 30	9.13	2,900	- 8,500	
Sept. 3	9.00	3,200	-11,700	DOWN
Sept. 4	8.88	2,100	-13,800	DOWN
Sept. 5	8.75	1,200	-15,000	DOWN
Sept. 6	8.88	2,200	-12,800	
Sept. 9	8.75	600	-13,400	
Sept. 10	8.50	1,500	-14,900	
Sept. 11	8.75	1,400	-13,500	
Sept. 12	8.50	1,400	-14,900	
Sept. 13	8.13	4,100	-19,000	DOWN
Sept. 16	7.63	4,600	-23,600	DOWN
Sept. 17	8.13	4,200	-19,400	
Sept. 18	8.13	1,800	-19,400	
Sept. 19	8.75	3,400	-16,000	
Sept. 20	9.63	3,800	-12,200	UP
Sept. 23	10.13	5,300	- 6,900	UP
Sept. 24	11.00	6,600	- 300	UP
Sept. 25	10.88	2,400	- 2,700	
Sept. 26	10.63	2,200	- 4,900	
Sept. 27	9.75	1,600	- 6,500	
Sept. 30	9.75	2,600	- 6,500	
Oct. 1	10.75	5,000	- 1,500	
Oct. 2	10.75	1,000	- 1,500	
Oct. 3	10.25	1,200	- 2,700	
Oct. 4	9.75	2,200	- 4,900	
Oct. 7	10.38	3,700	- 1,200	UP
Oct. 8	10.75	2,000	- 800	UP
Oct. 9	10.63	600	200	
Oct. 10	11.25	5,100	5,300	UP
Oct. 11	11.63	2,500	7,800	UP
Oct. 14	11.88	2,100	9,900	UP
Oct. 15	11.13	3,400	6,500	
Oct. 16	11.00	400	6,100	
Oct. 17	10.88	1,400	4,700	
Oct. 18	10.75	1,100	3,600	
Oct. 21	10.50	2,300	1,300	
Oct. 22	10.75	3,400	4,700	
Oct. 23	10.88	400	5,100	
Oct. 24	10.50	2,700	2,400	
Oct. 25	10.13	1,700	700	DOWN
Oct. 28	9.13	2,400	- 1,700	DOWN
Oct. 29	9.13	5,100	- 1,700	DOWN
Oct. 30	9.38	1,300	- 400	
Oct. 31	9.50	1,200	800	

Date	Closing Price	Daily Volume	On–Balance Volume	
Nov. 1	9.25	1,300	- 500	
Nov. 4	9.25	1,600	- 500	
Nov. 5	9.00	1,900	- 2,400	DOWN
Nov. 6	8.88 (ex-dividend)	3,700	- 2,400	DOWN
Nov. 7	9.00	400	- 2,000	
Nov. 8	9.13	1,900	- 100	
Nov. 11	9.50	2,500	2,400	UP
Nov. 12	9.13	1,100	1,300	
Nov. 13	9.38	1,000	2,300	
Nov. 14	9.25	700	1,600	
Nov. 15	9.00	1,400	200	DOWN
Nov. 18	8.88	1,500	- 1,300	DOWN
Nov. 19	9.38	1,000	- 300	
Nov. 20	9.38	500	- 300	
Nov. 21	9.00	1,100	- 1,400	DOWN
Nov. 22	9.13	1,100	- 300	
Nov. 25	9.00	100	- 400	
Nov. 26	9.00	3,600	- 400	
Nov. 27	9.00	500	- 400	
Nov. 29	9.00	No Trades	- 400	
Dec. 2	9.00	2,000	- 400	
Dec. 3	9.00	500	- 400	
Dec. 4	8.75	300	- 700	
Dec. 5	8.63	1,800	- 2,500	DOWN
Dec. 6	8.63	1,600	- 2,500	DOWN
Dec. 9	8.50	1,300	- 3,800	DOWN
Dec. 10	8.63	1,100	- 2,700	
Dec. 11	8.88	1,700	- 1,000	
Dec. 12	8.88	2,100	- 1,000	
Dec. 13	8.88	2,100	- 1,000	
Dec. 16	8.75	5,100	- 6,100	DOWN
Dec. 17	8.88	4,200	- 1,900	
Dec. 18	9.00	2,100	200	UP
Dec. 19	9.50	3,800	4,000	UP
Dec. 20	9.63	3,200	7,200	UP
Dec. 23	10.88	7,700	14,900	UP
Dec. 24	11.38	6,600	21,500	UP
Dec. 26	11.63	5,600	27,100	UP
Dec. 27	11.88	2,000	29,100	UP
Dec. 30	12.50	6,000	35,100	UP
Dec. 31	10.88	9,100	26,000	
Jan. 2	11.25	2,400	28,400	
Jan. 3	11.50	3,900	32,200	
Jan. 6	11.75	11,000	43,300	UP
Jan. 7	11.38	2,000	41,300	
Jan. 8	12.38	9,800	51,100	UP

As the table shows, an important volume alert occurred on December 19, when the OBV came up and bettered the previous UP reading of November 11. A second and stronger alert occurred the next day when OBV jumped to

7,200, now within easy reach of bettering the key OBV high of 9,900 recorded on October 14. The key change and assured buy signal took place on December 23 when OBV advanced to 14,900, *clearing everything seen previously in the entire table!* Thereafter, all price resistance crumbled, and as the OBV made a further unimpeded rise to a new high at 51,500 the price easily rose to 12 3/8. Now note that the price had stood at 12 1/2 on December 30 with an OBV reading of 35,100. The stock is technically *stronger* on January 8 at 12 3/8 because OBV is at the *higher* reading of 51,100. Inasmuch as volume precedes price, the OBV here was saying GO. A few months later stock was over 14.

THE STUDY OF VELOCITY

The *velocity* of a stock can be measured by recording cumulative volume as a percentage of the capitalization. Now don't confuse cumulative volume with on-balance volume. Cumulative volume is a straight adding up of each day's volume regardless of price. In other words, velocity can also be defined as how many times a stock turns its capitalization. If a stock has a capitalization of 10,000,000 shares and records cumulative volume as 10,000,000 shares, it has therefore recorded 100% velocity, having turned over the capitalization once. Now, by adding on-balance volume as a percentage of the capitalization, one can view the impact of accumulation as a percentage of the whole as well as see its relationship to the velocity.

In the *Key* book in 1963 some interesting questions pertaining to velocity and OBV were asked which resulted in the construction of the Spring Principle. If a stock is constantly changing ownership with no clearly defined supply or demand patterns, it could turn its entire capitalization several times with no particular impact on the price. However, if a stock is under *persistent accumulation* (here a clearly defined demand pattern) measured by rising on-balance volume, there is a *mathematical limit* to the accumulation. The limit of course is the size of the capitalization and thus the importance of expressing OBV as a percentage of the capitalization. There is no limit to velocity *until it is related* to OBV. The Spring Principle maintained that as long as a stock maintained accumulation (rising OBV) there was a limit to velocity. Every time the stock turned over its entire capitalization, it was like a giant spring getting tighter and tighter. When the OBV *approached 100%* of the capitalization, the spring would have to snap and the price breakdown would be severe. The laboratory case presented was the great advance in American Motors back in 1958 and 1959, the stock rising in that period from 8 5/8 to 95 1/4. American Motors at that time had a capitalization of 6,000,000 shares. By the time the stock topped out at

95 1/4 in November, 1959, it had racked up a cumulative volume of 22,742,500 shares which was a velocity of 379%. In other words, the capitalization had completely turned over 3.79 times. The spring broke because that super-high velocity was related to an OBV reading of 4,892,400 at the peak which was 81.5% of the capitalization.

What was also shown was an additional characteristic of the Spring Principle—the *acceleration in the price rise as velocity increases providing accumulation is maintained*. At that time the following very revealing figures were given in support of that principle:

Date	Velocity	Stock Price Rise
Jan. 1958	7.5%	8.6%
Feb. 1958	11.4	1.0
Mar. 1958	15.0	1.0
Apr. 1958	32.9	28.9
May 1958	51.1	49.2
June 1958	62.1	49.2
July 1958	73.8	62.2
Aug. 1958	88.9	89.8
Sept. 1958	105.0	137.5
Oct. 1958	142.4	272.2
Nov. 1958	165.5	305.5
Dec. 1958	184.3	356.3
Jan. 1959	202.9	330.2
Feb. 1959	228.7	243.3
Mar. 1959	243.6	302.6
Apr. 1959	263.0	334.5
May 1959	277.1	347.6
June 1959	295.2	418.5
July 1959	309.3	444.6
Aug. 1959	318.0	450.4
Sept. 1959	348.2	567.7
Oct. 1959	374.1	826.9
Nov. 1959	379.0	1003.7

One of the most interesting theoretical questions is what happens when on-balance volume equals the capitalization? Can OBV equal the capitalization? In the case of American Motors on the 1958-59 rise OBV did get up to 81.5% of the capitalization before the spring snapped. In answer to the first question, all those who are going to buy the stock have already bought it. The accumulators have complete control. Any additional buyers will have to get their stock from the original accumulators and thus there can be no further *net* buying, no further rise in OBV, because of this. Therefore, any approach of OBV toward equalling the capitalization (not many cases on record) *must end the price rise*. In answer to the second question, the *Key* book cited the case of NAFI Corp. where the OBV rose to 104.22% of the capitalization, at which point the price broke sharply.

It is not clearly ascertained at what point OBV has to rise to as a percentage of capitalization in order to experience a runaway on the upside such as in the famous case of American Motors. One thing is clear, however: *Rising OBV and velocity have a profound effect on price.*

Now, in the case *of a much more heavily capitalized* stock, perhaps the necessary OBV requirements and velocity requirements *do not involve such higher percentages.* The figures pertaining to *Occidental Petroleum* were of great interest to this writer because the accumulation was every bit as persistent as it was in American Motors back in 1958 and 1959. To illustrate this, an OBV study is given here covering the period from September 16, 1974, to May 21, 1975. From this study one will note that the price of the stock *doubled* between September 16, 1974, and February 12, 1975, with OBV as a percentage of capitalization at only 6.2% and velocity at 20.7%. From these preliminary figures I would have to venture a guess that the stock will advance far above the May, 1975 levels and will serve as a future laboratory example of how far the percentages can range in the case of a heavily capitalized stock under persistent long-term accumulation. In this respect the work is incomplete, but it presents an interesting project for future technicians.

Capitalization: 55 Million Shares

Occidental Petroleum

Date	On–Balance Volume		OBV as a % of Capitalization	Cumulative Total Volume	Velocity	Price
Sept. 16, 1974	0		0	0	0	7.50
Sept. 17	42,600		1.0	42,600	0.1	7.63
Sept. 18	70,400		0.1	70,400	0.1	7.75
Sept. 19	122,600		0.2	122,600	0.2	8.25
Sept. 20	64,000		0.1	181,200	0.3	8.00
Sept. 23	38,500		0.1	206,700	0.3	7.88
Sept. 24	107,400		0.2	275,600	0.5	8.50
Sept. 25	221,100	UP	0.4	389,300	0.7	9.00
Sept. 26	192,700		0.3	417,700	0.7	8.75
Sept. 27	192,700		0.3	439,700	0.8	8.75
Sept. 30	162,900		0.3	469,500	0.8	8.25
Oct. 1	162,900		0.3	490,900	0.9	8.25
Oct. 2	138,000		0.2	515,800	0.9	8.13
Oct. 3	138,000		0.2	538,700	0.9	8.13
Oct. 4	185,900		0.3	586,600	1.0	8.25
Oct. 7	209,600		0.4	610,300	1.1	8.63
Oct. 8	184,600		0.3	635,300	1.1	8.50

Occidental Petroleum (Continued)

Date	On–Balance Volume		OBV as a % of Capitalization	Cumulative Total Volume	On–Balance Volume	
Oct. 9	275,800	UP	0.5	726,500	1.3	9.25
Oct. 10	191,600		0.3	810,700	1.5	8.88
Oct. 11	291,100	UP	0.5	910,200	1.7	9.75
Oct. 14	350,000	UP	0.6	969,100	1.8	10.00
Oct. 15	280,000		0.5	1,039,100	1.9	9.88
Oct. 16	253,100		0.4	1,066,000	1.9	9.25
Oct. 17	293,000		0.5	1,105,900	2.0	9.38
Oct. 18	336,800		0.6	1,149,700	2.1	9.75
Oct. 21	411,100	UP	0.7	1,224,000	2.3	10.38
Oct. 22	539,000	UP	1.0	1,351,900	2.5	10.50
Oct. 23	470,600		0.8	1,420,300	2.6	10.13
Oct. 24	413,200		0.7	1,477,700	2.7	10.00
Oct. 25	413,200		0.7	1,519,500	2.8	10.00
Oct. 28	491,100		0.9	1,597,400	2.9	10.25
Oct. 29	689,300	UP	1.2	1,795,600	3.3	11.00
Oct. 30	907,900	UP	1.6	2,014,200	3.7	11.38
Oct. 31	814,900		1.5	2,107,200	3.9	10.75
Nov. 1	870,000		1.6	2,162,300	4.0	10.88
Nov. 4	815,300		1.5	2,217,000	4.1	10.75
Nov. 5	890,200		1.6	2,291,900	4.2	11.13
Nov. 6	1,176,800	UP	2.1	2,578,500	4.7	11.38
Nov. 7	1,398,800	UP	2.6	2,800,500	5.2	12.38
Nov. 8	1,960,200	UP	3.8	3,361,900	6.2	13.75
Nov. 11	1,649,100		3.0	3,673,000	6.8	13.38
Nov. 12	1,429,200		2.6	3,892,900	7.2	12.25
Nov. 13	1,732,400		3.2	4,196,100	7.7	13.00
Nov. 14	2,067,500	UP	3.8	4,531,200	8.4	13.38
Nov. 15	2,642,000	UP	4.9	5,105,700	9.4	14.13
Nov. 18	2,385,000		4.4	5,362,700	9.9	12.88
Nov. 19	2,212,800		4.1	5,534,900	10.1	12.63
Nov. 20	2,274,500		4.1	5,596,600	10.1	12.75
Nov. 21	2,430,200		4.5	5,752,300	10.5	13.50
Nov. 22	2,632,500		4.9	5,954,600	10.9	13.75
Nov. 25	2,632,500		4.9	6,032,000	11.0	13.75
Nov. 26	2,632,500		4.9	6,146,300	11.2	13.75
Nov. 27	2,632,500		4.9	6,263,000	11.4	13.75
Nov. 29	2,632,500		4.9	6,290,500	11.5	13.75
Dec. 2	2,580,700		4.8	6,342,300	11.6	13.25
Dec. 3	2,694,500	UP	5.0	6,456,100	11.8	13.50
Dec. 4	2,753,300	UP	5.1	6,514,900	11.9	13.38 ex
Dec. 5	2,697,200		5.0	6,571,000	12.0	13.00
Dec. 6	2,583,600		4.8	6,684,600	12.2	12.25
Dec. 9	2,513,100	DOWN	4.7	6,755,100	12.3	12.13
Dec. 10	2,580,100		4.8	6,822,100	12.4	12.88
Dec. 11	2,580,100		4.8	6,901,600	12.5	12.88
Dec. 12	2,535,200		4.7	6,946,500	12.6	12.38
Dec. 13	2,535,200		4.7	6,989,800	12.7	12.38

Occidental Petroleum (Continued)

Date		On−Balance Volume		OBV as a % of Capitalization	Cumulative Total Volume	Velocity	Price
Dec.	16	2,506,700	DOWN	4.7	7,018,300	12.7	12.25
Dec.	17	2,603,400	UP	4.8	7,115,000	12.9	13.00
Dec.	18	2,725,500	UP	5.0	7,237,100	13.1	13.25
Dec.	19	2,686,700		4.9	7,275,900	13.2	13.00
Dec.	20	2,651,900		4.9	7,310,700	13.3	12.63
Dec.	23	2,651,900		4.9	7,367,400	13.4	12.63
Dec.	24	2,670,100		4.9	7,385,600	13.4	12.88
Dec.	26	2,670,100		4.9	7,420,400	13.4	12.88
Dec.	27	2,634,200	DOWN	4.9	7,456,300	13.4	12.50
Dec.	30	2,696,100	UP	5.0	7,518,200	13.5	12.63
Dec.	31	2,755,500	UP	5.1	7,577,600	13.6	12.75
Jan.	2, 1975	2,876,700	UP	5.3	7,698,800	13.8	13.13
Jan.	3	2,801,400		5.2	7,774,100	13.9	12.88
Jan.	6	2,980,300	UP	5.5	7,953,000	14.2	13.75
Jan.	7	3,153,900	UP	5.8	8,126,600	14.5	14.25
Jan.	8	3,069,800		5.7	8,210,700	14.6	13.75
Jan.	9	3,137,600		5.8	8,278,500	14.7	13.88
Jan.	10	3,338,100	UP	6.1	8,479,000	15.0	14.00
Jan.	13	3,038,100	UP	6.1	8,573,600	15.5	14.00
Jan.	14	3,179,700		5.9	8,732,000	15.8	13.50
Jan.	15	3,284,000		6.0	8,836,300	16.0	14.00
Jan.	16	3,390,600	UP	6.2	8,942,900	16.2	14.13
Jan.	17	3,337,200		6.1	8,996,300	16.3	14.00
Jan.	20	3,289,300		6.0	9,044,200	16.4	13.88
Jan.	21	3,245,300		6.0	9,088,200	16.5	13.75
Jan.	22	3,389,100		6.2	9,232,000	16.7	14.38
Jan.	23	3,033,700	DOWN	5.7	9,587,400	17.4	13.88
Jan.	24	3,164,100		5.9	9,717,800	17.6	14.13
Jan.	27	3,335,800		6.1	9,889,500	17.8	14.50
Jan.	28	3.204,700		5.9	10,020,600	18.2	14.13
Jan.	29	3,285,300		6.0	10,101,200	18.3	14.38
Jan.	30	3,143,700	DOWN	5.8	10,242,800	18.5	14.13
Jan.	31	3,219,500		5.9	10,318,600	18.7	14.38
Feb.	3	3,219,500		5.9	10,392,100	18.8	14.38
Feb.	4	3,127,100	DOWN	5.7	10,484,900	19.0	14.25
Feb.	5	3,309,200	UP	6.0	10,667,000	19.3	14.38
Feb.	6	3,066,800	DOWN	5.6	10,909,400	19.7	14.25
Feb.	7	3,125,100		5.7	10,967,700	19.8	14.63
Feb.	10	3,125,100		5.7	11,172,200	20.2	14.63
Feb.	11	3,183,400		5.8	11,230,500	20.3	14.75
Feb.	12	3,415,300	UP	6.2	11,462,400	20.7	15.38
Feb.	13	3,193,300		5.8	11,684,400	21.1	15.00
Feb.	14	3,279,800		5.9	11,770,900	21.2	15.25
Feb.	18	3,165,400	DOWN	5.7	11,885,300	21.4	14.88
Feb.	19	3,165,400	DOWN	5.7	11,957,700	21.7	14.88
Feb.	20	3,246,300		5.9	12,038,600	21.8	15.13
Feb.	21	3,140,400	DOWN	5.7	12.144,500	22.0	15.00
Feb.	24	3,087,700	DOWN	5.6	12,197,200	22.1	14.75

Occidental Petroleum (Continued)

Date		On–Balance Volume	OBV as a % of Capitalization		Cumulative Total Volume	Velocity	Price
Feb.	25	2,981,800	DOWN	5.5	12,303,100	22.3	14.25
Feb.	26	3,071,500		5.6	12,392,800	22.5	14.75
Feb.	27	3.071,500		5.6	12,432,000	22.6	14.75
Feb.	28	3,144,500		5.7	12,505,000	22.7	14.88
Mar.	3	3,144,500		5.7	12,568,300	22.8	14.88
Mar.	4	3,047,100		5.6	12,665,700	23.0	14.38 xα
Mar.	5	2,961,000	DOWN	5.5	12,751,800	23.2	13.88
Mar.	6	3,009,200		5.5	12,800,000	23.2	14.13
Mar.	7	2,964,200		5.5	12,845,000	23.3	14.00
Mar.	10	2,893,200	DOWN	5.3	12.916,000	23.4	13.63
Mar.	11	2,737,800	DOWN	5.0	13.072,400	23.7	13.13
Mar.	12	2,832,700		5.1	13,167,300	23.9	13.50
Mar.	13	2,856,500		5.2	13,191,100	23.9	13.63
Mar.	14	2,916,000		5.3	13,250,600	24.0	14.00
Mar.	17	2,855,900		5.2	13,310,700	24.2	13.75
Mar.	18	2,781,700		5.0	13,384,900	24.3	13.50
Mar.	19	2,745,600		5.0	13,421,000	24.3	13.25
Mar.	20	2,787,800		5.0	13,463,200	24.4	13.38
Mar.	21	2,787,800		5.0	13,502,800	24.5	13.38
Mar.	24	2,724,900	DOWN	4.9	13,565,700	24.6	13.00
Mar.	25	2,669,400	DOWN	4.8	13,621,200	24.7	12.75
Mar.	26	2,765,400		5.0	13,717,200	24.9	13.50
Mar.	27	2,804,400		5.0	13,756,200	24.9	13.63
Mar.	31	2,772,500		5.0	13,788,100	25.0	13.38
April	1	2,745,500		5.0	13,815,100	25.0	13.25
April	2	2,768,700		5.0	13,838,300	25.1	13.38
April	3	2,768,700		5.0	13,858,100	25.1	13.38
April	4	2,768,700		5.0	13,873,400	25.2	13.38
April	7	2,745,200	DOWN	5.0	13,896,900	25.2	13.25
April	8	2,716,000	DOWN	4.9	13,926,100	25.3	13.13
April	9	2,809,700	UP	5.0	14,019,800	25.4	13.75
April	10	2,987,500	UP	5.4	14,197,600	25.8	14.63
April	11	3,304,100	UP	6.0	14,514,200	26.3	15.25
April	14	3,304,100	UP	6.0	14,769,300	26.8	15.25
April	15	3,145,600		5.7	14,927,800	27.1	14.63
April	16	3,145,600		5.7	15,015,700	27.2	14.63
April	17	3,318,200	UP	6.0	15,188,300	27.6	14.75
April	18	3,395,000	UP	6.1	15,265,100	27.7	15.00
April	21	3,294,400		5.9	15,365,700	27.9	14.75
April	22	3,167,900		5.7	15,492,200	27.9	14.13
April	23	3,114,600	DOWN	5.6	15,545,500	28.2	13.88
April	24	3,204,400		5.8	15,635,300	28.4	14.63
April	25	3,094,100	DOWN	5.6	15,745,600	28.6	14.50
April	28	3.034,800	DOWN	5.5	15,804,900	28.7	14.38
April	29	2,951,600	DOWN	5.3	15,888,100	28.8	14.25
April	30	3,004,700		5.4	15,941,200	28.9	14.63
May	1	3,004,700		5.4	16,029,800	29.1	14.63

Occidental Petroleum (Continued)

Date	On–Balance Volume		OBV as a % of Capitalization	Cumulative Total Volume	Velocity	Price
May 2	3,236,600	UP	5.8	16,261,700	29.5	14.88
May 5	3,308,600	UP	6.0	16,333,700	29.7	15.13
May 6	3,178,300		5.7	16,464,000	29.9	14.75
May 7	3,178,300		5.7	16,501,800	30.0	14.75
May 8	3,248,000		5.8	16,571,500	30.1	14.88
May 9	4,039,800	UP	7.3	17,363,300	31.6	16.38
May 12	4,386,900	UP	7.9	17,710,400	32.2	16.50
May 13	4,201,600		7.6	17,895,700	32.5	16.38
May 14	4,201,600		7.6	18,160,100	33.0	16.38
May 15	4,008,700		7.3	18,353,000	33.3	16.25
May 16	3,948,500		7.2	18,413,200	33.4	16.00
May 19	4,045,800		7.3	18,510,500	33.5	16.25
May 20	3,960,600		7.2	18,595,700	33.6	16.13
May 21	3,960,600		7.2	18,688,500	33.9	16.13

At this point the stock became extremely active and higher.

VOLUME MUST PRECEDE PRICE

As further decisive proof that volume is the overriding factor in the technical analysis of a stock, let us consider the case of *Howard Johnson* as it approached the major bottom of late 1974, and then made a decisive turn for the better. Here are the starting figures dated from November 5, 1974. The OBV figures here are the same ones which were used in my weekly stock letter inasmuch as it makes no difference where an OBV line is picked up, one either starting at zero or adopting a previously established series of figures.

Date	Closing Price	OBV	Designation	Date	Closing Price	OBV	Designation
11/ 5	5.38	-386,300	UP	1/ 2	4.75	-609,900	UP
11/ 6	5.25	-488,400		1/ 3	5.00	-583,900	UP
11/ 7	5.25	-488,400		1./ 6	5.13	-565,100	UP
11/ 8	5.00	-612,400	DOWN	1/ 7	5.25	-543,900	UP
11/11	5.38	-595,900		1/ 8	5.13	-601,900	
11/12	5.13	-627,400	DOWN	1/ 9	5.00	-632,800	
11/13	5.38	-606,600		1/10	5.75	-396,300	UP
11/14	5.25	-615,900		1/13	5.63	-476,600	
11/15	5.50	-585,900	UP	1/14	5.25	-652,700	DOWN
11/18	5.13	-624,700		1/15	5.25	-652,700	DOWN
11/19	5.00	-662,200	DOWN	1/16	5.25	-652,700	DOWN
11/20	4.88	-680,000	DOWN	1/17	5.13	-664,700	DOWN
11/21	4.75	-690,900	DOWN	1/20	5.38	-649,500	
11/22	5.00	-675,700		1/21	5.13	-663,700	

Date	Closing Price	OBV	Designation	Date	Closing Price	OBV	Designation
11/25	5.00	-675,700		1/22	5.25	-657,600	UP
11/26	5.00	-675,700		1/23	5.63	-594,900	UP
11/27	4.88	-687,000		1/24	6.38	-483,100	UP
11/29	4.88	-687,000		1/27	6.63	-291,500	
12/ 2	4.88	-687,000		1/28	6.63	-387,900	UP
12/ 3	4.63	-695,500	DOWN	1/29	6.75	-239,100	
12/ 4	4.63	-695,500	DOWN	1/30	6.38	-320,500	
12/ 5	4.50	-710,500	DOWN	1/31	6.63	-240,500	UP
12/ 6	4.50	-710,500	DOWN	2/ 3	7.25	- 99,800	
12/ 9	4.50	-710,500	DOWN	2/ 4	7.00	-172,700	
12/10	4.63	-693,600		2/ 5	7.13	-143,300	UP
12/11	4.38	-716,600	DOWN	2/ 6	7.25	- 38,800	UP
12/12	4.50	-701,400		2/ 7	7.50	48,800	
12/13	4.25	-718,500	DOWN	2/10	7.38	13,100	UP
12/16	4.13	-746,900	DOWN	2/11	7.50	49,000	UP
12/17	4.25	-715,100		2/12	8.25	156,700	UP
12/18	4.13	-726,500		2/13	8.75	444,000	UP
12/19	4.13	-726,500		2/14	8.75	444,000	
12/20	4.13	-726,500		2/18	8.50	379,000	
12/23	4.13	-726,500		2/19	8.50	379,000	
12/24	4.13	-726,500					
12/26	4.25	-714,300	UP				
12/27	4.25	-714,300	UP				
12/30	4.38	-672,300	UP				
12/31	4.50	-628,700	UP				

The first rule to remember is that we do not buy a stock *until it is under accumulation.* A stock cannot be under accumulation if it is making new lows and thus, adding to the first rule, *we do not buy a stock which is making new lows.* Convinced, however, that a new bull market was underway dating from the October 4, 1974 bottom, here is how my stock letter handled Howard Johnson in the November 22, 1974 letter:

> (4 7/8)—Stock recorded a new OBV low on November 20th at -680,000. Remaining convinced that we are in a new bull market, stock can be held for recovery. *HOLD.*

The stock continued to zigzag lower, bottoming at 4 1/8 on December 16 with an OBV low at -746,900. Still showing no sign of a turnaround, the December 6 letter made the following statement:

> (4 5/8)—Stock recorded a new OBV low on December 3rd and 4th at -695,500. Still no sign whatsoever of a turnaround. *HOLD.*

After December 16 something changed, and let us see what it was and what came first. As the review table shows, the stock moved up to 4 1/4 on

December 17 on a volume of 31,800 shares, raising the OBV from -746,900 to -715,100. On December 18, it fell back to 4 1/8 again but did so on a *lighter* volume of 11,400 shares. That put the December 18 OBV at -726,500. Right at this point it must be said that the stock did not make a new low and was technically stronger at 4 1/8 than it was on December 16 at 4 1/8. This point was observed in the December 20 issue of the stock letter:

> (4 1/8)—OBV at new low of -746,900 on December 16th. Still no sign yet of a turnaround although stock technically stronger on December 18th at 4 1/8 than on December 16th. *HOLD.*

Inasmuch as the stock went up on December 17 on more volume than it went down on the next day, it must be concluded that *demand exceeded supply*. Stocks do not rise in price unless demand exceeds supply. Demand is measured in *volume* and thus *volume must precede price*.

After remaining unchanged at 4 1/8 at an *improved* OBV level between December 18 and 24, the stock moved back up to 4 1/4 again on December 26, raising the OBV to -714,300. Since that figure was above the previous high of -715,100 recorded on December 17, it is seen as an *OBV upside breakout* deserving of an UP designation. OBV is higher on December 26 at 4 1/4 than it was on December 17 at 4 1/4, and now we can advance our volume thesis another important step. The casual and uninformed market observer is not going to notice that Howard Johnson was showing steady technical improvement after December 16 because such observers are only influenced by *price,* not realizing that the higher prices they were waiting for *were already being signalled by volume.* The forecasted price improvement began to slowly emerge, getting up to 4 1/2 by December 31, the OBV putting together four consecutive UP designations as the table shows. This was duly noted in the January 3, 1975 issue of the stock letter:

> (4 1/2—This is the first time the stock has been able to put four OBV upside designations together in months, suggesting that the major bottom has at last been recorded. OBV stood at -628,700 on December 31st. *BUY.*

I was already convinced that *accumulation* was at last underway, thus qualifying the stock as a buy. However, *proof positive* of accumulation comes when the stock enters the *first rising field* trend following the bottom. The field trend is determined by looking at the columns marked *Designation,* which simply lists the OBV upside and downside breakouts. Always going by the last UP or DOWN in a series, we can see that Howard Johnson between November 5 and December 16 was in a FALLING field trend which is shown by a downward zigzag in the OBV figures. As the table shows, we had an UP at -386,300, a down at -627,400, an UP at -585,900 and a DOWN at -746,900. To alter that pattern it was necessary for OBV to come up and better the -585,900 reading of November 15th. This it did on January 3 when it reached -583,900. At that point the *field trend* had *improved* from FALLING to DOUBTFUL. In order to get a RISING field trend it was necessary to see a *rising zigzag* in the OBV clusters. OBV in this case would have to make a series of DOWN designations holding above the December 16 level and then a new series of UP designations bettering the previous series of UP designations. Here is what happened: The initial UP series terminated on January 10 at the improved level of -396,300 and the expected down series began on January 14, OBV on that day moving under the previous *closest* low of January 9 (-652,700 moving under -632,800). To this writer it was already obvious that the stock has made the major turn and the comment in the January 17 issue of the stock letter with the stock at 5 1/4 was jubilant:

> (5 1/4)—Confirmed turn at last! OBV bottomed at -746,900 on December 16th and the hint of the impending turn was given here in the last letter as stock showed improved strength on December 18th while still priced at 4 1/8. Series of new up designations started on December 16th, carrying OBV up to -396,300 on January 10th which broke through previous OBV high of -585,900 recorded on November 15th when stock was priced at 5 1/2. Stock then reverted to series of new down designations, OBV down to -652,700 on January 15th, holding well above December 16th OBV low. *BUY.*

The down series at -664,700 on January 17, and the expected new series of up designations got underway on January 23. As OBV moved sharply ahead to -291,500 on January 27, bettering the previous high of -396,300 recorded on January 10, the field trend shifted from DOUBTFUL to RISING. This was the important *confirmation* that the stock was under important *accumulation*. The rising field trend can be seen by looking at the following dates in the table: December 16, January 10, January 17, and January 27, OBV zigzagging higher from -746,900 to -396,300 to -664,700 to -291,500. Now that all the *technical groundwork* had been accomplished, the stock was free to make a more rapid price recovery, *a recovery so ably blueprinted by volume.* The following comments were made in the January 31 and February 14 market letters:

> *January 31*
> (6 3/4—Major buy recommendation at 4 1/2 in January 3rd letter with confirmed major turn reported in January 17th letter. OBV now in strong rising field trend, a new recovery high recorded on January 29th at -239,100. *BUY.*

February 14
(8 1/4)—Major buy recommendation in January 3rd letter at 4 1/2. The OBV uptrend here is *exceedingly powerful!* It moved out to a new high of 156,700 on February 12th. *BUY.*

Date	Closing Price	OBV	Designation	Date	Closing Price	OBV	Designation
2 /20	8.50	379,000		3/18	9.88	458,000	DOWN
2 /21	8.00	305,500		3/19	10.00	494,500	
2 /24	7.88	252,800		3/20	9.75	433,900	DOWN
2 /25	7.63	202,700		3/21	9.63	364,200	DOWN
2 /26	8.25	269,000		3/24	9.25	307,300	DOWN
2 /27	8.13	243,000		3/25	9.50	365,700	
2 /28	8.75	303,800	UP	3/26	9.88	393,700	
3 / 3	9.00	333,900	UP	3/27	10.50	449,100	
3 / 4	9.25	482,300	UP	3/31	10.63	495,700	UP
3 / 5	9.88	499,200	UP	4/ 1	10.00	473,600	
3 / 6	10.88	690,400	UP	4/ 2	9.88	440,700	
3 / 7	11.00	819,200	UP	4/ 3	10.50	613,000	UP
3 /10	10.75	727,800		4/ 4	10.38	587,800	
3 /11	9.88	643,300		4/ 7	10.13	555,100	
3 /12	9.75	465,000		4/ 8	10.13	555,100	
3 /13	10.25	507,900		4/ 9	10.13	555,100	
3 /14	10.38	537,600		4/10	10.63	796,100	UP
3 /17	10.25	503,500		4/11	12.00	1,028,200	UP

The above OBV figures for Howard Johnson illustrate how easy it is to read a stock once it gets firmly in the grip of a *strong rising field trend.* Look at those field trend figures again:

Date	Price	OBV	Designation	Field Trend
12/16/74	4.13	- 746,900	DOWN	FALLING
1/10/75	5.75	- 396,300	UP	DOUBTFUL
1/17/75	5.13	- 664,700	DOWN	DOUBTFUL
3/ 7/75	11.00	+ 819,200	UP	RISING
3/24/75	9.25	+ 307,300	DOWN	RISING
4/17/75	12.50	+1,114,200	UP	RISING
4/29/75	11.63	+ 987,500	DOWN	RISING
5/ 5/75	13.25	+1,185,300	UP	RISING

Go back and review the OBV table, and you will note that it was possible to catch the rising field trend on January 27, 1975, when the price of the stock stood at 6 5/8

WORKING EXAMPLES OF ON-BALANCE VOLUME IN ACTION

For the most thorough grounding possible in working out a *mechanical* system of buying and selling stocks for constant trading profits, the reader is now presented with additional examples of on-balance volume in action. What we are seeking to find out here are the most advantageous ways to use OBV so as to maximize profits and keep losses to a minimum. Is a perfectly mechanical system possible? We hope to find out. In each example we will experiment with a number of buying and selling timing techniques and find out which ones embrace most of the examples. Each significant OBV move will be discussed as it took place, and then the *subsequent* action will be shown, discussed, and analyzed to see whether it conformed to the movement previously suggested by the OBV action.

In using on-balance volume we are dealing with *patterns* which fall into three categories—negative, neutral, or positive. A negative pattern must show on-balance volume downside breakouts, creating down designations below previous down designations and upside on-balance volume breakouts below the level of previous upside breakouts. When we see that pattern we know that the stock is in this negative posture, what I call a falling field trend. The second pattern is a trendless one. We can't find a pattern of an upward zigzag in the OBV breakouts or a pattern of a downward zigzag. The OBV tends to remain within easily defined parameters. The stock is judged to be neutral. It is neither under accumulation or distribution. It is awaiting a signal. The third pattern is the one we are always looking for, the positive pattern. Here we immediately detect OBV upside breakout designations going above previous upside breakout designations, suggesting *a change of pattern*, either jumping directly from a negative or neutral previous pattern.

This raises an immediate, obvious question. Do we buy the stock on that pattern-breaking upside OBV breakout, or do we wait for the next down designation to see if the down holds above the previous down? Well, we're going to find out. We are going to do both, testing out when the best time is to buy following a change to a positive OBV pattern. Conversely, a similar question is raised as to the best time to sell. Obviously we are not going to sell a stock which demonstrates that it is still trending upward. The first OBV indication to sell would come on *a change of pattern*, OBV making a down designation below a previous down designation. The question is do we sell on that first change of pattern down designation, or do we wait to see the next series of up designations fail to better the previous series of up designations? The answer to that will also derive from experimentally doing both and then seeing which method produces the best results.

To flatly say that a downward zigzag in the OBV upside and downside breakout levels is bearish can be downright misleading. In some of the strongest stocks this phenomenon occurs *within a small volume band,* and soon thereafter the stock reverts to a very bullish rising field trend. Those little downward zigzags in strong stocks or little upside zigzags in weak stocks are perfect illustrations of the market's attempts to camouflage the trends, to throw you off the trail of what the smart money is doing.

At this point I want to emphasize the action of on-balance volume in terms of *breathing*. It is probably the best way to express normality. If a stock is showing a pattern of higher OBV upside breakouts and higher downside breakouts, it can be said that the stock is "breathing normally." All stocks trending higher do so in these normal rising zigzags, and all stocks trending lower "breathe lower" in terms of descending OBV zigzags. If a stock has been trending higher (breathing normally), and then we see a downside OBV breakout putting the OBV below a previous down designation, we would have to report at that point that the stock is no longer breathing normally, the exhalation was greater than the previous intake. The positive pattern is destroyed.

Case History

City Investing

We start below with a few preliminary figures covering the period of October 1, 1974 through December 30, 1974:

Date	Closing Price	OBV	Designation	Date	Closing Price	OBV	Designation
10/ 1/74	5.88	0		11/14/74	5.63	- 25,600	
10/ 2/74	6.00	9,400		11/15/74	5.63	- 25,600	
10/ 3/74	5.88	- 7,000		11/18/74	5.50	- 45,900	DOWN
10/ 4/74	6.00	11,900	UP	11/19/75	5.50	- 45,900	DOWN
10/ 7/74	6.00	11,900	UP	11/20/74	5.25	- 57,500	DOWN
10/ 8/74	6.13	26,300	UP	11/21/74	5.00	- 78,300	DOWN
10/ 9/74	6.38	38,500	UP	11/22/74	5.00	- 78,300	DOWN
10/10/74	6.63	57,300	UP	11/25/74	5.13	- 59,500	
10/11/74	6.75	67,300	UP	11/26/74	5.13	- 59,500	
10/14/74	7.00	93,900	UP	11/27/74	5.13	- 59,500	
10/15/74	6.63	72,300		11/29/74	5.13	- 59,500	
10/16/74	6.38	60,400		12/ 2/74	5.00	-143,700	DOWN
10/17/74	6.38	60,400		12/ 3/74	4.75	-156,900	DOWN
10/18/74	6.63	68,800		12/ 4/74	5.00	-132,300	
10/21/74	6.63	68,800		12/ 5/74	4.50	-169,100	DOWN
10/22/74	6.75	75,800		12/ 6/74	4.63	-124,300	UP
10/23/74	6.38	63,800		12/ 9/74	4.50	-140,200	
10/24/74	5.75	30,800	DOWN	12/10/74	4.63	-120,400	UP
10/25/74	5.63	6,500	DOWN	12/11/74	4.88	-103,900	UP
10/28/74	5.50	- 6,100	DOWN	12/12/74	4.88	-103,900	UP
10/29/74	5.88	- 1,400		12/13/74	4.63	-118,700	
10/30/74	5.75	-12,500	DOWN	12/16/74	4.75	-104,600	
10/31/74	5.88	800	UP	12/17/74	4.63	-119,900	DOWN
11/ 1/74	5.75	- 9,700		12/18/74	4.63	-119,900	DOWN
11/ 4/74	5.63	-19,000	DOWN	12/19/74	4.50	-130,800	DOWN
11/ 5/74	5.88	- 4,900		12/20/74	4.38	-155,900	DOWN

Date	Closing Price	OBV	Designation	Date	Closing Price	OBV	Designation
11/ 6/74	5.88	- 4,900		12/23/74	4.38	-155,900	DOWN
11/ 7/74	5.75	-13,100		12/24/74	4.38	-155,900	DOWN
11/ 8/74	5.88	5,600	UP	12/26/74	4.63	-119,100	
11/11/74	5.75	-20,800	DOWN	12/27/74	4.38 xd	-119,100	
11/12/74	5.50	-40,200	DOWN	12/30/74	4.38	-119,100	
11/13/74	5.63	-25,600					

We start out here with a cluster of up designations in early October, *but this in itself is never enough evidence to tell us to buy the stock.* We always need some frame of reference, and so we must await additional up and down designations so as to know whether the stock is in a falling field trend, a doubtful or neutral field trend, or a rising field trend. This frame of reference on City Investing was clear by November 4, 1974. On that day a new down designation occurred which showed the stock to be in a falling field trend. The downward zigzag creating that falling field is shown by the OBV readings of October 14 at 93,900, October 30 at -12,500, October 31 at 800, and November 4 at -19,000. Now note carefully what happened next. On November 8 the OBV rose to 5,600, moving above the previous up designation of 800. That changed the field trend from falling to doubtful, breaking the pattern of downward OBV zigzags. Was this pattern-changing move a buy signal? The answer is no for the following reasons: (1) A rather isolated case of one up designation bettering a previous one is not enough technical evidence to quality as a buy signal. The test here is found *in the previous OBV parameters.* In other words, was there anything dramatic about OBV jumping to 5,600? Looking at the previous figures and seeing OBV considerably down from the 93,900 reading of October 14, the November 8 upswing did nothing to suggest a change in the OBV parameters, the parameters thus far in this case being 93,900 on the upside and -19,000 on the downside. Bearing out that analysis, OBV dropped to a new low the next day at -20,800 on November 11.

The remainder of the past performance figures continued to rule against buying up through December 30, 1974, a string of down designations taking place followed by a cluster of up designations which were well under the previous ups. The table concludes with a fresh string of down designations. However, note that by December 24, the OBV downs *had not broken under the December 5 low.* Wouldn't a new up designation now take on more significance? Of course it would. OBV would only have to move up from the -119,100 level and surpass the -103,900 level of December 12 to put the stock in a *rising* field trend. Let us see what happened next.

Date	Closing Price	OBV	Designation	Date	Closing Price	OBV	Designation
12/31	4.63	-75,600	UP	1/14	5.50	- 6,700	
1/ 2	5.00	-61,400	UP	1/15	5.75	5,500	

Date	Closing Price	OBV	Designation	Date	Closing Price	OBV	Designation
1/ 3	5.00	-61,400	UP	1/16	5.88	17,100	UP
1/ 6	5.25	-47,400	UP	1/17	5.88	17,100	UP
1/ 7	5.50	-27,600	UP	1/20	5.50	5,200	
1/ 8	5.38	-38,000		1/21	5.50	5,200	
1/ 9	5.38	-38,000		1/22	5.75	14.600	
1/10	5.50	-13,300	UP	1/23	5.75	14,600	
1/13	5.63	12,300	UP				

On December 31, 1974, the stock graduated from a doubtful field trend
to a rising field trend, the upward OBV zigzag apparent in the readings of
December 5 at -169,100, December 12 at -103,900, December 24 at
-155,900, and December 31 at -75,600. Achieving a rising field trend in a
depressed stock where the price range has been very narrow for months *must
be considered a buy signal.* While the OBV did not widen the existing
parameters, *the clue to significant change here is seen by comparing the OBV
levels with the price levels.* For instance, the price of City Investing stock
advanced from 4 3/8 to 4 5/8 on December 31, nothing significant there on
the surface. However, *now look at the OBV readings every time the stock
had closed at 4 5/8.* The first closing at that price occurred on December 6
with OBV at -124,300. We then see that the stock closed again at 4 5/8 on
December 10, but this time the OBV is -120,400. Another similar closing
occurred on December 13 with OBV at -118,700. OBV was a hair weaker at
-119,900 on December 17 and 18, and a hair stronger at -119,100 on
December 26, *and sharply improved at -75,600 on December 31.* Upon this
evidence and the shift to a rising field trend do we base our buy signal of
December 31.

By May 7, 1975, OBV was at a new high of 133,900 with the price at 7.

Case History

Consolidated Oil & Gas

We start out with a few preliminary figures covering the period from
October 1, 1974, through November 11, 1974, to get a feeling on the
technical background for some frame of reference.

Date	Closing Price	OBV	Designation	Date	Closing Price	OBv	Designation
10/ 1	5.38	0		10/22	7.00	85,000	UP
10/ 2	5.88	8,300		10/23	6.63	76,800	
10/ 3	5.50	3,500		10/24	6.25	67,800	
10/ 4	5.63	10,800	UP	10/25	6.38	71,100	
10/ 7	5.88	15,000	UP	10/28	6.63	75,300	
10/ 8	5.63	8,300		10/29	6.88	87,300	UP
10/ 9	5.75	22,500	UP	10/30	6.50	83,400	
10/10	5.75	22,500	UP	10/31	6.63	88,300	UP
10/11	5.88	27,700	UP	11/ 1	6.50	87,100	

Date	Closing Price	OBV	Designation	Date	Closing Price	OBV	Designation
10/14	6.38	37,800	UP	11/ 4	6.25	85,900	
10/15	6.25	28,400		11/ 5	6.63	94,800	UP
10/16	6.50	38,400	UP	11/ 6	6.38	90,500	
10/17	6.50	38,400	UP	11/ 7	6.50	97,300	UP
10/18	6.63	55,000	UP	11/ 8	6.88	98,100	UP
10/21	6.75	59,400	UP	11/11	7.38	123,900	UP

Here we see as clear a picture as is possible of a stock under *accumulation*. This is the almost perfect pattern to watch for, a depressed stock showing steady OBV gains *while still moving in a depressed price range*. There is still time to advantageously act, *but not too much time*. Again following the rule of not buying a stock simply on the evidence of a string of up designations, *we must await a definitive OBV signal*. We know the stock is under accumulation but if we await a definitive OBV signal we may be able to buy in at under the November 11 closing price of 7 3/8. Now let us look ahead and see if such a definitive OBV signal was forthcoming.

Date	Closing Price	OBV	Designation	Date	Closing Price	OBV	Designation
11/12	7.00	109,500		11/27	6.50	101,600	UP
11/13	6.75	98,600		11/29	6.38	99,600	
11/14	6.88	108,900		12/ 2	6.00	98,700	
11/15	6.75	102,000		12/ 3	6.00	98,700	
11/18	6.38	95,600	DOWN	12/ 4	6.25	101,500	
11/19	6.13	90,700	DOWN	12/ 5	5.75	98,400	DOWN
11/20	5.88	82,500	DOWN	12/ 6	5.50	95,100	DOWN
11/21	6.13	87,800		12/ 9	5.63	97,000	
11/22	6.38	99,000		12/10	5.50	94,300	DOWN
11/25	6.25	96,200		12/11	5.63	98,100	UP
11/26	6.38	98,300		12/12	5.50	94,600	
12/13	5.50	94,600		12/19	5.25	93,000	
12/16	5.38	92,800	DOWN	12/20	5.38	96,900	UP
12/17	5.50	96,500		12/23	5.25	91,500	DOWN
12/18	5.25	93,000		12/24	5.38	94,100	

Here we see an extremely interesting technical phenomenon-*the OBV downside fakeout occurring just prior to a dynamic upside move*. If the stock is under heavy accumulation and this phenomenon occurs, plunge right in with both feet and buy! In the above figures we see that an up occurred on November 27 at 101,600, a down on December 10 at 94,300, an up on December 11 at 98,100, and a down on December 16 at 92,800. You can see with the eye that this creates a *falling* field trend. That falling field trend condition was in force up through December 24, the OBV up and down designations continuing to zigzag lower. This had to be a fakeout on the downside for the following reasons: (1) The entire extent of the downside zigzag movement took the OBV from 101,600 down to 91,500, *an extremely narrow range of volume* in relation to the previous OBV buildup from 0 to 123,900 in the first review period. When you see an entire falling field trend crammed into such a short space of time involving a very narrow volume range, you can assume it to be a downside fakeout. (2) The downward OBV zigzags created after November 27 saw the OBV remaining well above the 82,500 down level of November 20. I would have been inclined to accept the technical evidence as it stood on December 23 to buy the stock, paying 5 3/8 the next day.

One might not be satisfied that this constituted a definitive buy signal, awaiting still stronger evidence of technical strength. Let us go on and see what happened next.

Date	Closing Price	OBV	Designation	Date	Closing Price	OBV	Designation
12/26	5.63	99,300	UP	1 /10	6.00	115,400	
12/27	6.00	118,400	UP	1 /13	6.00	115,400	
12/30	6.00	118,400	UP	1 /14	5.63	113,200	
12/31	6.50	130,100	UP	1 /15	5.75	116,500	UP
1/ 2	6.38	127,000		1 /16	6.13	123,400	UP
1/ 3	6.25	124,400		1 /17	7.13	259,600	UP
1/ 6	6.13	116,700		1 /20	8.25	394,600	UP
1/ 7	5.88	112,700		1 /21	7.75	322,100	
1/ 8	6.00	115,400		1 /22	9.25	460,300	UP
1/ 9	6.00	115,400		1 /23	9.00	339,000	

Here the OBV pattern changes abruptly. Confirming the previous downside OBV fakeout, the OBV on December 26, moved out above the previous up of December 20, thus changing the field trend from falling to doubtful. One could even say that the December 26 evidence constituted a definitive buy signal. What happened immediately thereafter removed any doubts, OBV smashing through to 130,100 on December 31, easily clearing the November 11 high of 123,900. Even then one was paying 6 1/2 or lower which was under the 7 3/8 closing of November 11, *but was doing so also on a definite OBV buy signal.* One also had three opportunities to buy the stock *under* 6 on January 7, January 14, and January 15, on the clear evidence that the stock, having already given a major buy signal, was "breathing normally" between December 31 and January 15. *A stock is showing great strength when it starts another series of up designations without having any down designations in between.* One could have bought in on January 15 on that evidence alone, paying less than 6. The major upthrust that occurred thereafter was more than ample reward for following any of the previous buy signals.

Case History

Hershey Foods

In the case of Hershey Foods, the stock was chosen because it was in a definite base pattern, paid a rich dividend (which is really irrelevant) and would probably be a stock which would show some marked recoveries when the price of sugar broke in late 1974. It was monitored on a daily basis and the preliminary figures bore out the contention that the stock was ripe for accumulation. The amazing thing here is that, being so attractive on so many counts, the stock traded in such low volume. However, it is chosen here to illustrate that *any pattern of proven accumulation is valid regardless of very low volume.* Such a pattern invariably gives way to higher volume days later on as more people become attracted to the increasingly obvious strength. Here are the preliminary figures covering the period from October 1, 1974, to November 18, 1974:

Date	Closing Price	OBV	Designation	Date	Closing Price	OBV	Designation
10/ 1	8.88	1,300		10/25	9.50	9,700	DOWN
10/ 2	8.88	1,300		10/28	9.63	10,000	
10/ 3	9.00	2,000		10/29	9.63	10,000	
10/ 4	9.00	2,000		10/30	9.63	10,000	
10/ 7	9.75	6,400		10/31	9.50	8,500	DOWN
10/ 8	9.88	7,700		11/ 1	9.25	6,400	DOWN
10/ 9	10.00	12,200		11/ 4	9.13	6,200	DOWN
10/10	10.00	12,200		11/ 5	9.00	5,500	DOWN
10/11	10.50	13,900		11/ 6	9.00	5,500	DOWN
10/14	10.50	13,900		11/ 7	9.63	10,800	UP
10/15	10.25	12,600		11/ 8	10.13	15,600	UP
10/16	10.25	12,600		11/11	10.13	15,600	UP
10/17	9.75	10,300		11/12	9.88	14,300	
10/18	10.13	11,500		11/13	9.88	14,300	
10/21	10.00	11,100		11/14	9.63	13,500	
10/22	9.75	10,400		11/15	10.75	17,700	UP
10/23	9.75	10,400		11/18	10.75	17,700	UP
10/24	9.75	10,400					

It must be surmised from the above set of figures that by November 11, the stock was in a rising field trend in view of the fact that one can observe the larger rising zigzag. Since the last down designation stopped at 5,500 on November 6, and was followed by a cluster of up designations (the 5,500 figure holding above the early October levels), the first series of ups provided a technically valid buy signal, November 8 providing the specific signal. On that day the OBV cleared the October highs, implying the near-term price breakout above the 10 1/2 recorded on October 11 and 14. A few days later the stock made the price breakout predicted by the on-balance volume figures, OBV moving out to a new high of 17,700, fully confirming the validity of the price breakout. So here we encounter a buy signal first on the November 8 *OBV breakout* followed up by a more forceful buy signal on the *confirmed price breakout* of November 15.

The technical groundwork in that period from October 1, 1974, to November 18, 1974, showed more than sufficient strength to withstand any kind of pullback. In the days that followed, these normal pullbacks occurred:

Date	Closing Price	OBV	Designation	Date	Closing Price	OBV	Designation
11/19	10.00	14,700		12/23	8.88	11,300	
11/20	10.13	15,800		12/24	9.25	13,100	
11/21	9.75	13,300	DOWN	12/26	9.88	16,700	
11/22	9.88	13,900		12/27	10.13	19,600	
11/25	9.75	13,200	DOWN	12/30	10.00	16,100	
11/26	10.13	15,400	UP	12/31	9.75	11,200	DOWN
11/27	10.25	18,500	UP	1/ 2	10.63	14,400	
11/29	9.63	16,900		1/ 3	10.75	15,500	
12/ 2	9.63	16,900		1/ 6	11.50	19,100	
12/ 3	9.13	15,700		1/ 7	11.25	17,600	
12/ 4	9.00	13,500		1/ 8	10.75	16,000	
12/ 5	8.88	12,700	DOWN	1/ 9	11.25	17,500	
12/ 6	9.13	14,200		1/10	12.25	21,600	UP
12/ 9	8.63	12,200	DOWN	1/13	12.38	23,700	UP
12/10	8.88	14,700	UP	1/14	12.13	21,500	
12/11	9.00	16,500	UP	1/15	12.38	24,900	UP
12/12	8.88	15,000		1/16	12.50	26,200	UP
12/13	8.75	10,300	DOWN	1/17	12.75	27,600	UP
12/16	8.88	12,200		1/20	12.75	27,600	UP
12/17	9.00	13,600		1/21	12.75	27,600	UP
12/18	9.13	17,400	UP	1/22	12.75	27,600	UP
12/19	9.50	21,300	UP	1/23	12.75	27,600	UP
12/20	9.00	17,300		1/24	13.00	29,900	UP

The stock encountered a normal cluster of down designations following the assured upside breakouts, OBV holding well above the previous down designations. By November 27, the stock was seen to be in an assured rising field trend. Following this we note that the stock then went into a *falling* field trend by December 13, and that in no way constituted any sell signals. There is a double test involved here which quickly clears the air as to whether such a downside movement has any technical validity. First of all, the entire OBV downswing from November 27, to December 13, was from 18,500 to 10,300, too narrow a band of volume to upset the overall pattern of accumulation. Secondly, do a quick price/OBV check at each critical level to see whether technical strength was maintained. The first down designation calling for such a quick checkout was that of December 5, when OBV moved under the previous down designation level of November 25. Since the stock had closed down at 8 7/8 with OBV at 12,700, we simply run our finger back to the last time the stock closed at 8 7/8 and find that this was on October 2, when OBV stood at 1,300. So we can make a statement here that the stock was technically stronger on December 5 at 8 7/8 than it was on October 2nd at 8 7/8. Similar comparisons on the down designation days of December 9 and 13 met the same positive conclusions.

Almost invariably the stock quickly awards the holder with renewed strength if he failed to be concerned with the little fakeout movement, another characteristic of a strong stock. Note how quickly the stock reverted to the upside, posting a new OBV high on December 19. Even then it did pull back once more to 8 7/8 on December 23. Note on that date that the OBV stood at 11,300, under the December 16 level when the stock was last at 8 7/8. One might ask why that wasn't showing the stock to be technically weaker. Inasmuch as there was no down designation posted on December 23, the small OBV pullback could not be questioned. The next posted down designation occurred on December 31, and that was above the previous one of December 13. By January 13 the stock was back in a rising field trend.

Date	Closing Price	OBV	Designation	Date	Closing Price	OBV	Designation
1/27	13.00	29,900	UP	2/18	13.00	24,300	
1/28	12.50	23,800		2/19	13.63 xd	29,600	UP
1/29	12.63	25,600		2/20	14.13	39,200	UP
1/30	12.63	25,600		2/21	14.00	34,700	
1/31	12.38	22,600	DOWN	2/24	14.00	34,700	
2/ 3	12.63	25,400		2/25	14.00	34,700	
2/ 4	12.50	17,000	DOWN	2/26	14.38	37,100	
2/ 5	12.63	18,800		2/27	14.88	46,200	UP
2/ 6	13.13	22,300		2/28	14.75	42,200	
2/ 7	13.00	20,900		3/ 3	16.25	53,200	UP
2/10	13.13	23,100	UP	3/ 4	16.00	40,100	DOWN
2/11	13.13	23,100	UP	3/ 5	15.88	37,000	DOWN
2/12	13.25	24,700	UP	3/ 6	15.75	32,400	DOWN
2/13	13.88	28,300	UP	3/ 7	15.75	32,400	DOWN
2/14	13.00	24,300		3/10	15.88	39,700	

Being in the grip of such a clearly defined rising field trend, Hershey had no trouble in zigzagging considerably higher, reaching 20 1/4 by April 22, and OBV at 141,400. It was another case of stock going begging in the 9 to 10 area, with outstanding bullish signals being flashed, and more than doubling a few months later.

MEASURING OBV POWER BY EIGHTHS

We have learned that volume is infinitely more important than price. This being true, we can then express this volume power in terms of the *price eighths* so as to determine the falsity of some downside price swings as well as the approaching finality of price tops. For instance, if a stock is undergoing a very strong price run-up and the volume per eighth is reasonably constant, then it is likely that the upswing has not terminated. However, suppose that volume *per eighth* makes a decided decline as the price run-up continues. That would mean that *the price was then outrunning the volume.* For instance, suppose the stock jumped 1/2 a point on Monday on 30,000 shares, 1 1/2 points on Tuesday on 50,000 shares, and 3 1/2 points on Wednesday on 75,000 shares. In terms of *volume per eighth,* the power increments would be 7,500 on Monday, 4,166 on Tuesday, and 2,678 on Wednesday. That reveals *a loss of strength* even though OBV in this case jumped from 30,000 to 80,000 and then to 155,000.

Let us now add this technique to the daily monitoring of stocks we are most interested in following and demonstrate how it worked out in the following case history.

Case History

Merrill Lynch

In the fall of 1974, Wall Street was wondering if the market would ever go up again. Merrill Lynch was a natural stock to start following as a bellwether inasmuch as one could see how the Street was treating the stock of the world's largest brokerage house right in the face of all the bad news and worsening economic statistics. As the figures below will show, the stock was being *heavily accumulated* at the market lows, and as the news got worse after early October, *the accumulation became still more pronounced.*

Date	Closing Price	OBV	Designation	Volume Per Eighth	Cumulative	Designation
10/ 1	7.88	45,900		+ 6,557	6,557	
10/ 2	8.00	96,200		50,300	56,887	
10/ 3	7.75	83,500		- 6,350	50,537	
10/ 4	7.63	62,000		-20,500	30,037	
10/ 7	8.00	89,700		+ 9,233	39,270	
10/ 8	8.00	89,700		0	39,270	
10/ 9	8.25	135,500	UP	+22,900	62,170	UP
10/10	8.75	231,400	UP	+23,975	86,145	UP
10/11	8.63	187,500	UP	- 43,900	42,245	
10/14	9.00	283,100	UP	+ 31,866	74,111	
10/15	9.00	283,100	UP	0	74,111	
10/16	9.00	283,100	UP	0	74,111	
10/17	9.00	283,100	UP	0	74,111	
10/18	9.00	283,100	UP	0	74,111	
10/21	9.88	334,200	UP	+ 7,300	81,411	
10/22	10.00	428,500		+ 94,300	175,711	UP
10/23	9.50	391,100		- 7,480	168,231	
10/24	9.25	350,600		- 20,250	147,981	
10/25	9.13	312,400		- 38,200	109,781	
10/28	9.25	342,500		+ 30,100	139,881	
10/29	9.75	405,000		+ 15,625	155,506	
10/30	9.75	405,000	UP	0	155,506	

Date	Closing Price	OBV	Designation	Volume Per Eighth	Cumulative	Designation
10/31	10.00	493,100	UP	+ 44,050	199,556	UP
11/ 1	10.00	493,100		0	199,556	UP
11/ 4	9.75	455,800	UP	- 18,650	180,906	
11/ 5	10.50	570,700	DOWN	+ 19,150	200,056	UP
11/ 6	10.38	427,000		-143,700	56,356	DOWN
11/ 7	10.50	537,900		+110,900	167,256	
11/ 8	10.50	537,900	UP	0	167,256	
11/11	10.88	601,000		+ 21,033	188,289	
11/12	10.63	512,000		- 44,500	143,789	
11/13	10.50	466,300		- 45,700	98,089	
11/14	10.75	505,400	DOWN	+ 19,550	117,639	
11/15	10.25	462,300	DOWN	- 10,775	106,864	
11/18	9.25	404,300	DOWN	- 7,250	99,614	
11/19	9.13	345,800		- 58,500	41,114	DOWN
11/20	9.25	369,400		+ 23,600	64,714	
11/21	9.88	410,400		. 8,200	72,914	
11/22	10.13	427,500		+ 8,550	81,464	
11/25	10.00	385,300		- 42,200	39,264	DOWN
11/26	10.63	441,100	UP	+ 11,160	50,424	
11/27	10.13	413,200		- 6,975	43,449	
11/29	10.13	413,200		0	43,449	
12/ 2	9.75	396,700		- 5,500	37,949	DOWN
12/ 3	9.63	379,800	DOWN	- 16,900	21,049	DOWN
12/ 4	9.88	402,300		+ 11,250	32,299	
12/ 5	9.50	394,500		- 2,600	29,699	
12/ 6	8.88	360,700	DOWN	- 6,760	22,939	
12/ 9	9.00	412,900	UP	+ 52,200	75,139	UP
12/10	9.38	440,300	UP	+ 9,133	84,272	UP
12/11	9.63	519,200	UP	+ 26,300	110,572	UP
12/12	9.25	483,200		- 12,000	98,572	
12/13	9.25	483,200		0	98,572	
12/16	9.50	509,200		+ 13,000	111,572	UP
12/17	10.25	561,700	UP	+ 8,750	120,322	UP
12/18	10.13	519,900		- 41,800	78,522	DOWN
12/19	10.38	543,300		+ 11,700	90,222	
12/20	10.13	515,100	DOWN	- 14,100	76,122	DOWN
12/23	9.75	484,600	DOWN	- 13,500	62,622	DOWN
12/24	10.38	510,100		+ 5,100	67,722	
12/26	10.38	510,100		0	67,722	
12/27	10.13	473,800	DOWN	- 18,150	49,572	DOWN
12/30	10.38	515,200	UP	+ 20,700	70,272	UP
12/31	11.00	587,100	UP	+ 14,380	84,652	UP
1/ 2	10.88	533,200		- 53,900	30,752	DOWN
1/ 3	10.50	495,700		- 12,500	18,252	DOWN
1/ 6	10.75	531,800		+ 18,050	36,302	
1/ 7	10.75	531,800		0	36,302	
1/ 8	10.38	501,500		- 10,100	26,202	
1/ 9	10.75	533,500	UP	+ 10,666	36,868	UP
1/10	11.00	597,600	UP	+ 32,050	68,918	UP
1/13	11.00	597,600	UP	0	68,918	UP
1/14	11.13	629,600	UP	+ 32,000	100,918	UP
1/15	11.38	678,200	UP	+ 23,800	124,718	UP
1/16	11.50	710,200	UP	+ 32,000	156,718	UP

Date	Closing Price	OBV	Designation	Volume Per Eighth	Cumulative	Designation
1/17	11.13	678,200		- 10,666	146,052	
1/20	12.00	770,200	UP	+ 13,142	159,194	UP
1/21	11.63	708,200		- 20,666	138,528	DOWN
1/22	12.38	752,200		+ 7,333	145,861	
1/23	12.50	936,600	UP	+184,400	330,261	UP
1/24	12.63	992,500	UP	+ 55,900	386,161	UP
1/27	13.38	1,226,600	UP	+ 39,016	425,177	UP
1/28	12.88	1,007,300		- 54,825	370,352	
1/29	13.25	1,094,100		+ 28,933	399,285	
1/30	13.13	1,009,800		- 84,300	314,985	DOWN
1/31	13.75	1,085,600		+ 15,160	330,145	
2/ 3	14.00	1,180,600	UP	+ 47,500	377,645	
2/ 4	13.75	975,000	DOWN	-102,800	274,845	DOWN
2/ 5	14.25	1,053,600		+ 19,850	294,695	
2/ 6	14.50	1,199,300	UP	+ 72,850	367,545	
2/ 7	14.75	1,275,100	UP	+ 37,900	405,445	UP
2/10	14.50	1,202,900		- 36,100	369,345	
2/11	14.50	1,202,900	UP	0	369,345	
2/12	15.25	1,283,900	UP	+ 13,500	382,845	
2/13	16.00	1,491,000	UP	+ 34,615	417,460	UP
2/14	16.25	1,660,400	UP	+ 84,400	501,860	UP
2/18	15.75	1,554,000		- 26,600	475,260	

Case History

Royal Crown Cola

We start below with a series of preliminary figures:

Date	Closing Price	OBV	Designation	Date	Closing Price	OBV	Designation
10/ 1/74	7.63	0		11/ 8/74	7.75	-12,700	
10/ 2/74	7.63	0		11/11/74	7.50	-16,500	
10/ 3/74	8.13	2,500		11/12/74	7.25	-24,100	DOWN
10/ 4/74	7.75	- 1,900		11/13/74	7.25	-24,100	DOWN
10/ 7/74	8.13	- 500		11/14/74	7.50	-18,000	
10/ 8/74	8.25	3,100	UP	11/15/74	7.75	-13,500	
10/ 9/74	8.50	5,900	UP	11/18/74	7.38	-19,100	
10/10/74	8.38	- 1,200		11/19/74	7.25	-23,400	
10/11/74	8.00	- 8,300	DOWN	11/20/74	7.25	-23,400	
10/14/74	9.00	4,900		11/21/74	7.13	-27,400	DOWN
10/15/74	8.63	1,600		11/22/74	7.00	-32,800	DOWN
10/16/74	8.38	400		11/25/74	7.13	-30,600	
10/17/74	8.50	1,900		11/26/74	7.13	-30,600	
10/18/74	8.75	3,200		11/27/74	7.25	-28,500	
10/21/74	9.00	5,500	UP	11/29/74	7.25	-28,500	
10/22/74	9.00	5,500	UP	12/ 2/74	7.13	-33,200	DOWN
10/23/74	8.63	4,200		12/ 3/74	7.13	-33,200	DOWN
10/24/74	8.50	2,500		12/ 4/74	7.38	-23,300	UP
10/25/74	8.13	1,800	DOWN	12/ 5/74	7.13	-25,000	
10/28/74	8.00	,000	DOWN	12/ 6/74	7.00	-39,500	DOWN
10/29/74	8.25	400		12/ 9/74	6.75 xd	-39,500	DOWN

Date	Closing Price	OBV	Designation	Date	Closing Price	OBV	Designation
10/30/74	7.88	- 4,900	DOWN	12/10/74	6.75	-39,500	DOWN
10/31/74	7.75	- 7,400	DOWN	12/11/74	6.88	-36,400	
11/ 1/74	7.63	-10,400	DOWN	12/12/74	6.75	-40,200	DOWN
11/ 4/74	7.75	6,900		12/13/74	6.88	-35,800	UP
11/ 5/74	7.63	-11,300	DOWN	12/16/74	6.75	-39,300	
11/ 6/74	7.38	-17,000	DOWN	12/17/74	6.75	-39,300	
11/ 7/74	7.75	-12,700					

For the period covered from October 1, 1974, to December 17, 1974, we can easily see that Royal Crown was in a falling field trend, the stock "breathing" negatively. The up designation of October 21 and 22 was below that of October 9, and the down designations that followed dropped well below the down designation level of October 11. The up designation of December 4 was well under that of October 22, and the down designation of December 12 was under the previous one of December 3. The up designation of December 13 was under the previous one of December 4. At no time during that period did the stock deviate from that negative OBV pattern.

The pattern changed on December 18. On that day the stock advanced 1/8 point on volume of 57,100 shares. Thinking in terms of *price,* nobody is going to be startled into action by a stock moving up from 6 3/4 to 6 7/8. The key to dynamic change in the pattern of stock price movements must lie in the *volume* changes, bearing out my long contention that *volume precedes price.* Let us now see what the December 18 trading volume of 57,100 shares did for Royal Crown at that point and thereafter. Adding the figure 57,100 to the -39,300 OBV level of December 17, we come up with an OBV reading of +17,800 for December 18. That exceeded the immediate previous OBV high of -35,800, and thus we get a new up designation on the December 18 reading. But lo and behold, the December 18 OBV reading of +17,800 busted through the earlier up designation level of -23,300 recorded on December 4, and we also see as we run our eye back over all the other OBV levels that the OBV of December 18 *cleared all previous hurdles.* Here then had to be *a significant change of pattern.* On that one day the stock got out of the falling field trend, the trend improving to doubtful. I use the expression "doubtful" simply because as yet Royal Crown had not shown an OBV pattern *zigzagging* higher. To get into a rising field trend, the down designations after December 18 would have to hold above the December 12 level, and this would have to be followed by new up designations above the December 18 level. Now let us see what happened after the December 18 change of pattern:

Date	Closing Price	OBV	Designation	Date	Closing Price	OBV	Designation
12/18/74	6.88	17,800	UP	1/ 7/75	10.38	111,900	UP
12/19/74	7.13	24,600	UP	1/ 8/75	10.50	118,000	UP
12/20/74	7.38	39,700	UP	1/ 9/75	10.50	118,000	UP
12/23/74	7.38	39,700	UP	1/10/75	10.75	123,900	UP
12/24/74	7.63	41,400	UP	1/13/75	10.75	123,900	UP
12/26/74	7.75	47,400	UP	1/14/75	10.63	120,300	
12/27/74	8.50	61,900	UP	1/15/75	10.50	119,000	
12/30/74	8.88	81,900	UP	1/16/75	10.50	119,000	
12/31/74	9.00	93,000	UP	1/17/75	9.38	111,100	
1/ 2/75	9.63	98,100	UP	1/20/75	9.88	112,800	
1/ 3/75	9.75	103,600	UP	1/21/75	9.88	112,800	
1/ 6/75	10.13	109,400	UP	1/22/75	9.50	110,000	DOWN

The stock immediately took off in an impressive series of daily OBV upside breakouts. No new down designation showed up until January 22, 1975. Thus far we have to conclude that the key buy signal occurred on December 18, buying on the first OBV up designation *that changed the previous OBV pattern.* If one waited until the first down designation after the pattern-breaking up designation, then one would have paid the higher price of 9 1/2 as against the lower price of 7 1/8 paid the day after the December 18 signal. For the record then, the stock was bought on the December 18 signal and up through January 22, 1975, was not sold. The down designation of January 22 showed the OBV standing at 110 000, sharply *above* the previous down designation of December 12, 1974. So then, the pullback on January 22, 1975, was *perfectly normal,* the stock "breathing normally."

EXPLORE UNPOPULARITY

I cannot accent enough the extreme attraction of *unpopularity.* It goes against the grain to buy a stock at a time when very few people want it. Most people won't do it, and *therein lies the principal reason why most people will never make maximum profits in the stock market.* Over and over you must repeat BUY LOW–SELL HIGH, BUY LOW–SELL HIGH, BUY LOW–SELL HIGH until your market thinking is completely reoriented to "smart money" thinking. If a stock is popular and has been rising for some time it is obviously not low. Stocks in the low category usually reflect a negative aura generally associated with unfavorable developments which put them in the low category. It would seem that at such a time nobody wants them. Baron Rothschild often said that the time to buy stocks is when nobody wants them. In the original *Strategy* book I cited that Rothschild statement as being theoretically correct market doctrine. I added, however, that a stock is not under accumulation when it is making new lows every day. If a stock is making new lows every day, it is more unwanted than a stock not making new lows. Therefore it is important to make a significant revision in the Rothschild statement; it should now read as follows: The time to buy stocks is when *most people don't want them* and when the technical evidence shows that *some people,* a small informed minority, *do want them.* The stocks must therefore be *in the earliest stages of informed accumulation.* That is an important distinction. Otherwise, one might think one could automatically buy into any situation where a stock is hit by very bad news and commences to make a series of new lows. One would soon go broke doing that because, as stated above, such stocks are not under accumulation, *and at no time should a stock be bought unless there is evidence of accumulation.*

So what we are looking for are *unpopular* stocks *under accumulation.* This means that no matter how bad the news is about those stocks they are no longer making new lows. The most reliable evidence we have that such stocks are under accumulation is found in the on-balance volume figures. When we see unpopular stocks coming off their lows in the face of bad news with on-balance volume signifying a reversal of the previous downtrend, we can correctly assume that it is "smart money" buying because most people don't buy stocks when they are low since "low" implies bad news and unpopularity. By the same token we can say that *most* people SELL LOW and BUY HIGH, doing the opposite of the informed smart money crowd. I'm talking sheer numbers now because the individual identities among both the smart money minority crowd and the generally lesser informed larger crowd are constantly changing. Never forgetting the constant game going on between the informed and uninformed factions, constantly rehearse the logic of the game plan over and over to yourself before you make an important stock commitment. The game is only made possible by *two opposing factions.* No exchange of stock is possible unless one side buys and the other side sells. When stocks are very low and under accumulation, the smart money is buying and is only able to do this because the uninformed crowd is selling. The uninformed crowd is selling only because they must be gripped by fear, otherwise they wouldn't be selling at such low prices. The news is bad and the stocks are unpopular. We therefore know that if we are to maximize our profits we have to have a *complete reorientation* in our market thinking, getting into step with the smart money faction. We have to capitalize on public fear, exploit unpopularity and seek out the smart money movements at all times.

We should always be attracted to *market extremes* because such extremes imply near-term reversals. All extremes are motivated by either fear or greed. Here is a typical example: The price of sugar had been rising for several months during 1974 but after September soared straight upwards to stratospheric heights, the price movement on the commodity chart making a straightline vertical ascent. Now we know that when a chart shows such a *vertical* ascent that it is a *terminal* move. The soaring price of sugar had obviously hurt the soft drink industry. If sugar was going to come down, then the soft drink stocks would be going up. Here was a beautiful case of watching for accumulation in an unwanted stock group. Sure enough, it was there. It had already started in earnest with Dr. Pepper on October 28 when the stock had moved up from 7 1/8 to 7 1/2 on a large block of 246,800 shares. That implied smart money betting that the high price of sugar then prevailing could not be maintained. Sure enough, the price of sugar peaked in the third week of November, and that automatically spurred the smart money buying of the soft drink stocks and other industries heavily influenced by the price of sugar such as the confectioners. Anticipating this, I strongly recommended the purchase of Dr. Pepper, Hershey Foods, Coca Cola, Royal Crown, and others which produced gains ranging to as high as 80% in less than three months. So then, here was a typical case of buying them when *most* people did not want them, following a line of accumulation in an unpopular group.

Hundreds of case histories could be shown where unpopularity was exploited by the smart money, racking up percentage gains you would seldom ever see in a portfolio managed by a bank, for instance. The energy crisis had obviously hurt Howard Johnson in 1974, the stock having plummeted to 4 1/8 by December 16 of that year. However, accumulation was evident by the turn of the new year, and I heavily recommended purchase at 4 1/2. By May, 1975, the stock was trading at 14. The key word always is *accumulation* as measured by *on-balance volume.* No stock should ever be bought unless *it is under accumulation.*

Probably one of the most outstanding cases of exploited unpopularity was that of Merrill Lynch. At a time when 46% of the people according to the polls were looking for a depression and the pundits were betting that a complete crash in stock prices would wipe out a number of the important stock brokerage firms, important buying was noted in depressed Merrill Lynch, the world's largest brokerage house. When the Dow averages made their last confirmed bottom on October 4, 1974, Merrill Lynch stock was selling at 7 5/8. On the surface it would have seemed to the uninformed Wall Street observer the worst of times to buy stocks and especially the very worst of times to buy into a brokerage house, an obvious target of hard times if the market was headed into a complete crash. *But that was the time to buy.* The on-balance volume figures showed a steady rise commencing from that time of too obvious despair, and by mid-February of 1975 the stock had climbed to 16 1/4, *more than double the price of four months earlier.* Somebody took advantage of the stock's maximum unpopularity to start accumulating the issue. That somebody was the smart money. Such accumulation cannot be disguised. The volume of trading is reported every market day, and when a stock rises on more volume than it falls on, it is reflected by *rising on-balance volume,* the line of *accumulation.* If one had simply adopted the policy of being automatically attracted to unpopularity one would have noted the accumulation going on in Merrill Lynch stock and simply jumped on the bandwagon.

In a sense market technicians are parasites. It was not necessary to know WHY Merrill Lynch was being bought, only that it was *being* bought. When on-balance volume shows a depressed stock under accumulation, it is assumed that it is smart money buying, and the technically oriented buyer simply follows the action in a parasitic manner, living off of the knowledge of the most informed smart money buyers who started the line of accumulation. After the stock had more than doubled by February, 1975, there were circulated rumors that the stock was benefiting handsomely because the company was the middle man agent for the vast financial transactions of the rich Arab nations. Whether true or not, the price of the stock was real, and the short-term returns were better than 100% for those who noted the accumulation at a time of maximum unpopularity.

4

How You Can Win the Game
(The Grand Strategy
of Stock Trading)

INTRODUCTION

Now comes the actual testing of all the information contained in this book. No matter how good your timing is by virtue of correctly interpreting all the major indicators, you still have to choose the right stock, and this is where all the strategies are employed, *the fusion of timing with choice—* buying, or selling, *the right stock,* at the *right time.* It is at this problem level where the technically uninformed stock trader usually encounters confusion. Any number of things can go wrong without a knowledge of what you, the reader, now already know. The timing might be right but the wrong stock was purchased. The right stock might be bought but the timing was wrong. The right stock might be bought at the right time but sold at the wrong time, cancelling out all the advantages of the early success. So then, all the strategy will be aimed at achieving FUSION and eliminating con-fusion.

Stop, Look and Listen

Many people are able to make a good profit on their first stock purchase and, unfortunately, begin to feel that this qualifies them as being fully experienced speculators. It would actually be better if many people lost money on their first trade so that the next time they came to the railroad crossing of choice they would stop, look, and listen rather than keep trying to beat the train. A series of starting successes without a knowledge of why they happened to be successes is likened to a person forever beating trains at crossings. His early demise via a railroad accident is inevitable.

A series of such easy gains makes the blood pressure go up and the judgment go down. The amateur stock trader always tends to overplay his hand. Early success without the guiding whys prompts him to raise the stakes, one good failure neutralizes all the previous successes, and the unfortunate amateur has no idea what went wrong. The following material is provided in order that its guidance will give you a technical know-how second to none and free you from the trading mistakes common to amateurs.

"Never" Never Happens

No theory of market timing is so infallible that it allows for 100% success. The use of the indicators and techniques described here will weight the odds heavily in your favor. Of course you will lose money on some trades, but your on-balance results should start showing some handsome profits. You not only will be able to make money on seven out of every ten stocks you trade in, but you will be able to minimize the losses on the three losing trades. The technique will show you how it will be almost impossible to ride a stock all the way down in a sharp decline as long as you follow the directions the technical indicators provide. Therefore, we will accept losses 30% of the time and profits 70% of the time, but the losses will be MINIMIZED and the gains MAXIMIZED. If you carefully follow the indicators and stay up on your necessary homework, there is no reason why the above-mentioned seven out of ten performance can't be your MINIMUM objective.

You must know how to minimize your loss when a trade backfires. Oftentimes, just when an expected advance or decline seems most assured, the market will pull an unexpected fooler. As a market letter writer, the author might sometimes fall into traps others were warned to avoid. One of these was to never use the word "never" when talking about the market. Things have a way of happening when most people think they "never" will. The example given in the first *Strategy* book was James Buchanan, our first bachelor President. I remember facing the February, 1966 market with complete confidence that it couldn't top out that month because the market record had shown up until then that a major top had never been recorded during the month of February. So what does the market do? It tops out in February, 1966. It wasn't too many years ago when one might have said that a man would never set foot on the surface of the moon. Well, that became a reality in July, 1969; another "never" exploded. Back in the 1960's Treasury officials stated over and over that the price of gold would never be raised above $35 an ounce, another famous "never" down the drain. And who could have predicted that a President and a Vice President would have resigned within twelve months of each other. Incredible. So then, beware the "nevers." Market success demands flexibility, the quick adaptation to constant and sometimes total unexpected change.

Income Stocks Provide Income and Not Maximum Profits

No one makes a fortune from stock income if the fortune was not already there to begin with. We are concerned with percentage gains that *build* fortunes, not small gains which merely *preserve* fortunes. Applications of timing techniques will therefore be centered on stocks capable of producing large capital gains. If the timing techniques are correct it tends to put less emphasis on the otherwise added risks involved. Correct timing in itself greatly reduces risk, although it never completely eliminates it.

Public Blindness Almost Incredible in Its Dimensions

Technical indicators see what the public cannot, and the more blinded the public becomes the more clearly the indicators point the way. The public reacts to what it reads in the newspapers and hears and sees on radio and television, as well as what it is told by the authorities it most respects. Market indicators are not exposed to such possibly biased comment. Remember, if it is obvious to the public it is obviously wrong. Majority opinion can be moulded, but the technical indicators are beyond the reach of the majority opinion moulders. While one or two might get distorted, no powers that be are powerful enough to distort more than these one or two. In this respect the market always plays fair. It is not allowed a 100% coverup at any time. Its plan must always be revealed to those who know what they are looking for. The public looks at the market *casually*, never in depth. You are going to look at the market as a *business*, as serious a business as your own. If you will work at it with the same determination and persistence you would give your own business, you will be amazed with your better results. You may already think you have worked hard at trying to make some money in the market, but it may have been completely *misdirected* work, working at fundamentals, trying to analyze the news, etc. Now you are going to analyze the market in the only proper way, and you now know what I mean when I say *you are going to follow the market*.

Three Major Mistakes

These have already been covered throughout the book, but they cannot be over-emphasized. When you trade stocks for profit (and why else would you trade?) it is essential that you avoid the misplaced stress which the uninformed place on management, earnings, and dividends. These constitute three of the major stumbling blocks which account for most of the trading losses racked up by the technically uninformed trader.

Management is not a major factor in our considerations for maximum profits. There is a rule in real estate that speculators interested only in turning over a property for a quick profit may ignore management. The same applies in the market for a short-term move. The management may be the world's best, but if the stock is ready to go down it will go down. Remember, a poor quality stock bought at the right time is more profitable than a high quality stock bought at the wrong time. The public so often attempts to "trade" a stock on fundamental factors. These are among the poorest factors upon which to base a trading decision, and the reader now knows why.

A second mistake is to bank heavily on an earnings statement or a projection of future earnings. The reader now knows why, having been shown how the market and the course of earnings operate on *two different timetables.*

The third mistake is to follow dividend boosts as an attraction to buying a stock. Dividends are raised because earnings are rising. But, since rising earnings have generally shown a poor correlation with the course of the stock market, it follows that the raising of dividends will also have a poor correlation with the course of the stock market. Dividends are nice when they can be considered as income, but when they constitute nothing more than a return of your own capital in a losing situation, they tend to lose all their importance.

Two Gimmicks Which Fool the Naive

The tendency of human nature to want something for nothing attracts the public to stocks which split. *Anything which attracts the public deserves a second look.* In view of the fact that there is no "second public" upon which the public can pass its stock onto at large markups, it must be assumed that any stock the public is attracted to in a big way is being willingly distributed to them *by design.* You will have to be careful when it comes to holding a stock after a split has been announced. Remember some of the questions you have now promised to ask yourself following all market developments which may be designed to make YOU the sucker, questions such as "Why is this happening?" "Why is it happening NOW?" "Who gets the benefit?" and "What time is it on the market clock?"

You have been alerted to secondary offerings. These are offered to the investing public at a concession in order to move them, just like slow merchandise. The broker receives a larger commission in order to provide him with more incentive to sell the stock. Secondary offerings are more likely made in the midst of a rising market while the public is strongly imbued with a bullish attitude. The public by then is so busy buying stocks and is so impressed with a rising Dow-Jones Industrial Average that there is no time or opportunity to pay attention to the rising trend of secondary offerings.

So then, view splits and secondary offerings as the distribution gimmicks they usually are. You should stop, look, and listen. Check things out. The public usually doesn't, so you should.

THE SIMPLE LOGIC BEHIND CHART READING

There is no abracadabra or magic in the reading of a stock price chart. What a stock does follows a clearly defined line of logic. There is a very simple and fundamental reason why a stock advances after making an upside penetration of a previous high and declines after moving down from a high of $75 a share. When the stock rebounds to 75, all those who first bought the stock at 75 will be anxious to move out, glad to be even after previously racking up temporary paper losses. Perfectly logical. The price of 75 on the upswing from 50 becomes the level of resistance, the level of SUPPLY. If the buyer at 50 is not aware of this technical impediment to further advance, he might ride the stock right back down to 50 again. He still has no loss. However, if the price goes under 50, then he is concerned, and with the creation of a paper loss the temptation to sell is at hand. This situation is multiplied by all those who bought at 50, and thus the downside penetration brings in further selling.

Why did the price go under 50 in the first place? Because all those who observed the stock going from 50 to 75 no longer had confidence that the stock would do it again the next time it got down to 50. It is assumed that such confidence does exist (a double bottom at 50) unless proved otherwise by a move under 50. The move under 50 shows no confidence and this explains why selling comes in on a downside penetration of a previous support level, the level of DEMAND. A stock making a double bottom and then rising is understandably bullish because it shows that there is confidence that a stock will repeat a previous advance from a given demand level.

Now suppose that the stock reaches a lower support level (level where it was previously observed as having been bought for a rise which ensued) and turns around and again advances to 75. Suppose this time, however, the stock moves above the old high of 75. This means that all those who previously bought at 75 have enough confidence in the stock to not wish to move out even, despite the fact that in the meantime they have sustained paper losses and a long wait without profits to show for it. That is pretty strong confidence under such conditions, and thus explains why a move above a previous high point brings in strong buying. That constitutes the chart "breakout." Explained in these terms, however, the so-called magic of upside price breakouts and downside penetrations is quickly translated into terms of simple logic and readily understandable human psychology.

Test your own feelings at various price levels in a given stock you have purchased. See if your impulses to buy or sell don't tend to coincide with the graphically portrayed gyrations of that stock through previous levels of supply and demand, resistance and support.

The specific action you must take when buying or selling stocks according to what the stock price chart is telling you is to only buy the stock in a DEMAND AREA and sell it in a SUPPLY AREA. Question: How does one KNOW that a supply area might not turn out to be a new demand area? When this question was posed in the original *Strategy* book the writer had not constructed the on-balance volume theory as yet, and the original answer simply stated that the stock trader did NOT know. Now, however, OBV would be expected to provide more than ample advance technical knowledge of new demand areas emerging before a price chart could record them. One doesn't have to wait for price to provide evidence of supply area penetrations. Such supply areas would be first penetrated by OBV upside breakouts followed thereafter by the price breakthroughs on the chart. With this advance technical knowledge that a new demand area had been created, the trader would continue to hold the stock or make additional purchases. WE DON'T TRY TO GUESS AT TOPS AND BOTTOMS. WE LET THE STOCK EVIDENCE ACCUMULATION AFTER THE BOTTOM HAS BEEN RECORDED, AND WE LET THE STOCK EVIDENCE DISTRIBUTION AFTER THE TOP HAS BEEN RECORDED. The reader now knows what technical evidence is required.

THE MOST BULLISH LOOKING CHART PATTERNS

All your buying for maximum profits should be concentrated on stocks having the following types of chart patterns:

1. Long-term decline followed by a breakout
2. Flat base breakout
3. Coming off a double bottom
4. W Pattern
5. Growth
6. Cyclical at historic lows

These are now examined separately:

1. *Long-term Decline Followed by a Breakout*

This pattern is mentioned first because it is capable of producing *the greatest capital gains*. The pattern is exactly as described, a long-term decline (the longer the better) followed by an eventual bullish reversal above a previous declining peak. The stock gains an upside impetus *commensurate with the duration and extent of the previous decline*. The theory here is that the stock has been so utterly oversold that upon the first evidence of *accumulation* (using the OBV detection method) the stock will advance at a greater rate than it previously declined. Let me add—MORE GAINS OF 100% AND BETTER OVER A SHORT PERIOD OF TIME HAVE SPRUNG FROM THIS TYPE OF CHART FORMATION THAN FROM ANY OTHER. (A successful parlay of ten such gains could turn $1,000 into $250 000.)

2. *Flat Base Breakout*

The longer the price of a stock remains in a very restricted range of fluctuation the greater is the potential rise upon a breakout above that price range. If the line of *accumulation* (evidence contributed by OBV) is at the bottom of a previous long-term decline then so much the better. A stock coming off of a ten-year base is potentially ten times more bullish than a stock coming off of a one-year base. The base or plateau may be at a higher price level but the same principle holds, a move above that plateau being quite bullish. The higher priced the plateau is the less bullish it is, and the lower the base line is priced the more bullish it is. Suppose a stock was once priced at $40 a share and then went into a long-term decline down to $5 a share. Suppose for the next ten years it fluctuated between $5 and $10 and then one day managed to break out to $11 with strong accompanying OBV evidence of the new accumulation. The stock would be screaming to be bought, having evidenced a degree of strength unseen in a decade. That would constitute a classic flat base breakout, and the chances of catching a 100% gain or better over the near-term by buying at $11 a share would be excellent.

3. *Coming off a Double Bottom*

When a stock has met support (demand) at a given level following a decline, the stock must prove itself by holding at that level should it rise and fall back again. If it evidences accumulation near that same price bottom, then the stock is in a much improved position to make a more sustained advance. The astute trader buys the stock *after* the double bottom has been recorded and the stock has evidenced accumulation.

There are two observations to make regarding double bottoms:

(a) The lower the bottom the more bullish it is (providing there is accumulation evidence)

(b) The farther apart the bottoms are the more bullish it is (providing there is accumulation evidence)

4. W Pattern

By the very shape of the letter we can see that a double bottom with an upside follow-through traces out a letter W. The middle leg of the W represents a temporary level of supply (upside resistance), and when the right leg of the W exceeds the middle leg it constitutes a very important buy spot (OBV confirming of course).

5. Growth

The growth pattern is characterized by a long continuing advance in the on-balance volume and the price with a tendency toward acceleration on the upside in the latter stages of its growth pattern. The astute trader who is only aiming at maximum profits is only going to pay attention to this type of pattern during the later stages of the upside OBV and price acceleration.

6. Cyclical at Historic Lows

This pattern is listed last because it contains more stringent timing requirements, but the use of on-balance volume would provide the necessary accumulation data. If the timing is right, the gains can be very great. (Buying such stocks off the 1974 bottom is an excellent illustration.)

Gearing the Six Patterns to the Market

Isaac Newton would undoubtedly have been fascinated with the stock market as a vivid proof of his famous Law of Gravity. A brief glance at a number of individual stock charts would immediately confirm the ever-present workings of his Law. In brief, what goes up must come down. The Law works the best in bear markets. The sharpest downswings have always followed the sharpest previous rises. Knowing this, the astute market trader will avoid buying those issues having had the sharpest rises the year before. If the indicators say that a bull market is still in progress, he will buy into those stocks in the middle area, those stocks which have been in a good early

upswing but which have in no way matched the startling upward performance of those sharply ascending stocks which promise to top out first once
the bull market has ended. At this juncture he will not buy the most
depressed stocks, those stocks which have not advanced very far during the
bull swing, because he figures (and rightly so) that if they haven't advanced
by this stage of the bull market, then they are not going to rise appreciably
in the time remaining.

For best results, *the six types of charts must be geared to what time it is
on the stock market clock.* Only some types of chart patterns are followed in
the first phase of a bull market, other types being followed during the
second phase, and a still different type of chart pattern is adhered to in the
third and final phase of the bull market.

Let us now apply the chart patterns discussed to the three phases of a bull
market.

START OF A BULL SWING

1. *The trader buys any issue showing a long-term decline followed by an
upside breakout.* He is attracted to this type of situation on the assumption
that the further the stock has declined the higher it must rise in a new bull
market upswing. At the start of a bull swing *the Law of Gravity operates in
reverse:* What goes down must go up, and, opposite to the bear phase of the
gravity formula, the further it has gone down the further will be the eventual
rise.

Depressed issues are therefore the most attractive *in the first phase of a
bull upswing.* However, after a severe bear market most of the stocks could
be considered as depressed. Which ones should be bought? The choices are so
numerous at this point that we require some special standards so as to cut
down the field of choice. At the very start of a new bull market we will go
for *maximum percentage gain.* That will automatically limit our choices to a
very low price category, say $4 to $12 a share. Even though IBM may be a
whale of a buy at this point at $200 a share, its future percentage gain over
the next six months of perhaps as much as 25% cannot compete with the
successful selection of a $4 stock with six-month upside potential of going to
$12 a share. If this isn't the time to buy a $4 stock, when is a better time?
Now, we don't go for just any $4 stock. It has to be a *name* stock so as to
insure good marketability. We can either buy it after it has given *price*
evidence of a turn, or we can buy it *prior* to a price breakout on the evidence
given by the on-balance volume method of analysis. In either case there must
be some technical evidence of a turn before the stock is bought, and that is
why successful traders await such evidence. Anything short of that is just a

guess. We never advocate buying a stock simply because it is "low" or selling a stock simply because it is "high." The low-priced stock must show some evidence of *accumulation* to be bought and the high-priced stock must show some evidence of *distribution* to be sold. A stock having been in a long-term decline never goes down in a straight line on the chart but descends in a series of declining waves. The successful trader waits until the price of the stock has advanced to a level above the crest point of the previous declining wave. That constitutes a breakout, the first technical indication by price that the stock is now likely to move higher. (A 200-day moving average price line chart would confirm the validity of the price breakout, the price of the stock moving above the average line.) Now the use of *on-balance volume* enables traders and investors to spot stocks under accumulation sooner than using older methods based on price alone.

Here is a classic case of picking the right stock meeting all the necessary technical requirements: (1) A name stock, (2) Super-depressed, dropping to $4 a share in December, 1974, (3) Proven accumulation by very early January, 1975, at $4.50 a share, (4) Previous long-term decline followed by *first the volume breakout and then the price breakout,* and (5) Upside penetration of the 200-day moving average trendline. The stock is *Howard Johnson.* Now being familiar with the OBV technique, I will omit all the daily OBV statistics but merely show the field trend OBV levels to illustrate how depressed stocks under accumulation can be picked up well ahead of the crowd, even the *informed* crowd that only follows *price* movements.

Howard Johnson

Date	Closing Price	On—Balance Volume		Field Trend
Aug. 27, 1974	5.50	-324,800	DOWN	Falling
Aug. 30	5.75	-298,200	UP	Falling
Sept. 6	5.13	-421,200	DOWN	Falling
Sept. 9	5.25	-386,400	UP	Falling
Sept. 16	4.63	-463,300	DOWN	Falling
Sept. 20	6.00	-391,400	UP	Falling
Oct. 4	4.63	-558,500	DOWN	Falling
Oct. 14	5.88	-367,700	UP	Doubtful
Oct. 24	4.88	-525,400	DOWN	Doubtful
Oct. 29	5.00	-508,500	UP	Doubtful
Nov. 1	4.75	-532,800	DOWN	Falling
Nov. 5	5.38	-386,300	UP	Doubtful
Nov. 12	5.13	-627,400	DOWN	Doubtful
Nov. 15	5.50	-585,900	UP	Doubtful
Dec. 16	4.13	-746,900	DOWN	Falling
Jan. 10, 1975	5.75	-396,300	UP	Doubtful

The above figures show how a stock is properly "tracked" so as to be able to immediately take advantage of a significant change in on-balance volume when it occurs. Now, *stock buying decisions must always be related to the general market trend.* You will recall that the first Dow bottom in 1974 occurred on October 4. That was the last bottom confirmed by the Dow-Jones Transports. All such bottoms are later "tested" to see if they will hold. The test came on December 6 when the Dow industrial average broke to a new low. However, that new low lacked a confirmation by the Transports, and thus the downside testing was a total success. The new bull market was fully assured at that point. A bullish change in pattern for Howard Johnson was looked for *after* December 6. The first such change was noted in early January, 1975, when the field trend improved from falling to doubtful. However, the table simply gave the final up or down reading in each OBV series, and thus the first technical proof of significant change for the better occurred on the *first* bettering of the November 15, 1975 on-balance volume level. That occurred on January 3, 1975, when the stock closed at 5. *That is when the stock could clearly have been bought based on OBV.* However, the upside momentum was so clearly in evidence on the year-end strength when the OBV stood at -628,700 on December 31, 1974, with an up designation that this writer anticipated the obvious OBV breakout and heavily recommended the stock at 4.50 a share.

The last of the declining price peaks occurred on November 15, 1974, at 5.50. One awaiting a *price* breakout in order to buy took action on January 10, 1975, at 5.75. One awaiting still more impressive proof of change waited for the *double breakout* of January 24, 1975, paying 6.38 a share. That is when the stock advanced above the January 10 high after a minor pullback to the trendline. In terms of just the field trends, here is what happened next:

Date	Closing Price	On–Balance Volume		Field Trend
Jan. 10, 1975	5.75	- 396,300	UP	Doubtful
Jan. 17	5.13	- 664,700	DOWN	Doubtful
Mar. 7	11.00	819,200	UP	RISING
Mar. 24	9.25	307,300	DOWN	RISING
April 17	12.50	1,114,200	UP	RISING
April 29	11.63	987,500	DOWN	RISING

The stock went considerably higher thereafter. Notice the very large build-up in on-balance volume from the deep minus area to well over 1,000,000 by mid-April. These tremendous accelerations in OBV build-up *precede the best price swings* and provide the best proof that *volume precedes price.*

Using this identical technique, the trader would have purchased the following stocks in late 1974 or very early in 1975:

Stock	Price Recommended*	Price Less than Six Months Later	OBV Low	Later OBV
Boise Cascade	10.25	23.00	-395,200	808,200
City Investing	4.63	8.25	-169,100	133,900
Denny's	6.00	18.25	- 42,100	617,200
Dr. Pepper	7.13	14.00	- 14,200	831,800
Fleetwood Enterprises	8.88	18.38	- 66,500	1,182,600
Hershey Foods	9.13	20.38	- 1,300	141,400
Howard Johnson	4.50	14.25	-746,900	1,185,300
LTV Corp.	8.88	19.00	-211,000	1,153,900
Merrill Lynch	9.25	16.38	45,900	1,703,200
Occidental Petroleum	9.25	16.38	-369,900	3,207,000
Rucker	8.00	19.75	- 10,300	408,200
Ward Foods	4.25	8.75	25,000	100,000
Whittaker	2.00	3.75	-114,600	605,400

*Prices recommended in market letters published between October 1974 and January 1975.

Average gains here were well in excess of 100% in but a few months. No thought was given as to what business the company was engaged in or what quality rating the stock had. *It was simply a case of picking the stocks with the long-term previous declines followed by a breakout and buying them at the most advantageous time, the start of a bull swing.* As the Chinese say, a picture is worth a thousand words, and the chart pictures on those stocks all had one thing to say . . . . . . BUY.

There is no intent here to encourage reckless gambling. The issues chosen in the fall of 1974 were picked with two things in minds, their chart patterns and their OBV patterns. Gambling is defined as uninformed speculation. Buying stocks at the right time, stocks where the chart and OBV definitely spell out accumulation, cannot be labeled as the act of an uninformed person, and thus it can be said that traders with a full grasp of market technical factors do not gamble. They speculate, gambling and speculation having different meanings. One of the major purposes of this book is to reduce out-and-out gambling and substitute it with a far more intelligent method of trading or investing. It makes absolutely no sense to buy a stock unless it can be shown that that stock is being *accumulated.* The original *Strategy* book laid down the tenets of spotting such accumulation through the study of charts. Since then the pure chart method of such detection has been greatly enhanced by the addition of the on-balance volume studies which not only detect accumulation *sooner* than the chart methods, but spell it out to the *exact degree.*

2. The trader would also be looking for buying opportunities on the evidence of additional "breakouts." Some traders have found it more profitable to only buy on breakouts and thus are willing to *wait until the*

stock goes higher before buying it on the assumption that their purchase at the higher level has the additional TECHNICAL INSURANCE of a further uptrend ahead. The higher price paid includes this "insurance premium." While this method has its laudable points, the use of on-balance volume enables one to buy on OBV breakouts on the valid assumption that, volume preceding price, *a position will be taken in an uptrending stock at a lower price.*

3. The trader would also find the flat base stock pattern attractive from the speculative standpoint. When an issue breaks out of a previous long-term narrow price range, it is usually followed by a sharp move over the ensuing months in the direction dictated by the breakout. A breakout from a long flat base could send the stock as high as the base is long. Picture a measuring tape. All bunched together it is loose and has plenty of slack. It is capable of being stretched way out before any tension is created. This is like the flat base pattern. The stock has plenty of slack, and the breakout above that base signals that it is now going to be stretched out with a sharp rise. The stock will rise until tension is created, the tension being demonstrated when the stock has advanced commensurately with the length of the base. Once that has taken place, the stock, like a fully stretched out piece of measuring tape, has no place to go except down and thus recedes in order to recreate slack and start the process all over again.

4. Buying a stock having a *cyclical* chart pattern can only produce the maximum profits if bought at the start of a bull swing. This is understandable in view of the fact that it is the cyclical issues which are most depressed at the end of a bear market. A cyclical stock tends to rise and fall with the business cycle in rhythmical swings and is much more sensitive to news affecting the industry it represents.

In the four areas for bull market first phase stock selection, the keyword is BREAKOUT. Regardless of whether the stock is of high quality or low quality, has a large capitalization or a small one, is higher priced or very low-priced, *there has to be one thing in common that triggers the buying in every case,* either a *price breakout* or an *on-balance volume breakout.* Such breakouts break the previous pattern of price depression, showing that something is at last *different.* The trader has to be alerted to these breakouts, and it can only be done if the trader (1) *regularly subscribes to a good chart service,* (2) *keeps a running record of daily on-balance volume figures on several potentially promising situations,* (3) *scans the daily list of the 15 most active stocks,* and (4) *scans the daily list of stocks making new highs.* Those four requirements are a MUST for any trader who desires to maximize his trading profits.

I am most partial to the *Trendline Daily Basis Charts* (published by Standard & Poor, 345 Hudson Street, New York, N.Y. 10014). It is a weekly chart service, and each chart clearly shows the 200-day moving average trendline of the stock so one can apply the important 200-day rules in making important buying and selling decisions.

Whenever a chart is selected as promising (one of the four situations previously described for first phase bull market buying), one should take the time either to start keeping OBV figures on it or to working the figures back a couple of months. If it looks like a situation which could be triggered higher any time soon, then the OBV figures should definitely be worked back so as not to miss a buy signal which might have already been given or is just about to be given.

In a new bull market the number of promising situations are so numerous that one must have a method to constantly cut the field of choice down. That method is always "go with the action," restricting the number of stocks to those culled from the daily volume and price leaders. This is why it is essential always to study each day the list of the most active stocks and the stocks making new highs for the year. Inasmuch as the most valid upside breakouts are those accompanied by relatively *high volume,* the daily list of the 15 most active stocks enables the trader to immediately look up those 15 stocks in his chartbook and see where the volume occurred in each case. If it suggests a probable OBV breakout which would probably lead to a later key price breakout, he should then immediately set up an OBV profile on the stock. Likewise, the daily list of stocks making new highs would immediately alert him to check out those stocks in his chartbook, narrowing down the list of choices to those stocks where the new high was the *first* one in a probable *series* of new highs to come.

THE MIDDLE OF THE BULL SWING

By this time at least six, or more probably eight, months have passed since the major bottom. Stocks have largely returned to known values from their vastly oversold levels of six to eight months before. By this time traders are in a much better position to know where they stand. They are about to take some six month capital gains profits if they haven't already done so. This provides additional capital to *add to positions* in the most promising technical situations on *normal reactions.* The market is a bit more selective now, but this matters little because most of the major stock choices *have already been made.* It is merely a case of daily supervision now watching for OBV signals of important weakness. Between the sixth and twelfth month after the major bottom market, reactions are normal and relatively short-lived. The logic behind this is simply that those who tended to be late in recognizing the validity of the new bull market will not be adding to market selling pressures on capital gain selling simultaneously with the early smart money buyers. In that period we have a good "mix" of buyers and sellers which would tend to keep reactions small and normal. Between the twelfth and fifteenth month after the major bottom, however, we must expect and prepare for the REACTION THAT FOOLS THE MAJORITY. This is the more extended and oftentimes rather severe decline in the market that is seen in every bull market, tending to occur in the *middle* of the *second* phase of the bull swing. The logic here is that capital gain selling pressures will be much greater, *combining* the selling by smart early buyers and lesser informed later buyers. The least informed buyers are taking the stock off their hands. What kind of people are those late buyers? Those very late buyers are undoubtedly totally ignorant of market technical conditions and would generally be classed as fundamentalists and strong believers in what they read. At this juncture in the bull market they are probably impressed by government reports that the recession is over as well as influenced by several bullish reports regarding the future of corporate earnings. They now come into the market just in time to catch the first major reaction in the bull market, their buying unable to offset the selling pressures of all those who bought heavily during the first year of the bull market.

This large secondary decline may or may not activate the 50% Principle, but, when applying that Principle on this first major bull market reaction, it must be remembered that it is most valid when applied against *completed* bull or bear markets. Here is an example: In the first phase of the 1970-73 bull market the Dow moved strongly from 631 to 950 between May, 1970, and April, 1971. True to form, a bearish secondary downtrend developed in the middle of the second phase, bottoming in November, 1971, at Dow 797. The halfway point of the advance was at 790. If the Dow had broken 790 there would have been a strong temptation to predict a complete collapse to 631, but it would have been faulty reasoning because the move from 631 to 950 did not make a *complete* bull market. The technical outlook looked even more bullish, however, with the Dow holding up at 797 on the reaction.

The trader, having gotten in a very liquid position between the twelfth and fifteenth month after the major bottom, *is ready to make his final buying assault in the bull market.* Having continued to follow faithfully a number of stocks by recording and analyzing the OBV figures each day throughout the secondary decline, he moves in on the key OBV buying signals with the intention of holding his new positions for another six months. He may even wait until the price of the stock has made a new upside penetration of the 200-day trendline, but that decision will depend on the quality of the OBV figures. The recovery from the secondary reaction is usually quite sharp, and the trader generally finds himself with some newly found paper profits long before his six-month holding period is up. If the market recovers too rapidly into new high ground following that secondary reaction, the trader may wish to protect himself for tax purposes and go short against the box so as to be sure of maintaining his position for the required six months should he have fears that the market can't sustain the climb until then.

Very late in the second phase of the bull market, the Dow-Jones Industrial Average will have again made a key upside penetration of its own 200-day trendline and advanced far enough to effect *a new high for the bull market for the trendline.* To do that the average itself would reach new bull market highs first. The trader takes his six-month capital gains between the *twenty-first* and *twenty-fourth* month after the major bottom. The second phase of the bull market is concluded.

THE FINAL PHASE OF THE BULL SWING

The most logical question the trader would ask himself at this juncture is: what determines the dividing line between the second phase and the third phase of the bull market? How does he KNOW that the third phase is about to begin? In the *Strategy* book I said to look at the *low-priced stocks* and the *advance-decline line.* Low priced stocks and generally all stocks of lower quality tend to peak out at the end of the second phase. This being true, it removes a key segment of support for the advance-decline line, and thus that key indicator tends to make a major top. But now, my most recent researches reveal that, additionally, the Dow-Jones industrial stock 200-day moving average trendline makes *one large upward zigzagging movement* throughout the entire bull market and that when it breaks through to a new high on the final upward leg, that breakthrough marks *the beginning of the third phase of the bull market.* These upward breakthroughs by the trendline itself generally take place between the *twenty-second* and *twenty-fourth* month after the major bottom, *leaving anywhere from six to nine months left in the entire bull market.*

The trader now restricts himself to a much smaller buying program comprising only *the top blue chip stocks.* Remembering the Bathtub Analogy, the blue chip stocks are the last to top out in a bull market. Selling them in the *thirtieth* to *thirty-third* month after the major bottom, that final selling should pretty much coincide with the end of the third phase of the bull market.

The three-phase timing example of the 1957-59 bull upswing shows an amazing exactitude of a *mid-phase reaction* with the reaction in the middle of the second phase being the largest reaction:

Three Phases of the 1957-59 Bull Upswing

Phase	Duration	Terminated By	Mid-Way Reaction
First Phase	October 1957 to July 1958 (nine months)	End of upswing in the short interest short interest	February 1958 (4½ months from October 1957
Second Phase	July 1958 to April 1959 (nine months)	Topping out of low-priced issues coinciding with Stock Exchange campaign against speculation	November 1958 (4½ months from July 1958)
Third Phase	April 1959 to January 1960 (nine months)	Topping out of blue chip issues	August 1959 (4½ months from April 1959)

While those phases all tended to be an equal nine months in length, let us now examine the three phases of the 1970-73 bull upswing:

Three Phases of the 1970-73 Bull Upswing

Phase	Duration	Terminated By	Mid-Way Reaction
First Phase	May 1970 to April 1971 (ten months)	Peaking of advance-decline line	October 1970 (five months from May 1970)
Second Phase	April 1971 to March 1972 (eleven months)	Secondary peak in advance-decline line	October 1971 (six months from April 1971)
Third Phase	March 1972 to January 1973 (ten months)	Major A-D Line non-confirmation of record Dow high	August 1972 (five months from March 1972)

Noticing that the 1957-59 upswing covered roughly *27 months* broken up into three equal *nine-month* phases, the 1970-73 bull upswing covered *31 months* broken up into almost equal *ten to 11* month phases. Once again the mid-phase reactions occurred almost exactly on schedule with the largest of these occurring in the middle of the second phase. This suggests to the writer that *perhaps the length of the first phase of the bull market determines the length of the entire bull market by simply multiplying its duration by three.* It is an interesting concept and if true would greatly simplify the projection of bull market tops. However, being too pat, I would be suspicious; but it doesn't cost anything to take it into consideration.

I would like to inject another thought here: We, as technicians, often forget about the presence of the lesser informed public and make all our moves based purely on the dictation of the technical indicators. Because the public always reacts to change more slowly than what the technical indicators would precisely demand, we should take this *time factor* into consideration and *allow for the overruns of enthusiasm or depression.* In other words, if we see developing technical trouble in March, don't be surprised to see the Dow continue to rise into May. The time lag between technical expression and fundamental response causes these overruns. We must allow for them when making our buying and selling decisions.

FIRST PHASE OF A BEAR SWING

Having had the warning of the bull market third phase reaction, the trader is now assumed to be in a liquid position, dumping his blue chip stocks on the final bull market run-up. He now has several options open to him. He can consult his chart book and pick out a number of suitable short sales, the best candidates being those where the stock price has dropped through the 200-day trendline. Assuming that he has continued to follow several stocks in terms of their daily on-balance volume figures, he will be aware of which ones are showing definite technical weakness: rising field trends turning to doubtful, and doubtful field trends turning to falling. Short selling should be done on the Up designations in the falling field trends.

In terms of time, most of the short selling by the smart money is going to be done a few weeks after the top, after the Dow has declined rather sharply from the record peak and then made failing attempts to rebound. As shown in the description of the three bull market phases, there was a reaction occurring in the middle of each phase. Now, during the three bear market phases traders can expect a rallying movement occurring in the middle of each phase. It is on the rallying movement in the middle of the first phase of the bear market where most of the correct short selling will be done.

Bear markets never visit by appointment, ringing your front doorbell during the daylight hours. They come like a thief in the night, sneaking in the back door while the public sleeps the slumber of confidence. The general investing public doesn't follow 200-day trendlines, the advance-decline line, or the short interest and wouldn't know a field trend from a fieldmouse. The general public reads the newspaper, and it contains *basically fundamental data.* That means that they buy stocks late and sell stocks late, not aware of the stock market game at all. The market game, only made possible by the *lack of synchronization* between the technical and fundamental, reaches one of its most interesting junctures as a bear market gets underway. Since the market moves ahead of the news, ahead of business, ahead of everything, trading on tomorrow and technicians follow the market, they will sell their stocks to the fundamentally oriented majority who lean almost totally on the news, business developments, economics, etc. By the very definition of this *time lag* between the technical and the fundamental, the public will always be confident at a major market top because the earnings and dividend picture will be very bright, the economy will be strong and just about everything else that creates public confidence will be in place. But those factors from a timing standpoint are *meaningless*. If the market generally moves *nine months ahead of earnings,* what utility does an earnings statement have? *But if the market and earnings moved together there could be no market game.* Technicians would want to buy stocks, but so would the fundamentalists, and then who would be selling? At a market peak earnings would also be at a peak, economists would be projecting a downturn and then everybody would want to sell, technicians and fundamentalists, and then who would be buying to make that total selling possible? So then it is axiomatic that most of the time the technical and the fundamental must DISAGREE. They have to be on *different timetables* in order to make buying and selling possible.

So then there is no question about public confidence in the first phase of a bear market. The public is the only agency that can BUY stocks as the smart money SELLS. Now, since the public is following everything CURRENT, and nothing in the current picture suggests a bear market, the initial downswing of a bear market is going to be greeted with total public DISBELIEF. After all, if they believed, who would be buying to make the selling possible? It takes two to tango. *Any major event tending to make the public totally confident on the outlook for business and the economy at this time should be viewed with maximum suspicion.*

THE SECOND PHASE OF A BEAR SWING

Second phase movements tend to be tricky but one thing can be strongly banked on—the very strong rally occurring in the *middle* of the period, the RALLY THAT FOOLS THE MAJORITY. There are many reasons for it which seem to be common in every case. The smart shortsellers have had a field day and will want to nail down their profits. This in itself could start the rally. The still confident public, convinced that the decline to date has been a severe secondary downtrend in a continuing bull market, will believe that the rally started by heavy short covering signals the resumption of the bull trend because they WANT to believe it. They step up their buying and the rally starts to look very good. Just when the rally *looks* the best and many commentators are beginning to talk about a full market recovery, it breaks sharply as perhaps a very disturbing piece of business news hits the

Street. More bad news follows as the Dow-Jones Industrial Average plummets to a new low, breaking under the point at which the "Judas rally" started. It isn't until the subsurface signs of business deterioration are completely in view that one can be sure the third phase of the bear market is about to get underway. All through the second phase the Administration in Washington states repeatedly that there will be no recession, refusing to acknowledge what the market is starting to discount. By this time national polls clearly indicate that the general public, confident up until now, is turning increasingly pessimistic, the first of many advance signs which alert the smart money to the lateness of the bear cycle. Inasmuch as the obvious is obviously wrong, the public is going to now act in a very obvious fashion and become the predominant sellers in the market. They have to be the predominant sellers because the news is getting worse and worse, and the public acts in concert with the news.

THE THIRD PHASE OF A BEAR SWING

The market continues to make new lows as the negative news continues to worsen and become even more negative. The professional superbears are at the peak of their popularity-lecturing, giving seminars, writing books, and otherwise preaching a thesis of economic Armageddon, and the public is now eating it up. Anything bearish is popular. Late in this phase many stocks *stop going down*. Evidence of that will be a maximum number of individual new lows recorded followed by a *diminishing number* as the Dow continues to make new lows. The profound change underway as the third phase of the bear market gets started is that the smart money is making the great transition from pessimism to confidence at the same rate that the public shifted their psychological stance from confident to pessimistic. Traders refrain from any further shorting. Short selling is now too popular to be the correct thing to do as evidenced by a record short interest. Now traders are beginning to track one depressed stock after another, mentally anticipating which ones will be the first to move up in a new bull market looking increasingly close. Such tracking will again consist of keeping daily on-balance volume figures, the best candidates for future buying being those moving the furthest under their own 200-day moving average trendlines.

He might even start making some small selective purchases, not unduly disturbed should a late selling wave wipe out some early fractional gains. The keyword now is ACCUMULATION for the smart money crowd, and the cheaper the acquisition the better. The business press is now full of reports about flat or declining earnings, and the smart money trader, with such help from the media, is pretty sure of getting all the stock he wants at his price.

The time is perhaps now right for a major event to occur which will intensify public pessimism to such a point that the Dow-Jones Industrial Average will descend sharply to another series of new lows, below anything thought possible when the bear market began. In the face of it, the number of individual new lows will NOT exceed the previous record number, the smart traders certain now that the market itself is beginning to *contain* the bad news. From there on out the trader looks for one technical *non-confirmation* after another as the industrial average makes further new lows. Now he consults his market timetable and carefully measures off 48 to 54 months after the previous major bottom seen in the previous bear market. If the market is in that *timing ballpark*, then the smart money trader can confidently know that the bear market has at last ended. His fundamentally oriented friends will not believe him because they will point to the increasingly unfavorable fundamental news as well as the probable reluctant admission by the Administration that the country is in a recession. The tight little 4 to 4 1/2 year cycle is completed and now ready to be repeated.

CHART PATTERNS TO FOLLOW FOR SUCCESSFUL SHORT SELLING

In view of the fact that the maximum profits in a bear market are made by going short, the chart formations to look for will be *just the opposite of those adhered to in the bull upswing:*

1. Long-term advance followed by a major reversal
2. Flat Top Failure
3. Declining from a double top
4. M Pattern
5. Decay
6. Cyclical at Historic Highs

1. Long-term Advance Followed By a Major Reversal

This is the exact opposite of the bullish long-term decline followed by a breakout pattern. The breaking of the long-term rising trendline is a major signal for a further sustained decline ahead.

2. Flat Top Failure

This pattern is the exact opposite of the bullish flat base breakout. The stock has moved in a very narrow price range at an advanced level for a long period of time and, instead of making an upside price penetration of the plateau level, makes a downside penetration. *This calls for a very rapid falling out and makes for a profitable short sale.*

3. Declining From a Double Top

This is the exact opposite of the bullish advance from a double bottom. The double top indicates that the stock has failed twice to penetrate an important line of supply (upside resistance), and it is usually found that the second top falls a bit short of the first top.

4. M Pattern

This is the exact opposite of the bullish W pattern. Shown is the double top with the right leg of the decline falling below the temporary support level in the middle of the M formation. The key signal to go short is the decline past that middle point.

5. Decay

This is the antithesis of growth. The stock price keeps gradually eroding away, declining through one support level after another.

6. Cyclical At Historic Highs

The successful short seller is short of steels, motors, coppers, machine tools, agricultural equipments, rails, etc., as he was long on these very stocks on the way up.

Important Note:

Truth is never out of date and these chart patterns are still the ones for shortsellers to look for when the presence of a new bear market is confirmed. Nothing has changed in that respect since the *Strategy* book first came out in 1960. Now, however, the use of on-balance volume *tremendously sharpens the earlier techniques.* Major reversals after a long-term advance will be spotted in terms of the OBV figures *before* seen on the price chart. The OBV technique will be particularly effective in the case of the flat top failure, breaking below a significant low point long before the downside price breakout is apparent on the price chart. OBV will also be additionally revealing in the case of the decline from a double top. The second top, while almost matching pricewise, will be far short of the first one in terms of the on-balance volume, a dead giveaway of technical failure at the top. As for the M pattern, OBV will also drop below the middle of the M formation ahead of price, and shortsellers will have the jump on their technically oriented friends who follow price movements alone. As for the decay pattern, OBV will also show the steady OBV breakdown ahead of price. The same OBV technique applied to cyclical stocks at their highs should also be superior to awaiting the more obvious price breakdowns, the OBV breakdowns occurring first.

If you don't already have one, get hold of a good book of stock charts and check out all these patterns at major market tops and bottoms. Get to know them well. If you are NOT a stock trader but rather a slow-moving long-term investor, interested primarily in only the major swings or even totally restricted to interest in dividend income, it is also important to watch the stock charts and be aware of the market game which is being played over and over every 4 to 4 1/2 years, oftentimes at YOUR expense. Stocks you own which have paid dividends for years may decline 50% in a bear market, and perhaps the dividend income for the next 12 years will only restore your position to the time just before the 50% decline. You may think you are still getting income from that point on, but you will only be getting *a partial return of capital* and will be ludicrously taxed on that return as if it was income. Such people are only kidding themselves when they sit with stocks through bull and bear markets, oblivious to the game being repeatedly played and so often at their expense.

If you are averse to taking a short position, the appearance of any of the described bearish chart patterns should at least tell you to move out of the stock and avoid the decline coming that can more than offset the dividends you would be receiving covering several years.

The Flat Base Alone Is Not Enough

When examining stock charts showing the stock to be moving in an extended flat base, *don't make the mistake of buying before the stock has penetrated the top of that base.* That was the original advice *before* the on-balance volume concept. Now that advice can be revised to caution against buying until the *on-balance volume* has made an upside breakout above the range corresponding to the length of the price base. That breakout might occur simultaneously with the price breakout or separately, but in either case demand that the OBV breakout be in evidence before buying.

Don't Marry a Stock

Astute traders have absolutely no sentiment when it comes to stocks. When a stock is signalling that it should be sold, it gets sold, and immediately. Uninformed and generally unsuccessful traders often get attached to a stock because the company might be a favorite of theirs. They seemingly take an oath "till death do us part" and literally hug the stock all the way down a bear market decline. We have all done this on occasion. Successful stock traders study a stock chart and then run an OBV table going back two or three months, and *the name of the company is usually the least important thing in their decision as to buy or sell the stock.* They wouldn't even have to see the name of the stock were it not for the fact that the name is required on the order. It might as well be a number. In this game we are accumulating *things* simply because they *are* being accumulated by their own given signals, and we then distribute those things when they *are* being distributed by their own given signals.

A NEW LOOK AT APPLYING THE
SHORT INTEREST TO INDIVIDUAL STOCKS

In the original *Strategy* book I introduced the concept of using the short interest in an individual stock as a guide toward successful stock trading. The theory stated simply that when the monthly short interest in a stock showed *three* consecutive monthly increases, then the stock should be bought. Conversely, three consecutive monthly declines was a strikeout and the stock should be sold. The theory was utterly simple and wholly logical. If the short interest in a stock is going down, it means that people are growing bullish on the issue. The further the short interest falls the more bullish is the public opinion of the stock. Obviously the stock is losing technical power as it gains public popularity, and the chances are good that it can be sold at a high price because the falling short interest reflected short covering which contributed toward the higher price. Conversely, if the short interest in a stock is rising, it means that people are growing bearish on the issue. The further the short interest rises the more bearish the opinion of the public. Now the stock is obviously gaining technical power as it loses public popularity, and the chances are good that it can be bought at a low price because the rising short interest reflected selling pressure which contributed toward the lower price.

While attempts have been made by fundamentalists to destroy the validity of this theory, they only served to draw attention to an additional requirement. The short interest must be related to the average daily volume just as the monthly short interest for the entire big board is related to the average daily market volume, making up a significant monthly *ratio* in each case. That method would eliminate meaningless increases or decreases in the stock short interest and enable one to know when an increasing or decreasing short interest on a three-month trend basis was meaningful. So then, the original theory is revised to the extent that we *substitute the short interest ratio* for the monthly short interest, requiring three consecutive monthly increases or decreases to constitute a buy or sell signal.

Now we can superimpose the use of *on-balance volume* to either intensify the buy or sell signals or dilute them. Counting a *positive* point for each bullish posture of the two indicators, a *negative* point for each bearish posture of the two indicators and a *neutral* rating in cases where the OBV field trend is classed as doubtful, there are six possible combinations in weighing the value of buy or sell signals based on the combination of short interest ratio trends and on-balance volume field trends:

(1)	Short interest ratio rises for three months Stock is in a rising field trend	2 Points	Most Bullish Signal
(2)	Short interest ratio rises for three months Stock is in a doubtful field trend	1 Point	
(3)	Short interest ratio rises for three months Stock is in a falling field trend	0 Points	
(4)	Short interest ratio falls for three months Stock is in a rising field trend	0 Points	
(5)	Short interest ratio falls for three months Stock is in a doubtful field trend	-1 Point	
(6)	Short interest falls for three months Stock is in a falling field trend	-2 Points	Most Bearish Signal

THE 200-DAY MOVING AVERAGE PRICE LINE ANALYSIS

This was one of the more durable contributions from the *Strategy* book, a pioneering technique which caused a major revision in all stock chart books thereafter. It is still believed that the 200-day moving average line stock charts are the most informative and profitably reliable indicators of where a stock is headed, provided the *eight* basic ways of reading them are known and followed. Variations of the technique have resulted in charts with 10-day, 25-day, 50-day, or 100-day moving averages, but time has proven that the penetrations of the slower moving 200-day line have been more meaningful. The complete chart consists of the actual price line of the stock with a 200-day moving average price line superimposed over it.

The *eight* basic ways of trading successfully by using these 200-day moving average price charts are as follows:

(1) If the 200-day average line flattens out following a previous decline, or is advancing, and the price of the stock penetrates that average line on the upside, this comprises a major buying signal.

(2) If the price of the stock falls below the 200-day moving average price line while the average line is still rising, this also is considered to be a buying opportunity.

(3) If the stock price is above the 200-day line and is declining toward that line, fails to go through and starts to turn up again, this is a buying signal.

(4) If the stock price falls too fast under the declining 200-day average line, it is entitled to an advance back toward the average line, and the stock can be bought for this short-term technical rise.

(5) If the 200-day line flattens out following a previous rise, or is declining, and the price of the stock penetrates that line on the downside, this comprises a major selling signal.

(6) If the price of the stock rises above the 200-day moving average price line while the average line is still falling, this also is considered to be a selling opportunity.

(7) If the stock price is below the 200-day line and is advancing toward that line, fails to go through and starts to turn down again, this is a selling signal.

(8) If the stock price advances too fast above the advancing 200-day average line, it is entitled to a reaction back toward the average line, and the stock can be sold for this short-term technical reaction.

COMBINING THE THREE GREATEST STOCK TRADING TECHNIQUES

Run through your chart book of 200-day moving average trendline charts and select any stock clearly showing one of the four buy signals based on the 200-day line analysis. Once identified, now go back and record the on-balance volume figures for the past 60 to 90 days. In doing that, check if the stock is running a short interest and compute the ratio for the past three months. You now have in your possession the best total technical information with which to trade with. Let us suppose that you identified a stock making Buy Signal #1 according to the 200-day line analysis, the line having flattened out following a previous decline or slightly advancing with the stock making an upside penetration. Your on-balance volume figures may show a clearly defined pattern of accumulation, perhaps a strong rising field trend, and there might even be three consecutive monthly advances in the short interest ratio. Obviously the trader is better armed with this total information rather than any portion of it. So, while successful trading could be done using any one of the techniques, I would strongly advise checking out all promising 200-day line moves with on-balance volume. I couldn't make that statement in the original *Strategy* book. But now, if only one method was available, I would have to choose the following of on-balance volume superior to any other single technique. Adding its use to the earlier techniques, the modern trader can equip himself with the finest technical data possible. Everybody won't do this, so one doesn't have to ever worry about it NOT working. People are lazy by nature, and the most successful stock traders are going to be those who DO THEIR HOMEWORK. The use of OBV is tedious, involving long hours if many stocks are being followed. However, I have shown how to limit the list of stocks being followed by the concentration on the new names showing up in the most active stock list and the stocks making new highs.

THE IDEAL SITUATION

Picking the right general time to buy stocks is half the battle

As you more closely observe the market (especially studying what it has done in the past), pay particularly close attention to how often it offered a TRULY GREAT BUYING OPPORTUNITY, the times when all the major indicators for a sustained market rise were in GEAR. Such times did not occur too often, but when they did, *those who recognized the pattern made tremendous profits.* Those were the times when even the risk of buying the basest "cats and dogs" was at such a minimum that one might even have done well by employing nothing more than the "hatpin" method of selecting stocks. All those great times for buying had *several things in common.* If this book does nothing more for you other than alert you to recognize just one of these great opportunity periods, it will have achieved its purpose.

The Ideal Timing Conditions For a Sustained Major Advance

1. *Things look terrible.* Stocks have been declining for many months with no let-up. The news is so bad that one would have to seem crazy to risk money in the stock market. All the news media is bearish. Government economists are publicly pessimistic. However, it can be shown that a point had been reached *where stocks are no longer acting commensurately with the bad news.* A point in the Dow has been reached which just *might* later on be identified as a major bottom.
2. *A line is formed.* Following that point which might be identified as the bottom, the news background gets even worse, but stocks now are in a set trading range. There has been a small rally off the bottom, but it hasn't held. On the other hand, new declines are no longer creating a maximum number of new individual stock lows.

3. *The breakthrough.* Usually within four months from the designated bottom there is some clearly defined upside breakthrough. The Dow clears the trading range of the past three or four months. Of course the news is still bad.

4. *Major upside penetration of the Dow 200-day Line.* This move is the first rate evidence that the great buying opportunity is at hand. The opportunity now corresponds to November, 1962, January, 1967, August, 1970, and January, 1975.

5. *Four to four and one-half years have passed since the last major market bottom.* If one turns one's back on the clearly defined cyclical rhythms of the market, one will miss those not too frequent great opportunity periods. This time factor is all-important to take into consideration.

When these FIVE conditions are met, you are probably encountering one of those great buying periods. Obviously you must have mounting evidence that *technical* conditions are improving between the time of # 1 and #4.

The Ideal Timing Conditions For a Sustained Major Decline

1. *Things look terrific.* Stocks have been advancing for many months with no let-up. The news is so good that the last thing that would be thought of is a major decline in stocks. All the news media is bullish. Government economists are publicly optimistic, and the public has demonstrated great confidence in the stock market. However, it can be shown that a point has been reached *where stocks are no longer acting commensurately with the good news.* A point in the Dow has been reached which just *might* later on be identified as a major top.

2. *A line is formed.* Following that point which might be identified as the top, the news background even gets better, but stocks are now in a set trading range. There has been a small decline from the top but it has not carried very far. On the other hand, new rallies are no longer creating a maximum number of new individual stock highs.

3. *The breakthrough.* Usually within four months from the designated top there is some clearly defined downside breakthrough. The Dow cracks the trading range of the past three or four months on the downside. Of course the news is still good.

4. *Major downside penetration of the Dow 200-day Line.* This move clinches the great selling opportunity at hand, such selling opportunities seen in 1962, 1966, 1969, and 1973.

5. *At least 2 1/2 years have passed since the last major top at a minimum and more commonly something closer to four years.* It has already been

explained that there is a definite timing *irregularity* between major market tops, while major bottoms are timed with some cyclic regularity.

When these FIVE conditions are met you are probably encountering one of the great market selling opportunities. Obviously you must have mounting *technical* evidence of important market deterioration between the time of #1 and #4.

THE GRAND STRATEGY

The Grand Strategy of picking the right stock at the right time involves a checklist of all the highlights touched upon here. Two things must be rigorously inspected: (1) the technical position of the market and (2) the technical position of the stock. Familiarize yourself with this step-by-step technical inspection report. It can serve as your blueprint for greater market gains and fewer losses.

COMPLETE TECHNICAL INSPECTION

Step One

Determining Which Phase the Market Is In

Bull Phase One:	*Characteristics*
Advance-Decline Line	(a) Has traced out a previous long-term decline, has stopped going down and has moved above a previous interim high.
Highs and Lows	(b) It can be shown that sometime during the previous nine months there was a climax in the number of new lows, some maximum number achieved in the 500 to 900 area, and since that time the number of individual new highs has been consistently outnumbering the number of new lows.
Dow-Jones Industrials	(c) Some time during the previous six to nine months made a major bottom confirmed by the Dow-Jones Transports. Since then has either made an unconfirmed new low or a clear pattern of rising bottoms and tops.
Dow-Jones Transports	(d) Some time during the previous six to nine months made a major bottom confirmed by the Dow-Jones Industrials. Since then has

either made an unconfirmed new low or a clear pattern of rising bottoms and tops.

Time Indicator

(e) Check out the market long-term cyclic bottoms-1957, 1962, 1966, 1970, 1974. Assuming a continued 4 to 4 1/2 year cycle, market should be within one to nine months after the recording of one of those cyclic lows.

Dow-Jones Industrial 200-Day Trendline

(f) The Dow 200-day trendline for a long time has been in a protracted decline. To insure against a mere rally in a bear market, the decline in the line must have lasted longer than nine months. The Dow makes an upside penetration of that trendline roughly 4 to 4 1/2 years after a similar upside penetration in the first phase of the previous bull market.

The 50% Principle

(g) If the Dow-Jones Industrial Average has retraced more than 50% of the previous *completed* bear market decline then the evidence is most compelling that the market is in the first phase of a new bull market.

News

(h) News is bearish in the main. The first phase of a bull market is never ushered in by good news because that would abort the market game principle. The fundamentalists would be buying along with the technicians and there would be no sellers. The news is *most* bearish during the first three months of the first phase, gradually lessening thereafter. As is so often the case, the country is in an economic recession during a bull market first phase, and the bad news stemming from it provides the necessary cover for technically inspired buying while the bulk of the fundamentally-oriented public worries over the daily headlines. The first phase of a new bull market always shows the market shrugging off the bad news, climbing on a wall of worry. It is the best evidence we have that expresses the degree of public disbelief that the market can rise in the face of such poor fundamentals.

General Motors

(i) In the very earliest part of the bull market first phase, the price of General Motors stock drops to the lowest level seen in 4 to 4 1/2 years. When this occurs, immediately check out the technical evidence of a major market bottom having already been recorded inasmuch as General Motors, more often than not, has made its low *after* the Dow. Thereafter, stock has no difficulty in effecting the bullish GM-four month rule, refusing to make a new low for four months. Once it records that bullish confirmation market's bullish first phase generally has three months remaining.

Secondary Offerings

(j) Very few secondary offerings, this being an *accumulation* phase, not a *distribution* phase.

Stock Splits

(k) Few if any stock splits. Again, the time wouldn't be right for them. Stock prices are still too low and this is not the distribution period.

Short Interest

(l) Downgraded in importance since the original *Strategy* book. Is now seen as a maverick indicator, not necessarily high or low at the start of a new bull market. At the 1970 market bottom it was very high and also at the 1974 bottom it was very high, continuing to rise throughout the first bull phase. The short interest *ratio* is far more important but even that indicator is not always telling a perfect story. A ratio approaching the very bullish level of 2.00 is always dependable as a first phase bull confirmation.

Disparity

(m) Measured by the cumulative differential between the Dow and the Standard & Poor 500 Stock Index or the Dow and the New York Stock Exchange Index, disparity offers no serious problems during the bull market first phase. On the general pattern of the Dow industrials being the last to rise and the last to fall, there is usually negative disparity in the very earliest phase of a new bull market, tending toward zero around four months off the bottom. Around nine or ten months after the major bottom, there is enough positive disparity (the Dow moving up faster than the general market) to suggest the end of the first phase.

Margins	(n) Generally a few months have passed since a cut in margin requirements.
Corporate Mergers	(o) Very few important mergers.
Stock Exchange Seat Price	(p) Seat prices just starting to come up from the lows.
Odd-Lot Short Sales	(q) If it peaks at 15,000 to 50,000 a few weeks after a confirmed major bottom market definitely in bull phase one. Other than that, indicator remains rather dormant for life of bull market.

Several deletions have been made in making up the revised layout of the Technical Inspection. Notably absent, the Barron's Confidence Index is no longer considered a reliable indicator. It fell sharply during the fall of 1970, having no relativity to the stock price trend. It fell sharply in the spring of 1975, perhaps meaningful this time, perhaps not. Odd-lot trading is dropped. I feel the indicator is redundant at best; as much reliable technical information is obtainable from the remaining indicators. Even odd-lot short sales only tell a really important story once or twice at best during the entire bull cycle. Yields are deleted, not only because the indicator can be classed as fundamental, but because the first phase of a new bull market no longer strictly requires that stocks yield more than bonds. Interest rates are also deleted. Very low rates are not required to get a new bull market going. Relative change is the important thing. If rates start down from a very high plateau (as they did in late 1974) that is as bullish as if they had started down from a much lower level. Bull markets do require a favorable change in the interest rate structure, it being very basic. However, I would prefer sticking mostly here to technical indicators. The interest rate is classed as fundamental, undoubtedly the most important of all fundamental indicators, and technicians are really never unaware of what rates are doing. Total market volume as an indicator might have been added in the revised layout, but its characteristics are too subject to change in each bull and bear market. One bull market might start out with very low volume as classically expected by Dow Theorists while other equally valid bull market first phases may be characterized by very heavy volume.

Bull Phase Two:	*Characteristics*
Advance-Decline Line	(a) Advance-Decline Line made the first of two tops during the bull first phase. As Bull Phase Two gets underway, the A-D line is diverging, working temporarily lower, the strong first

phase upswing being digested. In the middle of the second phase, the more extended downward corrective movement called the DECLINE THAT FOOLS THE MAJORITY carries the A-D line just low enough to make it difficult for the line to do more than recover that loss. That second top may or may not be higher than the first phase top, and it occurs very late in the second phase, practically at the dividing line between the second and third phases. Regardless of whether the line is moving up rapidly or not in the second phase, the general pattern calls for one top in the first phase and one about equal or higher in the second.

Highs and Lows

(b) The number of new individual stock price highs may have topped out very late in the first bull phase if not reserved for a second phase peak. That largely depends on whether the first phase market movement was characterized by high or low volume. If first phase market volume was high and the advance in the Dow quite spectacular, then it is more probable that the number of new highs peaked late in the first phase. We never get as many new highs at one time in a bull market as we get simultaneous new lows in a bear market. The usual peaking in the number of new highs is done in the 300-400 area while climax figures for new lows run as high as the 550-900 area. Assuming the spectacular bull market first phase advance in the Dow on heavy volume, new highs now consistently run under the peak of the first phase, generally fluctuating in the 80 to 150 area. Following a more sluggish low volume bull phase one, new highs would not be expected to top out until late in phase two.

Dow-Jones Industrials

(c) May or may not exceed first phase high prior to mid-phase sharp downward correction. Will make a new bull market high very late in second phase after mid-phase correction.

Dow-Jones Transports

(d) No serious divergences from the industrials are expected to occur during the second phase unless it precedes the mid-phase corrective move. A failure to confirm the industrial upswing after the mid-phase correction would be deemed serious.

Time Indicator

(e) Ten to 20 months have gone by since a major confirmed market bottom has been recorded. An intermediate downtrend occurs approximately 15 to 18 months after such a major bottom.

Dow-Jones Industrial 200-Day Trendline

(f) Trendline remains under the first phase peak throughout the second phase of the bull market.

The 50% Principle

(g) Has no major function during second phase other than helping to pinpoint extent of mid-phase secondary reaction.

News

(h) While stock prices climbed the wall of worry during the first phase, news-oriented fundamentalists were stunned with disbelief. What usually starts the second phase of the bull market is a change in the news transforming that first phase public disbelief to BELIEF. If the country was in an economic recession during the first phase, a reported end or near-end to the recession would usher in the bull market second phase, and such ushering in would probably coincide with a market reaction as the public comes in and pays top dollar.

General Motors

(i) *Trends higher* through second phase, all reactions holding sharply above previous bear market low.

Secondary Offerings

(j) A normal flow of secondary offerings is now in progress.

Stock Splits

(k) Stock prices have generally returned to known values, having recovered about half of bear market losses. It is still too early for serious distribution patterns to emerge and thus only an occasional stock split is noted.

Short Interest

(l) Tends to drop from earlier peaks. Ratio tends to fluctuate between normal and bullish, 1.25 to 1.50.

Disparity

(m) Any positive disparities are eliminated on mid-phase secondary reaction. Thereafter, no problems should be seen here until during the third phase.

Margins	(n) Possibly raised late in second phase.
Corporate Mergers	(o) Mergers are increasing in number.
Stock Exchange Seat Price	(p) Several good increases seen in seat price.
Odd-Lot Short Sales	(q) Rather dormant indicator. Next possible function is to possibly aid in identifying mid-phase secondary reaction termination.

Bull Phase Three: *Characteristics*

Advance-Decline Line (a) Records major peak at end of bull market second phase and generally diverges from the Dow industrials all throughout the bull market third phase.

Highs and Lows (b) There is one final attempt by new highs to scale the earlier bull market peak, but it fails. There is an increase in the number of new lows but the figure would seldom come up and pass the number of new highs.

Dow-Jones Industrials (c) The Dow industrials are in their glory during the third bull phase, pulling away from all the broader indices. A series of new highs for the bull market is recorded with the usual terminal move characterized by a sharp final perpendicular rise to a record high, a move lacking confirmation by a number of the major indicators

Dow-Jones Transports (d) A serious divergence is expected during the third bull phase between the industrials and transports, one of the two averages failing to confirm the other. This is not absolutely required, however, to identify the third phase termination. It is possible that both averages could record a confirmed major top accompanied by a serious technical non-confirmation elsewhere, notably in the A-D Line and the number of new highs.

Time Indicator (e) Twenty-one to 33 months have gone by since a major confirmed market bottom has been recorded. By this indicator alone one would be warned that the bull market is aging, the time at hand to begin to look for the exits.

Dow-Jones Industrial 200-day Trendline (f) Here we have what I have defined as a clear signal agent for the timing of the bull market

third phase. When the trendline comes up
after the second phase reaction and zigzags
into new bull market high ground, that breakthrough signals the start of the bull market
third phase. The bull market from that point
usually has less than a year to run and many
times closer to six to eight months.

The 50% Principle   (g) Has no important applications during bull
                             third phase.

News   (h) Economic news is glowing and the public is
                             very bullish. Reflecting the industrial boom,
                             all kinds of extremely bullish earnings fore-
                             casts are being published. The bulk of the
                             market, however, is not responding well to the
                             very bullish news as seen in a slipping
                             advance-decline line.

General Motors   (i) General Motors has now topped out ahead of
                             the Dow Jones industrial average.

Secondary Offerings   (j) Secondary stock offerings in major stocks are
                             very frequent now. These are reported each
                             week in the Barron's Market Laboratory page.

Stock Splits   (k) Stock splits are now occurring with great
                             frequency, reflecting the heavy distribution of
                             stocks.

Short Interest   (l) While there is a normal expectation of a falling
                             short interest it is not mandatory in order to
                             identify this phase. The big drops may be
                             reserved for the first phase of the bear market.
                             The short interest ratio, while extremely use-
                             ful in calling market bottoms when it is high,
                             is not a reliable indicator on market tops, it
                             having been previously mentioned here how
                             many times the ratio has fallen to less than
                             1.00.

Disparity   (m) Almost invariably a big positive disparity devel-
                             ops between the Dow industrial average and
                             the broader indices during this bull market
                             phase. The more positive the disparity, the
                             more vulnerable the market.

Margins   (n) Margin requirements remain at a high level.
Corporate Mergers   (o) Mergers are very frequent now.
Stock Exchange Seat Price (p) Stabilized at a high level, far above prices
                             realized at previous bear market bottom.

Odd-lot Short Sales	(q) Running very low now, down in the 1,500 to 3,000 area.
Bear Phase One:	*Characteristics*
Advance-Decline Line	(a) Breaks under the low recorded just prior to the final bull market rally in the blue chips and is a clearly defined downtrend.
Highs and Lows	(b) The daily number of new lows climbs rapidly and surpasses the dwindling number of new highs. Consistently thereafter new lows outnumber new highs.
Dow-Jones Industrials	(c) First sharp declines in the industrial average from the major peak recorded. Strong attempt to rally back about 60 days later fails, the Dow then breaking the first important low point to record a very bearish-looking downward zigzag.
Dow-Jones Transports	(d) Commensurate sharp decline from major peak with inability to recover on later rally attempt.
Time Indicator	(e) Twenty-two to 34 months have gone by since the last major bear market bottom. A market top having all the earmarks of a major bull market peak must have been seen within the past one to five months.
Dow-Jones Industrial 200-day Trendline	(f) Previously rising 200-day line has flattened out and is just starting to turn down. The Dow-Jones Industrial Average has come down sharply and made a downside penetration of the trendline. Later the average might get back a bit over the line but promptly turns down again. This all usually happens during the first bear phase.
The 50% Principle	(g) The earlier this Principle is activated the more *valid it is likely to be.* If more than 50% of the previous completed bull market is retraced during the first bear phase, the record strongly points toward the previous bear market low being broken in this bear market. As shown in the section covering the Principle, it was activated too late on the 1966 downswing to be effective, thereby setting up a fooler. It effected a breakthrough during the first phase of the 1968-70 bear cycle, thereby predicting

a bottom below that of 1966. It effected a breakthrough during the second phase of the 1973-74 bear market and that also was followed by a bottom below that of 1970. Summing up, if the Principle is activated during either the first or second phase of the bear market it is likely to be very valid and thus a very bearish indication.

News

(h) The news definitely remains bullish, very favorable to business. Most economic indicators support the continuation of prosperous times. While the market responded to favorable news during the second phase of the bull market with rallies, shrugged off the good news and went sideways during the third phase of the bull market, the market now goes into sharp declines in the face of continuing good news.

General Motors

(i) General Motors is now in a very bearish falling field trend. The price of the stock has made a downside penetration of its own 200-day line, and the line itself has flattened out and is just starting to turn down.

Secondary Offerings

(j) Secondary offerings continue to occur with great frequency.

Stock Splits

(k) Stock splits are continuing to occur although with a bit less frequency.

Short Interest

(l) Sharp declines are recorded in the short interest.

Disparity

(m) The Positive disparity built up late in the bull market third phase may not go away too quickly, for as the Dow now drops sharply the general market drops just as sharply, and the positive disparity is generally retained which is very bearish.

Margins

(n) Margin requirements still at a high level.

Corporate Mergers

(o) Mergers continue to occur but less frequently.

Stock Exchange Seat Price

(p) First substantial drop in seat prices occurs.

Odd-lot Short Sales

(q) Starting to build, jumping up in the 5,000 to 8,000 area.

Bear Phase Two: *Characteristics*

Advance-Decline Line

(a) Turns up sharply on strong mid-phase rally and moves out of the down channel, but the move turns out to be transitory, the A-D Line soon thereafter breaking down even more sharply, breaking the previous low.

Highs and Lows

(b) New highs for the calendar year temporarily outnumber the new lows but soon gives way to the very bearish pattern of new lows consistently outnumbering new highs.

Dow-Jones Industrials

(c) On a number of rally attempts since the major peak, one or two Dow-Jones Industrial stocks actually get back to the old high, decciving many into thinking that perhaps the previous decline was a secondary reaction in a bull market after all. Such spotty strength soon gives way to the primary bearish trend. Maximum deception occurs on strong mid-phase rally.

Dow-Jones Transports

(d) Transports rally during mid-phase strength but fall woefully short of the peak and probably fail to confirm the industrial rise or visa versa.

Time Indicator

(e) Anywhere from seven to 14 months have passed since the major bull market peak.

Dow-Jones Industrial 200-day Trendline

(f) The trendline is coming straight down hard which made it easier for the Dow to make the deceptive upside penetration on the mid-phase rally, the RALLY THAT FOOLS THE MAJORITY.

The 50% Principle

(g) If the Principle is activated, and all the signs point to this being the second phase of the bear market, then the activation is very bearish, predicting a new low below that of the previous bear market.

News

(h) The news has soured and market responds to the change in the news with further sharp declines. During the mid-phase rally market goes up on talk of recovery, but the talk proves to be premature. Public continues to buy on all reactions, still confident that bull market can be revived.

General Motors

(i) General Motors is unable to tack on more than just a few points on mid-phase rally. The 200-day line is trending sharply lower and upside penetration of the line by the stock proves very temporary, the stock breaking to a new low thereafter.

Secondary Offerings	(j) Passed their frequency peak, it becoming more difficult to distribute stock.
Stock Splits	(k) Very few stocks splitting now. The bear market is effecting the same results.
Short Interest	(l) Short interest starts to go up again, experiencing one more large decline on mid-phase rally. That further weakens the technical position, making it easier for market to score new lows.
Disparity	(m) Positive disparity is eliminated, the Dow acting as weak as the general market.
Margins	(n) First cut in margin requirements (announced during sharp decline which follows abortive rally).
Corporate Mergers	(o) Mergers are rare but an occasional one occurs.
Stock Exchange Seat Price	(p) Continues to drop in price but then stabilizes.
Odd-Lot Short Sales	(q) Generally stays in the 5,000 to 8,000 area.
Bear Phase Three:	*Characteristics*
Advance-Decline Line	(a) Continues to zigzag to new lows with no let-up.
Highs and Lows	(b) List of new highs is running close to zero in number while new lows number in the hundreds, climaxing anywhere in the 500 to 900 area.
Dow-Jones Industrials	(c) Most Dow stocks making new lows with a small handful of them accounting for a majority of the losses.
Dow-Jones Transports	(d) Falling rapidly, keeping apace with the industrials on the downside, recording new lows for the bear market.
Time Indicator	(e) Market should be within 48 to 54 months since last major cyclic bottom and within 14 to 21 months since previous bull market top.
Dow-Jones Industrial 200-day Trendline	(f) The trendline continues to come down hard, and the Dow is now outpacing the trendline on the downside, dropping the maximum distance below it of any time during the bear market.
The 50% Principle	(g) If the Principle is activated during this phase, the chances are very strong that the Dow is close to the bottom and that the activation of the Principle will result in a key bear trap.

News   (h) Public has turned completely sour on the
                      market and responds to every bit of bad news
                      with heavy selling. Their previous misplaced
                      confidence has now turned to extreme pessi-
                      mism. The smart money, awaiting the collapse
                      of the public confidence, shifts their stance
                      from one of pessimism to one of confidence.

General Motors (i) This bellwether stock continues to make new
                      lows, there being virtually no support for the
                      stock.

Secondary Offerings (j) Virtually none being recorded, any stock to be
                      distributed having been done so in previous
                      bear market phases and the late phase of the
                      bull market.

Stock Splits   (k) Virtually none being recorded, the market
                      performing that function effectively now.

Short Interest (l) Rising rapidly now month after month. The
                      rapid rise adds a large number of new short-
                      sellers, those shorting on the obviously bad
                      news.

Disparity   (m) This indicator finally falls into negative terri-
                      tory, the Dow acting worse now than the
                      general market.

Margins   (n) Possible second cut in margin requirements
                      made to help revive collapsing market.

Corporate Mergers (o) Virtually no mergers announced.
Stock Exchange Seat Price (p) Price drops to a new bear market low.
Odd-Lot Short Sales (q) Possible sharp rise late in bear third phase, but
                      it may occur just after the Dow bottom. In
                      either case an indicator that must be closely
                      watched for unusual activity.

Step Two

Matching Right Type of Stock and Chart to Each Phase

Bull Phase One:

The maximum profit opportunities exist in this phase if you concentrate on the
following:

THE RIGHT CHARTS   1. Long-term decline followed by a breakout
                      2. Flat base breakout
                      3. Coming off a double bottom
                      4. Cyclical at historic lows

PRICE CATEGORY	Low-priced.
CAPITALIZATION	Thin (the thinner the better).
QUALITY	Stocks of secondary and tertiary quality desired because the correct timing has reduced the risk which would ordinarily be associated with stocks of that reduced quality.
ON-BALANCE VOLUME	Dramatic rise off of a long-term bottom evidencing important accumulation, the field trend having at least improved from an extensive falling field trend or having advanced to a rising status.
200-DAY LINE	Stock has either made an upside penetration of its own 200-day line or is about to, based on the strong OBV evidence of accumulation.
SHORT INTEREST	Preferably rising but not a necessary requirement.

This is the phase in which the highly speculative positions are most likely favored to work out for the astute trader who instantly recognizes this particular phase of the market. The trend which the trader must take advantage of for *maximum profits* calls for taking the *maximum risks* as the market moves up from an *important bottom.* As the market moves through each bull phase, the element of risk must be *gradually reduced by increasing the quality of the stock.*

If the trader or investor has correctly identified the first phase of a new bull market, his timing *substitutes for quality.* What I mean by that is simply that *he can take on risks which could not be tolerated in any other market phase.* If he finds it possible to buy a thinly capitalized stock coming off a major bottom, a stock considered of low or questionable quality, a stock evidencing definite accumulation, it will probably be a much better buy than any higher-priced blue chip stock. Many stocks in this period go from 2 to 10 in about nine months while higher priced issues about double on average, 400% rise as against 100%. So, you can go for quality if you choose to, but if you are interested in *maximum profits,* experience has shown that the time to be bold and acquire poorer quality stocks *which are ready to go* is during this bull market first phase. There won't be a similar opportunity for 4 to 4 1/2 years. So the unbeatable combination is looked for:

1. Thinly capitalized stock
2. Low-priced (somewhere under 10)*

---

* The number of low-priced stocks available during the first phase of a new bull market will largely depend on how severe the previous bear market was. A severe bear market would naturally create conditions for super-maximum profits, because then even stocks *of much higher quality* would be pounded down to prices under $10 a share. Following such severe bear markets the unbeatable buying combination would therefore include such higher quality stocks. The 1973-74 bear market was a severe one, producing dozens of super bargains selling under $10 a share, including such well-known company names as Dr. Pepper, Hershey Foods, Howard Johnson, Merrill Lynch, Occidental Petroleum, Radio Corp., Westinghouse, and many others.

3. Coming off a bottom according to any of the four chart patterns mentioned previously
4. Dynamic OBV pattern of accumulation
5. Breaking above the 200-day line or anticipated

Once purchases have been made, the next thing to be decided is how long to hold the stocks. You don't have to make the decision. The market will decide for you. Assuming you correctly identified the first phase of the bull market, the chosen stocks should encounter no serious difficulties until sometime late in the second phase of the bull market. This implies that you will be holding them approximately 18 to 21 months. In any case, you will qualify for a capital gain since it is highly unlikely that any undue technical weakness will be encountered prior to six months holding time. If weakness does develop in any of the chosen stocks, it will show up in the on-balance volume figures early enough to be advantageously switched to another stock flashing the ready signal. Stay loose. You're not marrying any of the stocks purchased. They are just numbers and not names. They don't know you and you don't want to know them, at least not long enough to have to call them relatives by marriage.

Bull Phase Two:

The maximum profit opportunities exist in this phase if you concentrate on the following:

THE RIGHT CHARTS	1. Long-term decline followed by a breakout (ALWAYS GOOD)
	2. Flat Base Breakout (ALWAYS GOOD)
	3. Coming Off a Double Bottom (ALWAYS GOOD)
	4. CYCLICAL STOCKS (The big feature in this phase)
PRICE CATEGORY	General price category for concentrating upon at this point is the $15 to $30 price range. The low-priced speculative vehicles purchased during the first bull phase will be sold at the end of this phase.
CAPITALIZATION	When a stock is ready to go, the one more thinly capitalized generally does better. However, stock selection during this phase should be more guided by which new names are showing up among the most active stocks as well as the stocks making new highs for the first time.
QUALITY	You will be looking now for the better grade cyclical stocks early in this phase, selling your "cats and dogs" at the end of the phase.

ON-BALANCE VOLUME   Having developed the essential daily habit of keeping on-balance volume records up to date, a great deal of time will be saved when buying decisions must be made. Even though most of the low-priced stocks have made good moves by now, an occasional new one jumps into the picture. When such a new face shows up with a promising chart, run an OBV check immediately.

200-DAY LINE   Most stocks by now have come up through their 200-day lines, and many of them have made normal retreats back toward the rising line. These stocks, providing the accumulation pattern is fully intact, are among the best buying candidates.

SHORT INTEREST   Enough time has elapsed now to expect that some technically strong stock will have developed a rising short interest trend. This is often an important technical "kicker" and enhances the upside prospects.

In this second phase of the bull market your first purchased stocks will probably be undergoing their greatest degree of capitalization on the bullish charts. It is very important now to recognize the transition from the second phase to the third phase of the bull swing, for it is at that point where you will generally take profits in the low-priced cats and dogs as well as the cyclical stocks. Throughout the first and second bull markets phases no short selling is recommended.

Bull Phase Three:

THE RIGHT CHARTS   Here you will rely heavily on high quality, blue chip issues of a counter-cyclical nature, stocks which have not made downside moves threatening their rising 200-day moving average trendlines. You will have switched out of cyclical capital goods stocks into such issues as American Brands, American Telephone, General Foods, Procter & Gamble, Sears Roebuck, Woolworth, etc. Any counter-cyclical equity in a rising trend is a candidate for potential profits in this phase. The Dow industrial stocks, being the last to top out in a bull market, will contain many of the stocks you should be in during this phase.

PRICE CATEGORY   Low-priced stocks are strictly out during this phase. If one can still be found there is obviously an impediment which has kept it low while the majority of the other low-priced stocks moved up during the first two phases of the bull market. Buying will be centered on stocks on the move in the $30 to $100 category.

CAPITALIZATION   Should not be a consideration during this phase. It is difficult, if not almost impossible, to find a combination of high quality and very low capitalization. However, stocks with the smallest capitalizations will be chosen among the list of blue chip stocks selected. (Of course stocks must pass inspection on all major technical counts: chart position, 200-day trendline position, OBV, and short interest.)

QUALITY   Maximum attention on high quality.

ON-BALANCE VOLUME   When this phase in the bull market is reached, most of the OBV patterns will be ones of maturity or near maturity. Great care must be taken when analyzing the OBV figures now because, unless one has available the figures going back through the first two phases of the bull market, one may not be able to detect this degree of technical maturity. OBV figures, like the advance-decline line, can be started at any given point in time, and during this phase it is essential that enough past performance data is available to avoid expensive errors of misinterpretation.

200-DAY LINE   Typical third-phase bull movements show the price of the stock consistently above the trendline, both of them rising fairly rapidly in *parallel* fashion. Stocks selected were already *above* the trendline when purchased. If the price of a stock is under the trendline during the third phase of the bull market, something is wrong with it, and it should not be touched. Now note carefully the *consistent distance* above the trendline maintained by the price. Now watch for an *upside deviation* in that distance, the price of the stock outrunning the rate of climb in the trendline. *When that occurs that will be the signalled time to sell the stocks.*

SHORT INTEREST   May or may not be falling as a total. However, stocks showing a falling short interest trend will be avoided as much as possible.

As the third phase of the bull market is traversed, you have adopted a selective policy with standards only a very few stocks can meet. Only the

STRONGEST TECHNICAL FEATURES OF STRENGTH WILL BE TOL-
ERATED. You are not going to be fooled by grandiose earnings estimates if
the stock does not measure up technically. You have been out of cats and
dogs for some time now, have sold all cyclical stocks, and are now in only a
few defensive blue chips which have met the rigorous technical standards
you require.

*During this phase you have permitted yourself to take a few selected short
positions in stocks where the price of the stock has obviously outrun the
trendline on the upside, or in stocks which have turned their trendlines
down, or in stocks which have shown sharply falling short interest trends, all
these situations evidencing pronounced distribution patterns in terms of
their on-balance volume figures.*

Bear Phase One:

THE RIGHT CHARTS

Charts are only looked at now with an eye to
selecting opportunities for profitable shortselling.
If you do not care to indulge in shortselling, no
common stocks are worthy to be held in a bear
market. You are out of the market for the rest of
the downturn. You might make some exceptions
during the third phase of the bear market, but,
unless you go short, you have nothing good to
look forward to in a bear market. Most stock
charts will now suggest short selling opportunities,
but the best choices will be where the price of the
stock has obviously outrun the trendline on the
upside, or where a downside penetration of the
trendline has just started to turn the trendline
itself down.

PRICE CATEGORY

Being the first phase of a bear market, you must
now view the market as the *exact opposite* of the
first phase of a bull market. While you were
searching out low-priced stocks under accumulation then, you are now looking for short sale
opportunities among high-priced stocks under distribution, stocks in the $50 to $100 range or
higher.

CAPITALIZATION

It is never wise, as a rule, to short thinly capitalized stocks. There will be so many short sale
opportunities available in this phase that it will be
easy to find plenty of candidates without having
to short a thin stock.

QUALITY

Quality is not a key consideration here since
stocks of varying qualities are going to go down in
a bear market.

ON-BALANCE VOLUME	This data is now especially valuable, confirming where the clearest patterns of distribution lie, revealing upside excesses, and forecasting drops below the trendlines before they actually occur.
200-DAY LINE	Usually a bear market hasn't been technically confirmed until after a number of stocks have already seen their highs and have made their initial sharp drop toward their trendlines. Therefore *most* of the shortsale candidates will be stocks making their initial downside penetrations of their trend-lines, penetrations turning the lines down. (This is why some short selling is permitted during the third phase of the bull market, catching those stocks at the maximum distance above their trendlines where OBV distribution patterns predicted their down-turn.)
SHORT INTEREST	Continue shorting stocks evidencing declining short interests or in other cases where there is virtually little or no short interest.

While the original *Strategy* book permitted some buying during the first phase of a bull market in special situations and the continued holding of some stocks in special cases, experience has shown that it is best to make no exceptions in a bear market. In a bear market the primary trend is down and you either must go short or get out. There is no safe middle road.

Bear Phase Two:

THE RIGHT CHARTS	The most predominant chart patterns in evidence at this time, charts suggesting continued short selling, will be those charts showing the stock coming down from the bull market peak, having then made the downside penetration of the 200-day line, falling sharply thereafter, *and then rebounding to a declining trendline.* Concentrate new short selling on this demonstrated movement, *catching the stock at the point it comes back and touches the declining trendline.*
PRICE CATEGORY	The higher the price the better. Many of the highest flyers have been cut down considerably from their bull market peaks, but now just about any stock still selling over $50 a share is ripe for short selling. It is open season on them all.
CAPITALIZATION	Continue to refrain from shorting thin stocks.
QUALITY	Quality provides no defense in this phase and thus stocks of all qualities are being shorted. The bear

	market has been merciless on stocks of low quality.
ON-BALANCE VOLUME	Invaluable during this phase in pinpointing the predicted upside failures on stocks advancing from initial reaction lows to the point at which they touch their declining trendlines.
200-DAY LINE	Practically all 200-day lines are now declining, best shortselling opportunities now seen as the majority of stocks hit the declining line and come down and break to new lows.
SHORT INTEREST	Reflecting a general rise in the short interest, it will be increasingly difficult to find stocks having declining short interest trends. However, at this point it is not an important consideration inasmuch as shortsellers are *shorting with the trend,* and thus there is no compulsion to cover. Using the short interest as a trading tool is more reliable in bull markets.

It must be kept in mind that a strong rally usually occurs during the second phase of a bear market. A close appraisal of the technical indicators should clearly signal when short sales should be covered. If one insists on buying into that rally, one must be guided almost completely by one's on-balance volume figures since most other considerations will remain generally bearish.

Bear Phase Three:
THE RIGHT CHARTS

The third phase of the bear market is the most vicious, stripping the public first and in the end entrapping the bears. During the steepest segment of this final downturn, short sale profits will accrue rapidly, and, while the bulk of short sales earlier in the bear market were in stocks of less than top quality, remaining short sale positions in this phase will largely be in stocks of blue chip status, the blue chips being the last to fall in a bear market. Charts will show price consistently under declining trendlines, *covering of shorts being done when price outruns the trendline on the downside,* creating downside distortions equal and opposite to the upside distortions seen in the third bull market phase. *Inasmuch as this is usually the shortest of the three bear market phases, the uppermost consideration now is not looking for new shortselling opportunities, but trying to ascer-*

	tain the best time for covering the short positions already held.
PRICE CATEGORY	Is of no consequence now. Short positions have been taken in blue chip stocks, traditionally the last to touch bottom.
CAPITALIZATION	Is of no consequence now. Short positions in the blue chips obviously imply high capitalizations.
QUALITY	All poorer quality stocks have virtually collapsed, only the blue chips having some distance to go until bottom is reached.
ON-BALANCE VOLUME	Again invaluable in identifying the downward acceleration typical of all approaching major bottoms. Such downside acceleration in the OBV figures will accompany the price/trendline spread seen at all major bottoms. When that twin phenomena shows up, *you will cover all your short positions.*
200-DAY LINE	Watch for price outrunning the line on the downside and then cover short sales.
SHORT INTEREST	Will be rising now in most stocks.

There are always existing tendencies for overlapping characteristics from one market phase to the next. The dividing lines are never so distinct that a trader can divorce himself entirely from some of the trading tactics successfully employed in the previous phase. The degree of discretion is dictated by the technical conclusions drawn. The third phases of both bull and bear markets have these overlapping characteristics in common, each one consisting of endings and beginnings side by side. After all, a bull market doesn't end when the Dow-Jones Industrial Average says it does anymore than a bear market ends on the Dow low. So, while you were permitted to take some selected short sale positions late in the third phase of the bull market in stocks having outrun their trendlines on the upside and showing initial distribution patterns as seen by OBV, *so then are you permitted to go long late in the bear market third phase in those stocks which have outrun their trendlines on the downside and are showing initial accumulation patterns as seen by OBV.*

5

A Look at the Future

I

How will the market game go in the future? Will most market followers continue to revolve around the market game board every 4 to 4 1/2 years, first getting their brains knocked out against their self-imposed hard wall of fear and later allowing themselves to drown in a sea of self-imposed euphoria and greed, while a much smaller and smarter group runs in the opposite direction, or will there be some degree of evolution? Are we constantly condemned to repeat the errors of the past on a constant plane of ignorance, or is there real progress despite ourselves? History says there is both, not only the constantly predictable pitfalls of human nature reacting the same way to all excesses of fear and greed, but simultaneously a perceptive evolution to a higher plane of intelligence, not only in an increasingly sophisticated population of market game players but in all things.

Maximum blindness to this encouraging truth occurs during periods of national excess, excesses of pessimism and optimism. This nation has always been blessed by being given great leaders during times of national peril. If such was not apparent at the time, the net evolution of the nation according to history has proved that even during critical times, when big name leadership might have been lacking, there was always a band of positive-thinking individuals working far outside the boundaries of self-interest who were willing to press on against great odds and make a timely contribution toward the evolution of this nation, helping to rekindle the fires of the imagination when the national spirit was low. The new ideas and the determination of these hardy souls survived the dogmatic defeatism which they were fortuitously brought on the scene to counter. Their counterparts are those who keep their head when all the world around them seem to be losing theirs.

There are parallels in nature. For years science couldn't explain the periodic migrations of the lemming, a small furry rodent common in northern Scandinavian countries, with a variety also known in North

244

America. Approximately every four years millions of lemmings in packs would migrate in a given direction, most of them drowning in the rivers and streams or the ocean they were unable to cross. They didn't deliberately commit suicide. A migration could start in any direction but, once started, always continued in a straight line. When a river or stream was approached, the lemmings simply followed their leaders into it, millions of them drowning. The explanation of the lemming cycle is simple and has a stock market correlation. Each year the female lemming has an average of three litters, each containing three to nine young. Every four years the lemming population reaches a peak, and there isn't enough food to go around. Simple animal instinct drives them to migrate in search of fresh food supplies, and that migration produces the downswing in the population curve. The few remaining lemmings that didn't follow the pack replenish the population, and the cycle is perpetuated. So the mysterious cyclical migration of the lemming was finally explained when it was shown that each migration followed a period of *excess* population. The lemmings refusing to follow the pack survived, but the keyword here is *excess*. The excess motivated the action.

A major market downturn invariably follows a period of *excess* optimism, and a major upturn generally follows a period of *excess* pessimism. Here also the keyword is *excess,* the triggering cause of cyclical change. The market pendulum always swings further than most people anticipate at the terminal points of all bull and bear markets, but in the generated national mood of optimism or despair, most people forget what the excess of feeling implies, succumbing instead to its total influence. During the Eisenhower Administration, Treasury Secretary George Humphrey, in 1957, predicted a depression coming that would "curl your hair." The prediction was made in August, 1957, and five weeks later the Dow bottomed out at 419, never to see that level again. The Dow plummeted so rapidly in the spring of 1962 that the ghost of 1929 again seemed to be stalking the Street, and there were some very vocal people at the time grandstanding on the national fear psychosis. On the exact day of the bottom, June 26, 1972, the now defunct *New York Herald Tribune* provided a typical memorial to the occasion with a huge feature on their financial page titled *"Wall Street's Favorite 50 Short Sales,"* extolling their virtues at the very worst of times. Less than four months later a new blanket of fear was spread across the nation as President Kennedy revealed the presence of deadly missiles in Cuba. The Dow threatened to break the June low, but financial disaster was averted but a handful of days later when Russia backed down in the confrontation and removed the deadly weapons, it proving to have been one of the finest buying opportunities on record, again a case of opportunity clothed in crisis. But there were many who sought to personally capitalize on the national fear, selling expensive backyard bombshelters. Many a sucker plunked down thousands of dollars for these unused reminders of once imagined missile attacks when they should have been buying stocks with the money. Again depression warnings were rife at the 1966 market bottom, but seldom was the spectre of national doom seemingly closer to reality than during the hair raising days leading up to the May, 1970 bottom. Wall Street was running in red ink, the nation was split wide open over Cambodia, campus riots were getting out of control, highlighted by the deaths at Kent State, the huge International Overseas Services mutual fund had collapsed, the Penn Central railroad went into bankruptcy, Chrysler was on the verge of bankruptcy and would have gone under without 11th hour loans. The Stock Exchanges were on the verge of closing their doors, the heads of the New York Exchanges, along with key Treasury and Federal Reserve officials and business leaders from across the land, were called to an emergency closed door meeting at the White House by President Nixon, and on that day the market turned, not to see those Dow levels again for over four years.

The 1973-74 downturn was in a class by itself as a maximum producer of national pessimism. The country was sickened over the Watergate scandal, shocked by the sharpest decline in stock prices since the 1929 crash, and frightened by an overadvertised international monetary crisis as well as an uncontrolled inflation and record high interest rates. The price of gold soared to all-time highs of close to $200 an ounce as people vented their fears, the Middle East was in turmoil, and after a year of the energy crisis the national polls showed that half of the country was looking for a depression. Of course that many people weren't going to be right, but the most vocal disciples of doom yet to come on the scene were having a field day preaching the hopelessness of the world situation and convincing the public that the pessimists were going to be right this time. They ranged from unschooled selfmade "experts" hawking their mimeographed newsletters for the first time to much more responsible individuals. They all had one thing in common—the desire to cash in on the national gloom whether it be by giving a gold seminar, writing a bestseller on a coming monetary crisis, selling "survival kits," or a range of other activities. The common theme, expressed by one of the participants who packed Carnegie Hall at the peak of the obsession, was "buy gold for safety, silver for profits, Swiss francs or maybe Dutch guilders for liquidity, and a gun for protection." They all began to sound like the 1962 sellers of bombshelters, and their timing was familiarly similar.

During the attack on all those who disagreed with their depression thesis, the market hit true internal bottom on September 13, 1974, the final confirmed Dow bottom on October 4, 1974, and a second unconfirmed lower industrial low on December 6, 1974. A new bull market was once again born in the trough of maximum national pessimism, and at the time anyone who was proclaiming a new bull market was taken as a nut. The gloom was so thick you could cut it with a knife. It was not going to go away in a hurry. As Detroit was in a virtual depression and New York City was approaching bankruptcy, as millions joined the unemployed and President Ford declared in his State of the Union address in January, 1975 ,that he had bad news to report, the stock market continued to climb on its wall of worry, but the worry warts weren't about to disappear. They had discovered a good thing in how readily a disillusioned public will cough up a $5 bill or more for a newsletter entirely devoted to attacking government policies under the guise of exploiting liberty, there still being a wide market for negativism. However, their prayed-for depression again failed to materialize, and their crash talk sounded increasingly hollow against the background of a Dow industrial average up the better part of 300 points by the spring of 1975. Their "Kondratieff" had failed them or, rather, their very faulty interpretation of the Russian economist's long wave projections contrived by them to fit the crash thesis they were selling to the public.

II

Now who was Kondratieff? Born Nikolai D. Kondratieff in 1892, he was a famous Russian economist who achieved world reknown by first postulating the existence of long range 50-54 year cycles in our economic life, using French, German, and U.S. statistics to prove his theory. He was Deputy Minister of Food in the Provisional (Kerensky) Government at the age of 25 and founded the Moscow Business Conditions Institute in 1920 under the Lenin regime where he continued to operate until 1928. Most of his books and papers were published between 1922 and 1928. Because of this Russian's recognition of the cyclical character of the capitalist economies, his views differed sharply with Marxist doctrine, and he was arrested in 1930 by the Russian secret police and made to appear in 1931 as a witness at one of the political trials of the enemies of the Stalinist regime. He was kept in prison where he died at an unknown date. Other accounts state that he was shipped off to Siberia.

He is best known for his 1926 monograph entitled "The Long Waves In Economic Life," but even that was little known until the translation appeared in the *Review of Economic Statistics* in November, 1935. Professor Kondratieff referred to the long range peaks in commodity prices as they occurred in the United States, those exact peaks taking place in November,

1814, August, 1864, and May, 1920. The rhythm of the long wave is present in the intervals between those dates. The peak in commodity prices that took place in February, 1974, and the subsequent decline immediately suggested another "Kondratieff" long-term peak. Radical advocates of gold buying are among those who seriously distorted Kondratieff's work to fit their timetable for imminent world depression. The truth of the matter is that Kondratieff's projection, as shown by Joseph Schumpeter's work, *does not call for any truly serious downturn until the mid-1980's.*

Below is a reproduction of the Kondratieff wave (p. 127 of Dr. Harry D. Schultz's *Panics and Crashes*). Spotting the 1929 crash on the chart, one can see that it occurred in the middle of the downslope of the long wave cycle. *That exact point on the Kondratieff wave does not occur again until the 1980's.*

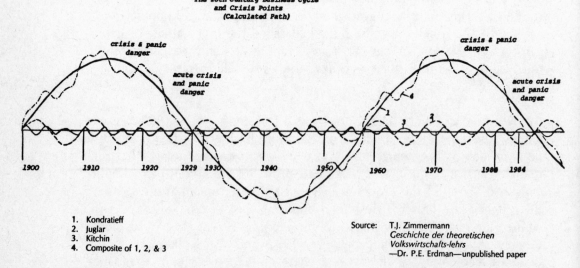

The 20th Century Business Cycle
and Crisis Points
(Calculated Path)

1. Kondratieff
2. Juglar
3. Kitchin
4. Composite of 1, 2, & 3

Source: T.J. Zimmermann
          Geschichte der theoretischen
          Volkswirtschafts-lehrs
          —Dr. P.E. Erdman—unpublished paper

There is no way that the 1973-74 downturn can be likened to the 1929 crash on a Kondratieff Wave timing basis. The true comparison is to use the historical peaks in commodity prices as did Kondratieff and then measure the Kondratieff downturns from those points. The four major spike formations in commodity prices stretching back to November, 1814, with the latest one occurring in February, 1974, contained double significance. The latest peak tended to negate the runaway inflation thesis, fear of inflation being the most common 1974 market fear, and solid historical evidence supported the contention that a major peak in commodity prices would soon be bullish for stocks, delaying any possibility of a true market crash until 1979 at the very earliest and more likely even later than that.

Within the remaining span of time could very well be contained the most prolonged period of speculation seen since the 1920's. Until the 1974 commodity peak, one had only three previous peaks to look at. The exact dates of those peaks in the wholesale commodity price index were November, 1814, August, 1864, and May, 1920. The time intervals are 49 years and nine months and 55 years and nine months. The time interval from May, 1920 to February, 1974, is 53 years and nine months. The first three peaks supported the Kondratieff theory of the long 50-54 year cycle, and the latest peak, occurring 53 years and nine months after the 1920 peak, introduced fresh supporting evidence.

It is important to point out that commodity price peaks do not coincide with stock market peaks. Important stock peaks have generally occurred during periods of low commodity prices. Following the 1814 commodity peak, commodity prices trended lower until 1842. Following the 1864 peak, commodity prices trended lower until 1898. Following the May, 1920 peak, commodity prices trended lower until 1932. Major breaks in stock prices occurred *several years* after each commodity peak. The famous 1873 panic occurred nine years after the major commodity peak, and the crash of 1929 occurred nine years after the major commodity peak. On a strict empirical basis there is no major comparable crash in the cards until nine years after February, 1974-or not until February, 1983. Such crashes occur after a prolonged period of speculative advance, and this wave analysis strongly supports the contention that the decade of the 70's is like the decade of the 20's, and that the 1974 bottom offered the same buying opportunities as those seen in 1921.

A particularly accurate analysis of the Kondratieff Wave as it applied to the decade ahead appeared in the May, 1973, issue of the *Bank Credit Analyst*. The three concluding paragraphs remain of interest:

"(1) The Kondratieff Wave, which spans a period of around 52-54 years on average from peak to peak, suggests that the business cycle peak of 1969 was the peak of the long wave and the 1969-70 experience was the "primary peak" recession to be followed by a gradually declining plateau. Characteristic of this plateau period is (a) a gentle deflation of prices, (b) mildly declining interest rates, (c) budget surpluses and tax cuts, (d) good but moderate business growth, (e) strong investment outlays and growing competition, (f) rising protectionism, and (g) lessening of social tensions and a continuation of a rightward swing in politics."

"(2) More specifically, the Kondratieff Wave suggests that we are not on the brink of imminent disaster but rather that we are in a difficult base-building period that reflects the re-adjustment problems arising from the end of the Viet Nam war and the primary peak recession of 1969-70. A big problem with the imminent doomsday thesis is that so many people believe it and large numbers of stock prices reflect it. Contrary Opinion Theory tells us that when something is widely forecast the odds of it happening are low. According to the long wave explanation, the "secondary peak" depression and period of significant debt liquidation will not come until the latter part of the 1970's, before which there should be a period of substantial prosperity."

"(3) The Kondratieff Wave is also consistent with the body of technical stock market analysts who feel that the technical readings are consistent with the formation of a major bottom area from which another great bull market could eventually evolve before real trouble begins."

A new bull market in stocks cyclically arrived in October, 1974, and by May, 1975, the Dow had risen 278 points off the bottom in the same type of power drive previously seen coming off of the previous cyclical low in May, 1970. Passing the halfway mark of the previous bear market decline on April 15, 1975, the 50% Principle (most reliable in bull markets) was predicting a full recovery back to the 1973 high of 1051.70. This move wrecked the thesis of the imminent doomsday crowd, those who had tried to fit the Kondratieff Wave to the 1973-74 downturn and make it flatly predict a worldwide depression. There were to be no more "killer waves" until at least the 1974-75 bull market was over, and normal cyclical projections did not call for an end to the bull market until very late 1976 or early in 1977. The next bear market would be expected to terminate in 1978, and this projected 1977-78 market downturn would not yet be expected to fit the Kondratieff Wave pattern probable "crash" date. The bull market of 1978-81 should be the really big one where speculation gets completely out of hand, leading up toward such a towering peak that only a Kondratieff-type 1929 bust could correct the excesses. The timing for the great decline may not set in until 1982, but here I'm thinking in terms of downturning markets the year after Presidential elections. So we're concerned with two sets of bad years, the 1977-78 period and the 1981-82 period. An empirical Kondratieff time measurement since 1929 would add 54 years and place the theoretical crash year as 1983, but one has to remember that the wave length has been described as anywhere from 50 to 54 years, and thus there is just an outside possibility that the market could be hit hard in 1979, if the bear market starting in 1977 is still in force. Summing up, I would have to say that the years 1979, 1980, 1981, 1982, and 1983 represent *the entire critical Kondratieff time span* wherein some maximum trouble must be expected to occur.

III

Speculation never dies. When it is ended in one area it simply moves to another. The 1972-74 gold fever was energized by the presence of the 1973-74 bear market and the worldwide fear of rampant inflation. It became the only game in town and, being such, it was driven to excess. The same terminating factor of greed was at work, and it broke the bubble regardless of how good the bubble might have looked. Over the years we have seen the big speculative plays in missile stocks, electronic stocks, bowling issues, savings and loan stocks, color TV, fried chicken, and nursing homes to mention only a few of the past bubbles. There was actually no reason to believe that the move in gold stocks would end any differently. The only difference was that it took a bear market to make the golds shine and build their speculative excesses to a boil. But the human psychology was the same. They were promised tremendous gains, and greed predominated to cut them short, far short of the widely predicted marks. Seeking to capitalize on the fears of inflation, many dozens of advisory services and commentators played a constant tune on the strings of fear and greed to induce the public to load up on gold stocks and to buy gold bullion, repeating over and over that the price of gold was going to $300, $400, $500, $1,000 and even $2,000 an ounce. The constant repetition of the message to buy gold produced the desired effect and prices rose. Bullish opinion increased geometrically until by January, 1974, it was virtually unanimous. Psychology had outrun the price of gold.

The unanimity of bullish opinion regarding gold stocks had reached obviously dangerous proportions by January, 1974, and between February and March it became technically obvious that the gold group of stocks had encountered ominous distribution patterns. The "Ides of March" were upon the gold stocks. Based strictly on chart formations, the group was seen to be headed for a nasty nosedive. By mid-February on-balance volume readings were clearly spelling out distribution. As is always the case, a group tops out amidst maximum popularity, and it is not strange that there were so many "gold forums" in January and February, 1974, conducted by the superbears who extolled the virtues of the gold shares right at the time when the charts were screaming *caveat emptor*. One should have been very suspicious when viewing so many "goldbug" ads in the financial press, all appearing at the same time. So many advisory services had increasingly devoted space to the golds that they virtually became letters totally on gold. The bursting gold bubble put many of them in a bind, the price they had be pay for the overconcentration on one subject that had seen its day. Those who bought gold shares at the January-February 1974 tops succumbed to the "greater fool" theory, secure in the belief that there would always be someone around to take the shares off their hands at a higher price. The tombstone chart formations should have alerted them to the serious possibility that buying gold stocks had at last reached the proportions of a "fad," and we all know what happens to a stock group after that. The group proved that it was not something special immune to the laws of supply and demand.

Also coinciding with the identifiable peak in the prices of gold shares, *National Geographic* came out with a key article on gold at the turn of the year, 1974, and the world's largest brokerage house, Merrill Lynch, finally came out with a detailed study of the gold shares right at the exact peak. Added to this, the gold mutual fund International Investors was turning down new business and doubling their floor space and staff right at the top, a dead giveaway that the whole gold buying process was dangerously overdone.

Perhaps the most telling evidence that the peak in gold had been reached was seen in the fantastic buying of gold in such small odd lots as the five-gram feather bar in Europe by the average housewife. Such odd lot buying of gold was akin to the odd lot buyer of stocks, that type of buying signifying a top.

Helping to create the obviously growing gold bubble were books such as Harry Browne's *You Can Profit from a Monetary Crisis,* and it was apparent that the public was eating it up inasmuch as the book was at the top of the best seller lists for months. The book played on the emotion of fear, inducing the reader to load up on gold and silver stocks. Similar timing was evident when Nicholas Darvas made the bestseller list with *How I Made Two Million in the Stock Market,* just a few months before the 1962 crash market. The stage was beautifully set for a massive long-term top in gold.

Amidst all this hoopla in favor of the gold stocks, the group ended its advance in January, 1974, even while the price of gold bullion was still rising. Gold stocks had already discounted the "hereafter" and were ripe targets for selling. Their distribution patterns became obvious by February, dropping on more volume and rebounding on lesser volume.

The ensuing downtrend immediately became a serious affair because technicians were aware of the fact that the January peak in 1974 had completed a major Elliot five-wave pattern, the fifth leg being the wild vertical finish. Even as that fifth leg was starting in November, 1973, Richard Russell, an outstanding proponent of gold at the time (he correctly turned bearish on the group later on as well as correctly bullish on the stock market), predicted that it would be a wild ride to the top. The goldbugs, however, were so married to their favorite subject that they refused to believe that the group had topped out, and they continued to tout the golds all the way down. The gold stocks had already signalled the peak that lay ahead in bullion prices.

The price of gold almost hit $200 an ounce in Europe following the death of French President Pompidou and then promptly hit the skids, making what looked like an orderly decline at first, but looking more like a rout in June and July. By early July, 1974, the price of gold in London was almost down to $130 an ounce, breaking one trendline after another in its precipitous slide.

But the group was to receive one last lease on life. The dream of all goldbugs was about to come true. Gold, after being an illegal holding in the United States since 1933, was about to become legalized. The goldbugs became more vocal than ever, driving the stocks to one final peak on the day President Ford signed the gold bill, August 14, 1974. That was the public moving in on the top. The smart money had sold out following the distribution patterns seen the previous February, and anything not yet sold was given to the public at top dollar on August 14, the typical "selling on the news." Thereafter the declines in the gold stocks were precipitous, locking in all those who bought the golds on the day President Ford signed the gold bill.

The price of gold bullion did not break thereafter because it had a floor, Americans expected to line up by the millions on January 1, 1975, and drive the price to a new all-time high. The price of bullion began to rise in anticipation of the expected American buying. It got up over $190 an ounce but couldn't stay there, the January 6 U.S. gold auction proving to be a dud. By late spring of 1975 the price had receded to around $162 an ounce.

There were many reasons explaining the drop in the gold share prices and the price of bullion, and some of them are of especial interest in view of what the stock market did after October, 1974. Here are some of the major reasons which explained the fall at the time:

(1) *Long Term Peak in Commodity Prices*—Long-term cyclical studies had long pointed toward a major top in commodity prices to occur early in the decade of the 1970's, such projections largely based on the work of Kondratieff. Inasmuch as gold is now a commodity and nothing more, it was not immune to this long-term cyclical decline in commodity prices. On the mid-1974 drop, gold had declined further in percentage than the Reuters Commodity Index, showing that it had outstripped all other commodities on average in its pronounced weakness. That was as it should be since (without its old monetary function) it is rated as the least valuable of all commodities, unable to sustain life and having no economic function unless it can be exchanged for other commodities.

(2) *Russian Gold Sales*—Back in 1921 Lenin wrote a short essay on gold entitled "The Significance of Gold, Now and After the Complete

Victory of Socialism." In that essay Lenin set forth the Russian gold policy, a policy being followed to the letter by the Russians thereafter. He simply said to hold gold until the price is high and then sell it to buy goods at the lowest price possible. Russia has perpetually produced more gold than she has sold, stockpiling what was estimated to be worth over $20 billion by 1974. Following the heavy sales of 1963, 1964, and 1965, sales were suspended for seven years (awaiting the higher price in accordance with the Leninist doctrine). With gold having begun to skyrocket in 1973, the Russians resumed selling gold from their vast hoard, dumping 300 tons in 1973 on the European market with another flood of 300 tons in 1974. Interestingly enough, the Russians did not have to sell gold in 1973 and 1974. They had one of the best wheat crops in years. Logic dictated that they sold simply because the price was too attractive not to take advantage of, and the second reason is that they expected the price to decline. Their expectations were absolutely correct and probably a mite sooner than they desired, having a great deal more gold to sell. Those Russian gold sales constituted one of the key factors contributing toward the peaking of the bullion price. The knowledge that the Russians were once again in the gold market kept the bullion price within bounds. It might be added here that, contrary to popular belief at the time, the Arabs were also selling gold early in 1974 rather than buying it, knowing in advance when the oil embargo was going to be lifted.

(3) *End of Heavy Gold Speculation*—Seeing the gold bubble burst, the entire psychology of buying gold for profit disappeared practically overnight. Large speculators who had previous snapped up over 600 tons on the free market now became sellers, seriously adding to the avalanche of supply. When the price of gold is not rising it becomes pretty expensive to hold it in a falling market, instantly ruining speculative appeal.

(4) *High Interest Rates*—At the time this was the new key deterrent to the speculative holding of gold bullion. It was all right while prices were skyrocketing but with gold then showing drops of several dollars an ounce per day, speculators had no choice but to jettison their shaky positions.

(5) *High Taxes*—In 1974 Ontario slapped a crushing tax on gold mining profits, serving as a grim reminder to producers what governments can do to future profits.

(6) *World Demonetization of Gold*—The International Monetary Fund in June, 1974, completely divorced gold from the international monetary

system, and that practically sounded the death knell for the goldbugs the world over. That information was very slow to sink into the public's awareness, not having been widely publicized and explained at the time. Now the price of gold is only supported in the free market by industrial and speculative demand.

Now subtracting gold from its old role as the ultimate money, we encounter some mind boggling supply figures. Gold has been mined for the past 6,000 years, but production figures show *geometrical* rates of increase. According to Timothy Green, more gold has been mined between 1800 and 1900 than in the previous 5,000 years. He also stated that 75% of all the gold in the world has been mined in the 20th century and two-thirds of this just since 1931. Most of this gold exists today in some shape or form. World production has now increased to an annual rate of about 46 million ounces, enough to replace everything in Fort Knox in five short years. Most of this gold was going into the hands of speculators and industrial users. The IMF dethronement of gold potentially opened up the flood of 6,000 years of production to satisfy industrial demand, speculative demand having seriously waned. Such a vast supply can only have a very depressing effect on the price of gold.

Prior to the start of the 1974 bull market in stocks, this writer had long contended that a break in the prices of gold stocks was required to serve as the precursor of a new bull market in stocks. Inasmuch as the fear of rampant inflation had served to puff gold up to its unrealistic price highs earlier in 1974, it followed that the decline of gold could signal an abatement of that fear, an advance indication that inflation was peaking. There is good evidence that interest rate peaks tend to coincide with commodity price peaks. It was therefore a simple case of relating the already achieved commodity price peak with an expected peak in the interest rate structure, the subsequent decline expected to usher in a new bull market in stocks. The cyclical evidence was of course excellent that a key turn was to be made in 1974 toward higher security prices, a pretty well defined 4 to 4 1/2 year cycle in evidence which, give or take a few months, had been apparent since the turn of the century.

Now what about the future of gold? Proponents of the idea of going back to an old-fashioned gold standard fail to point out that throughout 6,000 years of recorded history, the gold standard only worked for a very brief 50 years prior to 1914. Thereafter it broke down and a new monetary system had to evolve naturally, one not based on gold. It was not until the 1960's that the architects of the monetary structure made the first serious move toward a better solution to the world's liquidity problems, introducing the

Special Drawing Rights. These supplemented gold as reserves, but the system was still tied to gold. In June, 1974, the Special Drawing Rights were redefined, and the role of gold in the monetary system was reduced to zero, currencies no longer defined in terms of gold but purely in terms of the new SDRs.

This new evolvement in the monetary system seriously downgraded the future demand for gold. The United States government conveniently held off legalizing the buying and selling of gold by U.S. citizens until after this monumental decision, no longer concerned thereafter what U.S. citizens did about gold because by then it was no different than the U.S. government selling citizens copper from a large surplus stockpile. I had long contended that the move to legalize gold would kill off the speculative appeal for gold anyway, destroying the peculiar charisma gold had previously displayed. Such a move was expected to have a bad effect on the Swiss economy and on the Swiss franc, and advice was given at the proper time for people to rid themselves of any holdings in Swiss francs.

Gold as money was headed for destruction in principle because of the conflicting industrial use of gold. It created disturbing imbalances and was an uneconomical way to produce money, bookkeeping methods being far more efficient. Taking metal out of the ground and putting it into another hole in the ground had at last been recognized for the idiocy that it was.

Now that there is a threat of a world oversupply of gold, the increasing costs of producing an ounce of gold would naturally lead toward a coming decrease in world production. That would not lead toward a new rise in the price of gold because demand for gold will have dropped along with the drop in production.

According to the current situation as we cross into the latter half of the decade of the 70's, gold has been steadily going into the twilight stage. It is estimated that before the year 2000, South Africa will be producing less than 5 million ounces a year, an over 80% drop from what is currently coming out of that country's gold mines. Geologists have combed the African continent, looking for new fields with very little success. In order to keep up a high level of production, South Africa has stripped the supply of marginal ore practically clean and has gone deeper than ever before in the existing mines, where the heat and pressure are nothing short of unbearable. That considerably added to labor costs, and it is estimated that the cost of producing an ounce of gold in the South African gold mines would go far beyond $100 an ounce no later than 1976. With the current price of bullion steadily approaching those rising cost figures, a pretty dismal picture of future mining profits faces the South African gold producers. Similar problems are cropping up wherever gold is mined. Timothy Green estimated that very few of the 50 South African gold mines will be operating by the end of this century.

But Russia is something else. Before the end of this century *Russia is expected to be the number one gold producer.* That was inevitable. Everytime the price is right, the Soviets are expected to follow the dictates of their master and sell all they can at the highest price possible. There being many South African gold mining stocks available but no such thing as a Russian gold mining stock, you can derive some idea of the possible dismal future in that industry. Perhaps we have evolved beyond gold.

There are those people in this country who have totally accepted a dogma of defeat, completely convinced that there is absolutely no escape from a series of recurring crises and that a solution is beyond the power of government. *History does not agree.* We know there is an *evolution* on all planes of human endeavor, the basic urge to come up with something better. We can cite the evolutionary developments over the centuries in governments, philosophy, science, religion, or just about any other subject you can mention. Nothing has remained static. The search for something better and the will to achieve it resulted in the United States of America. Being concerned here with the stock market, a market that was pounded down and pummelled in 1973 and 1974 by fears of rampant inflation, distrust of government, impending monetary collapse, depression, and a multitude of other fears fanned out of all proportion by many disciples of doom, it would be well to examine some of the evolutionary aspects of economics and, more specifically, money. By so doing, one does not have to accept blindly a strict course of self-preservation which runs from the problem, but it rather behooves one to think more in terms of the national good. While that sounds unnaturally altruistic, a country that can put a man on the moon is capable by equal determination to check inflation without a depression both here and among the family of nations. To accept anything less is not in keeping with the provable evolution in all things.

We, the people, have the residual power to *force* a balanced budget by *law.* If the cost of a Federally financed power dam in Oregon is not matched by an equal amount of government income, the construction of the dam must be postponed until it can be paid for out of income. Only Congress can be held accountable for any unwise spending that puts the Federal Budget out of balance inasmuch as only Congress appropriates Federal funds. The Congress, the lawmaking body of government, can regulate such spending by law to conform to income if it genuinely reflects the will of the people. We don't have to any longer accept second best measures. Do it just once— balance the budget—and the dollar will quickly regain a degree of respect it hasn't held for years, and the fires of inflation will die out. The desire to invest in American business will be permanently revived, and all the nonsense you have read elsewhere about gold will be proved irrelevant to these evolutionary times.

American history offers countless examples of positive evolution, each problem a stepping stone toward a new solution. The ills of a state banking system gave way to a national banking system. The problems of an inelastic money supply led toward the creation of the Federal Reserve System. The gold standard worked rather well up until World War I only because it was never presented with a really major job to do. Faced with postwar problems which made it impossible to maintain the gold standard, the standard was dispensed with after futile attempts to return to it and has never been revised since. Those who advocate a return to a pure gold standard are totally unrealistic, living in the past. The magnitude of world trade has repeatedly demonstrated the increasing shortcomings of the gold exchange standard and the crying need for additional reserves. In an attempt to avoid the chaotic conditions of international finance which had plagued the years following World War I, the Bretton Woods conference in 1944 led to the creation of the International Monetary Fund which worked rather well for over 20 years. By the 1960's, however, highlighted by the problems of retaining former values of the British pound and the U.S. dollar (dramatized by a huge outflow of gold from the United States), it became apparent that the IMF required additional powers to create reserves. By 1968 the Special Drawing Rights (SDR'S) came into being and were in use by 1970. Gold began to play a lesser role, and the trend toward total international gold demonetization was underway. The latest act in this evolutionary monetary process was played out in June, 1974, when the last ties to gold were removed, currencies no longer defined in terms of gold. Gold had entered the twilight zone.

Inasmuch as supplies of domestic currencies were no longer tied to gold, the time had at last come to do the same for international means of payment. *Evolved* monetary thinking underscores the waste of resources to mine gold only to rebury it permanently in the vaults of a few dozen central banks. Book entries would do just as well, costing nothing to produce with total supply not limited by the factors that limit the total supply of gold. So the world took another giant step in monetary evolution, measuring a nation's true wealth not in terms of an otherwise worthless pile of metal, but in terms of *tradable gross national products.* When country A imports more from country B than it exports to country B, then country B gets a bookkeeping credit, a claim against a portion of country A's assets which then becomes a negotiable asset tantamount to international money.

Those who cannot grasp this thread of monetary evolution became totally addicted to an almost religious belief that the price of gold would continue to soar as it did in 1973. On the contrary, now that gold has reverted to being just another commodity, its supply will overhang the industrial market for many decades, and the price of gold will conform to that oversupply.

Perhaps the ultimate in stupidity was the widely disseminated notion that the Arabs, having a strangle-hold on the oil situation, would gobble up most of the available gold, drive the price of the metal out of sight and provoke an international monetary collapse, plunging the world into a depression. While it had the ring of some truth to it, it did not relate to the bear cycle of 1973-74 which blossomed into the bull market of 1974 at a time when the goldbugs and superbears were so positive their timetable for the great collapse was correct. How things change! Just a few months after the very peak of the oil crisis and gold fever, the Associated Press in May, 1975, made the following report:

MONETARY RESERVES REGAINED

Washington (AP)-May 5, 1975

The world's industrialized nations have regained most of the monetary reserves they had lost since the fourfold increase in the price of world oil, the International Monetary Fund reported Sunday.

The development appeared to end fears, at least temporarily, that the oil importing industralized world would be bankrupted by the high cost of oil imports.

Several oil exporting nations, including Iran, Algeria and Indonesia, have experienced a decline in their reserves in recent months, the IMF said, although the largest, Saudi Arabia, remains the third-ranking nation in terms of total financial reserves.

The IMF said the industrialized nations had total dollar reserves in March (1975) of $124.8 billion, an increase of 9.9 per cent since the first quarter of 1974 when the full impact of the oil price increase was being felt.

The March total also was higher than the $121.2 billion total reserves of these nations in the third quarter of 1973, before the big increase in world oil prices.

In terms of Special Drawing Rights-the IMF's international measure of value-the industrialized nations had reserves totaling 100 billion SDRs at the end of March, up from 94 billion SDRs a year earlier. The total was still slightly below the peak 100.5 billion SDRs in the third quarter of 1973.

One SDR is equal to about $1.25 in U.S. currency.

Among nations which have had steady increases in their reserves in recent months have been the United States, to a total of $16.7 billion; the United Kingdom $7.3 billion; France, $9.4 billion; Germany, $34.4 billion; Italy, $6.8 billion, and Japan, $14.2 billion.

Large borrowings by industrialized nations, the large flow of funds from oil producing nations, and an improved balance of payments position of some nations apart from the flows of borrowed money are some factors that led to the increase in reserves, the IMF said. (End of AP report)

You will notice that the word *gold* was totally absent from the IMF report. Having completely divorced gold from the international monetary system, the IMF report of May, 1975, reflected the new method of measuring reserves. Those who took the IMF historic action of June, 1974, lightly must have had second thoughts as they saw gold peak out along with the gold stocks shortly thereafter.

A NATIONAL LOTTERY—IS NOW THE TIME?

Almost 200 years ago, the citizens of our new nation willingly gambled their all on winning the war for their independence. The chips were down and there was no turning back. Our new nation was virtually broke, and it was essential that cash be raised immediately to buy the necessary military supplies with which to wage war. On November 18, 1776, in Philadelphia, the Congress approved a lottery bill to defray military expenses. There was no quibbling about the morality of holding lotteries. Our forefathers knew that something had to be done right away, and they decided that holding lotteries was the way to do it. We were in a war for our very existence as a nation, and in a time of great crisis anything that works is worthy of consideration.

Now almost 200 years later, our nation is again involved in a war. It is a total war involving every one of our citizens. It is the war against inflation. If our forefathers were alive today they would again not hesitate to implement any plan which showed excellent promise of working. Having used the national lottery idea successfully in their own time, why couldn't it work successfully in our time of crisis?

President Ford has committed himself to bring national inflation under control by July 4, 1976, a very tall order indeed. Many measures have been tried and they have mostly all failed. The time has surely arrived for more drastic action. If we aren't willing to experiment with bold departures from ineffective orthodox methods currently being employed, the President's ambitious timetable will never be effectively adhered to. There are too many cooks in the kitchen, each concocting his own pet formula, and the result is a confusing mixture of measures having no central theme.

This writer proposes a simple, double-barrelled plan that will not involve us in controversial wage and price controls which, in the past, have left much to be desired. Secondly, the plan is totally democratic and can prove of great benefit to all of us. In the third place, there is excellent evidence that it can work. However, we can't afford the luxury of taking too much time in order to make up our minds. The time is long past for dillydallying around with such a serious problem. The nation must come to grips with it immediately and not shrink from adopting bold new measures. Things were so bad back in 1932 that the country readily got behind Franklin Roosevelt's experimental programs, bold ventures to pull us out of the depression. At that time we couldn't make things worse. The only way left to go was up. This nation now stands at the crossroads where a choice must be made between bold new action taken immediately with a better than even chance for total success, or between an ineffective mixture of more of same, carrying with it the almost certain promise of dangerous failure with consequences the nation just cannot afford to face.

A Balanced Budget by Law

Don't tell me that this is just another proposal to balance the Federal budget? Good lord, man, it can't be done. Don't you know we only did it twice in the past 33 years? Yes, I know and that is why I make this compelling plea to get it balanced and keep it in balance. The time has come when it is so vitally important to balance the budget that we should entertain the idea of *enforcing* the balance. When you use the word enforce, you're talking *law*. A law should be passed compelling the Federal budget to be in balance every year. It sounds impossible, but let us give it a little thought.

You and I as individuals can do certain things in attempting to slow inflation, but unless the major effort is made on the Federal level, our individual efforts are as totally ineffective as a flea challenging an elephant to a wrestling match. Inflation is mostly generated and perpetuated on the Federal level, and if it is going to be stopped cold it has to be done on the Federal level.

The annual Federal budget is a massive thing to behold. To break it down into its component parts entails some 6,000 pages of microscopic statistics, the bound document weighing in at 60 pounds. With the thousands upon thousands of proposed expenditures listed in that book, it stands to reason that some of them are totally vital, some not so vital (where cuts are possible), and hundreds of expense items which could be totally eliminated that year *if the money was just not there.* For instance, suppose $30,000,000 was earmarked for a power dam in Oregon and the money to be spent was going to put the budget out of whack. The government would simply postpone the project until the money was available. It would *have to do this* because, if my proposal is acted upon, the Congress has passed a bill requiring the Federal budget to be in balance, and the President has signed the bill into law. No longer then can powerful lobbying interests get their pet projects into the budget, making heros out of local politicians in the eyes of their constituents at the devastating expense of the people as a whole. The past 33 years have proven the extreme difficulty in balancing the budget under the present system. We must now *know* it will be balanced with the same certainty that we know a red traffic light stops traffic at an intersection. If the question was brought up and presented to the people in a national referendum, the answer should be obvious. Uncontrolled inflation generated at the Federal level is wrecking our very way of life. The people are sick of it and sick from it. They will now seek virtually any possible cure. We are ready for nothing less!

Of course there are always the unexpected expenses stemming from such things as crop damage, floods, hurricanes and other acts of nature, but these must be budgeted contingencies. If they threaten to create a budgetary deficit, the other half of my double proposal will *guarantee* that the budget stay in balance and the new law upheld.

Effect of Balanced Budget

We have all seen over the years the havoc wreaked by a continuous series of annual deficits. Like a creeping disease, it has steadily eroded national and world confidence in our money, our national integrity, and it set a pattern now gripping every major nation in the free world. Lack of confidence in the dollar had become a permanent fixture because every nation in the world knew and expected the U.S. Federal budget to run a deficit every year. Until a similar disease had spread to many other countries making the dollar look a little stronger by comparison, the nation each year suffered the loss of vital substance, an efflux of money seeking safer harbors abroad. This only aggravated the problem, allowing it to feed on itself year after year until we can now no longer afford to drift. We are at the crossroads of having to make some immediate choices.

I would say this: balance the budget once, just ONCE, and the effect all over the world would be electrifying. Confidence in the dollar would be rapidly restored and capital from all over the free world would flow back into the United States seeking our safe harbor of new monetary integrity. The Federal engine of inflation would no longer be generating paper expense dollars fresh off the printing press unmatched by Federal income. Prices would stabilize, the stock market would recover and this nation could again have a prosperity based on a sound dollar. People here and all over the free world would again yearn to buy a piece of America, to invest in her productive future. But without this restored confidence born of a balanced budget, the nation faces only a disastrous road, well trodden by other nations that had accepted ineffective expedients in lieu of having the governmental guts to face the problem squarely and take the right action.

A Balanced Budget and a National Lottery
Go Hand in Hand

When one accepts that we are in a state of emergency in the thus far ineffective fight against inflation, one is then ready to give serious consideration to the benefits to be derived from a national lottery. Currently 17 of our states conduct lotteries, a highly successful method of producing revenue. However, the benefits of these more scattered fund-raising efforts on the state level have little or no effect in knocking out the core of the inflationary disease in this country. What is vitally needed now is a Federal lottery program with only one central objective: *serving as the back-up program and guarantee that the Federal budget will stay in balance.* In other words, I propose that all Federal lottery proceeds would go into a *National Disaster Fund* which could only be tapped with Congressional approval when any unforeseen emergency threatened to unbalance the budget.

Before you raise your eyebrows and dismiss the proposal too quickly, let's kick the idea around a little. We all grumble when we have to pay high excise and sales taxes. Actually, those taxes are *undemocratic.* Those taxes have to be paid by rich and poor alike. As to a Federal lottery ticket, however, you either buy it or you don't. Nobody is twisting your arm. It is a *democratic form of taxation* paid only by the participant who decides with his own free will whether or not to buy the ticket. *Any losing lottery ticket is a 100% tax.* Uncle Sam will get it all, but the proceeds from the sale of that ticket *will serve as a strong contribution by that individual to helping guarantee that the Federal budget will stay in balance.* So then, the purchase of lottery tickets by U.S. citizens, whether those tickets win or not, is the most *painless type of taxation.* On one hand we'll have government spending legislated to match government income, and on the other hand we'll have the Federal lottery program to soak up excess dollars in circulation and back up the balanced budget.

How Much Cash Could the Government Raise?

Eighty million people voted in the last presidential election. Using that number as a guide, I would conservatively estimate that the same number of people would eagerly participate in a weekly Federal lottery. Suppose tickets for these weekly drawings sold at $1 each and that many people bought an average of three tickets each week. That kind of weekly participation would produce about a quarter of a billion dollars a week in new revenue for Uncle Sam. Annualize those figures and *you've got $13 billion.* Deduct $1 billion for prizes and *you've got $12 billion as the first annual deposit into the*

National Disaster Fund. That is only the *first* year of the lottery program. In five short years the government could lock up $60 billion in that fund. It would be like the Federal Deposit Insurance Corp. which guarantees your bank deposits up to $20,000, but in this case it insures against an unbalanced Federal budget. The uses of such a fund are numerous, but the prime purpose at all times is *a guarantee against Federal deficit spending.* If the National Disaster Fund grows large enough after several years of balanced budgets, *a program of retiring outstanding government debt could be undertaken.* The benefits could be great beyond imagination and these would be benefits for all!

The Public Inducement

Would you buy a lottery ticket for $1 which, if it turned out to be a winning ticket, would pay you at least $250,000 tax free? Uncle Sam would take in so much on the lottery that all winnings paid out should be *tax free.* That is an important point because the inducement to buy a ticket should be *maximized* so as to guarantee that the demand for tickets will constantly be heavy. It is visualized that each week there would be about 80 winners paid an average of $250,000 a weekly payout of $20 million, amounting to an anual prize payout of $1 billion. Obviously, some people won't participate at all, millions upon millions of people will buy one to three tickets a week, and *millions more will buy considerably more than three tickets a week.* The projected $12 billion annual revenue for the government could turn out to be *well under the actual figure received.*

Each week the national lottery drawing *could be conducted on television in full view of the public.* (You can imagine what a spot commercial would be worth on that program!) I would certainly surmise that that would be the show of the week with record high Nielson ratings.

History of Lotteries

Lotteries have been conducted in many countries for hundreds of years. There is scarcely anything new about the lottery idea in itself. However, at no time does recorded lottery history tell us that a government conducted one in order to keep inflation under control for the good of the government and all its citizens. That idea is new. Lottery history tells us that it is unquestionably a successful method for raising funds. If properly controlled, it hurts nobody but benefits everybody.

The first lottery mentioned in English history occurred on May 6, 1569. It was held at the western door of St. Paul's Cathedral. It consisted of 40,000 lots at ten shillings for each lot. The prizes were pieces of plate and the profits of the lottery were used for repairing the English harbors. On June 29, 1612, a lottery was drawn in London for the benefit of the Virginia plantations, the profit amounting to 30,000 pounds. By 1630 lotteries in

England paid cash prizes for the first time, and by 1693 lotteries were officially sanctioned and conducted by the English government, yielding a large annual revenue to the crown for the next 130 years. One can imagine here Samuel Pepys confiding in his secret diary that he bought several lottery tickets after cash prizes started being paid in England after 1630. On April 5, 1753, the British parliament enacted that 20,000 pounds be raised by lottery to purchase the library of Sir Henry Sloan, deceased. That turned out to be the origination of the British Museum! On June 16, 1773, in London, an act was passed for the sale of buildings of the Adelphi by lottery.

One of the most colorful of all lotteries took place in Paris on January 26, 1879. It came to be known as The Great Lottery. The total value of the prizes amounted to $1,150,000, and 12 million tickets were sold. The lottery was organized to raise a fund to pay prizes to International Fair exhibitors and the expenses of the working men.

All these lotteries, however, lacked the serious intent of the ones conducted here in the United States at the time of the birth of the republic. Now approaching our 200th birthday as a nation, the national lottery idea is at last an idea whose time has come. Nobody can doubt the seriousness behind the proposal.

Is This Gambling?

This nation was built on a gamble. All life is a gamble, really. There are no rewards anywhere without risk. To shun the idea of a national lottery on the grounds that it is gambling overlooks the greater losses which are certain through inaction. If a man earns $20,000 a year he can expect about a 5% annual loss in dollar depreciation, just like throwing $1,000 away. If he spent $20 a week on lottery tickets and there was no inflation, *he would be no worse off.* So then, doing nothing about the problem is much more expensive than doing something, especially something that would have wide national appeal, benefitting government and citizen alike.

People are going to take chances every day in America—whether it be on the horses, dogs, jai alai, a card game, or bingo. There is a natural urge to gamble, officially recognized by the 17 states now conducting lotteries. This is the trend. Wouldn't it be so much better to funnel this urge into a constructive program to put this country's fiscal and monetary condition back into tip-top shape?

Our forefathers took the big gamble 200 years ago. Can we do anything less 200 years later?

A Closing Postscript

I have talked with hundreds of people in all walks of life about my idea for a national lottery and in every instance the response was *totally enthusiastic.* Those people readily understood that if nothing was done, they were going to lose about 5% of their capital every year. It didn't require a high IQ to figure out that it was better to wager a small portion of what they were otherwise *certain* to lose on the chance of winning $250,000 tax free, and at the same time protect their capital from further inflation shrinkage. They immediately saw the advantage of adopting this kind of plan in lieu of further painful taxation.

However, the history of great ideas shows that most of them were never readily accepted. They had to *evolve* in people's minds. They were eventually accepted when the world was ready to accept them. I surmise that by the time this book is in print and being read, the national lottery idea will be totally acceptable, the national acceptance spurred on by a series of events showing an unmistakable *trend* toward that ultimate acceptance. Indicative of this trend is the fact that New Jersey has already put the numbers on a legal basis in a daily lottery. It is such a certain trend on the state level that the logic almost dictates that in a matter of time it will go national. The pressing need for certain fund-raising without resorting to further painful taxation is prompting these breakthroughs.

By 1976 and 1977 the needs will be so pressing on the Federal level that ears, once deaf to such a proposal, will be listening and ready to adopt a bold new plan for national fiscal survival. The 1974-75 recession prompted massive government deficit spending of such record proportions ($68.8 billion deficit approved for fiscal year 1976 alone) that dire repercussions were virtually certain to erupt by late 1976 or early 1977 demanding bold new thinking and the adoption of plans previously thought unacceptable. Another skeleton rattling in the closet is the reportedly broke Social Security System, its funds having been repeatedly dipped into so often and not replaced that millions of people approaching retirement age are rightfully concerned as to whether the money will be there when they are ready to collect it. These are only some of the collective pressures which will be building up to a boil in the late 1970's, pressures which will demand the adoption of new ideas.

But to stick our heads in the sand and say there are no solutions is uncharacteristic of Americans. We are a *determined* people, and if we determine to do better, we will do better, as we have done in the past, as we face a crisis squarely head on. So, as there is the thread of monetary evolution, ideas meet with acceptance as thinking evolves to meet them.

So then, let's call a spade a spade: 67% of American adults gamble at least occasionally. Let us now harness that *majority impulse* to pull us out of the mire of perpetual inflation. The best comment I've ever read on gambling was made by Blackie Sherrodl: "If you bet on a horse, that's gambling. If you bet you can make three spades, that's entertainment. If you bet cotton will go up three points, that's business. See the difference?" Now, *let us bet on America's future.*

Glossary

Accumulation. Any stock which consistently evidences higher volume on upside days than on downside days is said to be under accumulation. Important price advances are generally preceded by accumulation. The most accurate measurement and evaluation of accumulation is effected by the use of on-balance volume.

Advance-Decline Line. The orthodox advance-decline line is a *net differential between the number of stocks advancing each day and the number of stocks declining each day kept on a cumualtive basis.* The word orthodox is used here because most people are still not aware of the *volume advance-decline line.* The orthodox advance-decline line is a measurement based on *price,* not volume. The advance-decline line is one of the *major* technical indicators having broad implications concerning the trend of stock prices. A declining advance-decline line implies that one should be far more selective when purchasing stocks and can even rule out purchase of stocks completely when such declines are in definite bearish configuration with other key indicators. A declining A-D line does not necessarily rule against new highs being made by the Dow-Jones Industrial Average during the first three phases of a bull market, but such unconfirmed highs spell out developing trouble. The market can usually sustain one or two unconfirmed new Dow highs for awhile, but a third Dow high lacking A-D Line confirmation is one of the clearest of all market get-out signals. While the advance-decline line has always peaked ahead of the Dow-Jones Industrial Average prior to the start of a bear market, *it is not a definite requirement for the line to reach bottom prior to the Dow at the start of a bull market.* The line was late on the 1962, 1966, 1970, and 1974 bottoms, the Dow having bottomed first.

Auction Market. Buyers attempt to buy at the lowest price and sellers attempt to sell at the highest price. No transaction occurs until the price satisfies both buyer and seller. The stock market is an auction market, bringing buyers and sellers together. A buyer alone can buy nothing. A seller alone can sell nothing. It takes two to tango—a balance, an equation. In the stock market they cannot both be right. The right side must beguile the wrong side into doing its bidding, giving the other what it wants on its terms, and that sets the stage for the eternal struggle—the game. *We are constantly being pressured by the other side to balance the market equation on its terms.* The pressures are often very subtle and close to being undetected and other times so obvious that their very obviousness blinds the unsuspecting. The media is the

267

unsuspecting tool in these pressure tactics, always making it easier for the right side of the market equation to beat the wrong side. When one is caught up in the buying or selling of stocks it is so easy to forget that the stock market is an auction market. When you make your move based on certain motivations, EXAMINE THE COUNTER-MOTIVATIONS WHICH MAKE YOUR MOVE POSSIBLE but not necessarily right.

Bar Chart. Prior to the use of on-balance volume, the bar chart was the orthodox method of recording volume with a stock price chart, a series of vertical lines depicting the daily volume. It is still being done and is an entirely unsatisfactory method of showing volume in a technically intelligent manner. Looking at that type of presentation one can only guess at possible accumulation or distribution trends. This writer maintains that the way to intelligently relate volume to price so as to identify accumulation or distribution is by on-balance volume.

Barb. A term employed here in the use of the A-B-C-D zigzagging Climax Indicator movements whereby the Dow-Jones Industrial Average makes new highs or lows on the C portion of the Climax Indicator zigzag, thereby impaling the unsuspecting on a technically insufficient spike, or "barb."

Bathtub Analogy. Used to depict the correct flow of money in the bull-bear cycle. At the beginning of a bull market the market bathtub is empty. The advance-decline line is at the bottom. The bathtub starts to refill with water, the first water entering the tub representing the smart money. The water level continues to rise until it crests, represented by the bull market peak in the advance-decline line. The last water to enter the tub is represented by the least informed money. Very late in the bull market the bathtub drain is opened, a fact which the uninformed money in generally unaware of. The smart money begins to make its exit and is the first water to leave the tub, first in and first out. The water level begins to recede as a majority of stocks begin to work lower as shown by a declining advance-decline line. The generally uninformed public, always mesmerized by what the Dow-Jones Industrial Average is doing, is not yet aware of the receding water level because the Dow is still making new bull market highs. The popularly followed Dow is generally the last to rise and the last to fall, being the surface water, the last water in the tub. When the bear market is at last recognized, the water level sinks more rapidly, and at the tail end of the bear market the water is sucked out of the tub rapidly, the smart money awaiting that sign as a signal that the tub is ready to be refilled again for another bath and a repetition of the complete cycle.

Bear Market. True bear markets tend to start "out of the blue" with the majority at a loss to explain the first downswing. Bear market means a declining market. A bear market is related to the bull market which it follows, thereby completing the entire bull-bear cycle, *but it has absolutely no relation to the bull market which follows after that bear market is completed.* That is a new ball game. Bear markets may or may not be accompanied by business recession. Bear market is a *market* term referring specifically to the opposite of a bull market. While varying greatly in terms of severity and duration, these things do correlate with the size and duration of the previous bull market. A bear market is obviously increasingly probable the older the previous bull market becomes. All market downturns after a bull market is 20 months old are suspect and deserve close examination. Downturns after a bull market is 30 months old are extremely dangerous and very likely are the real thing. Bear markets are always shorter in duration than the bull market preceding them. In estimating their length, always keep the 4 to 4 1/2 year market cycle in mind, major market bottoms very seldom being more that 4 1/2 years apart. A bull market lasting 33 months would therefore be expected to be followed by a bear market lasting from 15 to 21 months, but not beyond 21 months.

Bear Phases. Bull and bear markets tend to run in three distinct phases. The first bear phase outstanding characteristic is public *disbelief* in what is happening. The economy usually still looks strong, the news is generally bullish, and corporate earnings are usually still rising. However, the smart money has pulled the plug and is pessimistic while the public confidence in the market outlook is unimpaired. As the news worsens and the confident public begins to change their mind about the outlook, deciding to get out of many stocks, the market embarks on a very sharp rally lasting anywhere from a few weeks to a few months, the sharp rally characterizing the second phase of the bear market. Following a new collapse to new lows, the public confidence has by now completely eroded. The smart money, watching for such signs of collapse in the public confidence, now makes the key shift from their pessimism to confidence as prices now cascade down into the superdepressed bargain area. The public, having been fooled by the second phase, "rally that fools the majority," is in no mood to expect any new rallies in the final bear market phase. Their first phase disbelief has been transformed in the third phase to *belief,* belief that everything is going to get worse. When the next rally comes it usually starts a new bull market but by that time that would be the last thing the public could believe, thus the disbelief attached to the next phase, the first bull market phase.

Bear Trap. Any *technically unconfirmed* move to the downside encouraging the bulk of the investing and speculating public to be bearish. The most important bear traps terminate bear markets. In any case, they precede strong rallies.

Breakthrough (breakout). The terms *breakthrough* and *breakout* are interchangeable. This implies that either a stock price or average has moved above a previous high resistance level or has moved below a previous low support level. Such breakthroughs imply that the movement will be enhanced in the direction of the breakout on the physical principle of bodies in motion. The same terms apply to the more important on-balance volume movements through previous support or resistance levels on the demonstration that volume precedes price.

Bull Market. Any rising market might be called a bull market, but that would be a very loose definition. True bull markets imply a sweeping uptrend embracing many months duration with three definable phases. Like bear markets, bull markets vary widely in scope and duration. However, *a bull market has no relation to the bear market it follows,* and thus there is little to go on at first in estimating its length or importance. Since the time span between major market tops is a *complete variable,* unlike the more predictable cyclicality of major bottoms, one has to depend heavily on the bull phase characteristics (see bull phases) to estimate the probable duration of a bull market. But we do know that bull markets last longer than bear markets, and any bull market worthy of the name is going to last one to two years or longer with the accent on the "or longer."

Bull Phases. Running in three phases, the first bull phase is characterized by public *disbelief* in what is happening, disbelief that stock prices can rise importantly in the face of all the obviously bad news and bad fundamentals. The smart money, having turned confident during the third phase of the preceding bear market, is now more confident than ever in the face of the pessimistic public. All through the first bull phase the news is bad, and the public gapes in disbelief as prices climb the wall of worry. When the lagging fundamentals attempt to catch up and the public is told that there is light at the end of the tunnel, eliminating the earlier public disbelief in the rise, then the first bull phase is ending. The ending is technically shown by a topping out in the number of new individual highs, a topping out by the advance-decline line, one Dow stock after another having recorded an on-balance volume peak and other deteriorating technical phenomena. Just when the public confidence is given a shot in the arm and a little belief in the rise begins to replace the widespread pessimism, the market goes into a decline. At this point it is possible to project an approximate duration of the bull market, multiplying the duration of the first bull phase by three and adding the total time span to the last recorded major bottom. The outstanding characteristic of the second bull phase is the decline that fools the majority. The smart money, having taken the first easy profits at the end of the first bull phase, sells out to the public fooled by the shot in the arm burst of confidence. They sit back, awaiting the new buying opportunities on the wide second phase market decline. The public is still generally confused, getting whipsawed on the second phase decline. Fundamentals get more obviously stronger and the media helps to blow this up to boom proportions. Bull phase three is at hand. The outstanding characteristic of that phase is the public *belief* in what is happening. They now take over the bulk of the market buying as the smart money period of confidence comes to an end. When the next decline comes, it usually starts a bear market, but by that time it would be the last thing the public could believe, thus the disbelief attached to the next phase, the first bear market phase.

Bull Trap. Any *technically unconfirmed* move to the upside encouraging the bulk of the investing and speculating public to be bullish. The most important bull traps terminate bull markets. In any case, they precede important declines.

Buying Climax. A climax implies *an ending.* A buying climax is associated with such a sharp price run-up, with everything so heavily one-sided on the rise, that a move in the opposite direction becomes inevitable. Such a climax may be of the one-day variety ending a very short-term swing, or it could be of intermediate or final significance ending months of advance or even years of advance. All climaxes involve *increased* volume. While heavy volume is never a concern during the first two phases of a bull market, very heavy volume during the third phase is uninformed public buying, often ending in a buying climax. Beware of such climactic action late in a bull market.

Buy Column. When a stock is up in price at the end of a market trading session, all the volume generated during the session is recorded on the upside and the figure is placed in the BUY column.

Capitalization. This is the number of shares of common stock which constitutes the total issue held by stockholders of a particular company. The capitalization figure becomes important when determining (1) thinness, (2) marketability, (3) velocity, and (4) the effective application of the "Spring"principle.

Climactic. A term used to describe any movement which smacks of "excess," regardless of whether it is a price movement or a volume movement. Climactic moves are followed by moves in the *opposite* direction.

Climax Indicator. The Climax Indicator is the *net* number of on-balance volume breakouts among the 30 Dow-Jones Industrial stocks. It either confirms a move in the Dow average or fails to confirm. Non-confirmations are particularly meaningful at new high and low Dow levels. When the Net Field Trend is down, all high CLX readings of +20 and higher are excellent selling opportunities. When the Net Field Trend is up, all CLX readings of -20 and lower are excellent buying opportunities. It is an essential daily market indicator as well and an important intermediate and longer-range indicator.

Confidence Index. What is referred to here is the Barron's Confidence Index. This represents the ratio between the average yield on Barron's ten-highest grade corporate bonds and that on the Dow-Jones 40 Bonds (the ratio of primary to secondary bond yields). The ratio is high when investors demonstrate confidence by buying lower-grade liens, low when they take refuge in top-grade issues. For a long period of time the Confidence Index correlated with the movements of the Dow-Jones Industrial Average, the Index gaining a reputation as a highly sensitive forecasting instrument, predicting the extent as well as the timing of general price advances or declines. But, like any single indicator, it was not infallible, falling into disrepute in the years after 1966. It fell sharply in the fall of 1970, a false signal. It also fell sharply in the spring of 1975 and at this writing the outcome of that decline is in doubt.

Thinking in terms of the market game, any indicator measuring the extent of the public confidence would be suspect. As the game theory goes, public confidence goes hand in hand with smart money pessimism, and the smart money wins every time.

Contrary Opinion. Contrary opinion in itself is meaningless. *It depends on whose opinion it is contrary to.* If the public holds a widespread popular opinion about something then a minority contrary opinion is worth listening to. It is never the other way around because how could the huge public have a *minority* opinion about anything? Contrary opinion is most significant at all major market turning points. How do we know the market is at a major turning point? Check the 4 to 4 1/2 year market cycle and weigh the probabilities of the market either being in the third phase of a bear market or the third phase of a bull market.

Declining Tops. A pattern of declining tops implies a loss of upside energy and an ultimate decline. Each peak is less than the previous one, showing increasing weakness. The pattern is significant both in terms of price and on-balance volume.

Defensive. Anything which tends to remain relatively stable in a declining market is a *defensive* situation. A defensive technique involves the purchase of bonds in a bear market or some stock capable of going counter to the trend, perhaps a gold stock. During a period when high-priced stocks are under attack, it might be said that a move into very low-priced issues moving in a narrow range around their base lines would be a *defensive* measure. The best defense against a falling market is not to be in it.

Disparity. Specifically referred to here, disparity is measured by comparing the movements of the Dow-Jones Industrial Average with the movements of the Standard & Poor 500 Stock Index, keeping a cumulative record of the differentials between the two indices. Since the New York Stock Exchange Index was created in 1966, the latter serves as a still better measure of disparity, being the broadest of all averages. Positive disparity means that the Dow is moving up faster than the market, and that is bearish. It is an example of the Dow taking a solitary walk. It is soon yanked back on the true market path. Conversely, negative disparity has to be bullish inasmuch as it shows the market acting stronger than the Dow. The Dow will soon react to that technical stimulus and advance. Positive disparity is most dangerous and bearish when it develops during the third phase of a bull market. Negative disparity is most bullish when it develops during the third phase of a bear market.

Distribution. The opposite of accumulation. Distribution occurs when the market is high, accounting for the accommodation of the late bull market stock buyers, allowing the market equation to balance. It is often very subtle and not too easily detected, but the use of on-balance volume will clearly reveal its presence every time. Inasmuch as late bull market third phase public buying usually *generates a lot of volume,* distribution is the heaviest at such times, balancing off the heavy public buying *in the required market equation.* At such times one should ask: *who is doing the selling to make all this buying possible?* Distribution seeks to camouflage its presence by hiding behind GOOD NEWS.

Divergence. All market forecasts (forecasts made by the market) involve divergence. The high-low indicator is a divergence indicator. The advance-decline line is a divergence indicator. The Climax Indicator is a divergence indicator. In divergence something deviates from the norm, requiring a *market adjustment.*

Dividends. One of the market "hooks" to insure that somebody will be holding stocks in a bear market. In such markets the "dividend" buyer is getting no dividend at all, but merely a *partial return of his own capital,* a return the government considers "income" thus hitting the "dividend" buyer again. Notice how often companies raise their dividend payments at or near market tops, a move that often entraps many to buy at the wrong time.

Divisor. The key figure that determines the *volatility* of the Dow-Jones Industrial Average. Every time one of the 30 Dow-Jones industrial stocks splits or pays a stock dividend, the Dow-Jones industrial *divisor* is lowered. The average each day is computed by adding up the net rise or fall of the 30 stocks in terms of points and dividing by the divisor. Obviously a lower divisor increases the volatility of the average. In this respect a change (split or stock dividend) on any one of the thirty stocks *will affect them all.*

Dow-Jones Industrials. These are the 30 stocks which go to make up the Dow-Jones Industrial Average. On-balance volume is computed on these stocks each day in order to determine the daily readings of the Climax Indicator. The 30 industrials are as follows:

Allied Chemical	Esmark	Owens Illinois
Alcoa	Exxon	Procter & Gamble
American Brands	General Electric	Sears Roebuck
American Can	General Foods	Standard Oil of California
American Telephone	General Motors	Texaco
Anaconda	Goodyear	Union Carbide
Bethlehem Steel	International Harvester	United States Steel
Chrysler	International Nickel	United Technologies
DuPont	International Paper	Westinghouse Electric
Eastman Kodak	Johns Manville	Woolworth

Dow Theory. My respect for the Dow Theory has grown over the years, not lessened. Probably its greatest contribution is the *three-phase concept,* concentrating the attention on answering the major market question: what time is it on the market clock?

Down Column. When on-balance volume is being computed all the volume on downside days is placed in the DOWN column. This is a cumulative volume total. It is subtracted from the volume in the UP column and the result is the on-balance volume.

Double Bottom. This is the phenomenon of two prices coming into alignment at similar low points, points of technical support. The support is *implied* because the second bottom did not go below the level of the first. The advance off of a double bottom usually has greater upside impetus than if it had stemmed from a single low point. The reason for that is the observation that the first bottom was successfully tested. However, there are greater risks inherent in double bottoms because if they are broken the resulting declines are sharper than if a single bottom was broken. The "double bottom" phenomenon can also be observed in terms of the on-balance volume figures, also having the same inherent risks and opportunities.

Energy. This term is used in the book interchangeably with rising on-balance volume. It implies upside momentum, expanding technical strength.

Exhaustion. This occurs when buying pressure is no longer able to make a clear cut advance without obvious technical deterioration or when selling pressure is no longer able to effect a clear cut decline without obvious technical strength showing up. It is best detected either in terms of non-confirmations by the advance-decline line or non-confirmations by the Climax Indicator.

Field Trend. On-balance volume records upside breakouts and downside breakouts. When those breakouts trace out a rising zigzag there is then a *rising field trend.* When there is no evidence of a rising or falling zigzag in the clusters of breakouts the field trend is said to be *doubtful.* When the OBV breakouts record a downward zigzag, the field trend is said to be *falling.* The field trend mix of the 30-Dow-Jones industrial stocks is very important in determining the true trend of the Dow, comparing the number of stocks in rising field trends as against the number in falling field trends. The field trend is extremely important in determining when to buy or sell an individual stock.

Fifty Per Cent Principle. Based on the physical principle of a seesaw, the Principle states that if a previous decline in the market is more than 50% retraced on the next rally, then the market will ultimately retrace the entire decline. Conversely, if a previous advance is more than 50% retraced on the next decline, then the market will ultimately retrace the entire advance. It has a very good short term batting average, but in using it measured against entire bull and bear markets, it is most reliable in the early stages of a bull market when retracing more than 50% of the previous bear market. To avoid expensive miscalculations, only stress the halfway penetrations when measured against *completed* bull or bear markets. Such valid better than halfway retracements tend to be early in bull markets and late in bear markets.

First Phase Movement (individual stocks). Stocks tend to move up in three phases. The first phase is characterized by relatively static price movement but strong evidence of accumulation in the form of rising on-balance volume.

Flat Base. Some of the greatest percentage gains have stemmed from stocks breaking out from flat base formations. A flat base is made up of a long period of price fluctuations in a very narrow range. When accumulation can be detected, the flat base situation becomes very attractive from the technical standpoint.

Flat Base Breakout. This is the actual price move above the long range of narrow price fluctuations which have traced out the flat base formation. Such breakouts are always *preceded* by rising on-balance volume. The flat base description also can refer to the on-balance volume fluctuations, and an upside breakout from that narrow OBV range either predicts an imminent price breakout or both the OBV and price break out together. The results of such breakouts can only be bullish.

Floating Supply. This is a term used to describe how much stock is around which is not closely held, stock which is in the trading pool of available supply. Ths smaller the "float," the more susceptible the stock is to day-to-day supply and demand pressures. When the float becomes small enough and the price high enough, then maximum vulnerability to price decline is reached. To estimate the floating supply, subtract the on-balance volume from the capitalization. A real squeeze on the price of the stock is seen when *the short interest comes to equal or surpass the floating supply.*

Force. A term used synonymously with *energy* or rising on-balance volume.

Four Column Analysis. This is a separation of stock price analysis into *four* charts, a chart of the opening prices, the high prices, the low prices, and the closing prices. The theory here is that no price penetration is necessarily valid unless confirmed by the other three charts. The separate series can be shown in price *columns* and thus the term *four column* analysis.

Fundamental Data. Data comprising the entire gamut of economic intelligence-covering such things as the economy, stock earnings and dividends, price/earning ratios, new products, management changes and the computation of what a stock is worth, among other things. *Most of the time fundamental data is totally irrelevant to the market.* The market never speaks in terms of fundamentals. The market only speaks in *technical* terms. I have never ceased to be amazed at so much stress on the wrong things when it comes to the market. How can fundamental data be important when timing decisions are made when the market doesn't even speak the language? Nine times out of ten the overconcentration on fundamental data has resulted in losses. What the market does to the price of a stock is a *market function,* therefore, a *technical* function. When viewed in this light, the study of fundamental data as a prerequisite to making money in the market doesn't make much sense. Yet some very intelligent people have made the mistake of putting fundamental data ahead of technical data.

Gaps. These are visible separations or skips in either prices, on-balance volume, or both. Gaps set up targets for retracement, and it is not wise to ignore them. Gaps occurring early in a price upswing are not as bearish as those showing up in the third phase of the price movement, a definite technical characteristic suggesting the end of the line on the upside.

Genuity. A word coined in the original *Stragety* book to depict the degree of *genuineness* of a Dow move as checked out by the broader market averages.

Gravity. This word in technical analysis has the same meaning as it would in physics, that what goes up must come down. The effects of such gravity forces become irresistable late in the third phase of a price upswing.

Head and Shoulders. A chart formation showing three distinct rises, the first constituting the left shoulder, the second (and greatest rise) constituting the head, and the third rise advancing approximately as far as the left shoulder advanced, constituting the right shoulder. The base level of the three advances comprises the neckline. A head and shoulders chart formation depicts a probable market top, and the move under the neckline completes the formation with an ensuing sharp decline. Head and shoulders formations can be aborted, but experience has shown that *a true abortion consists of a rise above the head.* A higher right shoulder than left shoulder is not enough. One should especially be on guard to watch for such a bearish formation during the third phase of a bull market. The same rules apply to the very bullish reverse head and shoulders formation. These should be especially watched for very late in bear markets.

Leading Indicator. Any statistic which periodically turns down ahead of the market or turns up ahead of the market qualifies as a leading indicator, an indicator that "leads the way."

Logic. It is sometimes said that the market is illogical, not at all acting in a rational manner. Those who accuse it of such illogical moves are trying to relate two different time periods, the past or current events with the future. When something happens the market has not had time to discount, then the market *acts on a current events basis.* Everybody understands the market on such days because *they can relate it to the current events.* That is why the market is so one-sided on such days. Examples would include the Eisenhower heart attack market of 1955, the Kennedy assassination market of 1963, etc. When the market is viewed in retrospect, *its unerring logic is inescapable.* After all, millions of game players are trying to beat out millions of other game players, always thinking ahead, and only on those rare occasions does the news catch up with the market. Those who accuse the market of being illogical are themselves illogical.

M Pattern. This is the exact opposite of the W pattern. Shown is the double top with the right leg of the decline falling below the temporary support level in the middle of the

M formation. The key signal suggesting short selling is the decline below the middle point. The same conclusions can be drawn when the pattern is encountered using on-balance volume.

Maturity. A term associated with price movements in the third phase of a stock upswing, any price movement or OBV movement smacking of a vertical ascent.

Momentum. This is the *rate* of acceleration in price or volume expansion, best noted by developing gaps in velocity figures or gaps in an on-balance volume series. Upside *momentum* is the greatest just short of price maturity, and downside *momentum* tends to reach a peak at or near an important bottom.

Neckline. Term employed when describing the head and shoulders chart formation, the critical line of support at market tops which, when broken, results in sharp and extended declines. At market bottoms a reverse head and shoulders formation would depict the neckline as the critical line of resistance which, if penetrated, results in sharp and extended advances.

Net Differential. This is the difference between volume assigned to the *up* column and volume assigned to the *down* column. Obviously, *net differential* is the same as on-balance volume.

Net Field Trend. Major indicator depicting the true volume trend of the 30 Dow-Jones industrial stocks. It is simply the difference between the number of Dow stocks in rising field trends and the number of Dow stocks in falling field trends. For the correct interpretation of the daily Climax Indicator readings, one must take the Net Field Trend into consideration.

New York Stock Exchange Index. Created in 1966, this index comprises all stocks listed on the New York Stock Exchange and is thus the broadest measurement of what the market is doing. Its creation was prompted by mounting criticism of the Dow as a true reflector of the market.

OBV. This is the abbreviation for *on-balance volume.*

Odd Lot. Stock purchased or sold in lots of less than a round lot (100 shares) is called an odd lot.

Odd Lot Short Sales. This is the amount of stock sold short in odd lot amounts in expectation that the market is going lower. In major bull markets rising odd lot short sales tend to have strong bullish implications very early in the first phase when everyone thinks that a bear market is still in progress. This indicator was a big factor in identifying the 1962, 1966, and 1970 bottoms but was not a factor in identifying the 1974 bottom.

On-Balance. This is the difference between the pluses and the minuses in any situation.

On-Balance Volume. This is OBV, the result reached after subtracting all the volume on the downside from the volume on the upside. Readings can either be positive or negative.

Overbought. Price maturity and the term *overbought* are interchangeable descriptions. An overbought condition is detected when upside gaps show up in the velocity, price, and OBV. All vertical movements imply that a stock is overbought.

Overhead Supply. This is the total amount of shares traded in a stock at higher price levels through which the stock (after a decline) is trying to cut through on the recovery movement. Some chartists call it the *high volume zone.* High volume at higher prices presents a formidable resistance on recovery movements. To put it another way: too many people are waiting to move out of the stock the minute it returns to the higher levels at which they originally made their purchase. If a stock can cut back through overhead supply, it is a strongly bullish endorsement for a further upswing. Overhead supply can be measured, and when a decline has generated an equal number of shares with the overhead supply, then the decline is either over or just about to be terminated (overhead supply concept).

Oversold. This term is associated with *first phase* stock price movements. An oversold condition is detected by the presence of downside gaps in price and on-balance volume, or price returning to a key support level, or OBV reaching down to fill some gap overlooked on the way up.

Plurality. Term employed in describing the total advances and declines, assigning the *plurality* to one or the other.

Price/Earnings Ratios. A favorite tool of fundamental stock analysis which completely fails to take into account stock supply and demand patterns largely created by psychology. If p/e ratios contributed valid intelligence in making market decisions, then they would tend to be stable. Earnings would move up, the price of the stock would go up, and the p/e ratio would essentially remain the same. Instead, what happens? Earnings go up, the price of the stock stands still, and the p/e ratio drops; or earnings go up, the price of the stock goes down, and the p/e ratio plummets; or earnings move down, the price of the stock goes up, and the p/e ratio soars. So in actuality price/earnings ratios fluctuate widely and thus in themselves cannot provide any dependable guide to what the price of a stock is going to do. The fallacy of p/e ratios is explained by the *anachronism between price and earnings.* Earnings *lag* the market by about nine months. Price is current but tends to discount the *future.* So p/e ratios try to relate a current or *futuristic* statistic with a *lagging* statistic. Result? *Meaningless* fluctuations in the p/e ratio.

Price Maturity. This description fits all third phase stock price movements. The term maturity can refer to price or volume movements, the term here referring specifically to vertical price movements.

Primary Trend. The predominant trend of the market throughout bull and bear markets. When the primary trend turns bullish at the start of a bull market, it stays bullish until the bull market ends. When it turns bearish at the start of a bear market, it stays bearish until the bear market ends.

Pullback. Practically all advances of importance are tested with a subsequent "pullback" to or near the starting point of the advance. The price is easily seen as merely a pullback when the OBV reading is higher on the return trip price than it was the first time it was at that price.

Random Walk. Name given to the theory that stock movements have no memory and occur each day completely at random. Theory has no basis in fact and, at best, merely makes interesting reading. Proponents of the random walk obviously have no understanding of the market game, completely overlooking the planned strategies of stock accumulation and distribution, *obviously connected movements having total memory.* Cyclical analysis also disputes the random walk. Do major market bottoms in 1957, 1962, 1966, 1970, and 1974 look random? Hardly. A truly random series of market bottoms would run something like this, occurring in the following years: 1957, 1958, 1961, 1966, 1968, and 1972.

Resistance. Any barrier to progress is resistance. Once a price support level is broken, that support level becomes the *resistance* point on the recovery movement. The theory of resistance holds true in OBV movements.

Reverse Split. Being the opposite of a stock split, the move has bullish implications and smacks of accumulation. Anytime a reverse split is announced, one should start running an OBV on the stock, keeping in mind the *motives* behind a reverse split.

Rising Bottoms. The ability of a stock to turn up above each preceding important low point traces out a pattern of *rising bottoms,* a bullish formation. This is only half the formation, however. To be complete there should also be an accompanying series of rising tops. Rising bottoms (by definition) precede rising tops and are thus the first technical requirement which must be met if a situation is to be termed a bullish one. The same formation should be looked for in OBV.

Rising Tops. This is the typical pattern best seen in the second and third phase stock price movements. It must be seen in the first phase OBV movements, otherwise the later bullish unfoldment will not be seen. Rising tops beget rising tops until the gravity rule of the third phase stock price movement takes over.

Second Phase Stock Price Movement. This describes the orderly 30-degree angle price ascent which follows the price breakout from the first phase of accumulation. At the peak of this movement one of the commonest errors is to interpret the second phase price peak as the *final* peak of the typical three-phase stock price movement. For awhile (in retrospect) the second phase price peak will have all the appearances of a final peak inasmuch as final peaks are often preceded by sharp shake-outs, and, during that shake-out, the second phase pinnacle will look beyond attainment on a recovery move. The chief characteristic of the second phase stock price movement is *smoothness,* very few gaps (if any) between prices and rising OBV.

Secondary Offerings. Planned stock distributions, most numerous during late second phase of a bull market and throughout third phase.

Secondary Trend. Market movement in the opposite direction to the primary trend. Is often mistaken for a change in the primary trend. Chances of making that mistaken interpretation are greatly reduced by relating this opposite market movement to where it is occurring in the 4 to 4 1/2 year market cycle.

Sell Column. When a stock is down in price at the end of the trading session all the volume generated for the day is recorded on the downside, and the figure is placed in the SELL column.

Selling Climax. This is a situation that occurs when a clear majority of all stocks reach an oversold condition simultaneously. Selling climaxes have the following characteristics: (1) heavy volume, (2) decided plurality of declines over advances, (3) transactions reported long after they occur, the late tape, (4) a strong price reversal occurring before the session has ended, and (5) the move accompanied by a large number of odd lot short sales. If the market had not been closed after the brief period of hectic trading following the Kennedy assassination, it would undoubtedly have ended in such a selling climax. A selling climax implies *ending* and is one of the finest situations to buy into when seen. However, they have become increasingly less frequent in recent years. They are often triggered by *very bad news* which motivates the badly timed heavy public selling, thus the great buying opportunity.

Shake-Out. A healthy technical correction of an overbought situation, whether referring to the general market or a specific stock. The decline is sharp but comparatively short in duration. Shake-outs often terminate the second phase stock price movement. If one counts the shake-out as a full phase of the stock price movement, then it can be said that the bull cycle for individual stocks consists of four phases. Shake-outs in the general market have been falsely labeled as major bear markets many times, the surface appearances often being deceptively similar.

Short Interest. The total number of shares sold short and reported by the Stock Exchange once a month. A large short interest is basically bullish but is largely tempered by the volume of trading. Viewing the short interest, the question that must be answered is: are the shorts right or wrong on the market? A mere *quantity* of short sellers tells us nothing. Short sellers are wrong as a group in a bull market and right as a group in a bear market. Therefore, we must ascertain the primary trend *before* we attempt to weight the significance of the short interest. If the primary trend is judged to be bullish, then the short interest is significant, especially if it is rising in relation to the average daily volume. If the primary trend of the market is judged to be bearish, then a large short interest is of no help to the bulls because then the shorts are shorting *with* the trend, and there is no compulsion to cover their short sales. In a bull market there definitely is an increasing compulsion to cover, and that is a measurable bullish factor.

Short Interest Ratio. This is the ratio of monthly short interest to the average daily trading volume for that month. When the ratio is under 1.00 for a long period of time it is popularly construed to be bearish. A ratio above 1.00 is normal. If the ratio climbs above 1.50, that is bullish, and anything approaching 2.00 is wildly bullish. This indicator has been a poor one in helping to detect major market tops but has been among the best in detecting bottoms when the ratio approached the 2.00 level.

Short Selling. This is the process of selling a stock which is not owned with the expectation of buying it back (covering) at a lower price. The broker has to borrow the stock in order to make delivery. In a weak market, short selling becomes increasingly popular. When it becomes excessive, then the market either embarks upon a strong technical rally or starts a new bull market according to where the market stands in the 4 to 4 1/2 year market cycle (the shorts taking their profits by buying in or covering).

Shorting Against the Box. This is the process of going short on a stock already owned, a new transaction. To complete the transaction in the case of the stock going down in price, the originally owned stock is merely delivered. If the price goes up after the short sale, then the value of the original holding has also gone up the same amount, and no net loss is incurred. The purpose of shorting against the box is to stretch out the holding period for the originally bought shares so as to qualify for six month capital gains lower tax rates. Regardless of whether the price of the stock rises or falls on the shorting process, the holder "freezes" his position.

Snapback. A bullish technical property imparted to a stock if the price declines at a faster rate than the OBV. It implies that the stock has reached a true oversold position long before it would have under different circumstances. The price, being out of line with the OBV on the downside, therefore "snaps back."

Smart Money. Is on top of the market game, has read the market message correctly, is operating opposite to the public psychology and not in step with the news. Is accumulating stocks when the market says to accumulate. Is selling stocks when the markets says to distribute. Doesn't give a rap for fundamentals if the market dictates otherwise. May at times look like a nut to his friends, but laughs all the way to the bank.

Speculation Index. The ratio of total volume on the American Stock Exchange to the total volume on the New York Stock Exchange measured either weekly or monthly. The purpose of the indicator is to detect periods of overspeculation and underspeculation. When the ratio exceeds 45%, the market has entered an area of overspeculation, typical of the third phase of a bull market. Anything approaching 60% is 100% dangerous, as in 1968. While one can sell with confidence on the high Speculation Index readings, one cannot buy with confidence on the low readings because there is no clearly definable level which can be considered "low." Long before the 1973-74 bear market ended, the Speculation Index was at a very "low" level of over 20%, yet dropped all the way to about 9% by the time the bear market ended.

Spring Principle. Each turnover of capitalization accompanied by accumulation creates 100% of bullish velocity but at the same time winds up a spring which must by its own tightness eventually snap. The Spring Principle states that the price advance will accelerate percentagewise with each turn of the spring (each complete turnover of the capitalization) and that *in the later stages the percentage price rise will advance geometrically.* Velocity must be accompanied by rising OBV in order for the Principle to be valid.

Standard & Poor 500 Stock Index. Standard index used in computing disparity, the thumb rule being to multiply the index changes by ten and compare those results with the changes in the Dow-Jones Industrial Average.

Support. Any barrier to decline is called support. Once a resistance level has been successfully penetrated by a stock advance, the retreat from that level is expected to meet support at the old resistance level. The theory of support also holds true in OBV movements.

Tax Selling. Selling a stock for the purpose of recording a loss for tax purposes, tax selling is often a perfect camouflage for a developing new bull market, the majority mechanically fenced into a time period calling for inappropriate action. The tax selling period should also be related to where it occurs in the typical 4 to 4 1/2 year market cycle.

Technician. One who tries to follow the guidance of the greatest of all market advisors, the market itself. The technician is trained to understand the language of the market and is less prone to interpretive errors by restricting his analysis to this market language. The technician understands the constant struggle between the demand forces and the supply forces and knows that the outcome of that struggle determines prices and not earnings, news, p/e ratios, the economy, or anything else.

Tension. Any kind of disparity between price and OBV creates tension. If the price is outrunning OBV on the upside, then the created tension is distincly bearish. If the price is declining faster than the OBV, then the created tension is distinctly bullish. Bullish tension is the same as snapback.

Third Phase Stock Movement. The third phase movement of stock prices denotes maturity, finality, a vertical rise which cannot be sustained at that rate of climb. Accompanying characteristics of third phase stock movements are both price and OBV gaps.

Third Phase Stock Shake-Out. This is simply assigning the shake-out (which so often precedes the third phase stock run-up) to the third phase instead of numbering it as the third phase and necessitating the description of a fourth phase.

Three Phase Stock Movement. This is the whole price movement moving from first phase (base with accumulation), second phase (breakout from base through to the beginning of shake-out), and third phase (final price run-up preceded by brief but sharp shakeout). It is interesting to note that the three phase movement fits the Elliott Wave movement (UP-DOWN-UP-DOWN-UP, the first four waves matching the first and second phase price movement and the fifth wave corresponding to the third phase which denotes maturity. The five waves could be fitted to the following things previously described: First Wave—breakout from base, second Wave—normal pullback showing either double bottoms or rising bottoms, but always higher OBV on the pullback, third Wave—pinnacle reached prior to shakeout, fourth Wave—sharp shakeout, fifth Wave—final run-up to last price peak).

Topping Out. A term employed to denote loss of upside energy at the top after a long price run-up. Such a loss of energy would also show up in a pattern of declining tops or declining OBV.

Triple Bottom. The more often a stock or the market has met support in a given area the more reliable that area becomes as an important bottom on which an advance can be constructed. The most effective triple bottoms are those where it can be demonstrated that OBV is higher on each bottom. When encountering a triple bottom in the market, it is very important to try and relate it to the typical 4 to 4 1/2 year market cycle. If the third bottom occurs in a typical bear market third phase, then one can begin buying with confidence *even if that bottom is broken.* Some of the most effective bear traps have been seen on broken triple bottoms.

Triple Top. The more often a stock or the market has met resistance in a given area the more reliable that area becomes as an important top from which a decline will probably develop. The most ominous looking triple tops are those where it can be shown that OBV is lower on each of the tops, or, in the case of the general market, where the advance-decline line is lower on each of the tops. When encountering a triple top in the market, it is very important to try and relate it to the typical 4 to 4 1/2 year market cycle. If the third top occurs in the typical third phase of a bull market, then one can begin selling with conviction *even if the Dow comes up and breaks through the triple top.* Some of the most effective bull traps have been seen on penetrated triple tops. The last best example of this was the late 1972 upside breakout through a triple top, leading into the 1973-74 bear market.

Vacuum. This is another term having the same meaning as gap. It can either be a vacuum or gap in OBV or in price. Such vacuums or gaps are always potential targets to be filled in.

Velocity. This is the total cumulative volume expressed as a percentage of capitalization. Velocity only takes on meaning when it is accompanied by accumulation (rising OBV). It is an integral part of the Spring Principle.

Vertical Price Movement. A price run-up is a vertical movement, at high levels always being the chief characteristic of a stock's third phase movement of maturity or, at the very least, the topping out of the second phase price movement just prior to a sharp shakeout.

Volume Advance-Decline Line. Another way of expressing on-balance volume, simply substituting the more important volume factor.

Volume Breakout. A new high in a series of on-balance volume figures. Such breakouts tend to *precede* price breakouts.

Volume Ratio. A now antiquated method of detecting significant strength, completely superseded by the new concept of on-balance volume.

W Pattern. The opposite of the M-pattern, it is a formation seen either in terms of price or on-balance volume. The breakout above the middle leg on the upside as the W is being created is quite bullish.

The Appendix

TABLE I

For the benefit of those who desire to do additional research on the Climax Indicator, observing how it has acted every day for a period of ten years, the following figures should prove of some interest. Significant highs in the Climax Indicator, the 3-day moving average, the cumulative CLX readings, and the Dow are affixed with the letter H while significant lows are affixed with the letter L.

TABLE I

Ten Year Daily Record of the Climax Indicator

Date	Climax Indicator	3-day Moving Average	CLX Cumulative	Dow
March 25, 1965	- 5		- 5	898.34
March 26, 1965	-13		- 18	891.66
March 29, 1965	-12	-10.00	- 30	887.82
March 30, 1965	-10	-11.66	- 40	889.05
March 31, 1965	- 7	- 9.66	- 47	889.05
April 1, 1965	2	- 5.00	- 45	890.33
April 2, 1965	9	+ 1.33	- 36	893.38
April 5, 1965	6	+ 5.66	- 30	893.23
April 6, 1965	0	+ 5.00	- 30	891.90
April 7, 1965	- 1	+ 1.66	- 31	892.94
April 8, 1965	13	+ 4.00	- 18	897.90
April 9, 1965	16	+ 9.33	- 2	901.29
April 12, 1965	17 (H)	+15.33	+ 15	906.36
April 13, 1965	17 (H)	+16.66	+ 32	908.01
April 14, 1965	17 (H)	+17.00 (H)	+ 49	912.86
April 15, 1965	8	+14.00	+ 57	911.81
April 19, 1965	5	+10.00	+ 62	912.76
April 20, 1965	1	+ 4.66	+ 63	911.96
April 21, 1965	- 1	+ 1.66	+ 62	910.71
April 22, 1965	7	+ 2.33	+ 69	915.06
April 23, 1965	1	+ 2.33	+ 70	916.41

Date	Climax Indicator	3-day Moving Average	CLX Cumulative	Dow
April 26, 1965	4	+ 4.00	+ 74	916.86
April 27, 1965	4	+ 3.00	+ 78	918.16
April 28, 1965	0	+ 2.66	+ 78	918.86
April 29, 1965	2	+ 0.66	+ 76	918.71
April 30, 1965	5	+ 1.00	+ 81	922.31
May 3, 1965	3	+ 2.00	+ 84	922.11
May 4, 1965	10	+ 6.00	+ 94	928.22
May 5, 1965	11	+ 8.00	+105	932.22
May 6, 1965	8	+ 9.66	+113	933.52
May 7, 1965	4	+ 7.66	+117	932.52
May 10, 1965	4	+ 5.33	+121	931.47
May 11, 1965	2	+ 3.33	+123	930.92
May 12, 1965	0	+ 2.00	+123	934.17
May 13, 1965	5	+ 2.33	+128	938.87
May 14, 1965	1	+ 2.00	+129 (H)	939.62 (H)
May 17, 1965	- 6	.00	+123	930.67
May 18, 1965	- 6	- 3.66	+117	930.62
May 19, 1965	- 3	- 5.00	+114	932.12
May 20, 1965	- 8	- 5.66	+106	927.27
May 21, 1965	- 9	- 6.66	+ 97	922.01
May 24, 1965	-15	-10.66	+ 82	914.21
May 25, 1965	2	- 7.33	+ 84	921.09
May 26, 1965	- 6	- 6.33	+ 78	917.16
May 27, 1965	-12	- 5.33	+ 66	913.22
May 28, 1965	7	- 3.66	+ 73	918.04
June 1, 1965	-12	- 5.66	+ 61	908.53
June 2, 1965	-16	- 7.00	+ 45	904.06
June 3. 1965	-14	-14.00	+ 31	899.22
June 4, 1965	- 5	-11.66	+ 26	900.87
June 7, 1965	- 5	- 8.00	+ 21	902.15
June 8, 1965	-14	- 8.00	+ 7	889.05
June 9, 1965	-19	-12.66	- 12	879.84
June 10, 1965	-16	-16.33	- 28	876.49
June 11, 1965	- 5	-13.33	- 33	881.70
June 14, 1965	-15	-12.00	- 48	868.71
June 15, 1965	+ 5	- 5.00	- 43	874.57
June 16, 1965	+ 4	- 2.00	- 39	878.07
June 17, 1965	+ 7	+ 5.33	- 32	883.06
June 18, 1965	- 2	+ 3.00	- 34	879.17
June 21, 1965	- 1	+ 1.33	- 35	874.12
June 22, 1965	- 2	- 1.66	- 37	875.43
June 23, 1965	-11	- 4.66	- 48	870.22
June 24, 1965	-21	-11.33	- 69	857.76
June 25, 1965	-21	-17.66	- 90	854.42
June 28, 1965	-26 (L)	-22.66 (L)	-116	840.59 (L)
June 29, 1965	- 4	-17.00	-120 (L)	851.40
June 30, 1965	9	- 7.00	-111	868.03
July 1, 1965	10	+ 5.00	-101	871.59
July 2, 1965	7	+ 8.66	- 94	875.16
July 6, 1965	5	+ 7.33	- 89	873.18

Date	Climax Indicator	3-day Moving Average	CLX Cumulative	Dow
July 7, 1965	- 3	+ 3.00	- 92	870.77
July 8, 1965	6	+ 2.66	- 86	877.85
July 9, 1965	6	+ 3.00	- 80	879.49
July 12, 1965	- 3	+ 3.00	- 83	877.96
July 13, 1965	3	+ 2.00	- 80	876.97
July 14, 1965	9	+ 3.00	- 71	883.23
July 15, 1965	5	+ 5.66	- 66	880.98
July 16, 1965	0	+ 4.66	- 66	880.43
July 19, 1965	4	+ 3.00	- 62 (H)	880.26
July 20, 1965	-17	- 4.33	- 79	868.79
July 21, 1965	-13	- 8.66	- 92	865.01
July 22, 1965	-12	-14.00	-104	861.77
July 23, 1965	- 4	- 9.66	-108	863.97
July 26, 1965	- 6	- 7.33	-114	867.26
July 27, 1965	-10	- 6.66	-124 (L)	863.53
July 28, 1965	2	- 4.66	-122	867.92
July 29, 1965	3	- 1.66	-119	874.23
July 30, 1965	19 (H)	+ 8.00	-100	881.74
August 2, 1965	7	+ 9.66	- 93	881.85
August 3, 1965	5	+10.33	- 88	881.20
August 4, 1965	10	+ 7.33	- 78	883.88
August 5, 1965	2	+ 5.66	- 76	881.63
August 6, 1965	2	+ 4.66	- 74	882.51
August 9, 1965	- 4	.00	- 78	879.77
August 10, 1965	- 3	- 1.66	- 81	878.89
August 11, 1965	3	- 1.33	- 78	881. 47
August 12, 1965	3	+ 1.00	- 75	881.96
August 13, 1965	11	+ 5.66	- 64	888.82
August 16, 1965	11	+ 8.33	- 53	891.13
August 17, 1965	10	+10.66	- 43	894.26
August 18, 1965	9	+10.00	- 34	894.37
August 19, 1965	3	+ 7.33	- 31	891.79
August 20, 1965	- 2	+ 3.33	- 33	889.92
August 23, 1965	- 4	- 1.00	- 37	887.07
August 24, 1965	- 2	- 2.66	- 39	887.12
August 25, 1965	- 1	- 2.33	- 40	890.85
August 26, 1965	8	+ 1.66	- 32	896.18
August 27, 1965	1	+ 2.66	- 31	895.96
August 30, 1965	4	+ 4.33	- 27	895.63
August 31, 1965	- 3	+ 0.66	- 30	893.10
September 1, 1965	2	+ 1.00	- 28	893.60
September 2, 1965	10	+ 3.00	- 18	900.40
September 3, 1965	14	+ 8.66	- 4	907.97
September 7, 1965	11	+11.66 (H)	+ 7	910.11
September 8, 1965	5	+10.00	+ 12	913.68
September 9, 1965	7	+ 7.66	+ 19	917.47
September 10, 1965	5	+ 5.66	+ 24	918.95
September 13, 1965	6	+ 6.00	+ 30	920.22
September 14, 1965	1	+ 4.00	+ 31	916.59
September 15, 1965	9	+ 5.33	+ 40	922.95

Date	Climax Indicator	3-day Moving Average	CLX Cumulative	Dow
September 16, 1965	13	+ 7.66	+ 53	931.18
September 17, 1965	1	+ 7.66	+ 54	928.99
September 20, 1965	6	+ 6.66	+ 60	931.18
September 21, 1965	0	+ 2.33	+ 60	926.52
September 22, 1965	7	+ 4.33	+ 67	931.62
September 23, 1965	- 3	+ 1.33	+ 64	927.45
September 24, 1965	1	+ 1.66	+ 65	929.54
September 27, 1965	7	+ 1.66	+ 72	937.88
September 28, 1965	- 2	+ 2.00	+ 70	935.85
September 29, 1965	- 2	+ 1.00	+ 68	932.39
September 30, 1965	- 6	- 3.33	+ 62	930.58
October 1, 1965	- 6	- 4.33	+ 56	929.65
October 4, 1965	- 4	- 5.33	+ 52	930.86
October 5, 1965	6	- 1.33	+ 58	938.70
October 6, 1965	2	+ 1.33	+ 60	936.84
October 7, 1965	1	+ 3.00	+ 61	934.42
October 8, 1965	8	+ 3.66	+ 69	938.32
October 11, 1965	10	+ 6.33	+ 79	942.65
October 12, 1965	7	+ 8.33	+ 86	941.12
October 13, 1965	5	+ 7.33	+ 91	941.01
October 14, 1965	- 2	+ 3.33	+ 89	937.50
October 15, 1965	3	+ 2.00	+ 92	940.68
October 18, 1965	7	+ 2.66	+ 99	945.84
October 19, 1965	0	+ 3.33	+ 99	947.76
October 20, 1965	0	+ 2.33	+ 99	948.47
October 21, 1965	3	+ 1.00	+102	950.28
October 22, 1965	8	+ 3.66	+110	952.42
October 25, 1965	3	+ 4.66	+113	948.14
October 26, 1965	8	+ 6.33	+121	956.32
October 27, 1965	11	+ 7.33	+132	959.50
October 28, 1965	7	+ 8.66	+139	959.11
October 29, 1965	6	+ 8.00	+145	960.82
November 1, 1965	3	+ 5.33	+148 (H)	958.96
November 3, 1965	- 3	+ 2.00	+145	961.13
November 4, 1965	- 1	- 0.33	+144	961.85 (H)
November 5, 1965	1	- 1.00	+145	959.46
November 8, 1965	- 7	- 2.33	+138	953.95
November 9, 1965	- 3	- 3.00	+135	951.72
November 10, 1965	- 3	- 4.33	+132	951.22
November 11, 1965	1	- 1.66	+133	953.28
November 12, 1965	0	- 0.66	+133	956.29
November 15, 1965	2	+ 1.00	+135	955.90
November 16, 1965	1	+ 1.00	+136	956.51
November 17, 1965	3	+ 2.00	+139	956.57
November 18, 1965	- 2	+ 0.66	+137	950.50
November 19, 1965	- 2	- 0.33	+135	952.72
November 22, 1965	-12	- 5.33	+123	946.38
November 23, 1965	- 5	- 6.33	+118	948.94
November 24, 1965	- 3	- 6.66	+115	948.94
November 26, 1965	- 3	- 3.66	+112	948.16

Date	Climax Indicator	3-day Moving Average	CLX Cumulative	Dow
November 29, 1965	- 1	- 2.33	+111	946.93
November 30, 1965	- 7	- 3.66	+104	946.71
December 1, 1965	- 1	- 3.00	+103	947.60
December 2, 1965	- 4	- 4.00	+ 99	944.59
December 3, 1965	- 4	- 3.00	+ 95	946.10
December 6, 1965	-15	- 7.66	+ 80 (L)	939.53 (L)
December 7, 1965	4	- 5.00	+ 84	951.33
December 8, 1965	2	- 3.00	+ 86	946.60
December 9, 1965	0	+ 2.00	+ 86	949.55
December 10, 1965	2	+ 1.33	+ 88	952.72
December 13, 1965	1	+ 1.00	+ 89	951.55
December 14, 1965	6	+ 3.00	+ 95	954.06
December 15, 1965	6	+ 4.33	+101	958.74
December 16, 1965	8	+ 6.66	+109	959.13
December 17, 1965	6	+ 6.66	+115	957.85
December 20, 1965	1	+ 5.00	+116	952.22
December 21, 1965	11	+ 6.00	+127	959.46
December 22, 1965	13	+ 8.33	+140	965.86
December 23, 1965	9	+11.00 (H)	+149	966.36
December 27, 1965	- 2	+ 6.66	+147	959.79
December 28, 1965	- 2	+ 1.66	+145	957.96
December 29, 1965	2	- 0.66	+147	960.30
December 30, 1965	2	+ 0.66	+149	963.69
December 31, 1965	6	+ 3.33	+155	969.26
January 3, 1966	2	+ 3.33	+157	968.54
January 4, 1966	4	+ 4.00	+161	969.26
January 5, 1966	13	+ 6.33	+174	981.62
January 6, 1966	12	+ 9.66	+186	985.46
January 7, 1966	5	+10.00	+191	986.13
January 10, 1966	4	+ 7.00	+195	985.41
January 11, 1966	7	+ 5.33	+202	986.85
January 12, 1966	2	+ 4.33	+204	983.96
January 13, 1966	5	+ 4.66	+209	985.69
January 14, 1966	3	+ 3.33	+212	987.30
January 17, 1966	8	+ 5.33	+220	989.75
January 18, 1966	8	+ 6.33	+228	994.20
January 19, 1966	0	+ 5.33	+228	991.14
January 20, 1966	0	+ 2.66	+228	987.80
January 21, 1966	2	+ 0.66	+230	988.14
January 24, 1966	1	+ 1.00	+231 (H)	991.42
January 25, 1966	- 4	- 0.33	+227	991.64
January 26, 1966	- 5	- 2.66	+222	990.92
January 27, 1966	- 3	- 4.00	+219	990.36
January 28, 1966	- 7	- 5.00	+212	985.35
January 31, 1966	- 9	- 6.33	+203	983.51
February 1, 1966	-14	-10.00	+189	975.89
February 2, 1966	1	- 7.33	+190	982.29
February 3, 1966	0	- 4.33	+190	981.23
February 4, 1966	9	+ 3.33	+199	986.35
February 7, 1966	9	+ 6.00	+208	989.69

Date	Climax Indicator	3-day Moving Average	CLX Cumulative	Dow
February 8, 1966	6	+ 8.00	+214	991.03
February 9, 1966	10	+ 8.33	+224	995.15 (H)
February 10, 1966	4	+ 6.66	+228	990.81
February 11, 1966	- 1	+ 4.33	+227	989.03
February 14, 1966	- 3	.00	+224	987.69
February 15, 1966	- 7	- 3.66	+217	981.57
February 16, 1966	- 7	- 5.66	+210	982.40
February 17, 1966	-13	- 9.00	+197	975.27
February 18, 1966	-11	-10.33	+186	975.22
February 21, 1966	-14	-12.66	+172	966.48
February 23, 1966	-16	-13.66	+156	960.13
February 24, 1966	-16	-15.33 (L)	+140	950.66
February 25, 1966	- 4	-12.00	+136	953.00
February 28, 1966	- 7	- 9.00	+129	951.89
March 1, 1966	-19	-10.00	+110	938.19
March 2, 1966	-19 (L)	-15.00	+ 91	932.01
March 3, 1966	- 6	-14.66	+ 85	936.35
March 4, 1966	- 5	-10.00	+ 80	932.34
March 7, 1966	-17	- 9.33	+ 63	917.76
March 8, 1966	- 5	- 9.00	+ 58	919.90
March 9, 1966	4	- 6.00	+ 62	929.84
March 10, 1966	- 2	- 1.00	+ 60	929.23
March 11, 1966	- 5	- 1.00	+ 55	927.95
March 14, 1966	-14	- 7.00	+ 41	917.09
March 15, 1966	-14	-11.00	+ 27	911.08 (L)
March 16, 1966	0	- 9.33	+ 27	916.03
March 17, 1966	4	- 3.33	+ 31	919.32
March 18, 1966	4	+ 2.66	+ 35	922.88
March 21, 1966	11	+ 6.33	+ 46	929.17
March 22, 1966	13 (H)	+ 9.33 (H)	+ 59	934.52
March 23, 1966	- 3	+ 7.00	+ 56	929.00
March 24, 1966	- 3	+ 2.33	+ 53	928.61
March 25, 1966	- 1	- 2.33	+ 52	929.95
March 28, 1966	2	- 0.66	+ 54	932.62
March 29, 1966	- 6	- 1.66	+ 48	929.39
March 30, 1966	-13	- 5.66	+ 35	919.76
March 31, 1966	- 3	- 7.33	+ 32	924.77
April 1, 1966	0	- 5.33	+ 32	931.29
April 4, 1966	5	+ 0.66	+ 37	937.86
April 5, 1966	8	+ 4.33	+ 45	944.71
April 6, 1966	0	+ 4.33	+ 45	945.26
April 7, 1966	- 2	+ 2.00	+ 43	945.76
April 11, 1966	- 3	- 1.66	+ 40	942.42
April 12, 1966	- 9	- 4.66	+ 31	937.24
April 13, 1966	- 5	- 5.66	+ 26	938.36
April 14, 1966	- 3	- 5.66	+ 23	945.48
April 15, 1966	3	- 1.66	+ 26	947.77
April 18, 1966	- 4	- 1.33	+ 22	941.98
April 19, 1966	- 6	- 2.33	+ 16	941.64
April 20, 1966	11	+ 0.33	+ 27	951.28
April 21, 1966	4	+ 3.00	+ 31	954.73 (H)

Date		Climax Indicator	3-day Moving Average	CLX Cumulative	Dow
April	22, 1966	- 2	+ 4.33	+ 29	949.83
April	25, 1966	- 2	.00	+ 27	950.55
April	26, 1966	- 6	- 3.33	+ 21	947.21
April	27, 1966	- 9	- 5.66	+ 12	944.54
April	28, 1966	-13	- 9.33	- 1	937.41
April	29, 1966	-12	-11.33	- 13	933.68
May	2, 1966	- 9	-11.33	- 22	931.95
May	3, 1966	-22	-14.33	- 44	921.77
May	4, 1966	-18	-16.33	- 62	914.86
May	5, 1966	-22 (L)	-20.66 (L)	- 84	899.77
May	6, 1966	-12	-17.33	- 96	902.83
May	9, 1966	-16	-16.66	-112	886.80
May	10, 1966	9	- 6.33	-103	895.48
May	11, 1966	1	- 2.00	-102	895.43
May	12, 1966	-11	- 0.33	-113	885.57
May	13, 1966	-18	- 9.33	-131	876.11
May	16, 1966	-20	-16.33	-151	867.53
May	17, 1966	-19	-19.00	-170	864.14 (L)
May	18, 1966	- 1	-13.33	-171	878.50
May	19, 1966	- 6	- 8.66	-177	872.99
May	20, 1966	2	- 1.66	-175	876.89
May	23, 1966	8	+ 1.33	-167	882.46
May	24, 1966	10	+ 6.66	-157	888.41
May	25, 1966	7	+ 8.33	-150	890.42
May	26, 1966	6	+ 7.66	-144	891.75
May	27, 1966	10	+ 7.66	-134	897.04
May	31, 1966	- 9	+ 2.33	-143	884.07
June	1, 1966	- 6	- 1.66	-149	883.63
June	2, 1966	- 4	- 6.33	-153	882.73
June	3, 1966	6	- 1.33	-147	887.86
June	6, 1966	- 5	- 1.00	-152	881.68
June	7, 1966	- 7	- 2.00	-159	877.33
June	8, 1966	- 1	- 4.33	-160	879.34
June	9, 1966	0	- 2.66	-160	882.62
June	10, 1966	9	+ 2.66	-151	891.75
June	13, 1966	11 (H)	+ 6.66	-140	897.60
June	14, 1966	9	+ 9.66 (H)	-131	903.17 (H)
June	15, 1966	5	+ 8.33	-126	901.11
June	16, 1966	- 4	+ 3.33	-130	897.16
June	17, 1966	- 8	- 2.33	-138	894.26
June	20, 1966	- 8	- 6.66	-146	892.76
June	21, 1966	- 3	- 6.33	-149	894.98
June	22, 1966	2	- 3.00	-147	901.00
June	23, 1966	- 3	- 1.33	-150	896.49
June	24, 1966	2	+ 0.33	-148	897.16
June	27, 1966	-12	- 4.33	-160	888.97
June	28, 1966	-18	- 9.33	-178	880.90
June	29, 1966	-22 (L)	-17.33 (L)	-200	871.60
June	30, 1966	-11	-17.00	-211	870.10
July	1, 1966	1	-10.66	-210	877.06
July	5, 1966	- 1	- 3.66	-211	875.27

Date	Climax Indicator	3-day Moving Average	CLX Cumulative	Dow
July 6, 1966	7	+ 2.33	-204	888.86
July 7, 1966	7	+ 4.33	-197	891.64
July 8, 1966	5	+ 6.33	-192	894.04
July 11, 1966	5	+ 5.66	-187	893.09
July 12, 1966	1	+ 3.66	-186	886.19
July 13, 1966	- 7	- 0.33	-193	881.40
July 14, 1966	2	- 1.33	-191	887.80
July 15, 1966	7	+ 0.66	-184	889.36
July 18, 1966	- 1	+ 2.66	-185	888.41
July 19, 1966	- 7	- 0.33	-192	884.07
July 20, 1966	-15	- 7.66	-207	874.49
July 21, 1966	-14	-12.00	-221	873.99
July 22, 1966	-12	-13.66	-233	869.15
July 25, 1966	-22 (L)	-16.00 (L)	-255	852.53
July 26, 1966	-12	-15.33	-267	852.17
July 27, 1966	- 4	-12.66	-271	856.23
July 28, 1966	- 3	- 6.33	-274	854.06
July 29, 1966	- 3	- 3.33	-277	847.38
August 1, 1966	-19	- 8.33	-296	835.18
August 2, 1966	-14	-12.00	-310	832.57 (L)
August 3, 1966	5	- 9.33	-305	841.70
August 4, 1966	13	+ 1.33	-292	851.50
August 5, 1966	9	+ 9.00 (H)	-283	852.39
August 8, 1966	4	+ 8.66	-279	849.05
August 9, 1966	2	+ 5.00	-277	844.82
August 10, 1966	- 8	- 0.66	-285	838.53
August 11, 1966	- 2	- 2.66	-287	837.91
August 12, 1966	0	- 3.33	-287	840.53
August 15, 1966	- 3	- 1.66	-290	834.85
August 16, 1966	-17	- 6.66	-307	823.80
August 17, 1966	-19	-13.00	-326	819.59
August 18, 1966	-21	-19.00	-347	810.74
August 19, 1966	-18	-19.33	-365	804.62
August 22, 1966	-22 (L)	-20.33 (L)	-387	792.03
August 23, 1966	-18	-19.33	-405	790.14
August 24, 1966	- 2	-14.00	-407	799.55
August 25, 1966	- 8	- 9.33	-415	792.35
August 26, 1966	-17	- 9.00	-432	780.56
August 29, 1966	-21	-15.33	-453	767.03 (L)
August 30, 1966	- 2	-13.33	-455	775.72
August 31, 1966	+ 5	- 6.00	-450	788.41
September 1, 1966	+ 8	+ 3.66	-442	792.09
September 2, 1966	+ 5	+ 6.00	-437	787.69
September 6, 1966	- 3	+ 3.33	-440	782.34
September 7, 1966	-10	- 2.66	-450	777.39
September 8, 1966	- 9	- 7.33	-459	774.88
September 9, 1966	- 6	- 8.33	-465	775.55
September 12, 1966	+ 8	- 2.33	-457	790.59
September 13, 1966	+12	+ 4.66	-445	795.48
September 14, 1966	+12	+10.66	-433	806.23
September 15, 1966	+16 (H)	+13.33 (H)	-417	814.30 (H)

Date	Climax Indicator	3-day Moving Average	CLX Cumulative	Dow
September 16, 1966	+ 9	+12.33	-408	814.30
September 19, 1966	+ 1	+ 8.66	-407	810.85
September 20, 1966	- 5	+ 1.66	-412	806.01
September 21, 1966	-12	- 5.33	-424	793.59
September 22, 1966	- 2	- 6.33	-426	797.77
September 23, 1966	- 9	- 7.66	-435	790.97
September 26, 1966	- 5	- 5.33	-440	792.70
September 27, 1966	- 3	- 5.66	-443	794.09
September 28, 1966	-13	- 7.00	-456	780.95
September 29, 1966	-21 (L)	-12.33	-477	772.66
September 30, 1966	-13	-15.66	-490	774.22
October 3, 1966	-21 (L)	-18.33 (L)	-511	757.96
October 4, 1966	- 8	-14.00	-519	763.19
October 5, 1966	-11	-13.33	-530	755.45
October 6, 1966	-13	-10.66	-543	749.61
October 7, 1966	-15	-13.00	-558	744.32 (L)
October 10, 1966	- 1	- 9.66	-559 (L)	754.51
October 11, 1966	+ 2	- 4.66	-557	758.63
October 12, 1966	+11	+ 4.00	-546	778.17
October 13, 1966	+ 8	+ 7.00	-538	772.93
October 14, 1966	+ 4	+ 7.66	-534	771.71
October 17, 1966	+ 5	+ 5.66	-529	778.89
October 18, 1966	+12	+ 7.00	-517	791.87
October 19, 1966	- 1	+ 5.33	-518	785.35
October 20, 1966	0	+ 3.66	-518	783.68
October 21, 1966	+ 2	+ 0.33	-516	787.30
October 24, 1966	- 3	- 0.33	-519	787.85
October 25, 1966	+ 3	+ 0.66	-516	793.09
October 26, 1966	+11	+ 3.66	-505	801.11
October 27, 1966	+16 (H)	+10.00	-489	809.57
October 28, 1966	+ 5	+10.66 (H)	-484	807.96
October 31, 1966	- 1	+ 6.66	-485	807.07
November 1, 1966	+ 5	+ 3.00	-480	809.63
November 2, 1966	+ 2	+ 2.00	-478	807.29
November 3, 1966	- 2	+ 1.66	-480	804.34
November 4, 1966	+ 3	+ 1.00	-477	805.06
November 7, 1966	- 8	- 2.33	-485	802.22
November 9, 1966	+ 5	.00	-480	809.91
November 10, 1966	+10	+ 2.33	-470	816.87
November 11, 1966	+ 8	+ 7.66	-462	819.09
November 14, 1966	- 2	+ 5.33	-464	813.75
November 15, 1966	+ 2	+ 2.66	-462	815.31
November 16, 1966	+ 4	+ 1.33	-458 (H)	820.87 (H)
November 17, 1966	- 6	.00	-464	816.03
November 18, 1966	- 4	- 2.00	-468	809.40
November 21, 1966	-17 (L)	- 9.00	-485	798.16
November 22, 1966	-14	-11.33	-499	794.98
November 23, 1966	- 9	-13.33 (L)	-508	796.82
November 25, 1966	0	- 7.66	-508	803.34
November 28, 1966	- 1	- 3.33	-509	801.16
November 29, 1966	- 7	- 2.66	-516	795.26

Date	Climax Indicator	3-day Moving Average	CLX Cumulative	Dow
November 30, 1966	-11	- 6.33	-527	791.59
December 1, 1966	-11	- 9.66	-538	789.75
December 2, 1966	-12	-11.33	-550	789.47
December 5, 1966	- 3	- 8.66	-553	791.59
December 6, 1966	+ 8	- 2.33	-545	797.43
December 7, 1966	+10	+ 5.00	-535	808.01
December 8, 1966	+10	+ 9.33	-525	812.80
December 9, 1966	+ 7	+ 9.00	-518	813.02
December 12, 1966	+13 (H)	+10.00 (H)	-505	820.54 (H)
December 13, 1966	+ 3	+ 7.66	-502	816.70
December 14, 1966	+ 1	+ 5.66	-501	817.98
December 15, 1966	- 7	- 1.00	-508	809.18
December 16, 1966	- 5	- 3.66	-513	807.11
December 19, 1966	- 8	- 6.66	-521	798.99
December 20, 1966	- 8	- 7.00	-529	794.59
December 21, 1966	- 2	- 6.00	-531	797.43
December 22, 1966	0	- 3.33	-531	801.67
December 23, 1966	- 1	- 1.00	-532	799.10
December 27, 1966	- 6	- 2.33	-538	792.20
December 28, 1966	- 9	- 5.33	-547	788.58
December 29, 1966	-15 (L)	-10.00	-562	786.35
December 30, 1966	-14	-12.66 (L)	-576	785.69 (L)
January 3, 1967	- 8	-12.33	-584	786.41
January 4, 1967	- 2	- 8.00	-586 (L)	791.14
January 5, 1967	+ 8	- 0.66	-578	805.51
January 6, 1967	+10	+ 5.33	-568	808.74
January 9, 1967	+12	+10.00	-556	813.47
January 10, 1967	+ 9	+10.33	-547	814.14
January 11, 1967	+16	+12.33	-531	822.49
January 12, 1967	+20 (H)	+15.00	-511	829.95
January 13, 1967	+15	+17.00 (H)	-496	835.13
January 16, 1967	+ 7	+14.00	-489	833.24
January 17, 1967	+16	+12.66	-473	843.65
January 18, 1967	+10	+11.00	-463	847.49
January 19, 1967	+ 4	+10.00	-459	846.44
January 20, 1967	+ 4	+ 6.00	-455	847.16
January 23, 1967	+ 7	+ 5.00	-448	847.72
January 24, 1967	+ 1	+ 4.00	-447	847.72
January 25, 1967	- 5	+ 1.00	-452	840.59
January 26, 1967	- 2	- 2.00	-454	838.70
January 27, 1967	+ 5	- 0.66	-449	844.04
January 30, 1967	+ 6	+ 3.00	-443	848.11
January 31, 1967	+ 6	+ 5.66	-437	849.89
February 1, 1967	- 1	+ 3.66	-438	848.39
February 2, 1967	+ 9	+ 4.66	-429	853.12
February 3, 1967	+13	+ 7.00	-416	857.46
February 6, 1967	+ 6	+ 9.33	-410	855.12
February 7, 1967	+ 1	+ 6.66	-409	852.51
February 8, 1967	+11	+ 6.00	-398	860.97 (H)
February 9, 1967	+ 6	+ 6.00	-392	857.52
February 10, 1967	+ 2	+ 6.33	-390	855.73

Date	Climax Indicator	3-day Moving Average	CLX Cumulative	Dow
February 13, 1967	0	+ 2.66	-390	853.34
February 14, 1967	+10	+ 4.00	-380	856.90
February 15, 1967	+ 5	+ 5.00	-375 (H)	855.79
February 16, 1967	4	+ 3.66	-379	851.56
February 17, 1967	- 4	- 1.00	-383	850.84
February 20, 1967	- 5	- 4.33	-388	847.88
February 21, 1967	- 5	- 4.66	-393	844.10
February 23, 1967	- 4	- 4.66	-397	846.77
February 24, 1967	- 4	- 4.33	-401	847.33
February 27, 1967	-15 (L)	- 7.66	-416	836.64 (L)
February 28, 1967	- 8	- 9.00 (L)	-424	839.37
March 1, 1967	0	- 7.66	-424	843.49
March 2, 1967	+ 7	- 0.33	-417	846.71
March 3, 1967	+ 2	+ 3.00	-415	846.60
March 6, 1967	- 2	+ 2.33	-417	842.20
March 7, 1967	- 4	- 1.33	-421	841.76
March 8, 1967	- 4	- 3.33	-425	843.32
March 9, 1967	- 5	- 4.33	-430	844.15
March 10, 1967	+ 3	- 2.00	-427	848.50
March 13, 1967	- 3	- 1.66	-430	844.82
March 14, 1967	+ 1	+ 0.33	-429	844.27
March 15, 1967	+ 9	+ 2.33	-420	854.06
March 16, 1967	+24 (H)	+11.33	-396	868.49
March 17, 1967	+10	+14.33 (H)	-386	869.77
March 20, 1967	+ 6	+13.33	-380	870.43
March 21, 1967	- 3	+ 4.33	-383	866.59
March 22, 1967	+ 4	+ 2.33	-379	870.55
March 23, 1967	+12	+ 4.33	-367	876.67
March 27, 1967	+ 2	+ 6.00	-365	873.72
March 28, 1967	+ 1	+ 5.00	-364	875.28
March 29, 1967	- 5	- 0.66	-369	871.10
March 30, 1967	- 8	- 4.00	-377	869.99
March 31, 1967	-12	- 8.33	-389	865.98
April 3, 1967	-11	-10.33	-400	859.97
April 4, 1967	- 9	-10.66	-409	859.19
April 5, 1967	- 5	- 8.33	-414	861.19
April 6, 1967	- 7	- 7.00	-421	861.25
April 7, 1967	-12	- 8.00	-433	853.34
April 10, 1967	-21 (L)	-13.33 (L)	-454	842.43
April 11, 1967	- 6	-13.00	-460	847.66
April 12, 1967	- 8	-11.66	-468	844.65
April 13, 1967	0	- 4.66	-468 (L)	848.83
April 14, 1967	+ 8	.00	-460	859.74
April 17, 1967	+12	+ 6.66	-448	866.59
April 18, 1967	+13 (H)	+11.00	-435	873.00
April 19, 1967	+ 9	+11.33 (H)	-426	873.94
April 20, 1967	+ 6	+ 9.33	-420	878.62
April 21, 1967	+ 8	+ 7.66	-412	883.18
April 24, 1967	+10	+ 8.00	-402	887.53
April 25, 1967	+ 9	+ 9.00	-393	891.20
April 26, 1967	+ 6	+ 8.33	-387	889.03
April 27, 1967	+10	+ 8.33	-377	894.82

Date	Climax Indicator	3-day Moving Average	CLX Cumulative	Dow
April	28, 1967	+10	+ 8.66	-367	897.05
May	1, 1967	- 1	+ 6.33	-368	892.95
May	2, 1967	- 1	+ 2.66	-369	891.65
May	3, 1967	+ 3	+ 0.33	-366	896.77
May	4, 1967	+ 9	+ 3.66	-357	901.95
May	5, 1967	+11	+ 7.66	-346	905.96
May	8, 1967	+13 (H)	+11.00	-333 (H)	909.63 (H)
May	9, 1967	- 2	+ 7.33	-335	899.89
May	10, 1967	- 5	+ 2.00	-340	894.10
May	11, 1967	- 5	- 4.00	-345	896.21
May	12, 1967	-13	- 7.66	-358	890.03
May	15, 1967	-13	-10.33	-371	882.41
May	16, 1967	- 2	- 9.33	-373	885.79
May	17, 1967	- 9	- 8.00	-382	882.23
May	18, 1967	- 7	- 6.00	-389	877.34
May	19, 1967	-15	-10.33	-404	874.55
May	22, 1967	-14	-12.00 (H)	-418	871.05
May	23, 1967	- 2	-10.33	-420	868.71
May	24, 1967	- 9	- 8.33	-429	862.41
May	25, 1967	0	- 3.66	-429	870.71
May	26, 1967	- 2	- 3.66	-431	870.32
May	29, 1967	- 6	- 2.66	-437	864.97
May	31, 1967	-21 (L)	- 9.66	-458	852.55
June	1, 1967	+ 5	- 7.33	-453	864.98
June	2, 1967	+ 2	- 4.66	-451	863.31
June	5, 1967	-15	- 2.66	-466	847.77 (L)
June	6, 1967	+ 4	- 3.00	-462	862.71
June	7, 1967	+ 9	- 0.66	-453	869.19
June	8, 1967	+ 9	+ 7.33	-444	873.20
June	9, 1967	+ 8	+ 8.66	-436	874.89
June	12, 1967	+ 6	+ 7.66	-430	878.93
June	13, 1967	+ 5	+ 6.33	-425	886.15 (H)
June	14, 1967	- 3	+ 2.66	-428	880.61
June	15, 1967	+ 6	+ 2.66	-422	883.26
June	16, 1967	+ 6	+ 3.00	-416	885.00
June	19, 1967	0	+ 4.00	-416	884.54
June	20, 1967	+ 1	+ 2.33	-415	880.61
June	21, 1967	- 7	- 2.00	-422	877.66
June	22, 1967	- 8	- 4.66	-430	875.69
June	23, 1967	- 4	- 6.33	-434	877.37
June	26, 1967	-10	- 7.33	-444	872.11
June	27, 1967	-11	- 8.33	-455	869.39
June	28, 1967	-10	-10.33	-465	868.87
June	29, 1967	-12	-11.00 (L)	-477	861.94
June	30, 1967	- 7	- 9.66	-484	860.26
July	3, 1967	- 3	- 7.33	-487 (L)	859.69 (L)
July	5, 1967	+ 2	- 2.66	-485	864.94
July	6, 1967	- 2	- 1.00	-487	864.02
July	7, 1967	+ 6	+ 2.00	-481	869.05
July	10, 1967	+12	+ 5.33	-469	875.52
July	11, 1967	+10	+ 9.33	-459	879.45

Date	Climax Indicator	3-day Moving Average	CLX Cumulative	Dow
July 12, 1967	+ 2	+ 8.00	-457	878.70
July 13, 1967	+ 1	+ 4.33	-456	878.53
July 14, 1967	+ 4	+ 2.33	-452	882.05
July 17, 1967	+ 3	+ 2.66	-449	882.74
July 18, 1967	+11	+ 6.00	-438	896.09
July 19, 1967	+14 (H)	+ 9.33	-424	903.32
July 20, 1967	+12	+12.33 (H)	-412	908.69
July 21, 1967	+10	+12.00	-402	909.56
July 24, 1967	+ 1	+ 7.66	-401	904.53
July 25, 1967	- 1	+ 3.33	-402	901.29
July 26, 1967	+ 3	+ 1.00	-399	903.14
July 27, 1967	- 3	- 0.33	-402	903.14
July 28, 1967	0	.00	-402	901.53
July 31, 1967	+ 1	- 0.66	-401	904.24
August 1, 1967	+ 9	+ 3.33	-392	912.97
August 2, 1967	+14 (H)	+ 8.00	-378	922.27
August 3, 1967	+ 6	+ 9.66	-372	921.98
August 4, 1967	+ 6	+ 8.66	-366	923.77
August 7, 1967	0	+ 4.00	-366	920.37
August 8, 1967	+ 3	+ 3.00	-363	922.45
August 9, 1967	+ 6	+ 3.00	-357	926.72 (H)
August 10, 1967	+ 5	+ 4.66	-352 (H)	925.22
August 11, 1967	- 1	+ 3.33	-353	920.65
August 14, 1967	- 2	+ 0.66	-355	916.32
August 15, 1967	- 3	- 2.00	-358	919.15
August 16, 1967	- 8	- 4.33	-366	915.68
August 17, 1967	+ 2	- 3.00	-364	918.23
August 18, 1967	0	- 2.00	-364	919.04
August 21, 1967	- 9	- 2.33	-373	912.27
August 22, 1967	-14	- 7.66	-387	907.48
August 23, 1967	-14	-12.33	-401	905.11
August 24, 1967	-20	-16.00	-421	898.46
August 25, 1967	-20 (L)	-18.00 (L)	-441	894.07
August 28, 1967	-13	-17.66	-454	894.71
August 29, 1967	-13	-15.33	-467	894.76
August 30, 1967	- 6	-10.66	-473 (L)	893.72 (L)
August 31, 1967	+ 6	- 4.33	-467	901.29
September 1, 1967	+ 3	+ 1.00	-464	901.18
September 5, 1967	+ 5	+ 4.66	-459	904.13
September 6, 1967	+ 6	+ 4.66	-453	906.96
September 7, 1967	- 2	+ 3.00	-455	908.17
September 8, 1967	0	+ 1.33	-455	907.54
September 11, 1967	- 1	- 1.00	-456	909.62
September 12, 1967	+ 4	+ 1.00	-452	911.75
September 13, 1967	+13	+ 5.33	-439	923.77
September 14, 1967	+13	+10.00	-426	929.44
September 15, 1967	+ 8	+11.33	-418	933.48
September 18, 1967	+14 (H)	+11.66 (H)	-404	938.74
September 19, 1967	+ 1	+ 7.66	-403	930.07
September 20, 1967	0	+ 5.00	-403	929.79
September 21, 1967	+ 1	+ 0.66	-402	930.40

Date	Climax Indicator	3-day Moving Average	CLX Cumulative	Dow
September 22, 1967	+ 2	+ 1.00	-400	934.35
September 25, 1967	+ 8	+ 3.66	-392	943.08 (H)
September 26, 1967	- 6	+ 1.33	-398	937.19
September 27, 1967	-10	- 2.66	-408	933.14
September 28, 1967	-11	- 9.00	-417	929.38
September 29, 1967	-10	-10.33	-427	926.66
October 2, 1967	-12	-11.00 (L)	-439	921.00
October 3, 1967	- 3	- 8.33	-442	924.47
October 4, 1967	- 3	- 6.00	-445	921.29
October 5, 1967	+ 4	- 0.66	-441	927.13
October 6, 1967	+ 5	+ 2.00	-436	928.74
October 9, 1967	+ 4	+ 4.33	-432	933.31
October 10, 1967	- 3	+ 2.00	-435	926.61
October 11, 1967	- 7	- 2.00	-442	920.25
October 12, 1967	- 8	- 6.00	-450	913.20
October 13, 1967	- 6	- 7.00	-456	918.17
October 16, 1967	- 9	- 7.66	-465	908.42
October 17, 1967	- 9	- 8.00	-474	904.36
October 18, 1967	- 6	- 8.00	-480	903.49
October 19, 1967	- 5	- 6.66	-485	903.72
October 20, 1967	- 6	- 5.66	-491	896.73
October 23, 1967	- 7	- 6.00	-498	894.65
October 24, 1967	-15	- 9.33	-513	888.18
October 25, 1967	-12	-11.33 (L)	-525	886.73
October 26, 1967	- 3	-10.00	-528	890.89
October 27, 1967	- 8	- 7.66	-536	888.18
October 30, 1967	- 7	- 6.00	-543	886.62
October 31, 1967	- 9	- 8.00	-552	879.74
November 1, 1967	-14	-10.00	-556	867.08
November 2, 1967	-13	-12.00	-579	864.83
November 3, 1967	-20 (L)	-15.66	-599	856.62
November 6, 1967	-14	-15.66	-613	855.29
November 8, 1967	-18	-17.33 (L)	-631	849.57 (L)
November 9, 1967	- 6	-12.66	-637 (L)	856.97
November 10, 1967	+ 5	- 6.33	-632	862.81
November 13, 1967	+ 4	+ 1.00	-628	859.75
November 14, 1967	- 3	+ 2.00	-631	852.40
November 15, 1967	+ 3	+ 1.33	-628	855.18
November 16, 1967	+ 3	+ 1.00	-625	859.74
November 17, 1967	+ 3	+ 3.00	-622	862.11
November 20, 1967	- 7	- 0.33	-629	857.78
November 21, 1967	+ 2	- 0.66	-627	870.95
November 22, 1967	+ 5	.00	-622	874.02
November 24, 1967	+ 1	+ 2.66	-621	877.60
November 27, 1967	+ 1	+ 2.33	-620	882.11
November 28, 1967	0	+ 0.66	-620	884.88
November 29, 1967	+ 2	+ 1.00	-618	883.15
November 30, 1967	0	+ 0.66	-618	875.81
December 1, 1967	+ 3	+ 1.66	-615	879.16
December 4, 1967	+ 6	+ 3.00	-609	883.50
December 5, 1967	+ 6	+ 5.00	-603	888.12

Date	Climax Indicator	3-day Moving Average	CLX Cumulative	Dow
December 6, 1967	+ 9	+ 7.00	-594	892.28
December 7, 1967	+ 5	+ 6.66	-589	892.22
December 8, 1967	- 4	+ 3.33	-593	887.25
December 11, 1967	- 5	- 1.33	-598	882.05
December 12, 1967	- 3	- 4.00	-601	881.30
December 13, 1967	- 3	- 3.66	-604	882.34
December 14, 1967	- 8	- 4.66	-612	883.44
December 15, 1967	- 7	- 6.00	-619	880.61
December 18, 1967	- 7	- 7.33	-626	881.65
December 19, 1967	- 6	- 6.66	-632	881.36
December 20, 1967	+ 1	- 4.00	-631	886.90
December 21, 1967	+ 4	- 0.33	-627	888.35
December 22, 1967	+ 3	+ 2.66	-624	887.37
December 26, 1967	+ 5	+ 4.00	-619	888.12
December 27, 1967	+11	+ 6.33	-608	894.94
December 28, 1967	+10	+ 8.66	-598	897.83
December 29, 1967	+13 (H)	+11.33 (H)	-585	905.11
January 2, 1968	+10	+11.00	-575	906.84
January 3, 1968	+ 6	+ 9.66	-569	904.13
January 4, 1968	- 1	+ 5.00	-570	899.39
January 5, 1968	+ 4	+ 3.00	-566	901.24
January 8, 1968	+11	+ 4.66	-555	908.92 (H)
January 9, 1968	+ 3	+ 6.00	-552	908.29
January 10, 1968	+ 1	+ 5.00	-551 (H)	903.67
January 11, 1968	- 1	+ 1.00	-552	899.79
January 12, 1968	- 2	- 0.66	-554	898.98
January 15, 1968	- 7	- 3.33	-561	892.74
January 16, 1968	-11	- 6.66	-572	887.14
January 17, 1968	-13	-10.33	-585	883.79
January 18, 1968	-11	-11.66	-596	882.80
January 19, 1968	-15	-13.00	-611	880.32
January 22, 1968	-19 (L)	-15.00	-630	871.71
January 23, 1968	-18	-17.33 (L)	-648	864.77
January 24, 1968	-13	-16.66	-661	862.23
January 25, 1968	- 7	-12.66	-668	864.25
January 26, 1968	- 4	- 8.00	-672	865.06
January 29, 1968	- 5	- 5.33	-677	863.67
January 30, 1968	- 8	- 5.66	-685	859.57
January 31, 1968	- 7	- 6.66	-692	855.47
February 1, 1968	+ 3	- 4.00	-689	861.36
February 2, 1968	+ 2	- 0.66	-687	863.56
February 5, 1968	- 3	+ 0.66	-690	861.13
February 6, 1968	- 1	- 0.66	-691	861.25
February 7, 1968	- 3	- 2.33	-694	859.92
February 8, 1968	-11	- 5.00	-705	850.23
February 9, 1968	-18	-10.66	-723	840.03
February 13, 1968	-18	-15.66	-741	831.76
February 14, 1968	- 6	-14.00	-747	837.37
February 15, 1968	- 1	- 8.33	-748	839.22
February 16, 1968	- 8	- 5.00	-756	836.50
February 19, 1968	0	- 3.00	-756	839.11

Date	Climax Indicator	3-day Moving Average	CLX Cumulative	Dow
February 20, 1968	+ 6	- 0.66	-750	843.10
February 21, 1968	+13	+ 6.33	-737	849.23
February 23, 1968	+ 6	+ 8.33	-731	849.81
February 26, 1968	+ 4	+ 7.66	-727	841.78
February 27, 1968	+ 5	+ 5.00	-722	846.68
February 28, 1968	- 2	+ 2.33	-724	844.72
February 29, 1968	- 9	- 2.00	-733	840.50
March 1, 1968	- 8	- 6.33	-741	840.44
March 4, 1968	-16	-11.00	-757	830.56
March 5, 1968	-19	-14.33	-776	827.03
March 6, 1968	0	-11.66	-776	837.21
March 7, 1968	+ 1	- 6.00	-775	836.22
March 8, 1968	+ 2	+ 1.00	-773	835.24
March 11, 1968	+13	+ 5.33	-760	842.98
March 12, 1968	+ 2	+ 5.66	-758	843.22
March 13, 1968	0	+ 5.00	-758	842.23
March 14, 1968	-16	- 4.66	-774	830.91
March 15, 1968	- 2	- 6.00	-776	837.55
March 18, 1968	+ 1	- 5.66	-775	840.09
March 19, 1968	- 8	- 3.00	-783	832.99
March 20, 1968	- 8	- 5.00	-791	830.85
March 21, 1968	-21 (L)	-12.33	-812	825.13 (L)
March 22, 1968	- 6	-11.66	-818	826.05
March 25, 1968	- 5	-10.66	-823	827.26
March 26, 1968	- 4	- 5.00	-827 (L)	831.54
March 27, 1968	+ 5	- 1.33	-822	836.57
March 28, 1968	0	+ 0.33	-822	835.12
March 29, 1968	+ 8	+ 4.33	-814	841.09
April 1, 1968	+19 (H)	+ 5.66	-795	861.25
April 2, 1968	+10	+12.33	-785	863.97
April 3, 1968	+15	+14.66 (H)	-770	869.11
April 4, 1968	+ 9	+11.33	-761	872.52
April 5, 1968	- 2	+ 7.33	-763	865.81
April 8, 1968	+11	+ 6.00	-752	884.42
April 10, 1968	+ 5	+ 4.66	-747	892.57
April 11, 1968	+13	+ 9.66	-734	905.69
April 15, 1968	+ 7	+ 8.33	-727	910.49
April 16, 1968	+ 6	+ 8.66	-721	907.08
April 17, 1968	+ 6	+ 6.33	-715	908.47
April 18, 1968	+ 6	+ 6.00	-709	909.21
April 19, 1968	- 6	+ 2.00	-715	897.65
April 22, 1968	- 9	- 3.00	-724	891.99
April 23, 1968	+ 1	- 4.66	-723	897.48
April 24, 1968	+ 2	- 2.00	-721	898.46
April 25, 1968	+ 2	+ 1.66	-719	905.57
April 26, 1968	+ 1	+ 1.66	-718	906.03
April 29, 1968	+ 3	+ 2.00	-715	908.34
April 30. 1968	0	+ 1.33	-715	912.22
May 1, 1968	+ 1	+ 1.33	-714	913.20
May 2, 1968	+ 8	+ 3.00	-706	918.05
May 3, 1968	+ 3	+ 4.00	-703	919.21

Date	Climax Indicator	3-day Moving Average	CLX Cumulative	Dow
May	6, 1968	- 1	+ 3.33	-704	914.53
May	7, 1968	+ 6	+ 2.66	-698	919.90 (H)
May	8, 1968	0	+ 1.66	-698	918.86
May	9, 1968	-10	- 1.33	-708	911.35
May	10, 1968	- 1	- 3.66	-709	912.91
May	13, 1968	- 3	- 4.66	-712	909.96
May	14, 1968	- 4	- 2.66	-716	908.05
May	15, 1968	- 2	- 3.00	-718	907.81
May	16, 1968	- 8	- 4.66	-726	903.72
May	17, 1968	- 6	- 5.33	-732	898.98
May	20. 1968	-12	- 8.66	-744	894.18
May	21, 1968	- 4	- 7.33	-748	896.37
May	22, 1968	- 4	- 6.66	-752	896.84
May	23, 1968	- 7	- 5.00	-759	893.20
May	24, 1968	- 3	- 4.66	-762	895.28
May	27, 1968	- 7	- 5.66	-769	891.60 (L)
May	28, 1968	+ 1	- 3.00	-768	896.78
May	29, 1968	- 3	- 3.00	-771	895.33
May	31, 1968	+ 3	+ 0.33	-768	899.12
June	3, 1968	+13	+ 4.33	-755	905.38
June	4, 1968	+16 (H)	+10.66 (H)	-739	916.63
June	5, 1968	0	+ 9.66	-739	907.42
June	6, 1968	+ 5	+ 7.00	-734	910.13
June	7, 1968	+ 7	+ 4.00	-727	914.88
June	10, 1968	+ 2	+ 4.66	-725	913.38
June	11, 1968	+ 4	+ 4.33	-721	917.95
June	13, 1968	- 3	+ 1.00	-724	913.86
June	14, 1968	- 5	- 1.33	-729	913.62
June	17, 1968	-11	- 6.33	-740	903.45
June	18, 1968	- 8	- 8.00	-748	900.20
June	20, 1968	- 7	- 8.66	-755	898.28
June	21, 1968	- 2	- 5.66	-757	901.05
June	24, 1968	- 4	- 4.33	-761	901.83
June	25, 1968	- 4	- 3.33	-765	901.35
June	27, 1968	- 5	- 4.33	-770	898.76
June	28, 1968	- 3	- 4.00	-773	897.80
July	1, 1968	- 4	- 4.00	-777	896.35
July	2, 1968	0	- 2.33	-777	896.84
July	3, 1968	+ 8	+ 1.33	-769	903.52
July	8, 1968	+10	+ 6.00	-759	912.61
July	9, 1968	+13	+10.33	-746	920.49
July	11, 1968	+14	+12.33	-732	922.82
July	12, 1968	+ 9	+12.00	-723	922.46
July	15, 1968	+ 6	+ 9.66	-717	923.72 (H)
July	16, 1968	+ 2	+ 5.66	-715	921.20
July	18, 1968	- 1	+ 2.33	-716	917.95
July	19, 1968	- 3	- 0.66	-719	914.22
July	22, 1968	-10	- 4.66	-729	900.62
July	23, 1968	- 6	- 6.33	-735	898.10
July	25, 1968	-14	-10.00 (L)	-749	885.47
July	26, 1968	- 7	- 9.00	-756	888.47

Date	Climax Indicator	3-day Moving Average	CLX Cumulative	Dow
July 29, 1968	- 8	- 9.66	-764	883.36
July 30, 1968	- 5	- 6.66	-769	883.18
August 1, 1968	-10	- 7.66	-779	878.07
August 2, 1968	-11	- 8.66	-790	870.91
August 5, 1968	- 5	- 8.66	-795	872.53
August 6, 1968	+ 1	- 5.00	-794	877.28
August 8, 1968	- 9	- 4.33	-803	871.02
August 9, 1968	- 5	- 4.33	-808	869.65 (L)
August 12, 1968	+ 8	- 2.00	-800	882,10
August 13, 1968	+ 8	+ 3.66	-792	885.76
August 15, 1968	- 4	+ 4.00	-796	879.51
August 16, 1968	+ 4	+ 2.66	-792	885.89
August 19, 1968	+10	+ 3.33	-782	887.68
August 20, 1968	+ 7	+ 7.00	-775	888.67
August 22, 1968	+ 2	+ 6.33	-773	889.04
August 23, 1968	+ 6	+ 5.00	-767	892.34
August 26, 1968	+ 7	+ 5.00	-760	896.13
August 27, 1968	+ 6	+ 6.33	-754	893.65
August 29, 1968	+ 4	+ 5.66	-750	894.33
August 30, 1968	+ 8	+ 6.00	-742	896.01
September 3, 1968	+11	+ 7.66	-731	900.36
September 4, 1968	+16	+11.66	-715	907.01
September 5, 1968	+17 (H)	+14.66	-698	917.52
September 6, 1968	+13	+15.33 (H)	-685	921.25
September 9, 1968	+14	+14.66	-671	924.98
September 10, 1968	+ 6	+11.00	-665	919.38
September 12, 1968	+ 3	+ 7.66	-662	915.53
September 13, 1968	+ 1	+ 3.33	-661	917.15
September 16, 1968	+ 2	+ 2.00	-659	921.94
September 17, 1968	+ 2	+ 1.66	-657	923.05
September 19, 1968	+ 1	+ 1.66	-656	923.98
September 20, 1968	+ 3	+ 2.00	-653	924.42
September 23, 1968	+11	+ 5.00	-642	930.45
September 24, 1968	+10	+ 8.00	-632	938.28
September 25, 1968	- 2	+ 6.33	-634	933.12
September 27, 1968	+ 2	+ 3.33	-632	933.56
September 30, 1968	+ 1	+ 0.33	-631	935.79
October 1, 1968	+ 6	+ 3.00	-625	942.32
October 3, 1968	+11	+ 6.00	-614	949.47
October 4, 1968	+14 (H)	+10.33	-600	952.95
October 7, 1968	+11	+12.00 (H)	-589	956.68
October 8, 1968	+ 7	+10.66	-582	956.24
October 10, 1968	- 4	+ 4.66	-586	949.78
October 11, 1968	- 3	.00	-589	949.59
October 14, 1968	+ 2	- 1.66	-587	949.06
October 15, 1968	+ 6	+ 1.66	-581	955.31
October 17, 1968	+ 2	+ 3.33	-579	958.91
October 18, 1968	+ 7	+ 5.00	-572	967.49
October 21, 1968	+ 6	+ 5.00	-566	967.49
October 22, 1968	+ 2	+ 5.00	-564	963.14
October 24, 1968	0	+ 2.66	-564	956.68

Date	Climax Indicator	3-day Moving Average	CLX Cumulative	Dow
October 25, 1968	0	+ 0.66	-564	961.28
October 28, 1968	- 4	- 1.33	-568	957.99
October 29, 1968	- 5	- 3.00	-573	951.08
October 31, 1968	+ 2	- 2.33	-571	952.39
November 1, 1968	- 6	- 3.00	-577	948.41
November 4, 1968	- 3	- 2.33	-580	946.23
November 6, 1968	+ 1	- 2.66	-579	949.52
November 7, 1968	+ 1	- 0.33	-578	950.65
November 8, 1968	+12 (H)	+ 4.66	-566	958.98
November 12, 1968	+12	+ 8.33	-554	964.20
November 13, 1968	+ 7	+10.33 (H)	-547	967.43
November 14, 1968	+ 4	+ 7.66	-543	963.89
November 15, 1968	+ 5	+ 5.33	-538	965.88
November 18, 1968	- 1	+ 2.66	-539	963.76
November 19, 1968	0	+ 1.33	-539	966.75
November 21, 1968	- 3	- 1.33	-542	964.69
November 22, 1968	+ 4	+ 0.33	-538	967.06
November 25, 1968	+ 9	+ 3.33	-529	971.35
November 26, 1968	+11 (H)	+ 8.00	-518	979.49
November 27, 1968	+ 2	+ 7.33	-516	976.32
November 29, 1968	+ 8	+ 7.00	-508	985.08
December 2, 1968	+ 6	+ 5.33	-502	983.34
December 3, 1968	+ 1	+ 5.00	-501 (H)	985.21 (H)
December 5, 1968	- 4	+ 1.00	-505	977.69
December 6, 1968	- 3	- 2.00	-508	978.24
December 7, 1968	- 4	- 3.66	-512	979.36
December 10, 1968	- 1	- 2.66	-513	977.67
December 12, 1968	- 3	- 2.66	-516	977.13
December 13, 1968	+ 2	- 0.66	-514	981.98
December 16, 1968	- 2	- 1.00	-516	976.32
December 17, 1968	- 9	- 3.00	-525	970.91
December 19, 1968	0	- 3.66	-525	975.14
December 20, 1968	- 4	- 4.33	-529	967.25
December 23, 1968	-15	- 6.33	-544	953.75
December 24, 1968	-11	-10.00	-555	952.32
December 26, 1968	- 4	-10.00	-559	954.25
December 27, 1968	- 6	- 7.00	-565	952.51
December 30, 1968	-11	- 7.00	-576	945.11
December 31, 1968	-14	-10.33	-590	943.75
January 2, 1969	- 3	- 9.33	-593	947.73
January 3, 1969	+ 4	- 4.33	-589	951.89
January 6, 1969	-13	- 4.00	-602	936.66
January 7, 1969	-20 (L)	- 9.66	-622	925.72
January 8, 1969	-17	-16.66 (L)	-639	921.24 (L)
January 9, 1969	- 3	-13.33	-642	927.46
January 10, 1969	- 4	- 8.00	-646	925.53
January 13, 1969	- 4	- 3.66	-650	923.11
January 14, 1969	+ 5	- 1.00	-645	928.33
January 15, 1969	+ 7	+ 2.66	-638	931.75
January 16, 1969	+ 7	+ 6.33	-631	938.59
January 17, 1969	- 1	+ 4.33	-632	935.54

Date	Climax Indicator	3-day Moving Average	CLX Cumulative	Dow
January 20, 1969	- 1	+ 1.66	-633	931.25
January 21, 1969	- 2	- 1.33	-635	929.82
January 22, 1969	+ 5	+ 0.66	-630	934.17
January 23, 1969	+10	+ 4.33	-620	940.20
January 24, 1969	+ 3	+ 6.00	-617	938.58
January 27, 1969	+ 2	+ 5.00	-615	937.46
January 28, 1969	+ 2	+ 2.33	-613	938.40
January 29, 1969	+ 1	+ 1.66	-612	938.09
January 30, 1969	0	+ 1.00	-612	942.13
January 31, 1969	+ 2	+ 1.00	-610	946.05
February 3, 1969	+ 5	+ 2.33	-605	948.29
February 4, 1969	+ 3	+ 3.33	-602	945.11
February 5, 1969	+ 1	+ 3.00	-601	945.98
February 6, 1969	+ 7	+ 3.66	-594	946.73
February 7, 1969	+ 7	+ 5.00	-587	947.85
February 11, 1969	+10	+ 8.00	-577	948.97
February 12, 1969	+ 6	+ 7.66	-571	948.97
February 13, 1969	+ 4	+ 6.66	-567	952.70 (H)
February 14, 1969	+ 3	+ 4.33	-564	951.95
February 17, 1969	- 7	.00	-571	937.72
February 18, 1969	-12	- 5.33	-583	930.82
February 19, 1969	-16	-11.66	-599	925.10
February 20, 1969	-19	-15.66	-618	916.65
February 24, 1969	-22 (L)	-19.00	-640	903.97
February 25, 1969	-18	-19.66 (L)	-658	899.80 (L)
February 26, 1969	- 6	-15.33	-664	905.77
February 27, 1969	- 8	-10.66	-672 (L)	903.03
February 28, 1969	+ 4	- 3.33	-668	905.21
March 3, 1969	+ 3	- 0.33	-665	907.14
March 4, 1969	+13	+ 6.66	-652	919.51
March 5, 1969	+12	+ 9.33	-640	923.11
March 6, 1969	+ 2	+ 9.00	-638	913.54
March 7, 1969	- 2	+ 4.00	-640	911.18
March 10, 1969	+ 4	+ 1.33	-636	917.14
March 11, 1969	+ 5	+ 2.33	-631	920.94
March 12, 1969	+ 1	+ 3.33	-630	917.52
March 13, 1969	- 9	- 1.00	-639	907.14
March 14, 1969	- 8	- 5.33	-647	904.28
March 17, 1969	- 7	- 8.00	-654	904.03
March 18, 1969	0	- 5.00	-654	907.38
March 19, 1969	+ 4	- 1.00	-650	912.11
March 20, 1969	+ 8	+ 4.00	-642	920.13
March 21, 1969	+ 4	+ 5.33	-638	920.00
March 24, 1969	0	+ 4.00	-638	917.08
March 25, 1969	+ 1	+ 1.66	-637	917.08
March 26, 1969	+ 8	+ 3.00	-629	923.30
March 27, 1969	+11	+ 6.66	-618	930.88
March 28, 1969	+12	+10.33	-606	935.48
April 1, 1969	+ 4	+ 9.00	-602	933.08
April 2, 1969	+ 2	+ 6.00	-600	930.92
April 3, 1969	0	+ 2.00	-600	927.30

Date		Climax Indicator	3-day Moving Average	CLX Cumulative	Dow
April	7, 1969	-12	- 3.33	-612	918.78
April	8, 1969	0	- 4.00	-612	923.17
April	9, 1969	+ 2	- 3.33	-610	929.25
April	10, 1969	- 1	+ 0.33	-611	932.89
April	11, 1969	+ 2	+ 1.00	-609	933.46
April	14, 1969	+ 3	+ 1.33	-606	932.63
April	15, 1969	+ 3	+ 2.66	-603	931.94
April	16, 1969	-11	- 1.66	-614	923.49
April	17, 1969	- 3	- 3.66	-617	924.12
April	18, 1969	+ 4	- 3.33	-613	924.82
April	21, 1969	- 7	- 2.00	-620	917.51
April	22, 1969	- 5	- 2.66	-625	918.59
April	23, 1969	- 6	- 6.00	-631	917.64
April	24, 1969	- 4	- 5.00	-635	921.20
April	25, 1969	+ 2	- 2.66	-633	924.00
April	28, 1969	+ 1	- 0.33	-632	925.08
April	29, 1969	+10	+ 4.33	-622	934.10
April	30, 1969	+18 (H)	+ 9.66	-604	950.18
May	1, 1969	+13	+13.66	-591	949.22
May	2, 1969	+17	+16.00 (H)	-574	957.17
May	5, 1969	+10	+13.33	-564	958.95
May	6, 1969	+10	+12.33	-554	962.06
May	7, 1969	+ 5	+ 8.33	-549	959.60
May	8, 1969	+ 3	+ 6.00	-546	963.68
May	9, 1969	- 5	+ 1.00	-551	961.61
May	12, 1969	- 9	- 3.66	-560	957.86
May	13, 1969	+ 5	- 3.00	-555	962.97
May	14, 1969	+10	+ 2.00	-545	968.85 (H)
May	15, 1969	- 1	+ 4.66	-546	965.16
May	16, 1969	+ 2	+ 3.66	-544 (H)	967.30
May	19, 1969	-11	- 3.33	-555	959.02
May	20, 1969	-15	- 8.00	-570	949.26
May	21, 1969	- 1	- 9.00	-571	951.78
May	22, 1969	- 5	- 7.00	-576	950.10
May	23, 1969	- 3	- 3.00	-579	947.51
May	26, 1969	- 4	- 4.00	-583	946.94
May	27, 1969	-11	- 6.00	-594	938.66
May	28, 1969	-10	- 8.33	-604	936.92
May	29, 1969	- 2	- 7.66	-606	937.56
June	2, 1969	-13	- 8.33	-619	933.17
June	3, 1969	- 9	- 8.00	-628	930.78
June	4, 1969	-10	-10.66	-638	928.84
June	5, 1969	- 2	- 7.00	-640	930.71
June	6, 1969	- 9	- 7.00	-649	924.77
June	9, 1969	-12	- 7.66	-661	918.05
June	10, 1969	-16	-12.33	-677	912.49
June	11, 1969	-19	-15.66	-696	904.60
June	12, 1969	-25 (L)	-20.00 (L)	-721	892.58
June	13, 1969	-13	-19.00	-734	894.84
June	16, 1969	-10	-16.00	-744	891.16
June	17, 1969	-17	-13.33	-761	885.73

Date	Climax Indicator	3-day Moving Average	CLX Cumulative	Dow
June 18, 1969	- 8	-11.66	-769	887.09
June 19, 1969	-14	-13.00	-783	882.37
June 20, 1969	-14	-12.00	-797	876.16
June 23, 1969	-14	-14.00	-811	870.86
June 24, 1969	- 4	-10.66	-815	877.20
June 25, 1969	-11	- 9.66	-826	874.10
June 26, 1969	-11	- 8.66	-837	870.28
June 27, 1969	- 8	-10.00	-845	869.76
June 30, 1969	0	- 6.33	-845	873.19
July 1, 1969	+ 6	- 0.66	-839	875.90
July 2, 1969	+ 9	+ 5.00	-830	880.69
July 3, 1969	+10	+ 8.33	-820	886.12
July 7, 1969	- 2	+ 5.66	-822	883.21
July 8, 1969	-10	- 0.66	-832	870.35
July 9, 1969	-15	- 9.00	-847	861.62
July 10, 1969	-23 (L)	-16.00	-870	847.79
July 11, 1969	- 7	-15.00	-877	852.25
July 14, 1969	-12	-14.00	-889	843.14
July 15, 1969	-12	-10.33	-901	841.13
July 16, 1969	0	- 8.00	-901	849.34
July 17, 1969	+ 5	- 2.33	-896	853.09
July 18, 1969	- 2	+ 1.00	-898	845.92
July 22, 1969	-12	- 3.00	-910	834.02
July 23, 1969	-15	- 9.66	-925	827.95
July 24, 1969	-11	-12.66	-936	826.53
July 25, 1969	-14	-13.33	-950	818.06
July 28, 1969	-22 (L)	-15.66	-972	806.23
July 29, 1969	-17	-17.66 (L)	-989	801.96 (L)
July 30, 1969	- 9	-16.00	-998	803.58
July 31, 1969	+ 2	- 8.00	-996	815.47
August 1, 1969	+ 5	- 0.66	-991	826.59
August 4, 1969	+ 4	+ 3.66	-987	822.58
August 5, 1969	- 1	+ 2.66	-988	821.23
August 6, 1969	+ 9	+ 4.00	-979	825.88
August 7, 1969	+ 7	+ 5.00	-972	826.27
August 8, 1969	+ 4	+ 6.66	-968	824.46
August 11, 1969	- 4	+ 2.33	-972	819.83
August 12, 1969	-10	- 3.33	-982	812.96
August 13, 1969	-16	-10.00	-998	809.13
August 14, 1969	- 1	- 9.00	-999	813.23
August 15, 1969	+10	- 2.33	-989	820.88
August 18, 1969	+10	+ 6.33	-979	827.68
August 19, 1969	+13 (H)	+11.00 (H)	-966	833.69
August 20, 1969	+ 5	+ 9.33	-961	833.22
August 21, 1969	+ 8	+ 8.66	-953	834.87
August 22, 1969	+ 5	+ 6.00	-948	837.25
August 25, 1969	- 6	+ 2.33	-954	831.44
August 26, 1969	- 8	- 3.00	-962	823.52
August 27, 1969	- 6	- 6.66	-968	824.78
August 28, 1969	- 1	- 5.00	-969	828.41
August 29, 1969	+ 9	+ 0.66	-960	836.72

Date	Climax Indicator	3-day Moving Average	CLX Cumulative	Dow
September 2, 1969	+ 3	+ 3.66	-957	837.71 (H)
September 3, 1969	+ 1	+ 4.33	-956	835.60
September 4, 1969	- 9	- 1.66	-965	825.30
September 5, 1969	-14	- 7.33	-979	819.50
September 8, 1969	-21 (L)	-14.66 (L)	-1000	811.84
September 9, 1969	- 8	-14.33	-1008	815.67
September 10, 1969	+ 3	- 8.66	-1005	828.01
September 11, 1969	+ 4	- 0.33	-1001	825.77
September 12, 1969	+ 3	+ 3.33	-998	824.25
September 15, 1969	+ 3	+ 3.33	-995	830.45
September 16, 1969	+ 5	+ 3.66	-990	831.64
September 17, 1969	- 3	+ 1.66	-993	826.56
September 18, 1969	+ 3	+ 1.66	-990	831.57
September 19, 1969	+ 5	+ 1.66	-985	830.39
September 22, 1969	+ 2	+ 3.33	-983	831.77
September 23, 1969	+ 2	+ 3.00	-981	834.81
September 24, 1969	+ 1	+ 1.66	-980	834.68
September 25, 1969	- 8	- 1.66	-988	829.92
September 26, 1969	-12	- 6.33	-1000	824.18
September 29, 1969	-14	-11.33	-1014	818.04
September 30, 1969	-16	-14.00	-1030	813.09
October 1, 1969	-17	-15.66 (L)	-1047	806.89
October 2, 1969	- 2	-11.66	-1049	811.84
October 3, 1969	-11	-10.00	-1060	808.41
October 6, 1969	- 7	- 6.66	-1067	809.40
October 7, 1969	- 5	- 7.66	-1072	806.23
October 8, 1969	-12	- 8.00	-1084	802.20 (L)
October 9, 1969	- 8	- 8.33	-1092	803.79
October 10, 1969	- 4	- 8.00	-1096 (L)	806.96
October 13, 1969	+ 6	- 2.00	-1090	819.30
October 14, 1969	+18 (H)	+ 6.66	-1072	832.43
October 15, 1969	+12	+12.00	-1060	830.06
October 16, 1969	+18 (H)	+16.00 (H)	-1042	838.77
October 17, 1969	+ 3	+11.00	-1039	836.06
October 20, 1969	+ 6	+ 9.00	-1033	839.23
October 21, 1969	+11	+ 6.66	-1022	846.89
October 22, 1969	+18 (H)	+11.66	-1004	860.36
October 23, 1969	+ 4	+11.00	-1000	855.73
October 24, 1969	+ 7	+ 9.66	-993	862.26
October 27, 1969	- 1	+ 3.33	-994	860.28
October 28, 1969	- 5	+ 0.33	-999	855.06
October 29, 1969	- 6	- 4.00	-1005	848.34
October 30, 1969	- 2	- 4.33	-1007	850.51
October 31, 1969	+ 4	- 1.33	-1003	855.99
November 3, 1969	+ 3	+ 1.66	-1000	854.54
November 4, 1969	+ 1	+ 2,66	-999	853.48
November 5, 1969	0	+ 1.33	-999	854.08
November 6, 1969	- 1	.00	-1000	855.20
November 7, 1969	+ 5	+ 1.33	-995	860.48
November 10, 1969	+ 1	+ 1.66	-994	863.05 (H)
November 11, 1969	0	+ 2.00	-994 (H)	859.75

Date	Climax Indicator	3-day Moving Average	CLX Cumulative	Dow
November 12, 1969	- 5	- 1.33	-999	855.99
November 13, 1969	- 8	- 4.33	-1007	849.85
November 14, 1969	- 4	- 5.66	-1011	849.26
November 17, 1969	-11	- 7.66	-1022	842.53
November 18, 1969	- 3	- 6.00	-1025	845.17
November 19, 1969	-11	- 8.33	-1036	839.96
November 20, 1969	-18	-10.66	-1054	831.38
November 21, 1969	-19	-16.00	-1073	823.13
November 24, 1969	-21	-19.33	-1094	812.90
November 25, 1969	-24 (L)	-21.33	-1118	807.29
November 26, 1969	-12	-19.00	-1130	810.52
November 28, 1969	-11	-15.66	-1141	812.30
December 1, 1969	-14	-12.33	-1155	805.04
December 2, 1969	-15	-13.33	-1170	801.35
December 3, 1969	-20	-16.33	-1190	793.36
December 4, 1969	- 8	-14.33	-1198	796.53
December 5, 1969	- 5	-11.00	-1203	793.03
December 8, 1969	-11	- 8.00	-1214	785.04
December 9, 1969	-10	- 8.66	-1224	783.79
December 10, 1969	- 6	- 9.00	-1230	783.99
December 11, 1969	- 7	- 7.66	-1237	783.53
December 12, 1969	+ 1	- 4.00	-1236	786.69
December 15, 1969	- 8	- 4.66	-1244	784.04
December 16, 1969	-14	- 7.00	-1258	773.82
December 17, 1969	-11	-11.00	-1269 (L)	769.92 (L)
December 18, 1969	+ 5	- 6.66	-1264	783.78
December 19, 1969	+ 7	+ 0.33	-1257	789.85
December 22, 1969	- 3	+ 3.00	-1260	785.97
December 23, 1969	- 2	+ 0.66	-1262	783.79
December 24, 1969	+ 6	+ 0.33	-1256	794.15
December 26, 1969	+ 7	+ 3.66	-1249	797.65
December 28, 1969	- 7	+ 2.00	-1256	792.37
December 30, 1969	+ 5	+ 1.66	-1251	794.68
December 31, 1969	+13 (H)	+ 3.33	-1238	800.36
January 2, 1970	+13	+10.33	-1225	809.20
January 5, 1970	+ 9	+11.66 (H)	-1216 (H)	811.31 (H)
January 6, 1970	- 2	+ 6.66	-1218	803.66
January 7, 1970	- 4	+ 1.00	-1222	801.81
January 8, 1970	- 2	- 2.66	-1224	802.07
January 9, 1970	- 8	- 4.66	-1232	798.11
January 12, 1970	-13	- 7.66	-1245	790.52
January 13, 1970	-15	-12.00	-1260	788.01
January 14, 1970	-10	-12.66	-1270	787.16
January 15, 1970	- 9	-11.33	-1279	785.05
January 16, 1970	- 8	- 9.00	-1287	782.60
January 19, 1970	-10	- 9.00	-1297	776.07
January 20, 1970	- 5	- 7.66	-1302	777.85
January 21, 1970	0	- 5.00	-1302	782.27
January 22, 1970	+ 1	- 1.33	-1301	786.10
January 23, 1970	-12	- 3.66	-1313	775.54
January 26, 1970	-17	- 9.33	-1330	769.88

Date	Climax Indicator	3-day Moving Average	CLX Cumulative	Dow
January 27, 1970	-17	-15.33	-1347	763.99
January 28, 1970	-16	-16.66	-1363	758.84
January 29, 1970	-23 (L)	-18.66 (L)	-1386	748.35
January 30, 1970	-14	-17.66	-1400	744.06 (L)
February 2, 1970	0	-12.33	-1400 (L)	746.44
February 3, 1970	+ 6	- 2.66	-1394	757.46
February 4, 1970	- 1	+ 1.66	-1395	754.42
February 5, 1970	- 3	+ 0.66	-1398	750.26
February 6, 1970	+ 1	- 1.00	-1397	752.77
February 9, 1970	+ 7	+ 1.66	-1390	755.68
February 10, 1970	- 8	.00	-1398	746.63
February 11, 1970	+10	+ 3.00	-1388	757.33
February 12, 1970	+ 5	+ 2.33	-1383	755.61
February 13, 1970	- 2	+ 4.33	-1385	753.30
February 16, 1970	+ 3	+ 2.00	-1382	753.70
February 17, 1970	- 4	- 1.00	-1386	747.43
February 18, 1970	+13	+ 4.00	-1373	756.80
February 19, 1970	+ 5	+ 4.66	-1368	757.92
February 20, 1970	+ 5	+ 7.66	-1363	757.46
February 24, 1970	+ 2	+ 4.00	-1361	754.42
February 25, 1970	+15	+ 7.33	-1346	768.28
February 26, 1970	+ 1	+ 6.00	-1345	764.45
February 27, 1970	+12	+ 9.33	-1333	777.59
March 2, 1970	+14	+ 9.00	-1319	780.23
March 3, 1970	+16 (H)	+14.00 (H)	-1303	787.42
March 4, 1970	+ 6	+12.00	-1297	788.21
March 5, 1970	+ 6	+ 9.33	-1291 (H)	787.55 (H)
March 6, 1970	- 1	+ 3.66	-1292	784.12
March 9, 1970	-10	- 1.66	-1302	778.31
March 10, 1970	- 4	- 5.00	-1306	779.70
March 11, 1970	- 9	- 7.66	-1315	778.12
March 12, 1970	- 8	- 7.00	-1323	776.47
March 13, 1970	- 7	- 8.00	-1330	772.11
March 16, 1970	-16 (L)	-10.33 (L)	-1346	765.05
March 17, 1970	- 8	-10.33	-1354	767.42
March 18, 1970	- 4	- 9.33	-1358	767.95
March 19, 1970	- 7	- 6.33	-1365	764.98
March 20, 1970	- 8	- 6.33	-1373	763.66
March 23, 1970	- 6	- 7.00	-1379	763.60 (L)
March 24, 1970	+10	- 1.33	-1369	773.76
March 25, 1970	+22 (H)	+ 8.66	-1347	790.13
March 26, 1970	+16	+16.00 (H)	-1331	791.05
March 30, 1970	+ 3	+13.66	-1328	784.65
March 31, 1970	- 1	+ 6.00	-1329	785.57
April 1, 1970	+ 9	+ 3.66	-1320	792.04
April 2, 1970	+ 6	+ 4.66	-1314	792.37
April 3, 1970	+ 3	+ 6.00	-1311	791.84
April 6, 1970	- 3	+ 2.00	-1314	791.18
April 7, 1970	+ 1	+ 0.33	-1313	791.64
April 8, 1970	+ 5	+ 1.00	-1308	791.64
April 9, 1970	+ 5	+ 3.66	-1303 (H)	792.50 (H)

Date	Climax Indicator	3-day Moving Average	CLX Cumulative	Dow
April 10, 1970	- 5	+ 1.66	-1308	790.46
April 13, 1970	-11	- 3.66	-1319	785.90
April 14, 1970	- 9	- 8.33	-1328	780.56
April 15, 1970	- 6	- 8.66	-1334	782.60
April 16, 1970	-14	- 9.66	-1348	775.87
April 17, 1970	- 8	- 9.33	-1356	775.94
April 20, 1970	-10	-10.66	-1366	775.87
April 21, 1970	-12	-10.00	-1378	772.51
April 22, 1970	-17	-13.00	-1395	762.61
April 23, 1970	-24 (L)	-17.66	-1419	750.59
April 24, 1970	-20	-20.33	-1439	747.29
April 27, 1970	-24 (L)	-22.66 (L)	-1463	735.15
April 28, 1970	-24 (L)	-22.66 (L)	-1487	724.33
April 29, 1970	- 3	-17.00	-1490	737.39
April 30, 1970	- 3	-10.00	-1493	736.07
May 1, 1970	- 3	- 3.00	-1496	733.63
May 4, 1970	-15	- 7.00	-1511	714.56
May 5, 1970	-12	-10.00	-1523	709.81
May 6, 1970	- 1	- 9.33	-1524	718.40
May 7, 1970	+ 1	- 4.00	-1523	723.07
May 8, 1970	- 1	- 0.33	-1524	717.73
May 11, 1970	- 7	- 2.33	-1531	710.07
May 12, 1970	-12	- 6.66	-1543	704.59
May 13, 1970	-17	-12.00	-1560	693.84
May 14, 1970	-22 (L)	-17.00 (L)	-1582	684.79
May 15, 1970	- 1	-13.33	-1583	702.22
May 18, 1970	+ 2	- 7.00	-1581	702.81
May 19, 1970	-10	- 3.00	-1591	691.40
May 20, 1970	-20 (L)	- 9.33	-1611	676.62
May 21, 1970	-20 (L)	-16.66	-1631	665.25
May 22, 1970	-14	-18.00 (L)	-1645	662.17
May 25, 1970	-21 (L)	-18.33 (L)	-1666	641.36
May 26, 1970	-21 (L)	-18.66 (L)	-1687 (L)	631.16 (L)
May 27, 1970	+ 4	-12.66	-1683	663.20
May 28, 1970	+13	- 1.33	-1670	684.15
May 29, 1970	+12	+ 9.66	-1658	700.44
June 1, 1970	+15 (H)	+13.33 (H)	-1643	710.36
June 2, 1970	+12	+13.00	-1631	709.61
June 3, 1970	+ 9	+12.00	-1622	713.86 (H)
June 4, 1970	0	+ 7.00	-1622	706.53
June 5, 1970	- 5	+ 1.33	-1627	695.03
June 8, 1970	- 3	- 2.66	-1630	700.23
June 9, 1970	- 2	- 3.33	-1632	700.16
June 10, 1970	-11	- 5.33	-1643	694.35
June 11, 1970	-17 (L)	-10.00	-1670	684.42
June 12, 1970	-12	-13.33 (L)	-1682	684.21
June 15, 1970	- 3	-10.66	-1685	687.36
June 16, 1970	+13	- 0.66	-1672	706.26
June 17, 1970	+10	+ 6.66	-1662	704.68
June 18, 1970	+ 9	+10.66	-1653	712.83
June 19, 1970	+15 (H)	+11.33 (H)	-1638	720.57 (H)

Date	Climax Indicator	3-day Moving Average	CLX Cumulative	Dow
June 22, 1970	+ 4	+ 9.33	-1634 (H)	716.11
June 23, 1970	- 9	+ 3.33	-1643	698.11
June 24, 1970	-11	- 5.33	-1654	692.29
June 25, 1970	- 7	- 9.00	-1661	693.59
June 26, 1970	-10	- 9.33	-1671	687.84
June 29, 1970	-15 (L)	-10.66 (L)	-1686	682.91
June 30, 1970	- 6	-10.33	-1692	683.53
July 1, 1970	- 5	- 8.66	-1697	687.64
July 2, 1970	- 2	- 4.33	-1699	689.14
July 6, 1970	-16	- 7.66	-1715	675.66
July 7, 1970	-17	-11.66	-1732 (L)	669.36 (L)
July 8, 1970	+ 2	-10.33	-1730	682.09
July 9, 1970	+11	- 1.33	-1719	692.77
July 10, 1970	+ 9	+ 7.33	-1710	700.10
July 11, 1970	+ 8	+ 9.33	-1702	702.22
July 14, 1970	+ 7	+ 8.00	-1695	703.04
July 15, 1970	+10	+ 8.33	-1685	711.66
July 16, 1970	+13	+10.00	-1672	723.44
July 17, 1970	+22 (H)	+15.00	-1650	735.08
July 20, 1970	+11	+15.33 (H)	-1639	733.91
July 21, 1970	- 5	+ 9.33	-1644	722.07
July 22, 1970	+ 2	+ 2.66	-1642	724.67
July 23, 1970	+ 8	+ 1.66	-1634	732.68
July 24, 1970	- 1	+ 3.00	-1635	730.22
July 27, 1970	- 4	+ 1.00	-1639	730.08
July 28, 1970	- 1	- 2.00	-1640	731.45
July 29, 1970	+ 9	+ 1.33	-1631	735.56 (H)
July 30, 1970	+ 1	+ 3.00	-1630	734.73
July 31, 1970	+ 5	+ 5.00	-1625 (H)	734.11
August 3, 1970	- 8	- 0.66	-1633	722.96
August 4, 1970	+ 2	- 0.33	-1631	725.90
August 5, 1970	- 4	- 3.33	-1635	724.81
August 6, 1970	- 7	- 3.00	-1642	722.82
August 7, 1970	+ 4	- 2.33	-1638	725.70
August 10, 1970	-11	- 4.66	-1649	713.92
August 11, 1970	-11	- 6.00	-1660	712.55
August 12, 1970	- 7	- 9.66	-1667	710.64
August 13, 1970	-12 (L)	-10.00	-1679	707.35 (L)
August 14, 1970	- 1	- 6.66	-1671	710.84
August 17, 1970	- 9	- 7.33	-1680 (L)	709.06
August 18, 1970	+10	.00	-1670	716.66
August 19, 1970	+11	+ 4.00	-1659	723.99
August 20, 1970	+12	+11.00	-1647	729.60
August 21, 1970	+22 (H)	+15.00	-1625	745.41
August 24, 1970	+22 (H)	+18.66 (H)	-1603	759.58
August 25, 1970	+11	+18.33	-1592	758.97
August 26, 1970	+ 9	+14.00	-1578	760.47
August 27, 1970	+ 8	+ 9.33	-1570	759.79
August 28, 1970	+12	+ 9.66	-1558	765.81
August 31, 1970	+11	+10.33	-1547	764.58
September 1, 1970	- 2	+ 7.00	-1549	758.15

Date	Climax Indicator	3-day Moving Average	CLX Cumulative	Dow
September 2, 1970	- 4	+ 1.66	-1553	756.64
September 3, 1970	+ 7	+ 0.33	-1546	765.27
September 4, 1970	+ 4	+ 2.33	-1542	771.15
September 8, 1970	+ 8	+ 6.33	-1534 (H)	773.14 (H)
September 9, 1970	- 2	+ 3.33	-1536	766.43
September 10, 1970	-10	- 1.33	-1546	760.75
September 11, 1970	- 2	- 4.66	-1548	761.84
September 14, 1970	- 6	- 6.00	-1554	757.12
September 15, 1970	-13 (L)	- 7.00	-1567	750.55
September 16, 1970	- 2	- 7.00	-1569	754.31
September 17, 1970	0	- 5.00	-1569	757.67
September 18, 1970	0	- 0.66	-1569	758.49
September 21, 1970	-10	- 3.33	-1579	751.92
September 22, 1970	-13 (L)	- 7.66 (L)	-1592 (L)	747.47 (L)
September 23, 1970	+ 1	- 7.33	-1591	754.38
September 24, 1970	+ 8	- 1.33	-1583	759.31
September 25, 1970	+10	+ 6.33	-1573	761.77
September 28, 1970	+ 3	+ 7.00	-1570	759.97
September 29, 1970	+ 4	+ 5.66	-1566	760.88
September 30, 1970	+ 4	+ 3.66	-1562	760.68
October 1, 1970	+ 1	+ 3.00	-1561	760.68
October 2, 1970	+ 5	+ 3.33	-1556	766.16
October 5, 1970	+12	+ 6.00	-1544	776.70
October 6, 1970	+16 (H)	+11.00	-1528	782.45
October 7, 1970	+13	+13.66 (H)	-1515	783.68 (H)
October 8, 1970	- 1	+ 9.33	-1516	777.04
October 9, 1970	- 3	+ 3.00	-1519	768.69
October 12, 1970	- 1	+ 1.66	-1520	764.24
October 13, 1970	- 8	- 4.00	-1528	760.06
October 14, 1970	- 2	- 3.60	-1530	762.73
October 15, 1970	+ 4	- 2.00	-1526 (H)	767.87
October 16, 1970	- 7	- 1.66	-1533	763.35
October 19, 1970	- 8	- 3.66	-1541	756.50
October 20, 1970	- 1	- 5.33	-1542	758.83
October 21, 1970	- 2	- 3.66	-1544	759.65
October 22, 1970	- 9	- 4.00	-1553	757.87
October 23, 1970	- 5	- 5.33	-1558	759.38
October 26, 1970	- 9	- 7.66	-1567	756.43
October 27, 1970	- 9	- 7.66	-1576	754.45
October 28, 1970	- 6	- 8.00	-1583	755.96
October 29, 1970	- 5	- 6.66	-1588 (L)	753.56 (L)
October 30, 1970	+ 3	- 2.66	-1585	755.61
November 2, 1970	- 1	- 1.00	-1586	758.01
November 3, 1970	+11	+ 4.33	-1575	768.07
November 4, 1970	+12	+ 7.33	-1563	770.81
November 5, 1970	+ 9	+10.66	-1554	771.56
November 6, 1970	+10	+10.33	-1544	771.97
November 9, 1970	+12	+10.33	-1532	777.66
November 10, 1970	+10	+10.66	-1522	777.38
November 11, 1970	+13 (H)	+11.66 (H)	-1509	779.50 (H)
November 12, 1970	- 2	+ 7.00	-1511	768.00

Date	Climax Indicator	3-day Moving Average	CLX Cumulative	Dow
November 13, 1970	-14 (L)	- 1.00	-1525	759.79
November 16, 1970	-10	- 8.66	-1535	760.13
November 17, 1970	- 7	-10.33 (L)	-1542	760.47
November 18, 1970	-11	- 9.33	-1553	754.24 (L)
November 19, 1970	- 3	- 7.00	-1556	755.82
November 20, 1970	+ 4	- 3.33	-1552	761.57
November 23, 1970	+ 7	+ 2.66	-1545	767.52
November 24, 1970	+ 8	+ 6.33	-1537	772.73
November 25, 1970	+11	+ 8.66	-1526	774.71
November 27, 1970	+20	+13.00	-1506	781.35
November 30, 1970	+25 (H)	+18.66	-1481	794.09
December 1, 1970	+16	+20.33 (H)	-1465	794.29
December 2, 1970	+13	+18.00	-1452	802.64
December 3, 1970	+16	+15.00	-1436	808.53
December 4, 1970	+18	+15.66	-1418	816.06
December 7, 1970	+10	+14.66	-1408	818.66
December 8, 1970	+ 2	+10.00	-1406	815.10
December 9, 1970	+ 7	+ 6.33	-1399	815.24
December 10, 1970	+10	+ 6.33	-1389	821.06
December 11, 1970	+10	+ 9.00	-1379	825.92
December 14, 1970	+ 4	+ 8.00	-1375	823.18
December 15, 1970	- 1	+ 4.33	-1376	819.62
December 16, 1970	+ 1	+ 1.33	-1375	819.07
December 17, 1970	+ 4	+ 1.33	-1371	822.15
December 18, 1970	+ 4	+ 3.00	-1367	822.77
December 21, 1970	- 2	+ 2.00	-1369	821.54
December 22, 1970	+ 2	+ 1.33	-1367	822.77
December 23, 1970	+ 3	+ 1.00	-1364	823.11
December 24, 1970	+ 7	+ 4.00	-1357	828.38
December 28, 1970	+10	+ 6.66	-1347	830.91
December 29, 1970	+18 (H)	+11.66	-1329	842.00
December 30, 1970	+ 9	+12.33	-1320	841.32
December 31, 1970	+ 6	+11.00	-1314	838.92
January 4, 1971	- 1	+ 4.66	-1315	830.57
January 5, 1971	+ 3	+ 2.66	-1312	835.77
January 6, 1971	0	+ 0.66	-1312	837.76
January 7, 1971	+ 1	+ 1.33	-1311	837.83
January 8, 1971	+ 3	+ 1.33	-1308	837.01
January 11, 1971	+ 2	+ 2.00	-1306	837.21
January 12, 1971	+ 9	+ 4.66	-1297	844.19
January 13, 1971	+ 3	+ 4.66	-1294	841.11
January 14, 1971	+ 5	+ 5.66	-1289	843.31
January 15, 1971	+ 9	+ 5.66	-1280	845.70
January 18, 1971	+10	+ 8.00	-1270	847.82
January 19, 1971	+ 7	+ 8.66	-1263	849.47
January 20, 1971	+ 3	+ 6.66	-1260	849.95
January 21, 1971	+ 7	+ 5.66	-1253	854.74
January 22, 1971	+ 7	+ 5.66	-1246	861.31
January 25, 1971	+ 9	+ 7.66	-1237	865.62
January 26, 1971	+ 9	+ 8.33	-1228	866.79
January 27, 1971	- 2	+ 5.33	-1230	860.83

Date	Climax Indicator	3-day Moving Average	CLX Cumulative	Dow
January 28, 1971	+ 3	+ 3.33	-1227	865.14
January 29, 1971	+ 2	+ 1.00	-1225	868.50
February 1, 1971	+12	+ 5,66	-1213	877.81
February 2, 1971	+ 5	+ 6.33	-1208	874.59
February 3, 1971	+ 3	+ 6.66	-1205	876.10
February 4, 1971	+ 2	+ 3.33	-1203	874.79
February 5, 1971	+ 7	+ 4.00	-1196	876.57
February 8, 1971	+ 8	+ 5.66	-1188	882.12
February 9, 1971	+ 5	+ 6.66	-1183	879.79
February 10, 1971	+ 5	+ 6.00	-1178	880.99
February 11, 1971	+ 9	+ 6.33	-1169	885.34
February 12, 1971	+12	+ 8.66	-1157	888.83
February 16, 1971	+10	+10.33	-1147	890.06
February 17, 1971	+ 5	+ 9.00	-1142	887.87
February 18, 1971	+ 1	+ 5.33	-1141	885.06
February 19, 1971	- 7	- 0.33	-1148	878.56
February 22, 1971	-17 (L)	- 7.66	-1165	868.98
February 23, 1971	- 9	-11.00 (L)	-1174	870.00
February 24, 1971	0	- 8.66	-1174	875.61
February 25, 1971	+ 2	- 2.33	-1172	881.98
February 26, 1971	0	+ 0.66	-1172	878.83
March 1, 1971	0	+ 0.66	-1172	882.53
March 2, 1971	+ 4	+ 1.33	-1168	883.01
March 3, 1971	- 2	+ 0.66	-1170	882.39
March 4, 1971	+ 8	+ 3.33	-1162	891.36
March 5, 1971	+11	+ 5.66	-1151	898.00
March 8, 1971	+12	+10.33 (H)	-1139	898.62
March 9, 1971	+ 6	+ 9.66	-1133	899.10
March 10, 1971	0	+ 6.00	-1133	895.88
March 11, 1971	0	+ 2.00	-1133	899.44
March 12, 1971	0	.00	-1133	898.34
March 15, 1971	+12	+ 4.00	-1121	908.20
March 16, 1971	+17 (H)	+ 9.66	-1104	914.64
March 17, 1971	+ 3	+10.66 (H)	-1101	914.02
March 18, 1971	+ 5	+ 8.33	-1096	916.83
March 19, 1971	- 2	+ 2.00	-1098	912.92
March 22, 1971	- 6	- 1.00	-1104	910.60
March 23, 1971	- 5	- 4.33	-1109	908.89
March 24, 1971	-13	- 8.00	-1122	899.37
March 25, 1971	- 6	- 8.00	-1128	900.81
March 26, 1971	- 6	- 8.33	-1134	903.48
March 29, 1971	- 4	- 5.33	-1138	903.48
March 30, 1971	- 7	- 5.66	-1145	903.39
March 31, 1971	0	- 3.66	-1145	904.37
April 1, 1971	- 1	- 2.66	-1146	903.88
April 2, 1971	- 3	- 1.33	-1149	903.04
April 5, 1971	+ 1	- 1.00	-1148	905.07
April 6, 1971	+ 5	+ 1.00	-1143	912.73
April 7, 1971	+ 7	+ 4.33	-1136	918.49
April 8, 1971	+ 8	+ 6.66	-1128	920.39
April 12, 1971	+ 9	+ 8.00	-1119	926.64

Date		Climax Indicator	3-day Moving Average	CLX Cumulative	Dow
April	13, 1971	+ 7	+ 8.00	-1112	927.28
April	14, 1971	+10	+ 8.66	-1102	932.55
April	15, 1971	+15 (H)	+10.66	-1087	938.17
April	16, 1971	+11	+12.00	-1076	940.21
April	19, 1971	+14	+13.33 (H)	-1062	948.85
April	20, 1971	+ 3	+ 9.33	-1059	944.42
April	21, 1971	- 2	+ 5.00	-1061	941.33
April	22, 1971	+ 2	+ 1.00	-1059	940.63
April	23, 1971	+ 2	+ 0.66	-1057	947.79
April	26, 1971	0	+ 1.33	-1057 (H)	944.00
April	27, 1971	- 1	+ 0.33	-1058	947.09
April	28, 1971	+ 1	.00	-1057	950.81 (H)
April	29, 1971	- 4	- 1.33	-1061	948.15
April	30, 1971	- 6	- 3.00	-1067	941.75
May	3, 1971	-10	- 6.66	-1077	932.41
May	4, 1971	+ 1	- 5.00	-1076	938.45
May	5, 1971	0	- 3.00	-1076	939.92
May	6, 1971	0	+ 0.33	-1076	937.39
May	7, 1971	+ 3	+ 1.00	-1073	936.97
May	10, 1971	- 4	- 0.33	-1077	932.55
May	11, 1971	+ 5	+ 1.33	-1072	937.25
May	12, 1971	+ 4	+ 1.66	-1068	937.46
May	13, 1971	+ 4	+ 4.33	-1064	936.34
May	14, 1971	+ 1	+ 3.00	-1063	936.06
May	17, 1971	-10	- 1.66	-1073	921.30
May	18, 1971	- 9	- 6.00	-1082	918.56
May	19, 1971	- 7	- 8.66	-1089	920.04
May	20, 1971	- 4	- 6.66	-1093	923.41
May	21, 1971	- 3	- 4.66	-1096	921.87
May	24, 1971	-13	- 6.66	-1109	913.15
May	25, 1971	-17	-11.00	-1126	906.69
May	26, 1971	- 7	-12.33 (L)	-1133	906.41
May	27, 1971	- 4	- 9.33	-1137	905.78
May	29, 1971	0	- 3.66	-1137	907.81
June	1, 1971	+ 4	.00	-1133	913.65
June	2, 1971	+ 6	+ 3.33	-1127	919.27
June	3, 1971	+ 5	+ 5.00	-1122	921.30
June	4, 1971	0	+ 3.66	-1122	922.15
June	7, 1971	+ 2	+ 2.33	-1120	923.06
June	8, 1971	-12	- 3.33	-1132	915.01
June	9, 1971	-11	- 7.00	-1121	912.46
June	10, 1971	+ 1	- 7.33	-1120	915.96
June	11, 1971	- 2	- 4.00	-1122	916.47
June	14, 1971	- 5	- 2.00	-1127	907.71
June	15, 1971	- 5	- 4.00	-1132	907.20
June	16, 1971	- 2	- 4.00	-1134	908.59
June	17, 1971	- 4	- 3.66	-1138	906.25
June	18, 1971	-18	- 8.00	-1156	889.16
June	21, 1971	-22 (L)	-14.66	-1178	876.53
June	22, 1971	-13	-17.66 (L)	-1191	874.42
June	23, 1971	- 3	-12.66	-1194	879.45

Date	Climax Indicator	3-day Moving Average	CLX Cumulative	Dow
June 24, 1971	- 1	- 5.66	-1195	877.26
June 25, 1971	- 3	- 2.33	-1198	876.68
June 28, 1971	- 3	- 2.33	-1201	873.10 (L)
June 29, 1971	+ 8	+ 0.66	-1193	882.30
June 30, 1971	+12 (H)	+ 5.66	-1181	890.99
July 1, 1971	+10	+10.00 (H)	-1171	893.03
July 2, 1971	+ 4	+ 8.66	-1167	890.19
July 6, 1971	+ 9	+ 7.66	-1158	892.30
July 7, 1971	+ 6	+ 6.33	-1152	895.88
July 8, 1971	+ 8	+ 7.66	-1144	900.99
July 9, 1971	+ 6	+ 6.66	-1138	901.80
July 12, 1971	+ 3	+ 5.66	-1135	903.40 (H)
July 13, 1971	-10	- 0.33	-1145	892.38
July 14, 1971	- 4	- 3.66	-1149	891.21
July 15, 1971	-12	- 8.66	-1161	888.95
July 16, 1971	- 7	- 7.66	-1168	888.51
July 19, 1971	-10	- 9.66	-1178	886.39
July 20, 1971	+ 3	- 4.66	-1175	892.30
July 21, 1971	- 3	- 3.33	-1178	890.92
July 22, 1971	- 3	- 1.00	-1181	886.68
July 23, 1971	+ 2	- 1.33	-1179	887.78
July 26, 1971	+ 1	.00	-1178	888.87
July 27, 1971	- 7	- 1.33	-1185	880.70
July 28, 1971	-14	- 6.66	-1199	872.01
July 29, 1971	-20 (L)	-13.66	-1219	861.42
July 30, 1971	-10	-14.66	-1229	858.43
August 2, 1971	- 2	-10.66	-1231	864.92
August 3, 1971	-12	- 8.00	-1243	850.03
August 4, 1971	-18	-10.66	-1261	844.92
August 5, 1971	- 5	-11.66	-1266	849.45
August 6, 1971	0	- 7.66	-1266	850.61
August 9, 1971	-11	- 5.33	-1277	842.65
August 10, 1971	- 6	- 5.66	-1283 (L)	839.59 (L)
August 11, 1971	+ 3	- 4.66	-1280	846.38
August 12, 1971	+14	+ 3.66	-1266	859.01
August 13, 1971	+ 5	+ 7.33	-1261	856.02
August 16, 1971	+20 (H)	+13.00 (H)	-1241	888.95
August 17, 1971	+12	+12.33	-1229	899.90
August 18, 1971	- 6	+ 8.66	-1235	886.17
August 19, 1971	- 9	- 1.00	-1244	880.77
August 20, 1971	- 4	- 6.33	-1248	880.91
August 23, 1971	+ 4	- 3.00	-1244	892.38
August 24, 1971	+ 9	+ 3.00	-1235	904.13
August 25, 1971	+ 6	+ 6.33	-1229	908.37
August 26, 1971	+ 4	+ 6.33	-1225	906.10
August 27, 1971	+ 5	+ 5.00	-1220	908.15
August 30, 1971	+ 1	+ 3.33	-1219	901.43
August 31, 1971	2	+ 1.33	-1221	898.07
September 1, 1971	- 3	- 1.33	-1224	899.02
September 2, 1971	+ 5	.00	-1219	900.63
September 3, 1971	+12	+ 4.66	-1207	912.75

Date	Climax Indicator	3-day Moving Average	CLX Cumulative	Dow
September 7, 1971	+10	+ 9.00	-1197	916.47
September 8, 1971	+13 (H)	+11.66 (H)	-1184	920.93 (H)
September 9, 1971	+ 4	+ 9.00	-1180 (H)	915.89
September 10, 1971	- 2	+ 5.00	-1182	911.00
September 13, 1971	- 2	.00	-1184	909.39
September 14, 1971	-10	- 4.66	-1194	901.65
September 15, 1971	- 4	- 5.33	-1198	904.86
September 16, 1971	0	- 4.66	-1198	903.11
September 17, 1971	+ 6	+ 0.66	-1192	908.22
September 20, 1971	- 7	- 0.33	-1199	905.15
September 21, 1971	- 6	- 2.33	-1205	903.40
September 22, 1971	-20 (L)	-11.00	-1225	893.55
September 23, 1971	-11	-12.33	-1236	891.28
September 24, 1971	-14	-15.00 (L)	-1250	889.31
September 27, 1971	-13	-12.66	-1263	883.47
September 28, 1971	- 4	-10.33	-1267	884.42
September 29, 1971	- 5	- 7.33	-1272	883.84
September 30, 1971	0	- 3.00	-1272	887.19
October 1, 1971	+ 7	+ 0.66	-1265	893.98
October 4, 1971	+ 8	+ 5.00	-1257	895.66
October 5, 1971	0	+ 5.00	-1257	891.14
October 6, 1971	+10	+ 6.00	-1247	900.41
October 7, 1971	+ 8	+ 6.00	-1239	901.80
October 8, 1971	- 5	+ 4.33	-1244	893.91
October 11, 1971	- 4	- 0.33	-1248	891.94
October 12, 1971	0	- 3.00	-1248	893.55
October 13, 1971	- 2	- 2.00	-1250	888.80
October 14, 1971	-19	- 7.00	-1269	878.36
October 15, 1971	-15	-12.00	-1284	874.85
October 18, 1971	-12	-15.33	-1296	872.44
October 19, 1971	-15	-14.00	-1311	868.43
October 20, 1971	-22 (L)	-16.33	-1333	855.65
October 21, 1971	-14	-17.00 (L)	-1347	854.85
October 22, 1971	-11	-15.66	-1358	852.37
October 25, 1971	-10	-11.66	-1368	848.50
October 26, 1971	- 9	-10.00	-1377	845.36
October 27, 1971	-12	-10.33	-1389	836.38
October 28, 1971	- 7	- 9.33	-1396	837.62
October 29, 1971	- 1	- 6.66	-1397	839.00
November 1, 1971	-12	- 6.66	-1409	825.86
November 2, 1971	- 7	- 6.66	-1416	827.98
November 3, 1971	+11	2.66	-1405	842.58
November 4, 1971	+ 5	+ 3.00	-1400	843.17
November 5, 1971	- 1	+ 5.00	-1401	840.39
November 8, 1971	+ 2	+ 2.00	-1399	837.54
November 9, 1971	+ 1	+ 0.66	-1398	837.91
November 10, 1971	- 8	- 1.66	-1406	826.15
November 11, 1971	-14	- 7.00	-1420	814.91
November 12, 1971	-15 (L)	-12.33	-1435	812.94
November 15, 1971	- 9	-12.66 (L)	-1444	810.53
November 16, 1971	+ 2	- 7.33	-1442	818.71

Date	Climax Indicator	3-day Moving Average	CLX Cumulative	Dow
November 17, 1971	+ 7	.00	-1435	822.14
November 18, 1971	- 3	+ 2.00	-1438	815.35
November 19, 1971	- 4	.00	-1442	810.67
November 22, 1971	-13 (L)	- 6.66	-1455	803.15
November 23, 1971	-12	- 9.66	-1467	797.97 (L)
November 24, 1971	- 7	-10.66 (L)	-1474 (L)	798.63
November 26, 1971	+ 7	- 4.00	-1467	816.59
November 29, 1971	+15	+ 5.00	-1452	829.73
November 30, 1971	+ 6	+ 9.33	-1446	831.34
December 1, 1971	+14	+11.66	-1432	846.02
December 2, 1971	+10	+10.00	-1422	848.79
December 3, 1971	+14	+12.66 (H)	-1408	859.59
December 6, 1971	+ 4	+ 9.33	-1404	855.72
December 7, 1971	+ 5	+ 7.66	-1399	857.40
December 8, 1971	0	+ 3.00	-1399	854.84
December 9, 1971	- 3	+ 0.66	-1402	852.15
December 10, 1971	+ 3	.00	-1399	856.75
December 13, 1971	+ 4	+ 1.33	-1395	858.79
December 14, 1971	- 3	+ 1.33	-1398	855.14
December 15, 1971	+ 8	+ 3.00	-1390	863.76
December 16, 1971	+10	+ 5.00	-1380	871.31
December 17, 1971	+10	+ 9.33	-1370	873.80
December 20, 1971	+18 (H)	+12.66 (H)	-1352	885.01
December 21, 1971	+ 8	+12.00	-1344	888.32
December 22, 1971	+ 4	+10.00	-1340	884.86
December 23, 1971	+ 2	+ 4.66	-1338	881.17
December 27, 1971	+ 4	+ 3.33	-1334	881.47
December 28, 1971	+15	+ 7.00	-1319	889.98
December 29, 1971	+ 7	+ 8.66	-1312	893.66
December 30, 1971	+ 2	+ 8.00	-1310	889.07
December 31, 1971	+ 4	+ 4.33	-1306	890.20
January 3, 1972	- 7	- 0.33	-1313	889.30
January 4, 1972	- 1	- 1.33	-1314	892.23
January 5, 1972	+14 (H)	+ 2.00	-1300	904.43
January 6, 1972	+13	+ 8.66	-1287	908.49
January 7, 1972	+ 8	+11.66 (H)	-1279	910.37
January 10, 1972	+ 4	+ 8.33	-1275	907.96
January 11, 1972	+ 4	+ 5.33	-1271	912.10
January 12, 1972	+ 1	+ 3.00	-1270 (H)	910.82
January 13, 1972	- 6	- 0.33	-1276	905.18
January 14, 1972	- 2	- 2.33	-1278	906.68
January 17, 1972	+ 1	- 2.33	-1277	911.12
January 18, 1972	+ 4	+ 1.00	-1273	917.22 (H)
January 19, 1972	- 1	+ 1.33	-1274	914.96
January 20, 1972	- 4	- 0.33	-1278	910.30
January 21, 1972	- 2	- 2.33	-1280	907.44
January 24, 1972	-14 (L)	- 6.66	-1294	896.82
January 25, 1972	-13	- 9.66	-1307	894.72
January 26, 1972	-13	-13.33 (L)	-1320 (L)	889.15 (L)
January 27, 1972	+ 2	- 8.00	-1318	899.84
January 28, 1972	+ 5	- 2.00	-1313	906.38

Date	Climax Indicator	3-day Moving Average	CLX Cumulative	Dow
January 31, 1972	- 1	+ 2.00	-1314	902.17
February 1, 1972	- 1	+ 1.00	-1315	901.79
February 2, 1972	+ 1	- 0.33	-1314	905.85
February 3, 1972	- 3	- 1.00	-1317	903.15
February 4, 1972	+ 1	- 0.33	-1316	906.76
February 7, 1972	- 1	- 1.00	-1317	903.97
February 8, 1972	+ 1	+ 0.33	-1316	907.13
February 9, 1972	+ 8	+ 2.66	-1308	918.72
February 10, 1972	+ 7	+ 5.33	-1301	921.28
February 11, 1972	0	+ 5.00	-1301	917.59
February 14, 1972	- 3	+ 1.33	-1304	910.90
February 15, 1972	+ 3	.00	-1301	914.51
February 16, 1972	+ 8	+ 2.66	-1293	922.94
February 17, 1972	0	+ 3.66	-1293	922.03
February 18, 1972	-10	- 0.66	-1303	917.52
February 22, 1972	- 7	- 5.66	-1310	913.46
February 23, 1972	- 8	- 8.33	-1318	911.88
February 24, 1972	+ 1	- 4.66	-1317	912.70
February 25, 1972	+ 5	- 0.66	-1312	922.79
February 28, 1972	+ 8	+ 4.66	-1304	924.29
February 29, 1972	+ 6	+ 6.33	-1298	928.13
March 1, 1972	+ 9	+ 7.66	-1289	935.43
March 2, 1972	+ 3	+ 6.00	-1286	933.77
March 3, 1972	+ 8	+ 6.66	-1278	942.43
March 6, 1972	+13 (H)	+ 8.00 (H)	-1265	950.18 (H)
March 7, 1972	+ 1	+ 7.33	-1264	946.87
March 8, 1972	+ 5	+ 6.33	-1259	946.19
March 9, 1972	- 2	+ 1.33	-1261	943.41
March 10, 1972	- 4	- 0.33	-1265	939.87
March 13, 1972	- 9	- 5.00	-1274	928.66 (L)
March 14, 1972	- 5	- 6.00 (L)	-1279	943.00
March 15, 1972	+ 1	- 4.33	-1278	937.31
March 16, 1972	- 1	- 1.66	-1279	936.71
March 17, 1972	+ 5	+ 1.66	-1274	942.83
March 20, 1972	- 3	+ 0.33	-1277	941.15
March 21, 1972	-10 (L)	- 2.66	-1287	934.00
March 22, 1972	- 5	- 6.00 (L)	-1292	933.92
March 23, 1972	+ 6	- 3.00	-1286	944.69
March 24, 1972	0	+ 0.33	-1286	942.28
March 27, 1972	- 3	+ 1.00	-1289	939.72
March 28, 1972	0	- 1.00	-1289	937.01
March 29, 1972	- 5	- 2.66	-1294	933.02
March 30, 1972	+11	+ 2.00	-1283	940.70
April 3, 1972	+ 1	+ 2.33	-1282	940.93
April 4, 1972	+ 6	+ 6.00	-1276	943.40
April 5, 1972	+13 (H)	+ 6.66	-1263	954.55
April 6, 1972	+11	+10.00	-1252	959.44
April 7, 1972	+10	+11.33 (H)	-1242	962.60
April 10, 1972	- 2	+ 6.33	-1244	958.08
April 11, 1972	+ 1	+ 3.00	-1243	962.60
April 12, 1972	0	- 0.33	-1243	966.96

Date	Climax Indicator	3-day Moving Average	CLX Cumulative	Dow
April 13, 1972	- 1	.00	-1244	965.53
April 14, 1972	+ 4	+ 1.00	-1240	967.72
April 17, 1972	+ 2	+ 1.66	-1238	966.59
April 18, 1972	+ 6	+ 4.00	-1232	968.92 (H)
April 19, 1972	- 1	+ 2.33	-1233	964.78
April 20, 1972	+ 2	+ 2.33	-1231 (H)	966.29
April 21, 1972	- 3	- 0.66	-1234	963.80
April 24, 1972	- 8	- 3.00	-1242	957.48
April 25, 1972	-18	- 9.66	-1260	946.49
April 26, 1972	-13	-13.00 (L)	-1273	946.94
April 27, 1972	- 7	-12.66	-1280	945.96
April 28, 1972	+ 1	- 6.33	-1279	954.17
May 1, 1972	- 8	- 4.66	-1287	942.28
May 2, 1972	-10	- 5.66	-1297	935.21
May 3, 1972	- 6	- 8.00	-1303	933.47
May 4, 1972	+ 3	- 4.33	-1300	937.31
May 5, 1972	- 1	- 1.33	-1301	941.23
May 8, 1972	- 1	+ 0.33	-1302	937.84
May 9, 1972	-20 (L)	- 7.33	-1322	925.12 (L)
May 10, 1972	- 4	- 8.33	-1326	931.07
May 11, 1972	- 3	- 9.00 (L)	-1329 (L)	934.83
May 12, 1972	+11	+ 1.33	-1318	941.83
May 15, 1972	+ 4	+ 4.00	-1314	942.21
May 16, 1972	+ 3	+ 6.00	-1311	939.27
May 17, 1972	+ 2	+ 3.00	-1309	941.15
May 18, 1972	+10	+ 5.00	-1299	951.23
May 19, 1972	+13 (H)	+ 8.33	-1286	961.54
May 22, 1972	+ 9	+10.66 (H)	-1277	965.30
May 23, 1972	+ 5	+ 9.00	-1272	962.30
May 24, 1972	+ 6	+ 6.66	-1266	965.46
May 25, 1972	+ 5	+ 5.33	-1261	969.07
May 26, 1972	+ 7	+ 6.00	-1254	971.25 (H)
May 30, 1972	+ 4	+ 5.33	-1250 (H)	971.18
May 31, 1972	-11 (L)	.00	-1261	960.72
June 1, 1972	- 6	- 4.33	-1267	960.72
June 2, 1972	- 6	- 7.66	-1273	961.39
June 5, 1972	- 5	- 5.66	-1278	954.39
June 6, 1972	- 9	- 6.66	-1287	951.46
June 7, 1972	-12	- 8.66	-1299	944.08
June 8, 1972	- 9	-10.00	-1308	941.30
June 9, 1972	-15 (L)	-12.00 (L)	-1323	934.53 (L)
June 12, 1972	-11	-11.66	-1334	936.71
June 13, 1972	-10	-12.00 (L)	-1344	938.29
June 14, 1972	- 1	- 7.33	-1345	946.79
June 15, 1972	+ 4	- 2.33	-1341	945.97
June 16, 1972	0	+ 1.00	-1341	945.06
June 19, 1972	- 1	+ 1.00	-1342	941.82
June 20, 1972	+ 8	+ 2.33	-1334	948.22
June 21, 1972	+ 4	+ 3.66	-1330	951.61 (H)
June 22, 1972	- 1	+ 3.66	-1331	950.71
June 23, 1972	- 6	- 1.00	-1337	944.76

Date	Climax Indicator	3-day Moving Average	CLX Cumulative	Dow
June 26, 1972	-14	- 7.00	-1351	936.41
June 27, 1972	-10	-10.00	-1361	935.28
June 28, 1972	-13 (L)	-12.33 (L)	-1374	930.76
June 29, 1972	-11	-11.33	-1385	926.25
June 30, 1972	- 5	- 9.66	-1390	929.03
July 3, 1972	- 5	- 7.00	-1395	928.65
July 5, 1972	0	- 7.33	-1395	933.48
July 6, 1972	+ 8	+ 1.00	-1387	942.13
July 7, 1972	+ 4	+ 4.00	-1383	938.07
July 10, 1972	- 4	- 2.66	-1387	932.12
July 11, 1972	- 7	- 2.33	-1394	925.87
July 12, 1972	- 5	- 5.33	-1399	923.69
July 13, 1972	-11 (L)	7.66	-1410	916.99
July 14, 1972	- 5	- 7.00	-1415	922.26
July 17, 1972	- 6	- 7.33	-1421	914.96
July 18, 1972	-10 (L)	- 7.00	-1431	911.72
July 19, 1972	+ 2	- 4.66	-1429	916.69
July 20, 1972	- 5	- 4.33	-1434 (L)	910.45 (L)
July 21, 1972	+ 9	+ 2.00	-1425	920.45
July 24, 1972	+18 (H)	+ 7.33	-1407	935.36
July 25, 1972	+ 7	+11.33 (H)	-1400	934.45
July 26, 1972	+ 3	+ 9.33	-1397	932.57
July 27, 1972	- 1	+ 3.00	-1398	926.85
July 28, 1972	+ 1	+ 1.00	-1397	926.10
July 31, 1972	- 4	- 1.33	-1401	924.74
August 1, 1972	+ 3	.00	-1398	930.46
August 2, 1972	+11	+ 3.33	-1387	941.15
August 3, 1972	+12	+ 8.66	-1375	947.70
August 4, 1972	+11	+11.33	-1364	951.76
August 7, 1972	+ 8	+10.33	-1356	953.12
August 8, 1972	+ 4	+ 7.66	-1352	952.44
August 9, 1972	+ 1	+ 4.33	-1351	951.16
August 10, 1972	+ 3	+ 2.66	-1348	952.89
August 11, 1972	+12	+ 5.33	-1336	964.18
August 14, 1972	+15 (H)	+10.00	-1321	973.51 (H)
August 15, 1972	+10	+12.33 (H)	-1311	969.97
August 16, 1972	+ 7	+10.66	-1304	964.25
August 17, 1972	+ 4	+ 7.00	-1300	961.24
August 18, 1972	+ 7	+ 6.00	-1293	965.83
August 21, 1972	+ 5	+ 5.33	-1288	967.19
August 22, 1972	+13 (H)	+ 8.33	-1275	973.51 (H)
August 23, 1972	+ 2	+ 6.66	-1273	970.35
August 24, 1972	- 8	+ 2.33	-1281	
August 25, 1972	- 3	- 3.00	-1284	
August 28, 1972	- 2	- 4.33	-1286	
August 29, 1972	- 9	- 4.66	-1295	
August 30, 1972	- 1	- 4.00	-1296	
August 31, 1972	+ 7	- 1.00	-1289	
September 1, 1972	+14	+ 6.66	-1275	970.05
September 5, 1972	+ 6	+ 9.00	-1269 (H)	969.37
September 6, 1972	- 3	+ 5.66	-1272	963.43

Date	Climax Indicator	3-day Moving Average	CLX Cumulative	Dow
September 7, 1972	0	+ 1.00	-1272	962.45
September 8, 1972	- 4	- 2.33	-1276	961.24
September 11, 1972	- 9	- 4.33	-1285	955.00
September 12, 1972	-13 (L)	- 8.66 (L)	-1298	946.04
September 13, 1972	- 1	- 7.66	-1299	949.88
September 14, 1972	+ 1	- 4.33	-1298	947.55
September 15, 1972	- 2	- 0.66	-1300	947.32
September 18, 1972	- 5	- 2.00	-1305	945.36
September 19, 1972	- 7	- 4.66	-1312	943.18
September 20, 1972	-12 (L)	- 8.00	-1324	940.25
September 21, 1972	-11	-10.00 (L)	-1335	939.49
September 22, 1972	- 5	- 9.33	-1340	943.04
September 25, 1972	- 5	- 7.00	-1345	935.66 (L)
September 26, 1972	+ 3	- 2.33	-1342	936.56
September 27, 1972	+14	+ 4.00	-1328	947.25
September 28, 1972	+15 (H)	+10.66	-1313	955.15 (H)
September 29, 1972	+ 4	+11.00 (H)	-1309	953.27
October 2, 1972	0	+ 6.33	-1309	953.27
October 3, 1972	+ 1	+ 1.66	-1308	954.47
October 4, 1972	- 3	- 0.66	-1311	951.31
October 5, 1972	-11	- 4.33	-1322	941.30
October 6, 1972	- 5	- 6.33	-1327	945.36
October 9, 1972	+ 1	- 5.00	-1326	948.75
October 10, 1972	+ 2	- 0.66	-1324	951.84
October 11, 1972	- 3	.00	-1327	946.42
October 12, 1972	- 9	- 3.33	-1336	937.46
October 13, 1972	-12	- 8.00	-1348	930.46
October 16, 1972	-18 (L)	-13.00 (L)	-1366	921.66 (L)
October 17, 1972	- 4	-11.33	-1370 (L)	926.55
October 18, 1972	+ 4	- 6.00	-1366	932.34
October 19, 1972	+ 4	+ 1.33	-1362	932.12
October 20, 1972	+12	+ 6.66	-1350	942.81
October 23, 1972	+20 (H)	+12.00	-1330	951.31
October 24, 1972	+14	+15.33 (H)	-1316	952.51
October 25, 1972	+ 7	+13.66	-1309	951.38
October 26, 1972	- 1	+ 6.66	-1310	950.56
October 27, 1972	- 7	- 0.33	-1317	946.42
October 30, 1972	- 3	- 3.66	-1320	946.42
October 31, 1972	+ 7	- 1.00	-1313	955.52
November 1, 1972	+ 9	+ 4.33	-1304	968.54
November 2, 1972	+13	+ 9.66	-1291	973.06
November 3, 1972	+16	+12.66	-1275	984.12
November 6, 1972	+15	+14.66	-1260	984.80
November 8, 1972	+ 7	+12.66	-1253	983.74
November 9, 1972	+ 5	+ 9.00	-1248	988.26
November 10, 1972	+ 8	+ 6.66	-1240	995.26
November 13, 1972	+ 2	+ 5.00	-1238	997.07
November 14, 1972	+13	+ 7.66	-1225	1003.16
November 15, 1972	0	+ 5.00	-1225	998.42
November 16, 1972	+ 5	+ 6.00	-1220	1003.69
November 17, 1972	+ 2	+ 2.33	-1218	1005.57

Date	Climax Indicator	3-day Moving Average	CLX Cumulative	Dow
November 20, 1972	+ 5	+ 4.00	-1213	1005.04
November 21, 1972	+12	+ 6.33	-1201	1013.25
November 22, 1972	+ 9	+ 8.66	-1192	1020.54
November 24, 1972	+ 7	+ 9.33	-1185	1025.21
November 27, 1972	- 4	+ 4.00	-1189	1017.76
November 28, 1972	+ 4	+ 2.33	-1185	1019.34
November 29. 1972	+ 5	+ 1.66	-1180	1018.81
November 30, 1972	+ 2	+ 3.66	-1178	1018.21
December 1, 1972	+ 8	+ 5.00	-1170	1023.93
December 4, 1972	+ 8	+ 6.00	-1162	1027.02
December 5, 1972	+ 2	+ 6.00	-1160	1022.95
December 6, 1972	+ 6	+ 5.33	-1154	1027.54
December 7, 1972	+ 8	+ 5.33	-1146	
December 8, 1972	+10	+ 8.00	-1136	
December 11, 1972	+12 (H)	+10.00 (H)	-1124	1036.27 (H)
December 12, 1972	0	+ 7.33	-1124 (H)	1033.19
December 13, 1972	5	+ 2.33	-1129	1030.48
December 14, 1972	7	- 4.00	-1136	1025.06
December 15, 1972	- 6	- 6.00	-1142	1027.24
December 18, 1972	-14	- 9.00	-1156	1013.25
December 19, 1972	-17 (L)	-12.33	-1173	1009.19
December 20, 1972	-13	-14.66 (L)	-1186	1004.82
December 21, 1972	-12	-14.00	-1198	1000.00 (L)
December 22, 1972	- 5	-10.00	-1203	1004.21
December 26, 1972	- 1	- 6.00	-1204	1006.70
December 27, 1972	- 1	- 2.33	-1205	1007.68
December 29, 1972	+11	+ 3.00	-1194	1020.02
January 2, 1973	+16 (H)	+ 8.66	-1178	1031.68
January 3, 1973	+14	+13.66 (H)	-1164	1043.80
January 4, 1973	+ 5	+11.66	-1159	1039.81
January 5, 1973	+ 9	+ 9.33	-1150	1047.49
January 8, 1973	+ 8	+ 7.33	-1142	1047.86
January 9, 1973	+ 2	+ 6.33	-1140	1047.11
January 10, 1973	0	+ 3.33	-1140	1046.06
January 11, 1973	+ 9	+ 3.66	-1131	1051.70 (H)
January 12, 1973	- 1	+ 2.66	-1132	1039.36
January 15, 1973	-10	- 0.66	-1142	1025.59
January 16, 1973	- 9	- 6.66	-1151	1024.31
January 17, 1973	- 4	- 7.66	-1155	1029.12
January 18, 1973	- 5	- 6.00	-1160	1029.12
January 19, 1973	-10	- 6.33	-1170	1026.19
January 22, 1973	-12	- 9.00	-1182	1018.81
January 23, 1973	- 6	- 9.33	-1188	1018.66
January 24, 1973	-19 (L)	-12.33	-1207	1004.59
January 26, 1973	-10	-11.66	-1217	1003.54
January 29, 1973	- 8	-12.33 (L)	-1225	996.46
January 30, 1973	- 8	- 8.66	-1233	992.92
January 31, 1973	0	- 5.33	-1233	999.03
February 1, 1973	-15 (L)	- 7.66	-1248	985.77
February 2, 1973	-10	- 8.33	-1258	980.81
February 5, 1973	- 8	-11.00 (L)	-1266	978.40

Date	Climax Indicator	3-day Moving Average	CLX Cumulative	Dow
February 6, 1973	- 3	- 7.00	-1269	979.91
February 7, 1973	-16 (L)	- 9.00	-1285	968.32
February 8, 1973	-16 (L)	-11.66 (L)	-1301	967.19
February 9, 1973	- 1	-11.00	-1302	979.46
February 12, 1973	+ 7	- 3.33	-1295	991.58
February 13, 1973	+11 (H)	+ 5.66	-1284	996.76
February 14, 1973	- 7	+ 3.66	-1291	979.91
February 15, 1973	- 4	.00	-1295	973.14
February 16, 1973	- 2	- 4.33	-1297	979.24
February 20, 1973	- 3	- 3.00	-1300	983.60
February 21, 1973	-10	- 5.00	-1310	974.34
February 22, 1973	- 8	- 7.00	-1318	971.78
February 23, 1973	-13	-10.33	-1331	959.89
February 26, 1973	-15 (L)	-12.00	-1346	953.79
February 27, 1973	-14	-14.00 (L)	-1360	947.92 (L)
February 28, 1973	- 3	-10.66	-1363	955.07
March 1, 1973	- 1	- 6.00	-1364 (L)	949.65
March 2, 1973	+ 8	+ 1.33	-1356	961.32
March 5, 1973	+ 9	+ 5.33	-1347	966.89
March 6, 1973	+23 (H)	+13.33	-1324	979.00
March 7, 1973	+13	+15.00 (H)	-1311	979.98 (H)
March 8, 1973	+ 2	+12.66	-1309	976.44
March 9, 1973	- 1	+ 4.66	-1310	972.23
March 12, 1973	- 2	- 0.33	-1312	969.75
March 13, 1973	+ 3	.00	-1309	976.07
March 14, 1973	+ 6	+ 2.33	-1303 (H)	978.85
March 15, 1973	- 6	+ 1.00	-1309	969.82
March 16, 1973	- 7	- 2.33	-1316	962.97
March 19, 1973	-10	- 7.66	-1326	952.51
March 20, 1973	- 5	- 7.33	-1331	949.43
March 21, 1973	-16	-10.33	-1347	938.37
March 22, 1973	-19 (L)	-13.33	-1366	925.20
March 23, 1973	-14	-16.33 (L)	-1380	922.71 (L)
March 26, 1973	- 3	-12.00	-1381 (L)	927.90
March 27, 1973	+10	- 2.33	-1373	944.91
March 28, 1973	+ 9	+ 5.33	1364	948.00
March 29, 1973	+12 (H)	+10.33 (H)	-1352	959.14 (H)
March 30, 1973	+ 4	+ 8.33	-1348	951.08
April 2, 1973	- 4	+ 4.00	-1352	936.18
April 3, 1973	- 7	- 2.33	-1359	927.75
April 4, 1973	- 5	- 5.33	-1364	925.04
April 5, 1973	- 7	- 6.33	-1371	923.46 (L)
April 6, 1973	+ 2	- 3.33	-1369	931.07
April 9, 1973	+10	+ 1.66	-1359	947.47
April 10, 1973	+14	+ 8.66	-1345	960.47
April 11, 1973	+16 (H)	+13.33 (H)	-1329	967.41 (H)
April 12, 1973	+ 3	+11.00	-1326	964.03
April 13, 1973	+ 1	+ 6.66	-1325	959.36
April 16, 1973	+ 2	+ 2.00	-1323	956.73
April 17, 1973	- 3	.00	-1326	953.42
April 18, 1973	+ 3	+ 1.66	-1323	958.31

THE APPENDIX

Date	Climax Indicator	3-day Moving Average	CLX Cumulative	Dow
April 19, 1973	+ 4	+ 1.33	-1319 (H)	963.20
April 23, 1973	- 5	+ 0.66	-1324	955.37
April 24, 1973	-10	- 3.66	-1334	940.77
April 25, 1973	-15	-10.00	-1349	930.54
April 26, 1973	- 5	-10.00	-1359	937.76
April 27, 1973	-14 (L)	-11.33 (L)	-1373	922.19
April 30, 1973	-10	- 9.66	-1383	921.43
May 1, 1973	- 5	- 9.66	-1388	921.21 (L)
May 2, 1973	+ 8	- 2.33	-1380	932.34
May 3, 1973	+11 (H)	+ 4.66	-1369	945.66
May 4, 1973	+10	+ 9.66 (H)	-1359	953.87
May 7, 1973	+ 3	+ 8.00	-1356	950.71
May 8, 1973	+11 (H)	+ 8.00	-1345	956.58 (H)
May 9, 1973	0	+ 4.66	-1345	949.05
May 10, 1973	- 7	+ 1.33	-1352	939.27
May 11, 1973	- 9	- 5.33	-1361	927.98
May 14, 1973	-18 (L)	-11.33 (L)	-1379	909.69
May 15, 1973	- 8	-11.66	-1387	917.44
May 16, 1973	- 4	-10.00	-1391	917.07
May 17, 1973	-11	- 7.66	-1402	911.72
May 18, 1973	-23 (L)	-12.66	-1425	895.16
May 21, 1973	-22	-18.66 (L)	-1447	886.51 (L)
May 22, 1973	- 9	-18.00	-1456	892.46
May 23, 1973	- 7	-12.66	-1463	895.02
May 24, 1973	+10 (H)	- 2.00	-1453	924.44
May 25, 1973	+ 8	+ 3.66	-1445	930.84 (H)
May 29, 1973	+ 3	˄ 7.00	-1442	925.57
May 30, 1973	- 6	+ 1.66	-1448	908.87
May 31, 1973	- 9	- 4.00	-1457	901.41
June 1, 1973	- 7	- 7.33	-1464	893.96
June 4, 1973	-13 (L)	- 9.66 (L)	-1477	885.91 (L)
June 5, 1973	+ 4	- 5.33	-1473	900.81
June 6, 1973	- 1	- 3.33	-1474	898.18
June 7, 1973	+11	+ 4.66	-1463	909.62
June 8, 1973	+16 (H)	+ 8.66	-1447	920.00
June 11, 1973	+ 6	+11.00	-1441	915.11
June 12, 1973	+14	+12.00 (H)	-1427	926.78 (H)
June 13, 1973	- 2	+ 6.00	-1429	915.49
June 14, 1973	-16	- 1.33	-1445	903.67
June 15, 1973	-20 (L)	-12.66	-1465	888.55
June 18, 1973	-20 (L)	-18.66 (L)	-1485	875.08
June 19, 1973	- 4	-14.66	-1489	881.55
June 20, 1973	- 3	- 9.00	1492	884.71
June 21, 1973	-11 (L)	- 6.00	-1503	873.65
June 22, 1973	+ 8	- 2.00	-1495	879.82
June 25, 1973	- 2	- 1.66	-1497	869.13 (L)
June 26, 1973	+ 8	+ 4.66	-1489	879.44
June 27, 1973	+ 5	+ 3.66	-1484	884.63
June 28, 1973	+ 8	+ 7.00	-1476	894.64
June 29, 1973	- 1	+ 4.00	-1477	891.71
July 2, 1973	-11	- 1.33	-1488	880.57

Date	Climax Indicator	3-day Moving Average	CLX Cumulative	Dow
July 3, 1973	- 8	- 6.66	-1496	874.17
July 5, 1973	- 5	- 8.00	-1501	874.32
July 6, 1973	-10	- 7.66	-1511 (L)	870.11
July 9, 1973	0	- 5.00	-1511	877.26
July 10, 1973	+ 9	- 0.33	-1502	888.32
July 11, 1973	+17 (H)	+ 8.66	-1485	908.19
July 12, 1973	+ 2	+ 9.33	-1483	901.94
July 13, 1973	- 7	+ 4.00	-1490	885.99
July 16, 1973	+ 2	- 2.33	-1488	897.58
July 17, 1973	+ 4	- 0.33	-1484	898.03
July 18, 1973	+11	+ 5.66	-1473	905.41
July 19, 1973	+ 7	+ 7.33	-1466	906.68
July 20, 1973	+11	+ 9.66 (H)	-1455	910.89
July 23, 1973	+ 5	+ 7.66	-1450	913.15
July 24, 1973	+ 4	+ 6.66	-1446	918.72
July 25, 1973	+14 (H)	+ 7.66	-1432	933.02
July 26, 1973	+ 6	+ 8.00	-1426	934.53
July 27, 1973	+ 2	+ 7.33	-1424	936.71 (H)
July 30, 1973	0	+ 2.66	-1424 (H)	933.78
July 31, 1973	- 2	.00	-1426	926.40
August 1, 1973	-15	- 5.66	-1441	912.18
August 2, 1973	- 7	- 8.00	-1448	910.14
August 3, 1973	- 4	- 8.66	-1452	908.87
August 6, 1973	- 5	- 5.33	-1457	912.78
August 7, 1973	- 4	- 4.33	-1461	911.95
August 8, 1973	- 9	- 6.00	-1470	902.02
August 9, 1973	- 6	- 6.33	-1476	901.19
August 10, 1973	-13	- 9.33	-1489	892.08
August 13, 1973	-20 (L)	-13.00	-1509	883.43
August 14, 1973	-19 (L)	-17.33 (L)	-1528	870.71
August 15, 1973	- 7	-15.33 (L)	-1535	874.17
August 16, 1973	-11	-12.33	-1546	872.74
August 17, 1973	-10	- 9.33	-1556	871.84
August 20, 1973	-14 (L)	-11.66	-1570	867.40
August 21, 1973	-18 (L)	-14.00	-1588	857.84
August 22, 1973	-16	-16.00 (L)	-1604	851.90 (L)
August 23, 1973	+ 2	-10.66	-1602	864.46
August 24, 1973	- 4	- 6.00	-1606 (L)	863.49
August 27, 1973	+ 5	+ 1.00	-1601	870.71
August 28, 1973	+ 4	+ 1.66	-1597	872.07
August 29, 1973	+16 (H)	+ 8.33	-1581	883.43
August 30, 1973	+10	+10.00	-1571	882.53
August 31, 1973	+13	+13.00 (H)	-1558	887.57
September 4, 1973	+12	+11.66	-1546	895.40
September 5, 1973	+ 8	+11.00	-1538	899.08
September 6, 1973	+ 8	+ 9.33	-1530	901.04
September 7, 1973	+ 2	+ 6.00	-1524	898.63
September 10, 1973	- 6	+ 1.33	-1530	891.33
September 11, 1973	- 6	- 3.33	-1536	885.76
September 12, 1973	- 7	- 6.33	-1543	881.32
September 13, 1973	- 3	- 5.33	-1546	880.57

Date	Climax Indicator	3-day Moving Average	CLX Cumulative	Dow
September 14, 1973	+ 1	- 3.00	-1545	886.36
September 17, 1973	+ 7	+ 1.66	-1538	892.98
September 18, 1973	+ 8	+ 5.33	-1530	891.26
September 19, 1973	+18	+11.00	-1512	910.37
September 20, 1973	+20 (H)	+15.33	-1492	920.53
September 21, 1973	+20 (H)	+19.33	-1472	927.91
September 24, 1973	+20 (H)	+20.00 (H)	-1452	936.71
September 25, 1973	+19	+19.66	-1433	940.62
September 26, 1973	+13	+17.33	-1420	949.50
September 27, 1973	+10	+14.00	-1410	953.26
September 28, 1973	+ 2	+ 8.33	-1408	947.09
October 1, 1973	+ 1	+ 4.33	-1407	948.82
October 2, 1973	+ 5	+ 2.66	-1402	956.81
October 3, 1973	+ 8	+ 4.66	-1394	964.40
October 4, 1973	+ 1	+ 4.66	-1393	955.75
October 5, 1973	+ 8	+ 5.66	-1385	971.10
October 8, 1973	+ 8	+ 5.66	-1377	977.65
October 9, 1973	+ 5	+ 7.00	-1372 (H)	974.19
October 10, 1973	- 9	+ 1.33	-1381	960.57
October 11, 1973	+ 2	- 0.66	-1379	976.07
October 12, 1973	+ 6	- 0.33	-1373	978.63
October 15, 1973	- 5	+ 1.00	-1378	967.04
October 16, 1973	- 3	- 0.66	-1382	967.42
October 17, 1973	- 2	- 3.33	-1384	962.53
October 18, 1973	- 9	- 4.66	-1393	959.75
October 19, 1973	+ 1	- 3.33	-1392	963.74
October 22, 1973	- 7	- 5.00	-1399	960.57
October 23, 1973	- 1	- 2.33	-1400 (L)	966.51
October 24, 1973	+ 3	- 1.66	-1397	971.85
October 25, 1973	+ 4	+ 2.00	-1393	974.48
October 26, 1973	+17 (H)	+ 8.00	-1376	987.05 (H)
October 29, 1973	+ 8	+ 9.66 (H)	-1368 (H)	984.80
October 30, 1973	- 8	+ 6.33	-1376	968.54
October 31, 1973	- 9	- 3.00	-1385	956.57
November 1, 1973	-15	-10.66	-1400	948.82
November 2, 1973	-17	-13.66	-1417	935.28
November 5, 1973	-20 (L)	-17.33	-1437	919.40
November 6, 1973	-16	-17.66 (L)	-1453	913.15
November 7, 1973	- 5	-13.66	-1458	920.00
November 8, 1973	+ 1	- 6.66	-1457	932.57
November 9, 1973	- 7	- 3.66	-1464	908.42
November 12, 1973	-14	- 6.66	-1478	896.00
November 13, 1973	-12	-11.00	-1490	883.40
November 14, 1973	-22 (L)	16.00	-1512	869.88
November 15, 1973	- 9	-14.33	-1521	874.55
November 16, 1973	+ 4	- 9.00	-1517	891.33
November 19, 1973	- 5	- 3.33	-1522	862.66
November 20, 1973	-11	- 4.00	-1533	844.90
November 21, 1973	- 5	- 7.00	-1538	854.98
November 23, 1973	- 2	- 6.00	-1540	854.00
November 26, 1973	-17	- 8.00	-1557	824.95

Date	Climax Indicator	3-day Moving Average	CLX Cumulative	Dow
November 27, 1973	-10	- 9.66	-1567	817.73
November 28, 1973	+ 7	- 6.66	-1560	839.78
November 29, 1973	- 8	- 3.66	-1568	835.11
November 30, 1973	- 8	- 3.00	-1576	822.25
December 3, 1973	-20 (L)	-12.00	-1596	806.52
December 4, 1973	-17	-15.00	-1613	803.21
December 5, 1973	-19	-18.66 (L)	-1632 (L)	788.31 (L)
December 6, 1973	+ 7	- 9.66	-1625	814.12
December 7, 1973	+14 (H)	+ 0.66	-1611	838.05
December 10, 1973	+12	+11.00 (H)	-1599	851.14 (H)
December 11, 1973	0	+ 8.66	-1599	834.23
December 12, 1973	- 7	+ 1.66	-1606	810.73
December 13, 1973	-10	- 5.66	-1616	800.43
December 14, 1973	- 2	- 6.33	-1618	815.65
December 17, 1973	- 1	- 4.33	-1619	811.11
December 18, 1973	+15	+ 4.00	-1604	829.48
December 19, 1973	+ 8	+ 7.33	-1596	829.56
December 20, 1973	+ 1	+ 8.00	-1595	828.10
December 21, 1973	- 3	+ 2.00	-1598	818.73
December 24, 1973	- 5	- 2.33	-1603	814.81
December 26, 1973	+12	+ 1.33	-1591	838.25
December 27, 1973	+13	+ 6.66	-1578	851.01
December 28, 1973	+ 3	+ 9.33	-1575	848.02
December 31, 1973	+ 8	+ 8.00	-1567	850.86
January 2, 1974	+ 4	+ 5.00	-1563	855.32
January 3, 1974	+20 (H)	+10.66	-1543	880.69 (H)
January 4, 1974	+ 7	+10.33	-1536	880.23
January 7, 1974	+ 6	+11.00 (H)	-1530 (H)	876.84
January 8, 1974	- 4	+ 3.00	-1534	861.78
January 9, 1974	-15 (L)	- 4.33	-1549	834.79
January 10, 1974	-12	-10.33 (L)	-1561	823.11 (L)
January 11, 1974	- 1	- 9.33	-1562	841.48
January 14, 1974	- 3	- 5.33	-1565	840.17
January 15, 1974	+ 4	.00	-1561	846.40
January 16, 1974	+ 6	+ 2.33	-1555	856.09
January 17, 1974	+12 (H)	+ 7.33 (H)	-1543	872.16
January 18, 1974	- 6	+ 4.00	-1549	855.47
January 21, 1974	- 5	+ 0.33	-1554	854.63
January 22, 1974	+ 4	- 2.33	-1550	863.47
January 23, 1974	+10 (H)	+ 3.00	-1540	871.00 (H)
January 24, 1974	+ 3	+ 5.66	-1537	863.08
January 25, 1974	+ 2	+ 5.00	-1535	859.39
January 28, 1974	- 9	- 1.33	-1544	853.01
January 29, 1974	-11	- 6.00	-1555	852.32
January 30, 1974	+ 4	- 5.33	-1551	862.32
January 31, 1974	- 8	- 5.00	-1559	855.55
February 1, 1974	-15	- 6.33	-1574	843.94
February 4, 1974	-23 (L)	-15.33	-1597	821.50
February 5, 1974	-13	-17.00 (L)	-1610	820.63
February 6, 1974	- 6	-14.00	-1616	824.62
February 7, 1974	+ 1	- 6.00	-1615	828.46

Date	Climax Indicator	3-day Moving Average	CLX Cumulative	Dow
February 8, 1974	- 8	- 4.33	-1623	820.40
February 11, 1974	-16 (L)	- 7.66	-1639	803.90 (L)
February 12, 1974	- 6	-10.00	-1645	806.63
February 13, 1974	- 1	- 7.66	-1646 (L)	806.87
February 14, 1974	+ 2	- 1.66	-1644	809.92
February 15, 1974	+10	+ 3.66	-1634	820.32
February 19, 1974	+ 7	+ 6.33	-1627	819.54
February 20, 1974	+13	+10.00	-1614	831.04
February 21, 1974	+18	+12.66	-1596	846.84
February 22, 1974	+21 (H)	+17.33 (H)	-1575	855.99
February 25, 1974	+ 9	+16.00	-1566	851.38
February 26, 1974	+17	+15.66	-1549	859.51
February 27, 1974	+12	+12.66	-1537	863.42
February 28, 1974	+ 4	+11.00	-1533	860.53
March 1, 1974	- 4	+ 4.00	-1537	851.92
March 4, 1974	+ 3	+ 1.00	-1534	853.18
March 5, 1974	+13	+ 4.00	-1521	872.42
March 6, 1974	+11	+ 9.00	-1510	879.85
March 7, 1974	- 3	+ 7.00	-1513	869.06
March 8, 1974	+ 9	+ 5.66	-1504	878.05
March 11, 1974	+14 (H)	+ 6.66	-1490	888.45
March 12, 1974	+ 6	+ 9.66 (H)	-1484	887.12
March 13, 1974	+ 8	+ 9.33	-1476	891.66 (H)
March 14, 1974	+ 2	+ 5.33	-1474 (H)	889.78
March 15, 1974	- 3	+ 2.33	-1477	887.83
March 18, 1974	-11	- 4.00	-1488	874.22
March 19, 1974	-15	- 9.66	-1503	867.57
March 20, 1974	- 8	-11.33	-1511	872.34
March 21, 1974	- 4	- 9.00	-1515	875.47
March 22, 1974	- 1	- 4.33	-1516	878.13
March 25, 1974	- 3	- 2.66	-1519	881.02
March 26, 1974	+ 2	- 0.66	-1517	883.68
March 27, 1974	- 8	- 3.00	-1525	871.17
March 28, 1974	-19 (L)	- 8.33	-1544	854.35
March 29, 1974	-19 (L)	-15.33	-1563	846.68
April 1, 1974	-17	-18.33 (L)	-1580	843.48
April 2, 1974	- 6	-14.00	-1586	846.61
April 3, 1974	2	- 7.00	-1584	858.03
April 4, 1974	+ 1	- 1.00	-1583	858.89
April 5, 1974	-11	- 2.66	-1594	847.54
April 8, 1974	-16	- 8.66	-1610	839.96
April 9, 1974	0	- 9.00	-1610	846.84
April 10, 1974	- 7	- 7.66	-1617	843.71
April 11, 1974	- 3	- 3.33	-1620	844.81
April 15, 1974	- 5	- 5.00	-1625	843.79
April 16, 1974	+13	+ 1.66	-1612	861.23
April 17, 1974	+ 9	+ 5.66	-1603	867.41
April 18, 1974	+10	+10.66 (H)	-1593	869.92
April 19, 1974	- 1	+ 6.00	-1594	859.90
April 22, 1974	- 7	+ 0.66	-1601	858.59
April 23, 1974	-16	- 8.00	-1617	845.98

Date		Climax Indicator	3-day Moving Average	CLX Cumulative	Dow
April	24, 1974	-22 (L)	-15.00	-1639	832.37
April	25, 1974	-19	-19.00 (L)	-1658	827.67 (L)
April	26, 1974	- 4	-15.00	-1662	834.64
April	29, 1974	- 2	- 8.33	-1664	835.42
April	30, 1974	- 1	- 2.33	-1665	836.75
May	1, 1974	+13 (H)	+ 3.33	-1652	853.88
May	2, 1974	+ 6	+ 6.00	-1646	851.06
May	3, 1974	- 2	+ 5.66	-1648	845.90
May	6, 1974	+ 1	+ 1.66	-1647	844.88
May	7, 1974	+ 5	+ 1.33	-1642	847.15
May	8, 1974	+ 9	+ 5.00	-1633	850.99
May	9, 1974	+17 (H)	+10.33 (H)	-1616	865.77 (H)
May	10, 1974	- 5	+ 7.00	-1621	850.44
May	13, 1974	- 6	+ 2.00	-1627	845.59
May	14, 1974	- 5	- 5.33	-1632	847.86
May	15, 1974	- 7	- 6.00	-1639	846.06
May	16, 1974	-11	- 7.66	-1650	835.34
May	17, 1974	-25 (L)	-14.33	-1675	818.84
May	20, 1974	-22	-19.33	-1697	812.42
May	21, 1974	-14	-20.33 (L)	-1711	809.53
May	22, 1974	-16	-17.33	-1727	802.57
May	23, 1974	-11	-13.66	-1738	805.23
May	24, 1974	+ 3	- 8.00	-1735	816.65
May	28, 1974	+ 2	- 2.00	-1733	814.30
May	29, 1974	-15 (L)	- 3.33	-1748 (L)	795.37 (L)
May	30, 1974	+ 1	- 4.00	-1747	803.58
May	31, 1974	0	- 4.66	-1747	802.17
June	3, 1974	+14	+ 5.00	-1733	821.26
June	4, 1974	+20 (H)	+11.33	-1713	828.69
June	5, 1974	+14	+16.00	-1699	830.18
June	6, 1974	+18	+17.33 (H)	-1681	845.35
June	7, 1974	+17	+16.33	-1664	853.72
June	10, 1974	+16	+17.00	-1648	859.67 (H)
June	11, 1974	+ 4	+12.33	-1644	852.08
June	12, 1974	+ 1	+ 7.00	-1643	848.56
June	13, 1974	+ 1	+ 2.00	-1642 (H)	852.08
June	14, 1974	- 4	- 0.66	-1646	843.08
June	17, 1974	-16	- 6.33	-1662	833.23
June	18, 1974	-18	-12.66	-1680	830.26
June	19, 1974	-16	-16.66	-1696	826.11
June	20, 1974	-18	-17.33	-1714	820.79
June	21, 1974	-22 (L)	-18.66 (L)	-1736	815.39
June	24, 1974	-11	-17.00	-1747	816.33
June	25, 1974	- 1	-11.33	-1748	828.85
June	26, 1974	-12	- 8.00	-1760	816.96
June	27, 1974	-15	- 9.33	-1775	803.66
June	28, 1974	-13	-13.33	-1788	802.41
July	1, 1974	- 7	-11.66	-1795	806.24
July	2, 1974	-20 (L)	-13.33	-1815	790.68
July	3, 1974	- 7	-11.33	-1822	792.87
July	5, 1974	- 8	-11.66	-1830	791.77

Date	Climax Indicator	3-day Moving Average	CLX Cumulative	Dow
July 8, 1974	-23 (L)	-12.66	-1853	770.57
July 9, 1974	-12	-14.33	-1865	772.29
July 10, 1974	-14	-16.33 (L)	-1879	762.12
July 11, 1974	-13	-13.00	-1892	759.62 (L)
July 12, 1974	+ 8	- 6.33	-1884	787.23
July 15, 1974	+ 5	.00	-1879	786.61
July 16, 1974	- 1	+ 4.00	-1880	775.97
July 17, 1974	+ 8	+ 4.00	-1872	784.97
July 18, 1974	+10 (H)	+ 5.66	-1862	789.19
July 19, 1974	+ 3	+ 7.00 (H)	-1859	787.94
July 22, 1974	+ 1	+ 4.66	-1858	790.36
July 23, 1974	+12 (H)	+ 5.33	-1846	797.72
July 24, 1974	+11	+ 8.00	-1835	805.77 (H)
July 25, 1974	- 4	+ 6.33	-1839	795.68
July 26, 1974	-10	- 1.33	-1849	784.57
July 29, 1974	-13	- 9.00	-1862	770.89
July 30, 1974	-14	-12.33	-1876	765.57
July 31, 1974	-14	-13.66	-1890	757.43
August 1, 1974	-14	-14.00 (L)	-1904	751.10
August 2, 1974	- 8	-12.00	-1912	752.58
August 5, 1974	0	- 7.33	-1912	760.40
August 6, 1974	+ 7	- 0.33	-1905	773.78
August 7, 1974	+15 (H)	+ 7.33	-1890	797.56
August 8, 1974	+ 1	+ 7.66	-1889	784.89
August 9, 1974	- 3	+ 4.33	-1892	777.30
August 12, 1974	- 7	- 3.00	-1899	767.29
August 13, 1974	-12	- 7.33	-1911	756.41
August 14, 1974	-15	-11.33	-1926	740.54
August 15, 1974	-11	-12.66	-1937	737.88
August 16, 1974	-17	-14.33	-1954	731.54
August 19, 1974	-18	-14.66 (L)	-1972	721.84
August 20, 1974	- 1	-12.00	-1973	726.85
August 21, 1974	- 8	- 9.00	-1981	711.28
August 22, 1974	-14	- 7.66	-1995	704.63
August 23, 1974	-18	-13.33	-2013	686.80
August 26, 1974	-11	-14.33	-2024	688.13
August 27, 1974	-15	-14.66	-2039	671.54
August 28, 1974	-17	-14.33	-2056	666.61
August 29, 1974	-18	-16.66 (L)	-2074	656.84
August 30, 1974	+ 4	-10.33	-2070	678.58
September 3, 1974	- 5	- 6.33	-2075	663.33
September 4, 1974	-21 (L)	- 7.33	-2096	647.92
September 5, 1974	+ 5	- 7.00	-2091	670.76
September 6, 1974	+16 (H)	.00	-2075	677.88
September 10, 1974	- 1	+ 4.00	-2076	658.17
September 11, 1974	- 8	- 4.00	-2084	654.72
September 12, 1974	-18	- 9.00	-2102	641.74
September 13, 1974	-24 (L)	-16.66 (L)	-2126	627.19 (L)
September 16, 1974	- 4	-15.33	-2130	639.78
September 17, 1974	+ 5	- 7.66	-2125	648.78
September 18, 1974	+ 5	+ 2.00	-2120	651.91

Date	Climax Indicator	3-day Moving Average	CLX Cumulative	Dow
September 19, 1974	+15 (H)	+ 8.33	-2105	674.05 (H)
September 20, 1974	+ 7	+ 9.00 (H)	-2098	670.76
September 23, 1974	- 4	+ 6.00	-2102	663.72
September 24, 1974	- 8	- 1.66	-2110	654.10
September 25, 1974	- 7	- 6.33	-2117	649.95
September 26, 1974	-10	- 8.33	-2127	637.98
September 27, 1974	-13	-10.00	-2140	621.95
September 30, 1974	-20 (L)	-14.33 (L)	-2160	607.87
October 1, 1974	- 9	-14.00	-2169	604.82
October 2, 1974	- 8	-12.33	-2177	601.53
October 3, 1974	-16	-11.00	-2193	587.61
October 4, 1974	-11 (L)	-11.66	-2204	584.56 (L)
October 7, 1974	+ 7	- 6.66	-2197	607.56
October 8, 1974	0	- 1.33	-2197	602.63
October 9, 1974	+18	+ 8.33	-2179	631.02
October 10, 1974	+16	+11.33	-2163	648.08
October 11, 1974	+13	+15.66	-2150	658.24
October 14, 1974	+22 (H)	+17.00 (H)	-2128	673.50 (H)
October 15, 1974	0	+11.66	-2128	658.40
October 16, 1974	- 6	+ 5.33	-2134	642.29
October 17, 1974	- 1	- 2.33	-2135	651.44
October 18, 1974	+ 3	- 1.33	-2132	654.88
October 21, 1974	+10	+ 4.00	-2122	669.82
October 22, 1974	- 7	+ 2.00	-2129	662.86
October 23, 1974	-13	- 3.33	-2142	644.95
October 24, 1974	-14 (L)	-11.33	-2156	636.26
October 25, 1974	-10	-12.33 (L)	-2166	636.19
October 28, 1974	-12	-12.00	-2178	633.84 (L)
October 29, 1974	+ 6	- 5.33	-2172	659.34
October 30, 1974	+12 (H)	+ 2.00	-2160	673.03 (H)
October 31, 1974	+ 6	+ 8.00	-2154	665.52
November 1, 1974	+ 8	+ 8.66	-2146	665.28
November 4, 1974	- 3	+ 3.66	-2149	657.23
November 5, 1974	+14 (H)	+ 6.33	-2135	674.75 (H)
November 6, 1974	- 5	+ 2.00	-2140	669.12
November 7, 1974	- 3	+ 2.00	-2143	671.93
November 8, 1974	- 6	- 4.66	-2149	667.16
November 11, 1974	+ 7	- 0.66	-2142	672.64
November 12, 1974	-12	- 3.66	-2154	659.18
November 13, 1974	- 4	- 3.00	-2158	659.18
November 14, 1974	- 1	- 5.66	-2159	658.40
November 15, 1974	-11	- 5.33	-2170	647.61
November 18, 1974	-26 (L)	-12.66	-2196	624.92
November 19, 1974	-24	-20.33	-2220	614.05
November 20, 1974	-18	-22.66 (L)	-2238	609.59
November 21, 1974	-12	-18.00	-2250	608.57 (L)
November 22, 1974	- 2	-10.66	-2252	615.30
November 25, 1974	- 6	- 6.66	-2258	611.94
November 26, 1974	+ 4	- 1.33	-2254	617.26
November 27, 1974	+ 7	+ 1.66	-2247	619.29
November 29, 1974	+ 1	+ 4.00	-2246	618.66

Date	Climax Indicator	3-day Moving Average	CLX Cumulative	Dow
December 2, 1974	- 9	- 0.33	-2255	603.02
December 3, 1974	-12	- 6.66	-2267	596.61
December 4, 1974	- 7	- 9.33	-2274	598.64
December 5, 1974	-17	-12.00	-2291	587.06
December 6, 1974	-19 (L)	-14.33	-2310	577.60 (L)
December 9, 1974	-10	-15.33 (L)	-2320	579.94
December 10, 1974	+ 4	- 8.33	-2316	593.87
December 11, 1974	- 1	- 2.33	-2317	595.35
December 12, 1974	+ 3	+ 2.00	-2314	596.37
December 13, 1974	- 5	- 1.00	-2319	592.77
December 16, 1974	- 5	- 2.33	-2324	586.83
December 17, 1974	+ 7	- 1.00	-2317	597.54
December 18, 1974	+ 8	+ 3.33	-2309	603.49
December 19, 1974	+ 3	+ 6.00	-2306	604.43
December 20, 1974	- 6	+ 1.66	-2312	598.48
December 23, 1974	-12 (L)	- 5.00	-2324 (L)	589.64 (L)
December 24, 1974	+ 2	- 5.33	-2322	598.40
December 26, 1974	+ 4	- 2.00	-2318	604.74
December 27, 1974	0	+ 2.00	-2318	602.16
December 30, 1974	0	+ 1.33	-2318	603.25
December 31, 1974	+13	+ 4.33	-2305	616.24
January 2, 1975	+21 (H)	+11.33	-2284	632.04
January 3, 1975	+15	+16.33	-2269	634.54
January 6, 1975	+13	+16.33 (H)	-2256	637.20
January 7, 1975	+11	+13.00	-2245	641.19
January 8, 1975	+ 3	+ 9.00	-2242	635.40
January 9, 1975	+13	+ 9.00	-2229	645.26
January 10, 1975	+22 (H)	+12.66	-2207	658.79
January 13, 1975	+11	+15.33	-2196	654.18
January 14, 1975	+ 2	+11.66	-2194	648.70
January 15, 1975	+ 9	+ 7.33	-2185	653.39
January 16, 1975	+ 4	+ 5.00	-2181	655.74
January 17, 1975	- 8	+ 1.66	-2189	644.63
January 20, 1975	- 2	- 2.00	-2191	647.45
January 21, 1975	- 7	- 5.66	-2198	641.90
January 22, 1975	0	- 3.00	-2198	652.61
January 23, 1975	+ 5	- 0.66	-2193	656.76
January 24, 1975	+15	+ 6.66	-2178	666.61
January 27, 1975	+28 (H)	+16.00	-2150	692.66
January 28, 1975	+19	+20.66	-2131	694.77
January 29, 1975	+19	+22.00 (H)	-2112	705.96
January 30, 1975	+ 3	+13.66	-2109	696.42
January 31, 1975	+ 8	+10.00	-2101	703.69
February 3, 1975	+13	+ 8.00	-2088	711.44
February 4, 1975	+ 7	+ 9.33	-2081	708.07
February 5, 1975	+12	+10.66	-2069	717.85
February 6, 1975	+ 7	+ 8.66	-2062	714.17
February 7, 1975	0	+ 6.33	-2062	711.91
February 10, 1975	- 4	+ 1.00	-2066	708.39
February 11, 1975	- 3	- 2.33	-2069	707.60
February 12, 1975	+ 2	- 1.66	-2067	715.03

Date	Climax Indicator	3-day Moving Average	CLX Cumulative	Dow
February 13, 1975	+10	+ 3.00	-2057	726.92
February 14, 1975	+14	+ 8.66	-2043	734.20
February 18, 1975	+ 9	+ 11.00	-2034	731.30
February 19, 1975	+ 9	+10.66	-2025	736.39
February 20, 1975	+10	+ 9.33	-2015	745.38
February 21, 1975	+13	+10.66	-2002	749.77
February 24, 1975	- 6	+ 5.66	-2008	736.94
February 25, 1975	- 9	0.66	-2017	719.18
February 26, 1975	- 2	5.66	-2019	728.10
February 27, 1975	0	- 3.66	-2019	731.15
February 28, 1975	+ 8	+ 2.00	-2011	739.05
March 3, 1975	+21 (H)	+ 9.66	-1990	753.13
March 4, 1975	+16	+15.00	-1974	757.74
March 5, 1975	+ 7	+14.66	-1967	752.82
March 6, 1975	+13	+12.00	-1954	761.81
March 7, 1975	+20 (H)	+13.33	-1934	770.10
March 10, 1975	+16	+16.33 (H)	-1918	776.13
March 11, 1975	+ 3	+13.00	-1915	770.89
March 12, 1975	- 6	+ 4.33	-1921	763.69
March 13, 1975	- 7	- 3.33	-1928	762.98
March 14, 1975	+ 8	- 1.66	-1920	773.47
March 17, 1975	+12 (H)	+ 4.33	-1908	786.53 (H)
March 18, 1975	+ 1	+ 7.00	-1907 (H)	779.41
March 19, 1975	- 9	+ 1.33	-1916	769.48
March 20, 1975	- 8	- 5.33	-1924	764.00
March 21, 1975	-10	- 9.00	-1934	763.06
March 24, 1975	-19 (L)	-12.33 (L)	-1953	743.43 (L)
March 25, 1975	- 4	-11.00	-1957	747.89
March 26, 1975	+10	- 4.33	-1947	766.19
March 27, 1975	+ 3	+ 3.00	-1944	770.26
March 31, 1975	+ 3	+ 5.33	-1941	768.15
April 1, 1975	- 7	- 0.33	-1948	761.58
April 2, 1975	- 8	- 4.00	-1956	760.56
April 3, 1975	-14	- 9.66	-1970	752.19
April 4, 1975	-12	-11.33	-1982	747.26
April 7, 1975	-15 (L)	-13.66 (L)	-1997	742.88 (L)
April 8, 1975	- 3	-10.00	-2000 (L)	749.22
April 9, 1975	+ 7	- 3.66	-1993	767.99
April 10, 1975	+ 7	+ 3.66	-1986	781.29
April 11, 1975	+10	+ 8.00	-1976	789.50
April 14, 1975	+18 (H)	+11.66	-1958	806.95
April 15, 1975	+13	+13.66	-1945	815.08
April 16, 1975	+10	+13.66 (H)	-1935	815.71
April 17, 1975	+ 7	+10.00	-1928	819.46
April 18, 1975	- 4	+ 4.33	-1932	808.43
April 21, 1975	+ 2	+ 1.66	-1930	815.86
April 22, 1975	- 2	- 1.33	-1932	814.14
April 23, 1975	-11	- 3.66	-1943	802.49
April 24, 1975	- 7	- 6.66	-1950	803.66
April 25, 1975	+ 2	- 5.33	-1948	811.80
April 28, 1975	- 1	- 2.00	-1949	810.00

Date	Climax Indicator	3-day Moving Average	CLX Cumulative	Dow
April 29, 1975	-10	- 3.00	-1959	803.04
April 30, 1975	+ 2	- 3.00	-1957	821.34
May 1, 1975	+11	+ 1.00	-1946	830.96
May 2, 1975	+18 (H)	+10.33	-1928	848.48
May 5, 1975	+16	+15.00 (H)	-1912	855.60 (H)
May 6, 1975	+ 1	+11.66	-1911	834.72
May 7, 1975	- 1	+ 5.33	-1912	836.44
May 8, 1975	+ 4	+ 1.33	-1908	840.50
May 9, 1975	+12 (H)	+ 5.00	-1896	850.13
May 12, 1975	+ 5	+ 7.00	-1891	847.47
May 13, 1975	+ 4	+ 7.00	-1887	850.13
May 14, 1975	+ 4	+ 4.33	-1883 (H)	858.73 (H)
May 15, 1975	- 6	+ 0.66	-1889	848.80
May 16, 1975	-12	- 4.66	-1901	837.61
May 19, 1975	- 9	- 9.00	-1910	837.69
May 20, 1975	-16	-12.33	-1926	830.49
May 21, 1975	-22 (L)	-15.66 (L)	-1948	818.68

TABLE II

A-B-C-D Climax Indicator Swings Culled From Table I, Swings Which Did Not

Culminate in Major Tops or Bottoms

Time Period	Point A	Point B	Point C	Point D	Dow Movement Thereafter
4 /14 to 5 /17 (65)	+17	- 2	+ 1	- 6	90—point decline
3 / 2 to 3 /21 (66)	-19	+ 4	-14	+11	27—point advance
3 /22 to 5 / 3 (66)	+13	-13	+ 4	-22	57—point decline
5 / 3 to 5 /24 (66)	-22	+ 9	-19	+10	15—point advance
5 /24 to 6 /27 (66)	+10	- 9	+ 9	-12	56—point decline
10/27 to 11/21 (66)	+16	- 8	+ 4	-17	9—point decline
11/21 to 12/ 6 (66)	-17	0	-12	+ 8	23—point advance
11/21 to 1 /11 (67)	-17	+13	-14	+16	87—point advance
5 /31 to 6 / 7 (67)	-21	+ 5	-15	+ 9	57—point advance
1 /22 to 2 /20 (68)	-19	+ 3	-18	+ 6	7—point advance
4 / 1 to 4 /19 (68)	+19	- 2	+ 7	- 6	6—point decline
6 / 4 to 7 /25 (68)	+16	-11	+ 6	-14	16—point decline
8 / 2 to 8 /12 (68)	-11	+ 1	- 5	+ 8	103—point advance
4 /30 to 5 /19 (69)	+18	- 9	+10	-11	157—point decline
9 / 8 to 10/13 (69)	-21	+ 5	-12	+ 6	44—point advance
10/22 to 11/13 (69)	+18	- 6	+ 1	- 8	80—point decline
11/25 to 12/18 (69)	-24	+ 1	-11	+ 5	27—point advance
7 /17 to 8 / 3 (70)	+22	- 5	+ 9	- 8	16—point decline
6 /21 to 8 /12 (71)	-22	+12	-20	+14	62—point advance
8 /16 to 9 /14 (71)	+20	- 9	+13	-10	104—point decline
10/20 to 11/29 (71)	-22	+11	-12	+15	139—point advance

Time Period	Point A	Point B	Point C	Point D	Dow Movement Thereafter
7 /24 to 8 /24 (72)	+18	- 4	+13	- 8	
5 /18 to 7 /11 (73)	-23	+16	-20	+17	29—point advance
7 /11 to 8 / 1 (73)	+17	- 7	+ 2	-15	60—point decline
8 /13 to 8 /23 (73)	-20	- 7	-16	+ 2	123—point advance
9 /24 to 11/ 1 (73)	+20	- 9	+17	-15	161—point decline
11/14 to 12/ 7 (73)	-22	+ 7	-19	+14	43—point advance
12/ 3 to 12/18 (73)	-20	+14	-10	+15	51—point advance
2 / 4 to 2 /14 (74)	-23	+ 1	-16	+ 2	82—point advance
2 /22 to 3 /18 (74)	+21	- 4	+ 8	-11	47—point decline
3 /29 to 4 /16 (74)	-19	+ 2	-16	+13	9—point advance
5 /17 to 6 / 3 (74)	-25	+ 3	-'5	+14	39—point advance
7 / 8 to 8 / 7 (74)	-23	+12	-14	+15	170—point decline
11/18 to 12/18 (74)	-26	+ 7	-19	+ 8	183—point advance
1 /27 to 2 / 24 (75)	+28	- 4	+13	- 6	18—point decline
3 / 7 to 3 /19 (75)	+20	- 7	+12	- 9	26—point decline

TABLE III

The theory here is that I am only interested in anything +10 or higher in the CLX or -10 or lower. All in-between readings are screened out.

Date	Industrials	Climax Indicator	Cum.	Comment (if any)
10/20/71	855.65	-22	- 22	
10/21/71	854.85	-14	- 36	
10/22/71	852.37	-11	- 47	
10/25/71	848.50	-10	- 57	
10/27/71	836.38	-12	- 69	
11/ 1/71	825.86	-12	- 81	
11/ 3/71	842.58	+11	- 70	
11/11/71	814.91	-14	- 84	
11/12/71	812.94	-15	- 99	
11/22/71	803.15	-13	-112	CLX Non-confirmation
11/23/71	797.97	-12	-124	CLX Non-confirmation
11/29/71	829.73	+15	-109	Large Upward Zigzag
12/ 1/71	846.02	+15	- 94	
12/ 2/71	848.79	+10	- 84	
12/ 3/71	859.59	+14	- 70	
12/16/71	871.31	+10	- 60	
12/17/71	873.80	+10	- 50	
12/20/71	885.01	+18	- 32	
12/28/71	889.98	+15	- 17	
1 / 5/72	904.43	+14	- 3	
1 / 6/72	908.49	+13	+ 10	
1 /24/72	896.82	-14	- 4	
1 /25/72	894.72	-13	- 17	
1 /26/72	889.15	-13	- 30	
2 /18/72	917.52	-10	- 40	

Date	Industrials	Climax Indicator	Cum.	Comment (if any)
3 / 6/72	950.18	+13	- 27	
3 /21/72	934.00	-10	- 37	
3 /30/72	940.70	+11	- 26	
4 / 5/72	954.55	+13	- 13	
4 / 6/72	959.44	+11	- 2	Loss of Strength
4 / 7/72	962.60	+10	+ 8	Loss of Strength
4 /25/72	946.49	-18	- 10	Large Downward Zigzag
4 /26/72	946.94	-13	- 23	
5 / 2/72	935.21	-10	- 33	
5 / 9/72	941.83	-20	- 53	
5 /12/72	941.83	+11	- 42	
5 /18/72	951.23	+10	- 32	
5 /19/72	961.54	+13	- 19	
5 /31/72	960.72	-11	- 30	
6 / 7/72	944.08	-12	- 42	
6 / 9/72	934.53	-15	- 57	
6 /12/72	936.71	-11	- 68	
6 /13/72	938.29	-10	- 78	
6 /26/72	936.41	-14	- 92	
6 /27/72	935.28	-10	-102	
6 /28/72	930.76	-13	-115	
6 /29/72	926.25	-11	-126	
7 /13/72	916.99	-11	-137	
7 /18/72	911.72	-10	-147	
7 /24/72	935.36	+18	-129	Large Upward Zigzag
8 / 2/72	941.15	+11	-118	
8 / 3/72	947.70	+12	-106	
8 / 4/72	951.76	+11	- 95	
8 /11/72	964.18	+12	- 83	
8 /14/72	973.51	+15	- 68	
8 /15/72	969.97	+10	- 58	
8 /22/72	973.51	+13	- 45	
9 / 1/72	970.05	+14	- 31	
9 /12/72	946.04	-13	- 44	
9 /20/72	940.25	-12	- 56	
9 /21/72	939.49	-11	- 67	
9 /27/72	947.25	+14	- 53	
9 /28/72	955.15	+15	- 38	
10/ 5/72	941.30	-11	- 49	
10/13/72	930.46	-12	- 61	
10/16/72	921.66	-18	- 79	Large Downward Zigzag
10/12/72	942.81	+12	- 67	
10/23/72	951.31	+20	- 47	
10/24/72	952.51	+14	- 33	
11/ 2/72	973.06	+13	- 20	
11/ 3/72	984.12	+16	- 4	
11/ 6/72	984.80	+15	+ 11	
11/14/72	1003.16	+13	+ 24	
11/21/72	1013.25	+12	+ 36	
12/ 8/72	1033.19	+10	+ 46	
12/11/72	1036.27	+12	+ 58	
12/18/72	1013.25	-14	+ 44	

Date	Industrials	Climax Indicator	Cum.	Comment (if any)
12/19/72	1009.19	-17	+ 27	
12/20/72	1004.82	-13	+ 14	
12/21/72	1000.00	-12	+ 2	
12/29/72	1020.02	+11	+ 13	
1 / 2/73	1031.68	+16	+ 29	
1 / 3/73	1043.80	+14	+ 43	
1 /15/73	1025.59	-10	+ 33	
1 /19/73	1026.19	-10	+ 23	
1 /22/73	1018.81	-12	+ 11	
1 /24/73	1004.59	-19	- 8	Large Downward Zigzag
1 /26/73	1003.54	-10	- 18	
2 / 1/73	985.77	-15	- 33	
2 / 2/73	980.81	-10	- 43	
2 / 7/73	968.32	-16	- 59	
2 / 8/73	967.19	-16	- 75	
2 /13/73	996.76	+11	- 64	
2 /21/73	974.34	-10	- 74	
2 /23/73	959.89	-13	- 87	
2 /26/73	953.79	-15	-102	
2 /27/73	947.92	-14	-116	
3 / 6/73	979.00	+23	- 93	Large Upward Zigzag
3 / 7/73	979.98	+13	- 80	
3 /19/73	952.51	-10	- 90	
3 /21/73	938.37	-16	-106	
3 /22/73	925.20	-19	-125	
3 /23/73	922.71	-14	-139	
3 /27/73	944.91	+10	-129	
3 /29/73	959.14	+12	-117	
4 / 9/73	947.47	+10	-107	
4 /10/73	960.47	+14	- 93	
4 /11/73	967.41	+16	- 77	
4 /24/73	940.77	-10	- 87	
4 /25/73	930.54	-15	-102	
4 /27/73	922.19	-14	-116	
4 /30/73	921.43	-10	-126	
5 / 3/73	945.66	+11	-115	
5 / 4/73	953.87	+10	-105	
5 / 8/73	956.58	+11	- 94	
5 /14/73	909.69	-18	-112	
5 /17/73	911.72	-11	-123	
5 /18/73	895.16	-23	-146	Large Downward Zigzag
5 /21/73	886.51	-22	-168	
5 /24/73	924.44	+10	-158	
6 / 4/73	885.91	-13	-171	
6 / 7/73	909.62	+11	-160	Large Upward Zigzag
6 / 8/73	920.00	+16	-144	
6 /12/73	926.78	+14	-130	
6 /14/73	903.67	-16	-146	
6 /15/73	888.55	-20	-166	
6 /18/73	875.08	-20	-186	
6 /21/73	873.65	-11	-197	
7 / 2/73	880.57	-11	-208	

Date	Industrials	Climax Indicator	Cum.	Comment (if any)
7 / 6/73	870.11	-10	-218	
7 /11/73	908.19	+17	-201	
7 /18/73	905.41	+11	-190	
7 /20/73	910.89	+11	-179	
7 /25/73	933.02	+14	-165	
8 / 1/73	912.18	-15	-180	
8 /10/73	892.08	-13	-193	
8 /13/73	883.43	-20	-213	
8 /14/73	870.71	-19	-232	
8 /16/73	872.74	-11	-243	
8 /17/73	871.84	-10	-253	
8 /20/73	867.40	-14	-267	
8 /21/73	857.84	-18	-285	
8 /22/73	851.90	-16	-301	
8 /29/73	883.43	+16	-285	Large Upward Zigzag
8 /30/73	882.53	+10	-275	
8 /31/73	887.57	+13	-262	
9 / 4/73	895.40	+12	-250	
9 /19/73	910.37	+18	-232	
9 /20/73	920.53	+20	-212	
9 /21/73	927.91	+20	-192	
9 /24/73	936.71	+20	-172	
9 /25/73	940.62	+19	-153	
9 /26/73	949.50	+13	-140	
9 /27/73	953.26	+10	-130	
10/26/73	987.05	+17	-113	
11/ 1/73	948.82	-15	-128	Large Downward Zigzag
11/ 2/73	935.28	-17	-145	
11/ 5/73	919.40	-20	-165	
11/ 6/73	913.15	-16	-181	
11/12/73	896.00	-14	-195	
11/13/73	883.40	-12	-207	
11/14/73	869.88	-22	-229	
11/20/73	844.90	-11	-240	
11/26/73	824.95	-17	-257	
11/27/73	817.73	-10	-267	Large Upward Zigzag
12/ 3/73	806.52	-20	-287	
12/ 4/73	803.21	-17	-304	
12/ 5/73	788.31	-19	-323	
12/ 7/73	838.05	+14	-309	Large Upward Zigzag
12/10/73	851.14	+12	-297	
12/13/73	800.43	-10	-307	
12/18/73	829.48	+15	-292	
12/26/73	838.25	+12	-280	
12/27/73	851.01	+13	-267	
1 / 3/74	880.69	+20	-247	
1 / 9/74	834.79	-15	-262	
1 /10/74	823.11	-12	-274	
1 /17/74	872.16	+12	-262	
1 /23/74	871.00	+10	-252	
1 /29/74	852.32	-11	-263	
2 / 1/74	843.94	-15	-278	

Date	Industrials	Climax Indicator	Cum.	Comment (if any)
2 / 4/74	821.50	-23	-301	Large Downward Zigzag
2 / 5/74	820.63	-13	-314	
2 /11/74	803.90	-16	-330	
2 /15/74	820.32	+10	-320	
2 /20/74	831.04	+13	-307	
2 /21/74	846.84	+18	-289	
2 /22/74	855.99	+21	-268	
2 /26/74	859.51	+17	-251	
2 /27/74	863.42	+12	-239	
3 / 5/74	872.42	+13	-226	
3 / 6/74	879.85	+11	-215	
3 /11/74	888.45	+14	-201	
3 /18/74	874.22	-11	-212	
3 /19/74	867.57	-15	-227	
3 /28/74	854.35	-19	-246	
3 /29/74	846.68	-19	-265	
4 / 1/74	843.48	-17	-282	
4 / 5/74	847.54	-11	-293	
4 / 8/74	839.96	-16	-309	
4 /16/74	861.23	+13	-296	
4 /18/74	869.92	+10	-286	
4 /23/74	845.98	-16	-302	
4 /24/74	832.37	-22	-324	
4 /25/74	827.67	-19	-343	
5 / 1/74	853.88	+13	-330	
5 / 9/74	865.77	+17	-313	
5 /16/74	835.34	-11	-324	
5 /17/74	818.84	-25	-349	
5 /20/74	812.42	-22	-371	
5 /21/74	809.53	-14	-385	
5 /22/74	802.57	-16	-401	
5 /23/74	805.23	-11	-412	
5 /29/74	795.37	-15	-427	
6 / 3/74	821.26	+14	-413	
6 / 4/74	828.69	+20	-393	
6 / 5/74	830.18	+14	-379	
6 / 6/74	845.35	+18	-361	
6 / 7/74	853.72	+17	-344	
6 /10/74	859.67	+16	-328	
6 /17/74	833.23	-16	-344	
6 /18/74	830.26	-18	-362	
6 /19/74	826.11	-16	-378	
6 /20/74	820.79	-18	-396	
6 /21/74	815.39	-22	-418	
6 /24/74	816.33	-11	-429	
6 /26/74	816.96	-12	-441	
6 /27/74	803.66	-15	-456	
6 /28/74	802.41	-13	-469	
7 / 2/74	790.68	-20	-489	
7 / 8/74	770.57	-23	-512	
7 / 9/74	772.29	-12	-524	
7 /10/74	762.12	-14	-538	

Date	Industrials	Climax Indicator	Cum.	Comment (if any)
7 /11/74	759.62	-13	-551	
7 /18/74	789.18	+10	-541	
7 /23/74	797.72	+12	-529	
7 /24/74	805.77	+11	-518	
7 /26/74	784.57	-10	-528	
7 /29/74	770.89	-13	-541	
7 /30/74	765.57	-14	-555	
7 /31/74	757.43	-14	-569	
8 / 1/74	751.10	-14	-583	
8 / 7/74	797.56	+15	-568	
8 /13/74	756.41	-12	-580	
8 /14/74	740.54	-15	-595	
8 /15/74	737.88	-11	-606	
8 /16/74	731.54	-17	-623	
8 /19/74	721.84	-18	-641	
8 /22/74	704.63	-14	-655	
8 /23/74	686.80	-18	-673	
8 /26/74	688.13	-11	-684	
8 /27/74	671.54	-15	-699	
8 /28/74	666.61	-17	-716	
8 /29/74	656.84	-18	-734	
9 / 4/74	647.92	-21	-755	
9 / 6/74	677.88	+16	-739	
9 /12/74	641.74	-18	-757	
9 /13/74	627.19	-24	-781	
9 /19/74	674.05	+15	-766	
9 /26/74	637.98	-10	-776	
9 /27/74	621.95	-13	-789	
9 /30/74	607.87	-20	-809	
10/ 3/74	587.61	-16	-825	
10/ 4/74	584.56	-11	-836	
10/ 9/74	631.02	+18	-818	
10/10/74	648.08	+16	-802	
10/11/74	658.24	+13	-789	
10/14/74	673.50	+22	-767	
10/21/74	669.82	+10	-757	
10/23/74	644.95	-13	-770	
10/24/74	636.26	-14	-784	
10/25/74	636.19	-10	-794	
10/28/74	633.84	-12	-806	
10/30/74	673.03	+12	-794	
11/ 5/74	674.75	+14	-780	
11/12/74	659.18	-12	-792	
11/15/74	647.61	-11	-803	
11/18/74	624.92	-26	-829	
11/19/74	614.05	-24	-853	
11/20/74	609.59	-18	-871	
11/21/74	608.57	-12	-883	
12/ 3/74	596.61	-12	-895	
12/ 5/74	587.06	-17	-912	
12/ 6/74	577.60	-19	-931	
12/ 9/74	579.94	-10	-941	

Date	Industrials	Climax Indicator	Cum.	Comment (if any)
12/23/74	589.64	-12	-953	
12/31/74	616.24	+13	-940	
1 / 2/75	632.04	+21	-919	
1 / 3/75	634.54	+15	-904	
1 / 6/75	637.20	+13	-891	
1 / 7/75	641.19	+11	-880	
1 / 9/75	645.26	+13	-867	
1 /10/75	658.79	+22	-845	
1 /13/75	654.18	+11	-834	
1 /24/75	666.61	+15	-819	
1 /27/75	692.66	+28	-791	
1 /28/75	694.77	+19	-772	
1 /29/75	705.96	+19	-753	
2 / 3/75	711.44	+13	-740	
2 / 5/75	717.85	+12	-728	
2 /13/75	726.92	+10	-718	
2 /14/75	734.20	+14	-704	
2 /20/75	745.38	+10	-694	
2 /21/75	749.77	+13	-681	
3 / 3/75	753.13	+21	-660	
3 / 4/75	757.74	+16	-644	
3 / 6/75	761.81	+13	-631	
3 / 7/75	770.10	+20	-611	
3 /10/75	776.13	+16	-595	
3 /17/75	786.53	+12	-607	
3 /21/75	763.06	-10	-617	
3 /24/75	743.43	-19	-636	
3 /26/75	766.19	+10	-626	
4 / 3/75	752.19	-14	-612	
4 / 4/75	747.26	-12	-624	
4 / 7/75	742.88	-15	-639	
4 /11/75	789.50	+10	-629	
4 /14/75	806.95	+18	-611	
4 /15/75	815.08	+13	-598	
4 /16/75	815.71	+10	-588	
4 /23/75	802.49	-11	-599	
4 /29/75	803.04	-10	-609	
5 / 1/75	830.96	+11	-598	
5 / 2/75	848.48	+18	-580	
5 / 5/75	855.60	+16	-564	
5 / 9/75	850.13	+12	-552	
5 /16/75	837.61	-12	-564	
5 /20/75	830.49	-16	-580	
5 /21/75	818.68	-22	-602	

Index